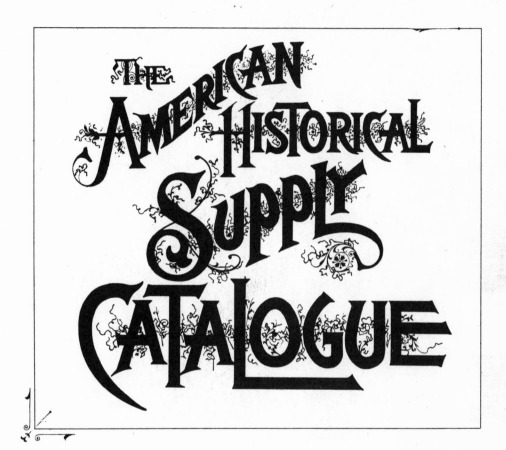

The American Historical Supply Catalogue

THE AMERICAN HISTORICAL SUPPLY CATALOGUE

A Nineteenth-Century Sourcebook

Alan Wellikoff

SCHOCKEN BOOKS
New York

First published by Schocken Books 1984
10 9 8 7 6 5 4 3 2   85 86 87
Copyright © 1984 by Alan Wellikoff

Library of Congress Cataloging in Publication Data
Wellikoff, Alan.
The American historical supply catalogue.
Includes index.
1. United States—Manufactures—Catalogs.
2. Americana—Catalogs.   I. Title.
TS199.W44   1984   745.1′075′073   84-5579

Photo credits: p. 30-Chamberstick and candlestick;
p. 48-Tankard; p. 49-All photos; p. 50-Plate (Courtesy
Henry E. Peach); p. 104-Buckboard (© 83 Jeffrey
P. Brand); p. 222 (Courtesy Laurie A. O'Neill)

❧

Designed by Richard Erlanger

Manufactured in the United States of America
ISBN 0-8052-0775-9

To my parents, Joseph and Anne,
and to the memory of Charlie Smith (1842–1979)

CONTENTS

Preface ix
Acknowledgments xiii
Structures and Plans 1
Building Supplies and Fixtures.......... 5
Furniture 13
Housewares 26
Crockery 44
Glassware and Silver................. 47
Lighting Supplies 51
Dry Goods 62
Decoration 68
Timepieces........................ 76
Stoves and Ranges 81
Farm and Garden.................... 89
Vehicles and Harness 102
Food and Drink 113
Wearing Apparel 123
Early Frontier Items (To 1845) 130
Late Frontier Items (1846–1893) 143
Military Goods 159
Books 175
Photographic Goods 186
Musical Instruments 190
Toys and Games 193
Remedies and Toilet Articles 201
Pipes and Tobacco 206
Nautical Items 211
Tours and Lodging 216
Christmas 226
Index 231
Index of Suppliers and Manufacturers.. 235

They shot the railway-train when it first came,
And when the Fords came they shot the Fords.
It could not save them. They are dying now
Or being educated, which is the same.
One need not weep romantic tears for them,
But when the last moonshiner buys his radio,
And the last, lost, wild-rabbit of a girl
Is civilized with a mail-order dress,
Something will pass that was American
And all the movies will not bring it back.

　　　　　　　　—Stephen Vincent Benét,
　　　　　　　　John Brown's Body, *1928*

PREFACE

IN AN ERA of rapid technological advance, record numbers of Americans are leaving the cities, growing their own produce, burning wood for heat, and otherwise incorporating elements characteristic of nineteenth-century life into that of the end of the twentieth. As "appropriate" technologies such as those of the windmill and wood stove help to conserve natural resources, the reasons for this are partly economic— encouraging the potbelly stove to supplant the nuclear reactor, the vegetable garden to answer the factory farm, and the short-haul railroad to take back some business from the Interstate Highway System.

But the historical aspects of this phenomenon can't be completely explained by economics. The high price of fuel won't go very far in helping us to understand the recent surges of interest in such things as black-powder hunting, horse ownership, Victorian architecture, Civil War reenactments, and antique country furniture. The fact is that in recent decades America's history has been restored to the landscape. But why?

Writing in the 1830s, Alexis de Tocqueville implied that Americans scorned history. Democratic peoples, he stated, arrange things so that "the woof of time is every instant broken, and the track of generations effaced." Perhaps it's partly the stress of modern life that has made us want to reverse this trait and gather our heritage around us for comfort. A prominent architect may have provided some insight here when he recently noted that a generation of modern architecture has brought about the most sustained interest in historical restoration that the country has ever seen.

We are a race barely removed from forest and farm, the descendants of those who for all time lived by hunting, by agriculture, and before the hearth. As our memory of this heritage is both organic and indelible, we bridle at being carried too rapidly away from it. So as technology advances, we correct it, reserving a place for the farmer, frontiersman, and firebuilder in us to find expression. Whatever became of those commuter autogyros that *Mechanics Illustrated* used to promise we'd all one day fly to work? Where are

those little pills that were to replace food? They're all part of a forgotten cargo of inappropriate technology, things either too complicated, expensive, unnatural, or plain incompatible with the joys of the hearth to be bothered with.

Late-twentieth-century society thus merges high technology with low. Today a man may own both a log cabin and a home computer without seeming to opt for the life of either Lincoln's parents or Superman's. Lately, notions of "past," "present," and "future" seem more intertwined than the myth of linear technological progress would have us believe. "Someone who today makes a buggy whip," said the humorist Jean Shephard, "performs a modern act." In other ways, the historical past can seem quite recent.

In *The Shootist,* one of John Wayne's last films, an old gunfighter, played by Wayne, seeks out the help of a doctor who tells him that he is dying, sick with "the cancer." It is the end of the nineteenth century, and the wildness of life in the western territories is rapidly being consumed by the advance of eastern civilization, for which the shootist's cancer stands as a metaphor. Stunned, yet bearing the dignity of one who has looked down the barrel of many a Remington and Colt, the dying gunfighter shambles back to his Carson City boardinghouse. There, the landlady sends his clothing—stiff with the dust of cattle towns and frontier camps—out to be drycleaned.

The history of the raw, germinative period of our nineteenth-century frontier is actually nearer than most of us imagine. If anything has made it seem as distant as it does, it's the commercial romanticizers—moviemakers and others—who have removed it to a praline candyland unconnected with the world in which we all go about daily. Louis Lamour, the well-known writer of western historical fiction, vividly remembers the smell of whiskey on Buffalo Bill Cody's breath when, as a toddler, Lamour was lifted by the old scout into his saddle and given a ride. Many of the veterans of the Indian Wars have only recently died; and in fact anyone old enough to read this is also old enough to have met a man who fought at the Battle of Vicksburg, a man who rode with Jesse James, or a man who himself could have met another who fought in the Revolutionary War.

So while the idea of a frontier gunfighter having his clothing dry-cleaned is a surprising one, it is also plausible. It *seems* more anachronistic than it really is. It serves to remind us that history is not made up of static, clearly segmented periods of time—but flows and is connected to the present. Bury it in the loam of succeeding events and the past will send up a green shoot to remind us of its proximity.

A compendium of nineteenth-century products now manufactured, *The American Historical Supply Catalogue* has been compiled with an eye to those durable goods that provide this sense of historical dimension. Some of the items included—like the Ace hard rubber combs that are exactly the same as those purportedly found in the pockets of Civil War dead—are surprising for their antiquity, while other currently manufactured products—like the replica Gatling gun—are startling to discover available new. Many other replicas, reproductions, and items in manufacture for almost a century or more are available to satisfy the contemporary yearning for substance, scale, and a sense of historical measure in everyday life. Assembled into a sourcebook intended as useful, informative, and entertaining, the compendium seeks to impart the feeling of an 1800s trade catalog, suddenly "come alive" from the past.

As this book comprises "nineteenth-century-style" products almost exclusively (several late-eighteenth- and early-twentieth-century items are included), some clarification of terminology is required. As the word is used in this sourcebook, a *replica* is an item that has been copied or replicated from one once made in the past. A *reproduction* differs in that to make it, a company (usually the original company) has resurrected old molds, dies, formulas, patterns, or plans to again produce an item as it once did, from the same materials. Finally, an item "in continual production" is made as it always has been for nearly a century or more, usually by the same firm. An example of this is the 200-year-old Hudson's Bay point blanket.

Both reproductions and items in continual manufacture are by definition authentic, leaving the replicas as the things to be watched. While it is invariably the shoddy replica that gives a bad name to this entire body of goods, for each manufacturer of bad merchandise there is another who, because of his good faith and devotion to the product and the period it represents, makes a superior-quality replica of detailed authenticity. While I've tried to limit the replica entries that follow to the latter, I've actually seen only a small portion of the products described and (in most cases) have been forced to rely on the intuition that one develops in doing this type of book. Where the suppliers themselves are quoted it is usually because their descriptions are interesting or succinctly informative; although sometimes their coyly worded copy is being passed on to the reader to use in judgment. It must be noted that neither the author nor the publisher makes any claims or guarantees regarding the quality or authenticity of any items described in this sourcebook.

Finally, as price and ordering information vary in accordance with the wishes of each individual supplier, not all prices have been quoted. While those cited are good through 1985, it is recommended that they be used only to infer true current prices and that the reader correspond directly with the supplier before sending any money. Many of the suppliers included in this book have small businesses, sensitive to the vagaries of the marketplace; thus prices are subject to change without notice, and some suppliers may even have gone out of business by the time this catalogue is in your hands. When ordering the products described, kindly note any postage and handling costs and include sales tax where appropriate.

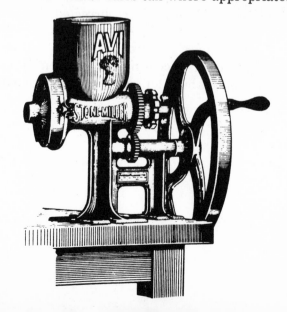

ACKNOWLEDGMENTS

FOR THEIR ROLES, direct and indirect, in helping to bring this book to print I want to express my gratitude to: Dr. Clarence Mondale, former chairman of the Department of American Civilization at the George Washington University; to my friend Denis Boyles, who gave me my first paying assignment as a journalist and who encouraged me to take the idea for this book to an agent; to that agent, Nick Ellison; to Ron Fraser of B. Dalton, Booksellers; and to Clem Labine, who runs the venerable *Old House Journal.*

Thanks as well to those extraordinarily helpful people whose companies' products are described herein: John Coolidge of the Plymouth Cheese Corporation, Dan Damon at Victorian Accents, Lucille DeRuvo at Caswell-Massey, Jay Frost at The Renovator's Supply, Ray Hillenbrand of Prairie Edge, Max Kelley of Heller-Aller, Eric Kindig at the Log Cabin Shop, Margo Koehler at the Briar Rose Farm, Karl Lipsky of Jenifer House, Rex Reddick at Crazy Crow Trading Post, Phil Spangenberger of Red River Frontier Outfitters, and Pat Tearney of La Pelleterie de Fort de Chartres.

For much of the lore I have included in this book I am indebted to Stuart Berg Flexner's *I Hear America Talking,* to the *Civil War Collector's Encyclopedia* by Francis A. Lord, to Clarence P. Hornung's *Treasury of American Antiques,* and to the *Dictionary of Americanisms,* edited by Mitford A. Mathews, which provided several of the quotations from nineteenth-century literature that have been used to illustrate many product entries.

I also deeply appreciate the help and support of my friends and relatives: Marc Arceneaux, Chris Blair, George Comtois, Ralph Cooper, Christy Cooper, Anne Diebold, Richard Erlanger, Judy Gitenstein, Liz Johnson, David Kelly, Ed Kritzler, Martha Landry, Betsy Snow, Margery Stein, Louis Wellikoff, and Michael Wellikoff. And especially the help of Susan Penick and Alan Rose, each of whom provided the kind of friendship that's only burnished by having had the touch put on it.

A.W.

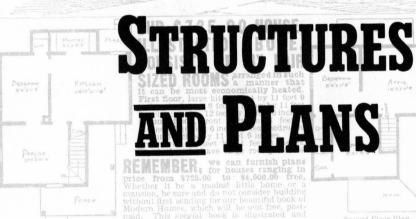

HENRY DAVID THOREAU. COURTESY THOREAU LYCEUM.

HENRY DAVID THOREAU'S WALDEN POND CABIN

Thoreau's motto, *multum in parvo*—much in little—survives in the New Age axiom that "less is more." Believing that the material comforts of life were not worth the amount of "life which is required to be exchanged" for them, Thoreau's sensual delight in living was made keener by the simple way he went about it. "This curious world which we inhabit," he said, "is more wonderful than it is convenient; more beautiful than it is useful; more to be admired and enjoyed than used."

This is essentially what Thoreau intended when he went to the woods to live "deliberately," in his well-remembered phrase. His life at Walden was, in the words of Joseph Wood Krutch, a "comic contrast with the cluttered and enslaved existence most men think it necessary to live"—an example, therefore, to the mass of men living their lives "of quiet desperation."

Using borrowed tools Thoreau built himself a ten- by fifteen-foot cabin on the banks of Walden Pond. His building materials were mostly acquired right at the site: pine saplings, second-hand brick, and the boards of a nearby shanty. The cost of the entire project,

Brochure available.

MOUNTAIN LUMBER COMPANY

Route 2
P.O. Box 43–1
Ruckersville, VA 22968
Tel. 804/295-1922

ORIGINAL LOG CABINS

Because of its intrinsic sturdiness and simplicity, the log cabin has come to be emblematic of the noblest American virtues—honesty, democracy, and independence. Perhaps it is for this reason that the structure is widely believed to be an American invention.

It isn't.

The first log cabin to appear on this continent was probably built by Scandinavian settlers at a place near the mouth of the Delaware River they called New Sweden. The year was 1683 and the Scandinavians were erecting structures similar to those they knew in the old world. But the North American frontier was a place so well suited to the log cabin that soon it was to be found everywhere. "It is not uncommon," Tocqueville wrote, "in crossing the new States of the West, to meet with deserted dwellings in the midst of the wilds; the traveller frequently discovers the vestiges of the log-house in the most solitary retreat, which bear witness to the power, and no less to the inconstancy, of man."

Traditional methods of log cabin building were relatively well understood until truncated by chain saws in our own generation. Today, while a suburban-hybrid line of descendants known generically as "log homes" enjoys much popularity, the old ways have almost been lost.

Mountain Lumber of Charlottesville, Virginia, reclaims original eighteenth- and nineteenth-century log cabins as part of their lumber business. After locating an original log house, the firm does not reflect as Tocqueville did . . . it dismantles the house for rebuilding at your site.

excluding his labor, was just over $28, a reasonable figure even today for anyone with similar access to both the land and the materials. But for others there's Roland Wells Robbins's replica of the Thoreau cabin that (using Mr. Robbins's construction drawings and wood frame) can be erected for about $4,000.

Any question regarding the authenticity of Mr. Robbins's recreation disappears with the knowledge that he is the same man who discovered the site of the original structure in 1945—exactly one hundred years after Thoreau first took axe to sapling there. Roland Robbins's work as an archeologist won him the admiration of Walt Robbins, an unrelated New Yorker, who in 1964 bequeathed him $20,000. "It was quite a welcome surprise," says Roland Robbins of the money that paid for the design and construction of the first replica Thoreau cabin at his home in Lincoln, Massachusetts.

This structure excited so much interest and drew so many inquiries that Mr. Robbins then decided to put his research to work and package a cabin that anyone could assemble. And so, after making arrangements with a local woodworking firm to replicate the original Walden post-and-beam cabin frame, Mr. Robbins's unique enterprise began.

Naturally, the replica Thoreau cabin can be built with the aid of contractors, but not before the Thoreau-quoting Roland Robbins may invoke this final bit of wisdom taken from the pages of *Walden:*

Who knows but if men constructed their dwellings with their own hands . . . the poetic faculty would be universally developed as birds univer-sally sing when they are so engaged? . . . Shall we forever resign the pleasure of construction to the carpenter?

For detailed information contact:

HOUSE OF THOREAU

P.O. Box 91
Concord, MA 01742
Tel. 617/259-8709

THE DOLLY BRYAN

GAZEBO With its lacy brackets, **fancy rails, and bell roof, Vintage Wood Works's Dolly Bryan Gazebo reflects** the intricate design of these Victorian structures. The company's solid-wood design is full size, measuring 11 feet by 11 feet including its tower. The Dolly Bryan Gazebo is easily erected and arrives with its side and roof sections already assembled.

Price: $2,995 (shipping included).

Catalog available, $2.

VINTAGE WOOD WORKS

P.O. Box 1157
Fredericksburg, TX 78624
Tel. 512/997-9513

TRADITIONAL AND VICTORIAN HOUSE PLANS

HISTORICAL REPLICATIONS

When native Mississippian Cecilia Reese Bullock despaired at the disappearance of the old-fashioned country homes of the South she loves, she did far more than become wistful, she went into business building them again. That's *build*, not restore.

These homes, which combined what are essentially modern floor plans with accurately reproduced traditional and Victorian exteriors, led her into her current business, designing and marketing plans for replicas of authentic late-nineteenth-century residences.

With camera in hand, Mrs. Bullock travels throughout Dixie seeking out houses that have for her a peculiar, not readily definable appeal. The popularity of the designs and plans that result from these journeys prove that Mrs. Bullock's instinct for proportion and grace is right on the mark. Among

these are plans for Cedar Lane, a farmhouse built in 1830 in Mount Pleasant, Georgia, by Solomon Graves, a political and social leader, and the Webb-Ginn House, an 1835 farmhouse in Gwinnett County, Georgia, with a front of lacy gingerbread "unparalleled for delicacy and grace." Others of Mrs. Bullock's plans have come directly from Victorian house-

plan books of the 1880s and 1890s. One of these, she notes, is again a best-seller after a hundred years.

Mrs. Bullock's portfolio includes working blueprints for home construction and is available for $10.

HISTORICAL REPLICATIONS, INC.

P.O. Box 31198, Dept. AHSC
Jackson, MS 39206

ANTIQUITY REPRINTS

Many of the questions faced by Victorian-era homebuilders were answered by the popular home magazines of the day, and by the contemporary architectural-plan, or "pattern" books. From these original sources Antiquity Reprints has assembled nineteenth-century house plans, home illustrations, construction details, and articles. These have been published in a series of softcover books for the Victorian home restorer, decorator, and enthusiast.

Brochure, "Yesterday's Home," available free with SASE.

ANTIQUITY REPRINTS

P.O. Box 370
Rockville Centre, NY 11571
Tel. 516/766-5585

5

SEARS, ROEBUCK & CO., (Incorporated), Cheapest Supply House on Earth, Chicago.

SEARS ROEBUCK & Co's
INCORPORATED.
BUILDER'S HARDWARE & MATERIAL

UNREASONABLE PROFITS are usually asked on goods in this line.

YOU WILL REQUIRE Doors, Sash, Building Paper, Paint, Lime, Hair, Cement, and Hardware, when you get ready to build a house, and most of the articles named when building a barn or granary or other building.

WE MAY NOT SELL YOU, but if you will have your carpenter make out a bill of just what goods you will require in this line, **we will quote you a price, delivered at your nearest railroad station**, and if we don't sell you, we will compel your local dealer to lose money and **sell the cheapest bill he ever sold** and in either case **we will save you money.**

LUMBER DEALERS often sell lumber on a small margin and make it up by charging unreasonably large profits on **Doors, Sash, Building Paper and Paint. Look out for your Lumber merchant** on these lines.

Look out for your Hardware merchant on **Locks, Door Knobs, Hinges, Latches, Sash Fixtures**, etc. These are big profit goods with retail dealers. **We can save you 25 to 50 per cent** on everything in this line, and no matter how little you wish to buy, **you will save enough** to well pay you for sending to Chicago for the goods.

Freight rates on hardware and Building Material are low and will amount to next to nothing compared with what you will save in price.

OUR TERMS ARE VERY LIBERAL. On all except **Doors and Sash**, which are always net cash with order, no discount, we will ship any goods by freight C. O. D., subject to examination, on receipt of **one-fourth** the amount of the bill, balance to be paid when received.

Three per cent. discount allowed if cash in full accompanies your order.

BUILDING SUPPLIES AND FIXTURES

Barn Door Hangers.

No. 13785. Common Barn Door Hanger, to run on half round rail. Bolts, screws or rails are not furnished free with hangers.
Diameter of wheel, inches, 3 4
Price, per pair,
Diameter of wheel, in
Price, per pair,

Check Back Barn Door Hangers.

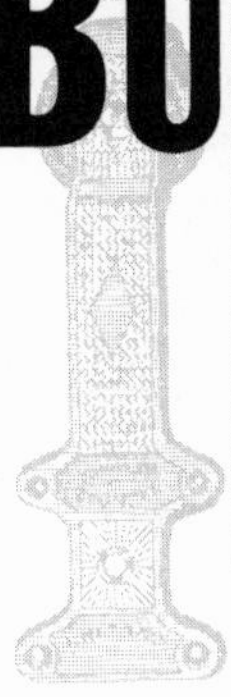

No. 13788. No screws or bolts furnished at the prices quoted.
Diameter of wheel in inches.

	3	4	5	6
Per pair,	$0.22	.25	.35	.45

No. 13786. Cast Iron Half Round Rail for above hangers comes in pieces 2 feet long. Price, per foot, without screws.......2c

No. 13789. Double flange Barn Door Rail to be used with above hangers, No. 13788 comes in pieces 2 feet long. No screws furnished at prices quoted. Per foot....2½c

Cronk's Anti-Friction Steel Barn Door Hanger.

No. 13790. This hanger is made from heavy steel, so it will carry the door with perfect ease and no trouble. We make a round bearing at the ends of the run, so if used on wider doors than made for, the axle will not wear into the rider bar, and the round bearings also make it run much easier than it otherwise would, or than any other hanger will that is not made this way. The groove is U shape, so it will not touch or grind on the edges and create friction, and also having a deep groove, will not jump the track. These hangers are marked with a gauge to put them up by, which saves time and insures getting them up right, even if done by a man not posted in the business. No screws or bolts furnished at prices quoted.

		Per pair.	Per doz. pair.
No. 1.	For 6 ft. run.	Price....50c	$5.40
No. 1½.	For 9 ft. run.	Price....60c	5.48
No. 2.	For 10 ft. run.	Price....70c	7.90
No. 3.	For 15 ft. run.	Price....80c	9.36

Cronk's Double Braced Steel Rail.

No. 13791.... Cronk's Double Braced Steel Rail.... is so made that it will not tremble. Guaranteed to hold a door weighing 2,000 pounds, and used in connection with our Anti-Friction Hangers will work perfectly on large or small doors. If ... the nail ... used it will hold any door ...

No. 13792. ... Barn Door Stay Rollers to screw, wrought iron shank. Weight, 14 oz. Price, each, 7c; per doz.......65c

No. 13796. Barn Door Stay Rollers, adjustable to any thickness of door. Will always stay in the right position. Price, each, 8c; per doz.......85c

No. 13797. Barn Door Pulls, extra heavy japanned. Weight, 10 oz. Price, each, 4c; per doz.......40c

Hinges.

Screws are not furnished with hinges at prices quoted. For screws see index.

No. 13805. Light wrought steel T Hinges. Size given is measure from joint to end of hinge.

Size, inches.	3	4	6	8
Size of screw used,	3	4	8	10
Weight, pair,	4 oz.	5 oz.	8 oz.	12 oz.
Price, pair,	$0.03	.04	.05	.07
Price, doz. pairs.	.33	.40	.54	.75

No. 13809. Extra heavy wrought steel T Hinges.

Size, inches,	6	8	10	12	14
Price, pair,	$0.09	.18	.20	.27	.35
Price, doz. pairs.	.98	1.40	2.12	2.12	3.65

No. 13816. Light wrought steel Strap Hinges. Size given is measurement from joint to end of hinge.

Size, inches,	3	4	5	6
Price, per pair,	$.03	.04	.05	.06
Price, doz. pairs.	.33	.44	.54	.56

No. 13817. Heavy wrought steel Strap Hinges, without screws.

Size, inches,	6	8	10	12
Price, per pair,	$0.08	.12	.18	.25
Price, per doz. pairs.	.80	1.26	1.92	2.88

No. 13818. Heavy wrought iron Screw Strap Hinges.

Size, inches,	10	12	14
Weight, per pair, lbs.,	3½	4½	5½
Price, per pair,	$0.12	.18	.22
Price, per doz. pairs.	1.28	1.75	2.00
Screws not furnished.

No. 13824. Narrow wrought steel Butts.

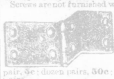

Length, inches	1	1¼	1½	2	2½
Width, open,	1¼	1¼	1½	1¾	1⅝
Size screw used	5	6	7	8	8
Weight per pair, oz.		3	4	4	7
Price, per pair,				.04	.04
				.20	.31

No. 13825. Wrought steel Back Flaps.

	⅞	1	1¼	1½	2
	2⅛	2¾	3¼	3¾	4½
	6	6	7	8	9
Price, per doz. pairs.	.20	.22	.23	.29	.35	.40
Screws are not furnished with Butts.

No. 13827. Wrought steel Chest Hinges. The 1½ inch size is 1½ inches wide and can be used on stuff ¾ inch thick. The 2 inch size is 2 inches wide and can be used on stuff ⅞ inch thick. 1½ inch, per pair, 5c; dozen pairs, 50c; 2 inch, per pair, 8c; dozen pairs.......70c

Hooks.

No. 13835. Wrought iron Hooks and Staples.

Length, inches	3	4	5	6
Weight, oz.	3	4	4	5
Price, each	$0.02	.02	.03	.03
Price, per doz.	.12	.16	.19	.22

No. 13836. Bright iron Wire Hooks and Screw Eyes.

Size, inches	2	2	3	4
Weight, oz.	2	2	4	
Price, each,	$0.02	.02	.03	.03
Price, per doz.	.15	.18	.23	
Price, per gross	1.15	1.50	1.88	

Hasps.

No. 13838. Wrought Iron Hasps and Staples complete with double hook.

Length, in.,	3	5	8	10
Weight, oz.,	4	5	9	13
Price, each,	$0.03	.03	.04	.05
Price, doz.,	.24	.28	.36	.50

No. 13839. Wrought Iron Hinge Hasps, like cut.

Length of hasp, in.,	3	4½
Whole length, in.,	5¾	7
	7	8
Price, each,	$0.06	.09
Price, per doz.,	.50	.66

Rings.

No. 13842. Wrought Iron Rings and Staples. Size given is diameter of rings.

Size, inches,	2	2½	3
Weight, oz.,	2	3	4
Each,	$0.03	.03	.03
Doz.	.15	.20	.25

No. 13843. Wrought Iron Staples only.

NINETEENTH-CENTURY LUMBER

For Europeans like the Massachusetts Bay colonists, being camped on the edge of a vast continental forest brought with it an equal expanse of ambivalence. The Puritans speculated endlessly about their situation: Had they, like Christ, been brought to a demonically wild place as a test of faith? Or was this the site of the New Jerusalem, and they the modern incarnation of the Hebrews, fleeing oppression through a wilderness that led to the establishment of a new covenant?

From Edward Johnson's 1654 *Wonder-Working Providence* to Robert Redford's more recent *Electric Cowboy*, a fascination with the American wilderness and its effect on our character has pervaded our literature and history. Yet during the same century when such men as Jefferson, Emerson, Parkman, and Muir were to extoll its enobling influences, the great

forest was inexorably depleted. When Frederick Jackson Turner stood before the American Historical Association in 1893 to deliver his famous thesis on "The Significance of the Frontier on American Life," his Chicago audience was unaware that it was participating in what would popularly be remembered as an event that signaled the close of that frontier.

With the western frontier closed, the eastern forest was a worn-out fabric, tattered and rent by agriculture. No longer did stands of huge spruce, hemlock, and fir extend solidly from northern New England along the high peaks down to Tennessee. Gone as well was the carpet of oak and chestnut that flourished from New Jersey to northern Virginia, and the pine and oak of the southern forests.

Longleaf pine, a softwood that grew primarily in the southernmost parts of Georgia, Mississippi, and Alabama, took 450 years to mature and yielded a heartwood so strong that the keel of the U.S.S. *Constitution* had been

made from a single plank. Frequently used during the 1800s in heavy construction, in shipbuilding, and for railroad bridges and coastal pilings, this steely wood was one of our leading exports.

Long since "timbered out," modern civilization has eliminated the conditions required by longleaf pine for regeneration, so today any of it found is likely to be reclaimed nineteenth-century lumber. The Mountain Lumber Company of Charlottesville, Virginia, specializes in this reclamation, salvaging the timber from torn-down structures. The company kiln-dries the wood and resaws it into a variety of sizes for paneling, flooring, and other uses.

Brochure available.

MOUNTAIN LUMBER COMPANY

Route 2
P.O. Box 43–1
Ruckersville, VA 22968
Tel. 804/295-1922

EARLY NEW ENGLAND POST-AND-BEAM CONSTRUCTION

Using native eastern hemlock, Vermont Frames of Hinesburg handcrafts house frames in accordance with traditional Yankee methods. The firm incorporates the requirements of individual families into its early New England two-story cape, saltbox, and partial-saltbox styles. **The cost** of erecting a frame at your site is $6.50 per square foot, excluding delivery charges.

Brochure available.

VERMONT FRAMES

P.O. Box 100
Hinesburg, VT 05461
Tel. 802/482-2722

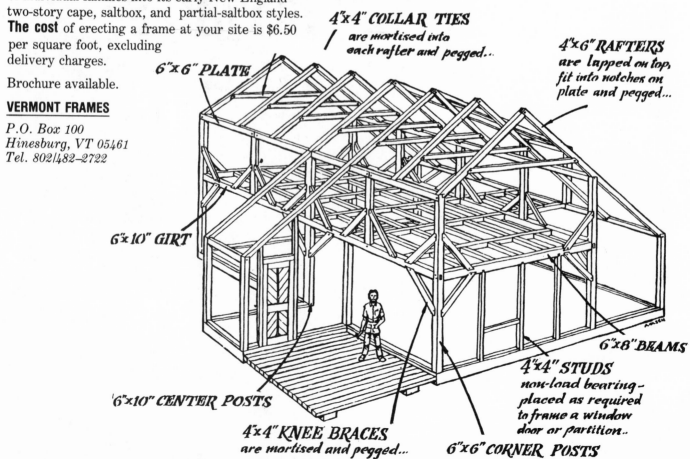

4"x4" COLLAR TIES are mortised into each rafter and pegged...

4"x6" RAFTERS are lapped on top, fit into notches on plate and pegged...

6"x6" PLATE

6"x10" GIRT

6"x10" CENTER POSTS

4"x4" KNEE BRACES are mortised and pegged...

6"x6" CORNER POSTS

4"x4" STUDS non-load bearing - placed as required to frame a window door or partition..

6"x8" BEAMS

VICTORIAN MILLWORK

CUMBERLAND WOODCRAFT

Cumberland Woodcraft offers a comprehensive line of interior and exterior Victorian millwork replicating the most intricate nineteenth-century originals. Unless special wood is ordered, the company uses premium-grade kiln-dried oak or poplar to turn out their pieces. Included are rails, spandrels, balustrades, brackets, corbels, posts, and wainscoating.

Catalog and price list available, $3.50.

CUMBERLAND WOODCRAFT COMPANY

*2500 Walnut Bottom Road
Carlisle, PA 17013
Tel. 717/243–0063*

VINTAGE WOODWORKS

"Heretofore seldom obtainable in this century," boasts Fredericksburg, Texas's Vintage Woodworks of its line of Victorian gingerbread and fretwork. The company offers a wide variety of authentic designs cut from traditional pine and ranging from small fret brackets to running porch rails and fleur-de-lys trim. The "Texas Special" bracket is a delightful Victorian interpretation of eternal Lone Star chauvinism. **Vintage Woodworks'** gingerbread is suitable for both indoor and outdoor use as part of the complete restoration of Victorian houses, gazebos, gateways, stables, barns, privies, etc. Special orders are welcomed by the firm.

Catalog available, $2.

VINTAGE WOODWORKS

*P.O. Box 1157
Fredericksburg, TX 78624
Tel. 512/997–9513*

HAND-HEWN
BEAMS

The Broad-Axe Beam Company is a family business in Vermont that produces beams of white pine, authentically hand-hewn with a broadaxe. The broad-axe—a chisel-bladed axe—remained the most convenient way to fashion beams even after the introduction of the water-powered sawmill, due to the mill's slowness (it used to be said that you could put a log on the carriage in the morning and then go off to lunch without having to worry about turning it for the next cut).

Broad-Axe Beam's structural timbers are 7-inch-square boxheart beams (meaning that the age rings radiate from the center toward the butt ends), and their decorative beams are simply structural beams sawed in half. All of the company's beams are air dried for six months. Custom hewing is available.

Structural beams come sawed one side or hewn on all four sides, approximately 7½ inches square, in lengths of 8, 12, 14, and 16 feet. Price: $5.25 per linear foot.

Decorative beams are approximately 3½ by 7½ inches in diameter, and come in lengths of 8, 12, 14, and 16 feet. Price: $3.50 per linear foot.

Shipping is by commercial trucker to your site.

BROAD-AXE BEAM COMPANY

R.D. 2, Box 181-E
Brattleboro, VT 05301
Tel. 802/257-0064

The Genuine   **Home-Made**

MILK PAINT

MILK PAINT Old-Fashioned Milk Paint's old-fashioned milk paint resulted from the company's search for an authentically Early American paint to use on its replica eighteenth- and nineteenth-century furniture. This product—essentially a refabrication of one commonly used prior to 1830—has again become popular for its unrefined old look and its use of authentic colors. Old-Fashioned Milk Paint comes as a dry powder to be mixed with water.

Colors available: barn red, pumpkin, mustard, bayberry, Lexington green, soldier blue, oyster white, and pitch black.

Prices: $5.50 per pint, $9.50 per quart, $28.50 per gallon (plus shipping charges).

Brochure available.

THE OLD-FASHIONED MILK PAINT COMPANY

P.O. Box 222
Groton, MA 01450

VICTORIAN
CEILING FANS

The success of Royal Windyne ceiling fans seems rooted in the company's determination to use traditional nineteenth-century materials and fabrication techniques. These are handmade fans, their designs based on extensive archival research, built of solid tulip poplar (the wood most often used for ceiling-fan blades throughout their late-nineteenth-century heyday), cut full width and individually sanded. Furthermore, as Royal Windyne's fans have been designed to operate at functional speeds, they effectively moderate room temperatures year round. Available in two models, with 39- and 53-inch-diameter blades respectively. Custom orders are welcomed by the firm.

Literature available, $1.

ROYAL WINDYNE LIMITED

1022 West Franklin Street
Richmond. VA 23220
Tel. 804/353–1812

PERIOD INTERIORS

The Architectural Antiques Exchange is a leader among the growing number of "urban excavators" who specialize in salvaging all that ornately carved woodwork that for too long was routinely destroyed when old buildings were demolished. Located in Philadelphia, a city that (in the East, anyway) has been in the forefront of the Victorian restoration movement, the company will not only restore, redesign, and install period interiors, but will also locate pieces per customer specification.

The Architectural Antiques Exchange's 30,000-square-foot warehouse provides visitors with a display of Victorian, western, and modern woodwork, ironwork, stained glass, fixtures, doors, and the like, including such one-of-a-kind pieces as a nineteenth-century railway ticket booth.

Brochure available.

ARCHITECTURAL ANTIQUES EXCHANGE

715 North 2nd Street
Philadelphia, PA 19123
Tel. 215/922–3669

TIN CEILINGS

A A Abingdon Ceilings of Brooklyn, New York, offers a large line of metal ceilings in modern and turn-of-the-century styles.

Brochure available.

A A ABBINGDON CEILINGS

2149 Utica Avenue
Brooklyn, NY 11234
Tel. 212/477–6505

CAST-IRON STAIRCASES

Steptoe & Wife Antiques of Ontario, Canada, offers a line of cast-iron Victorian staircases in kit form. These employ the structural and design features of various nineteenth-century originals, and include treads, risers, side panels, and center pole.

The Barclay model is a 5-foot-wide spiral staircase patterned after one purchased by Steptoe & Wife from an old Ottawa paper mill. It bolts together easily and has open fretwork and sides, with a closed step and ornate steel handrail supports. Each rise is 8⅛ inches.

The Kensington is claimed by Steptoe to be the only straight Victorian cast-iron staircase now available. It was adapted by the firm from the designs of several mid-nineteenth-century stairs found in the eastern U.S. and Canada (the staircase at Independence Hall in Wheeling, West Virginia, is cited as a particularly strong influence). The Kensington's riser and side panels are openwork; the tread is closed and employs a diamond-grid design. The stairs are 36 inches wide and have a 7⅝-inch rise. The stairs also have an optional brass railing and have a baked enamel finish.

Prices: Barclay Spiral Stairs, $185 per riser, $225 with brass handrail; Kensington Staircase, $185 per riser (prices include shipping and duty).

Catalog of architectural replicas available, $2.

STEPTOE & WIFE

36261 Victoria Park Avenue
Willowdale, ON
Canada M2H 3B2
Tel. 416/497–2989

BATHROOM FIXTURES

In December 1855 the big news in New York was not the ascendancy of the Know-Nothings in Congress, but the completion of the Vanderbilt Mansion, which for the first time set aside an entire room for bathing. This "bathroom," which contained both a bathtub and a commode, betokened the growing interest in personal hygiene that soon had Vassar College making each of its girls bathe twice weekly.

FROM SUNRISE SPECIALTY

CLAWFOOT BATHTUBS
Sunrise Specialty of Berkeley, California, offers clawfoot bathtubs of the type commonly used late in the 1800s. These are not reproductions but salvaged antiques, restored and refitted with new brass fixtures and oak rims. Sunrise Specialty uses the Chicago Faucet Company's taps exclusively. These have been continuously manufactured by that company since the nineteenth century and are the best available. Clawfoot tubs are obtainable in the Berkeley store or by special order.

PEDESTAL SINK
The Berkely model vitreous china pedestal sink is an exact replica of a sink manufactured around 1900.

Dimensions: 32 inches high, 24 inches wide, and 21 inches deep.

Color brochure available.

SUNRISE SPECIALTY

2210 San Pablo Avenue
Berkeley, CA 94702
Tel. 415/845-4751

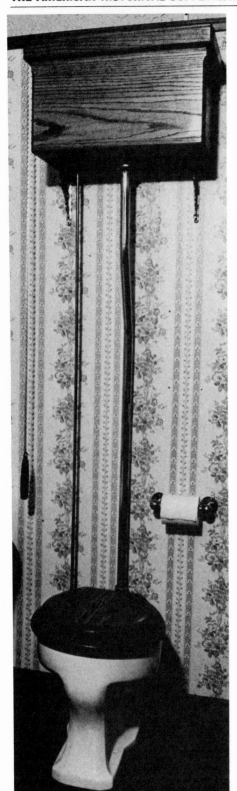

PULL-CHAIN
TOILET
The Rheinschild pull-chain toilet is an updated replica of a turn-of-the-century model. Its box is constructed of top-quality solid oak, and is lined with heavy-gauge stainless steel. The valve and flush mechanisms are solid-brass pieces.

The toilet comes with a rosewood flush handle and brass chain. The flush pipe is brass and built in the original offset shape. The bowl is made of first-quality new white china.

Price: $375 (50 percent deposit required; balance billed C.O.D.).

Brochure available, $1.35.

S. CHRIS RHEINSCHILD

2220 Carlton Way
Santa Barbara, CA 93109
Tel. 805/962–8589

HOT-AIR
REGISTERS
Michael and Anne Reggio manufacture traditional hot-air registers in a great variety for ceilings and floors, all made of either brass or cast iron. They will also accept special orders for custom-made grilles and registers.

Catalog available, $1.

THE REGGIO REGISTER COMPANY

P.O. Box 511
Ayer, MA 01432
Tel. 617/772–3493

COMMODE
SEAT
As part of their line of products that "you can bet your assets on," DeWeese Woodworking of Philadelphia, Mississippi, offers a solid-oak commode seat with solid-brass hinges. Standard and elongated styles are available.

Brochure available.

DEWEESE WOODWORKING COMPANY

P.O. Box 576
Philadelphia, MS 39350
Tel. 601/656–4951

COPPER
KITCHEN SINK
S. C. Rheinschild's kitchen sink is a replica of a standard nineteenth-century fixture. Formed from heavy-gauge copper, it has a hand-hammered top flange and soldered and riveted seams. Its overall size is approximately 22¼ inches by 32¼ inches by 6 inches; inside measurements are approximately 20 inches by 30 inches. Custom orders are welcome.

Price: $275 (plus packing and shipping charges).

Literature available, $1.35.

S. CHRIS RHEINSCHILD

2220 Carlton Way
Santa Barbara, CA 93109
Tel. 805/962–8598

COPPER WEATHER VANES

A ninth-century papal decree mandated that the image of a rooster be placed atop churches as evidence of good faith and to ward away evil. In time the rooster's talons would grip the roofs of people's homes as well, and throughout the Middle Ages he was a common sight, performing a religious as well as a decorative function there.

Following this tradition, the weathercock became king of the roost on colonial American homes and barns—but by then there were several other beasts in the menagerie. In nineteenth-century agricultural communities the rooster traced the wind rose along with a barnyard of other critters—cows, horses, sheep, and pigs. In seacoast towns, schools of swordfish, cod, and whales swam the wind currents from atop most buildings. During this period two other popular weather vanes were introduced: one was religious, the Angel Gabriel; the other patriotic, the American eagle.

Jenifer House, a popular storehouse of Americana located in Great Barrington, Massachusetts, offers more than twenty-four types of hand-hammered copper weather vanes, including two types of rooster in addition to the fish, whale, pig, and Angel Gabriel mentioned. These are New England made, fashioned from molds first used more than a century ago.

Gift catalog available.

JENIFER HOUSE

New Marlboro Stage
Great Barrington, MA 01230
Tel. 413/528–1500

$1⁹ IRON BEDS $12⁷⁵

BIG REDUCTION IN PRICES

AT $1.39 TO $12.75 We offer you finer iron beds than were ever before shown. Newest designs, first class material, construction and finish. Wonderful values. We challenge the world on quality and price. A lower price than ours means a poorer quality. THEY ARE INDESTRUCTIBLE AND WILL NEVER WEAR OUT.

THE METAL USED in the construction of our beds is strictly high grade throughout. No rusty scrap iron or corroded refuse metals. The highest and best quality of malleable iron, rolled Bessemer steel and drawn brass tubing.

THE CONSTRUCTION of our metal beds is the best that modern machinery, science and skilled workmanship, can possibly produce. Every part and parcel is carefully modeled, framed and jointed. The joints and chills carefully rounded and smoothed. The rails are made of Bessemer steel in angle shape and will not bend or break. Great care is taken in the fitting of the tongue and grooves by which the rail is fastened to the head and foot end.

THE FINISH of our iron beds, we guarantee the best that can be made. They stand firm and will support any weight of persons. The enamel which is used for the several coatings is the highest grade obtainable. Each coat, after being carefully and thoroughly applied, is baked in a large oven heated to a very high degree of temperature, then thoroughly smoothed and polished. This produces a finish that is impervious to water and all our iron beds can be cleaned of finger marks or other soiling by washing with soap and water.

THE BRASS TRIMMING which is used in the ornamentation and construction of our metal beds is of the highest quality of drawn brass tubing, highly polished and burnished, coated with the best quality of French lacquer, which absolutely preserves the polish and prevents tarnishing. Lacquer is to brass what varnish is to wood, it preserves the material.

COLOR BEDS. We furnish all our iron beds in white enamel unless ordered otherwise. Under the especial description of each bed it specifically states whether furnished in single solid color or in combination colors. Many designs of beds are much more attractive in single solid color only and for that reason we furnish certain patterns in single solid color only. When beds are ordered in colors, shipment will be made direct from factory near Chicago and from three days to one week's time is required before shipment can be made.

WE CALL YOUR SPECIAL ATTENTION to the fact that we furnish our iron beds shown on pages 428 and 429 in combination colors, with gilt decorated chills, as follows: Maroon and white, light blue and white, pea green and white, dark blue and white, pink and white, olive green and white or dark green and white. When you wish to order a bed in combination of colors, be sure to state colors desired.

WE ESPECIALLY RECOMMEND maroon and white, light blue and white, pea green and white, as the most effective and desirable combinations. When finished in combination colors the posts and top rods are finished in the first color mentioned above and the filling rods in white.

VERNIS MARTIN ALL GOLD FINISH. This beautiful high grade finish was recently popular. It derives its name from Vernis Martin. It is a three-coat finish, consisting of a priming foundation coat thoroughly baked, a second coat of high grade all bronze and, lastly, a third coat of the best quality varnish. The finish color is a transparent brass beds. To produce this handsome finish requires great care by the best skilled workmen. It must be seen, examined and compared with that offered by other dealers to be fully appreciated. We never fade or tarnish.

THE SIDE RAILS on all our iron beds are made of the best high carbon Bessemer steel to the bed with the reverse side up to allow the use of wood slats of regular extension end bar springs as desired. TO SET UP IRON BEDS, place the rail in the groove, lay a piece of wood on the shank of the rail and drive into the groove with hammer by striking the wood.

HOW TO ORDER. When ordering a metal bed, be sure to state the width wanted, also the color, otherwise white will be shipped. We illustrate our beds made up with bolster, mattress and covering, but the price quoted is for the bed only. Springs, mattress and pillows are illustrated and described on pages 431 to 435.

Adjustable Iron Bed Canopy.

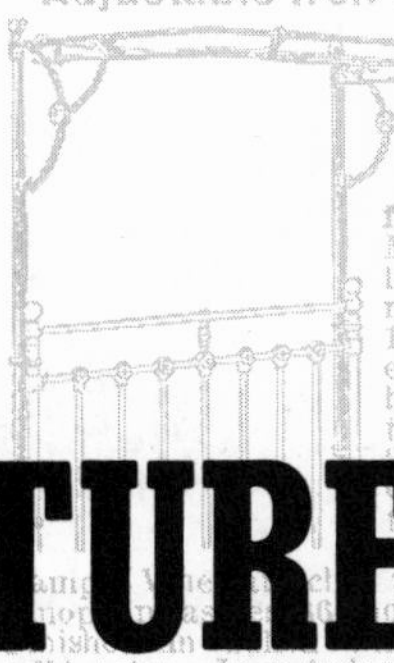

No. 1K2401 This illustration shows our adjustable canopy for iron beds. Made of best quality high carbon Bessemer steel. Posts, 1¼ inches in diameter. Solid steel hood rods, ¾ inch thick. Brass knobs, inches in diameter. be securely attached to bed posts four patent the bed the top of inches from the floor. enamel or any solid color. In ordering canopy be sure to give size of post, width of bed, and color wanted. Shipping weight, about 35 pounds.

Price, all sizes $3.25

$4⁹⁸ FOR THIS HANDSOME DESIGN HIGH GRADE, MASSIVE IRON BED complete with best quality

steel springs. The bed is one of our special three-piece combination beds which has no side rails. The long bar of the spring forms the side rail of the bed. One of the finest methods of construction known and offered exclusively by us. This method makes it possible to pack and ship the bed at less expense. We offer this combination outfit to show what it is possible for us to produce in a strictly high grade bed, spring and mattress at an extremely low price, which is offered only as a sample of the wonderful values we are giving in our entire bed line. Height of the head end of the bed, 56 inches, foot end, 44 inches. The corner posts are 1 5-16 inches in diameter and are mounted with massive smooth cast ornamental chills. The top rod and filling rods are ⅝ inch thick. These dimensions make an unusually substantial and massive bed. Finished throughout in best quality white enamel, thoroughly baked and hardened. The spring frame is made of high carbon steel angle bars, 1⅜ inches wide. The fabric is made of best quality heavy tinned wire interwoven and interlaced in what is called hairpin style, making it absolutely non-sagging and noiseless. The fabric is fastened to the steel frame at each end by fifteen high carbon steel spiral springs. This spring combines the greatest comfort and lasting qualities it is possible to obtain. The mattress is the finest of its kind that skill and our knowledge of mattress construction could enable us to produce. A combination mattress never before offered, suitable for use in any climate. The filling is made of white basswood excelsior, thoroughly screened and freed from all impurities. This forms the inner filling only. One side is covered with a thick layer of the best quality sanitary sea moss, which is not excelled for its hygienic and comfort giving qualities. The other side of the mattress is covered with thick layers of elastic felt of good quality. This makes the mattress suitable for cold or warm weather and furnishes a firm or soft bed as may be desired. The ticking is extra quality heavy twill, closely stitched and full bound. The mattress is made in the very latest and most up to date manner. Diamond tufted with leather tufts, and we place it in competition with mattresses sold throughout the country at $5.00 to $6.00.

No. 1K2395 Full size only. Price, Iron Bed and Spring.....$4.98
Shipping weight, about 110 pounds.

No. 1K2395 Full size only. Price, Mattress only.........$3.98
Shipping weight, about 50 pounds.

REDUCED TO $4⁹⁸

Iron Bed, High Grade Spring and Mattress.

No. 1K2395

$1.39

No. 1K2404 This Iron Bed is made of the best quality malleable iron and high carbon steel. Height, head end, 48 inches; height, foot end, 38 inches; corner posts, ⅞ inch thick; filling rods, ⅜ inch thick; finished in white enamel only. Wonderful value at our price. Furnished in 3 foot 6 inch, or 4 foot 6 inch widths. Shipping weight, 55 pounds. Be sure to state size desired. Price, all sizes...$1.39

$1.89

No. 1K2411 This Iron Bed has corner posts made of drawn steel tubing ¾ inch thick, filling rods, solid steel ½ inch thick. Height, head end, 50 inches; height, foot end, 45 inches. Finished in solid color white enamel only. Furnished in 3 foot, 3 foot 6 inch or 4 foot 6 inch widths. Exceptional value. Shipping weight, 60 pounds. Be sure to state size desired. Price, all sizes...$1.89

$2.69

No. 1K2415 This Iron Bed has corner posts 1 1-16 inches thick. Solid steel top rods and filling rods, ⅜ inch thick. Height, head, 56 inches; height, foot, 50 inches. Furnished only in solid color baked white enamel. Best quality casters. Made in 3 foot, 3 foot 6 inch, 4 foot or 4 foot 6 inch widths. Weight, 75 pounds. Be sure to state size desired. Price...$2.69

SIMMS & THAYER COUNTRY FURNITURE

Originally inspired by the functional simplicity of Shaker furniture, Bob and Sandra Sevigny of Simms & Thayer quickly realized that the Shakers' bent for uncluttered beauty and durable construction was a standard shared by most Early American cabinetmakers. But Shaker furniture was something that belonged to Shakers, they felt, so they moved on to the reproduction of non-sectarian eighteenth- and nineteenth-century American pieces. They did this, as they put it, with a devotion that is "worthy of the originals."

This devotion begins with the selection of the model pieces of furniture to be copied. ("We refrain from copying museum pieces as the good ones have usually been overdone," Sandra writes), and is carried through by the rigorously traditional construction and finishing techniques that Simms & Thayer employs. As a result there is something both anciently Yankee and curiously modern about the furniture produced, a quality that in its clean lines, honesty, and practicality transcends design.

PIE SAFE A large cabinet with shelves for holding breads and pies (even pies filled with meat), the pie safe (circa 1859) was kind of a specialized nineteenth-century Kelvinator. The most popular pie safes were made in the Middle West and West after 1830, and had pierced tin panels that would allow ventilation while keeping insects away. All of Simms & Thayer's pie safes are built of pine only, and mortised, tendoned, and pegged in the old way. The tin panels are hand-pierced.

Dimensions: 57 inches high, 40 inches wide, 18 inches deep.

APOTHECARY CHEST This early country cabinet, circa 1815, has ten drawers and was originally used for storing medicinal herbs and remedies. There are two shelves behind the hand-beaded two-panel door that has its own lock and key.

Dimensions: 34½ inches high, 23½ inches wide, and 17 inches deep.

Brochure available, $3.

SIMMS & THAYER, CABINETMAKERS

P.O. Box 35-AC
No. Marshfield, MA 02059
Tel. 617/585–8606 or 837–0271

HITCHCOCK CHAIRS

"L. Hitchcock—Hitchcocks-ville, Conn. Warranted," was the legend that Lambert Hitchcock inscribed on each of his chair's seat-backs, with each "N" curiously (if not quaintly) reversed. According to local legend, "warranted" meant that the chair had survived a fall from the third story of the factory building erected by Hitchcock in Riverton (Hitchcocksville), Connecticut, in 1826.

The chairs that Lambert Hitchcock manufactured at his factory had seats made of cat-o'-nine-tails rush, cane, or wood. The rush was harvested for him in late summer by local farmers, while the cane had to be imported. For ornamentation, Hitchcock would employ the stencil and striping techniques traditionally used by stagecoach decorators. Rockers, side chairs, and armchairs were all made in this way.

The quality of the Hitchcock chairs made them widely popular, although a few Yankees scoffed at them as "fancy chairs with fancy prices." But despite his success, Hitchcock in time became overextended and his factory had to end the manufacture of chairs shortly after his death in 1852.

Nearly a century later John T. Kenney was drifting lazily down the Farmington River on a fishing trip. There he came upon Hitchcock's forlorn chair

factory, padlocked and boarded up for decades. Virtually any New Englander would've been well familiar with the story of the Hitchcock chair, but Kenney had even received one as a wedding present. As he continued down the Farmington an idea came to Kenney: "Could it be," he wondered "that others would be as interested in a revived Hitchcock as I?" Market research soon affirmed Kenney's notion, and on October 17, 1946, the authentic reproduction of the Hitchcock chair was begun.

Hitchcock reproductions may be found at the factory store in Riverton, and at select furniture stores throughout New England. Write for further information:

THE HITCHCOCK CHAIR COMPANY

Riverton, CT 06065

HITCHCOCK'S SLATBACK SIDE AND ARM CHAIRS

ADIRONDACK LAWN CHAIR

ADIRONDACK LAWN CHAIR **According to Sally Packard, one of the principals of Lake Placid's Adirondack Store, the Adirondack lawn chair is derived** from the high-backed and wide-slatted chairs that were built by mountain guides and caretakers employed in the Adirondack forest's "Great Camps" (the rough-hewn mansions built there by the northeastern business aristocracy) during the turn of the century. Made from either pine or oak, these chairs graced broad porches and lawns, their back-slanted seats and generous proportions eliminating any need for cushions. As the Adirondack chair migrated to different parts, regional preferences traditionally saw them painted dark green in the North and white in the South.

The Adirondack Store's lawn chairs are made of seasoned oak and must be assembled from four pieces.

Dimensions: 39 inches high, 23 inches wide, and 35 inches deep.

Price: $88 (plus $10 for shipping, $14 on the West Coast). Checks, Master-Card, and VISA accepted.

Brochure available.

ADIRONDACK STORE AND GALLERY

109 Saranac Avenue
Lake Placid, NY 12946
Tel. 518/523-2646

BENT-HICKORY ROCKING CHAIR

BENT-HICKORY ROCKING CHAIR **As he relates it in his book** *The Pioneer Catalogue of Country Living* (Toronto: Personal Library, 1980), when Elmo Stoll married, he and his wife did what most new Amish householders do—they put a bent-hickory rocker high on their list of things to buy.

But Elmo, who now runs the Pioneer Place out of Alymer, Ontario, had a supply problem: these chairs were made only by Amish artisans, none of whom lived in Canada's small Mennonite community. Then the worthy John Martin stepped forward.

After traveling to Amish chair shops in Pennsylvania and Ohio to learn their methods, Martin returned to Ontario and set up shop. But once there he faced another problem: local supplies of the hickory sprouts needed to build the rockers were sparse. Martin appealed to the Canadian Ministry of Natural Resources to direct him to some good stands of the required shagbark hickory, but that, according to Elmo, "was like asking a bank manager if he knew of any good safes to crack."

Finally, word of Martin's plight reached an uncle who farmed in Iowa. He had shagbark aplenty, and Martin was welcome to all he could haul. "Iowa hickory sprouts," says Elmo, "have been used to build Ontario chairs ever since."

Price: $130, ppd.

Mail-order catalog available.

THE PIONEER PLACE

Route 2,
9938 County Road 39
Belle Center,
OH 43310

THE BRUMBY

ROCKER It was 1875 when the Brumby family of Marietta, Georgia, first built this rocking chair. Designed for both versatility and durability, the hand-hewn rocker would quickly be found in places far afield from its native South.

In those days it was said that it cost a man two weeks' work to buy a Brumby, but once he did, it was his for life. If this is so, it's primarily due to the fact that the Brumby mates Appalachian red oak (which tends to expand) with kiln-dried oak (which tends to contract) at key joints, thereby dampening the ravages of seasonal changes in temperature and humidity.

In 1942 the Brumby family discontinued the rocker's production because the war had made the Oriental canes they used for hand-weaving impossible to obtain; but twenty-five years later (after taking six years to trace and repurchase the Brumby's original wood presses and other special production tools) it was reborn. Today the Brumby rocker is crafted according to its original materials and specifications.

The Brumby Jumbo Rocker features gently curved back posts and runners with a slightly reversed rear arch (to resist tipping over), just as in 1875. Both seat and back are woven with "Blue Tie" cane, and the arms are made 5 inches wide to relieve shoulder stress.

Dimensions: overall height, 48 inches; outside arm span, 29½ inches; seat depth, 18 inches; runner length, 36 inches.

For price information contact:

THE ROCKER SHOP

1421 White Circle NW
P.O. Box 12
Marietta, GA 30061
Tel. 404/427-2618

"NASTURTIUM" BENCHES AND SEATS

"Nasturtium" benches and seats were first cast by the Coalbrookdale Company more than a century ago in commemoration of a popular flower of the time. They were first shown as part of the firm's display at the Great Exhibition, held at London's Crystal Palace in 1851.

Coalbrookdale has reproduced this detailed oak-and-iron furniture in limited numbers using, as ever, original patterns from the company's archives. Each piece comes with an identifying serial number.

Bench: 35¼ inches high, 39 inches long, 27 inches deep; weight 111 lbs.

Seat: 35½ inches high, 27¼ inches long, 27 inches deep; weight 98 lbs.

Literature available.

THE COALBROOKDALE COMPANY

American Sales Office
RFD 1, Box 477
Stowe, VT 05672
Tel. 802/253–9727

ALFRED STEVENS TABLE

This table was designed for the venerable Coalbrookdale Company by Alfred Stevens, a nineteenth-century Briton who is best known for his design of the Wellington Monument at St. Paul's Cathedral in London. The Stevens table was so admired at the time of its manufacture that several were sent to the South Kensington Museum to be put on display as examples of excellence in design.

Using the original nineteenth-century patterns, and marking each with a serial number, Coalbrookdale has reissued these tables for a limited period of time. The Stevens Table is 28½ inches high, 36¼ inches long, and 20 inches wide, and can be ordered with a top of either cast iron or polished English oak.

Literature available.

THE COALBROOKDALE COMPANY

American Sales Office
RFD 1, Box 477
Stowe, VT 05672
Tel. 802/253–9727

VICTORIAN PARK BENCH

Jenifer House's park bench features a heavy rococo cast-iron frame finished in black and holding teak slats.

Dimensions: 4 feet 3 inches long, 32 inches high, 27 inches deep. Shipped knocked down for United Parcel, the bench is easily assembled.

Price: $239 ppd. (add $10 west of the Mississippi).

Gift catalog available.

JENIFER HOUSE

New Marlboro Stage
Great Barrington, MA 01230
Tel. 413/528–1500

Victorian Park Bench

TURN-OF-THE-CENTURY FRENCH BISTRO TABLE

The Godin Foundry, one of the largest in France, has been in operation for a century. The bistro table first appeared in their catalog of 1903—the year Paris was a-twitter with the news of Boni de Castellone's marriage to the daughter of the great American railway baron, Jay Gould. The art nouveau table is a companion piece to Godin's remarkable Belle Époque stove (see section below on "Stoves and Ranges") and reflects the preeminence of cast-iron furniture during France's Second Empire period.

It was during this period that the Castellones founded the world's most famous restaurant—Maxim's. There's no record of it, but Maxim's may have provided a fitting debut for the bistro table.

For literature and details, write:

STONE LEDGE COMPANY

170 Washington Street
Marblehead, MA 01945
Tel. 617/631–8417

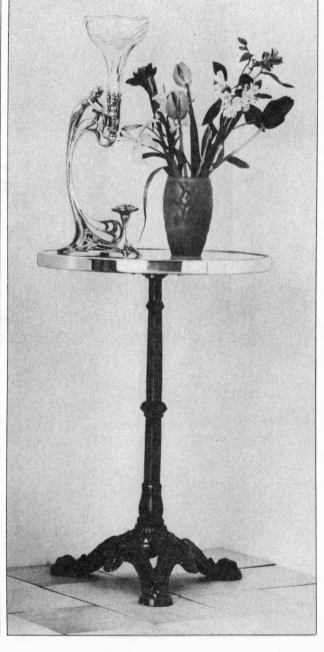

IRON AND BRASS BEDS

Brass beds, which reached the height of their popularity at around the turn of the century, have enjoyed a sustained revival of interest during the past twenty years. To the current standard of flimsy, brass-clad replicas, here are a couple of exceptions:

THE BEDPOST

THE BEDPOST The bedpost disdains the use of such "modern" materials as aluminum (invented in the 1880s, aluminum was used during the turn of the century, although not for bedframes) and keeps instead to cast iron, steel rods, and pipe. They also employ an antique-style bedframe design for its superior structural strength.

The company's iron and brass beds feature several types of ornamentation, the designs of which have been faithfully copied from originals. They estimate that their gauge of brass is about 25 percent heavier than the competition's. Both king- and queen-size models are available.

Packet of literature, $3.

THE BEDPOST

R.D. 1, Box 155
Pen Arygl, PA 18072
Tel. 215/588–3824

CHARLES P. ROGERS BRASS BEDS

CHARLES P. ROGERS BRASS BEDS Established in 1855, the Charles P. Rogers Brass Bed Company is the country's oldest manufacturer. Their solid-brass beds are available in a good range of antique styles and reflect in their structure and design the manufacturer's allegiance to traditional construction techniques.

Color catalog available, $3.

CHARLES P. ROGERS BRASS BEDS

149 West 24th Street
New York, NY 10011
Tel. 212/807–1989

Bedding House of CHAS. P. ROGERS & CO.,

248 Sixth Avenue, N. Y.

Corner 16th Street.

January 1st, 1890.

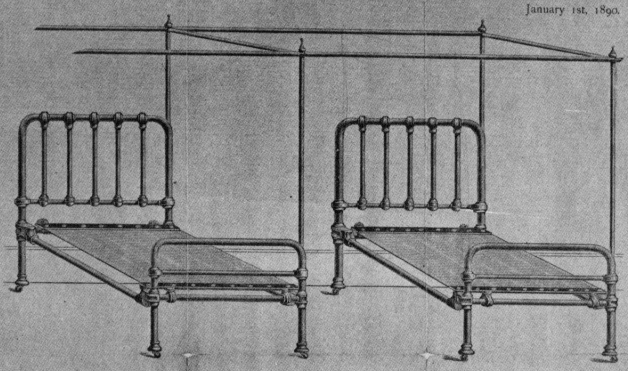

We would respectfully call your attention to

Our Improved Institution Iron Bedstead.

We refer by permission to the following Institutions where they are in use, and are found to meet all the requirements of a first-class **Hospital** or **Institution** Iron Bedstead.

References:—

Convent of the Sacred Heart, N. Y. City.
Isabella Home, N. Y. City.
Sisters of Charity, New Providence.

Franciscan Sisters of St. Mary's Brooklyn, N.Y.
Berachah Home, N. Y. City.
and many others.

This Bedstead is made of the best material throughout. The frames are made of inch tubing, with 1½ inch Tubular Sides and ends, are fitted with best quality woven wire, spring mattress with adjustable screws that prevent sagging, made with rubber feet, or castors and japanned, any plain color.

Sizes, - - - - 2 ft.-6.   2 ft.-9   3 ft.   3 ft.-6 wide.
Price, - - - -

We are prepared to furnish estimates for all kinds of Mattresses, Pillows, etc., suitable for **Institution** or Hospital use.

Mattresses and Pillows remade and renovated at short notice. (Special Prices.)

Shaker Furniture

"Purity of Life, Peace, Justice, Love." These are the principles of the Shaker orders as taught by Ann Lee, the religious sect's charismatic founder who emigrated to America from Manchester, England, in 1774.

Although their celibacy and unusual form of worship created suspicions in "worldly" society, by the mid–nineteenth century the Shaker sect could claim about 6,000 believers, settled into rural areas from Maine to Kentucky. The Shakers shook while they prayed, but through their honesty, fairness, and industriousness they earned a reputation that was rock solid. This simplicity and directness is reflected in the design of the furniture which, until their decline after the Civil War, Shaker communities produced.

Only two Shaker communities remain today, one in Canterbury, New Hampshire, and the other at Sabbathday Lake, Maine. Shaker furniture making is carried on entirely by private firms.

At Shaker Workshops, kits are produced by skilled craftsmen faithful to the specifications of Shaker pieces in museums and private collections. Each kit is preassembled, squared up, and pinned to ensure accurate fit; and only common tools are needed for their reassembly.

FROM SHAKER WORKSHOPS

ELDER'S CHAIR Richard Dabrowski, president of Shaker Workshops, writes that Shaker furniture was sometimes designed exclusively for sale to the "world's people," as nonbelievers were called. As the refreshing lack of xenophobia in this phrase indicates, the Shakers were tolerant of nonbelievers, even though they demanded all sorts of foolishness on the furniture that they bought. We suspect that this chair's slender rear-post finials and "mushroom" armrest turnings indicate that the elders who sat in this chair were worldly, and only shook when palsied. The chair has a rock maple frame.

Dimensions: 51½ inches high, 22 inches wide, and 18 inches deep.

Price: kit, $112.50 (plus $5.50 for shipping); finished piece, $225, ppd.

HANGING
SHELVES
A replica of a set of nineteenth-century shelves now in the collection of Hancock Shaker Village.

Made of clear pine with a height of 25 inches and a width of 27 inches, the three shelves are approximately 5, 6, and 7 inches deep, respectively.

Price: kit, $45 (plus $3.25 for shipping).

TOWEL RACK
Free-standing floor racks such as this were commonplace in Shaker retiring rooms, kitchens, and wash houses. Shaker Workshops' towel rack features unique octagonal rails.

Made of clear pine, the rack is 33½ inches high and 33⅛ inches wide.

Price: kit, $38.75 (plus $2.75 for shipping); finished piece, $77, ppd.

MOUNT LEBANON
SETTEE
"This piece would never have left the community," writes Mr. Dabrowski of the Shaker Mount Lebanon settee. Further described as "the rarest of all Shaker furniture," the double armchair that this settee replicates follows one originally built in the South Family chair shop at Mount Lebanon, New York, toward the end of the nineteenth century.

With a frame of rock maple, the settee has a height of 37½ inches, a width of 43½ inches, and a depth of 19 inches.

Price: kit, $200 (plus $7.55 for shipping); finished piece, $400, ppd.

WEAVER'S CHAIR Huge

Shaker handlooms demanded chairs with high seats to allow the weavers to sit close to their work. The same chairs were also used at shop desks, and laundry and ironing tables.

This weaver's chair is made of rock maple, and when finished stands 39 inches high (with a seat height of 26 inches) and 18¾ inches wide.

Price: kit, $65 (plus $4.25 for shipping); finished piece, $130, ppd.

LOW-BACK

CHAIR Reflecting Shaker practicality,

this chair was designed with a low back so that it could be tucked under the table following meals.

Made of rock maple, the low-back chair is 27 inches high, 18¾ inches wide, and 14 inches deep.

Price: kit, $60 (plus $3.75 for shipping); finished piece, $120, ppd.

SHOEMAKER'S

CANDLESTAND According

to the Shaker Workshops' catalog, this candlestand was found in a long-closed cobbler's shop at the Mount Lebanon community. It was resting there atop a bench in a room lined with shoe lasts, some bearing the names of long-dead Shaker brothers and sisters.

The 16½-inch candlestand is made entirely of rock maple. Its platform supports two candles and is adjustable by means of a threaded centerpost.

Price: kit, $37.50 (plus $2.75 for shipping).

Seasonal catalog available, 50¢.

SHAKER WORKSHOPS

P.O. Box 1028
Concord, MA 01742
Tel. 617/646-8985

SHAKER ROCKING CHAIR

The National Trust's Shaker rocking chair has been replicated from one at the Lyndhurst Estate in Tarrytown, New York. The 41-inch-high rocker is made of rock maple with a stain, oil, and wax finish. The seat is made of beige and butternut cotton webbing. The chair is shipped with rockers detached.

Price: $475.

Catalog available, $1.

PRESERVATION SHOPS

Department AH
National Trust for Historic
　　Preservation
1600 H Street NW
Washington, DC 20006
Tel. 202/673-4200

1890 CLOWN MIRROR

Three wagons, five horses, and a tent comprised the simple traveling show that John Robinson took through the Allegheny foothills in 1824. By the end of the century, when children flocked to the streets to see the parades of circuses like P. T. Barnum's "Greatest Show on Earth," the circus's humble beginnings must have seemed remote.

Victorian Accents offers a hand-cast replication of a clown-shaped mirror first made in 1890. Classically cherubic, the jester holds the reflecting glass across his belly like a huge drum.

　Dimensions: 9 inches by 12 inches.

　Price: $28.95 (plus $3.50 for shipping).

Catalog of Victoriana, $1.

WATTLE & DAUB'S VICTORIAN ACCENTS

661 West 7th Street
Plainfield, NJ 07060
Tel. 201/757-8507

HOUSEWARES

69c FOR THE IMPROVED PURITAN CHOPPER COMPLETE WITH FOUR CUTTERS AND COOK BOOK

THE CHOPPER THAT SAVES YOU MONEY. THE ONLY ONE YOU CAN'T AFFORD TO DO WITHOUT.

THE BEST AND MOST CONVENIENT CHOPPER on the market at anything like our price. Chops all kinds of raw or cooked meats, vegetables, fruits, etc. Each size chopper has three hand forged steel knives or cutters: coarse, medium and fine for meats and vegetables, and one nut butter cutter.

THE IMPROVED PURITAN FOOD CHOPPER is made of the finest material throughout, each working part is carefully finished so it will run smoothly and all exposed parts are heavily retinned, which makes it rustproof, easy to clean and sanitary. It is as carefully constructed as if intended to sell for twice the price. Simple, has few parts, and does the most satisfactory work in half the time usually required by other choppers.

THE PURITAN possesses all the good features found in other choppers with several valuable improvements of its own. It has a perfect drip spout which catches and saves the juice and prevents soiling the table or floor. It has an improved table clamp which holds fast. It quickly chops all kinds of food, meat, vegetables, fruit, etc., fine or coarse, and does not choke up. It is so easy to operate that a 10-year old girl can easily turn it. It is strong, durable and substantial, and with ordinary care will last a number of years.

OUR PURITAN FOOD CHOPPER will pay for itself in a short time by making it possible to utilize cold meats, "left overs," etc. We furnish with each Puritan Chopper a copy of our Puritan Food Chopper Cook Book which contains over 200 tested recipes and explains how to save time, labor, money and food by using a Puritan Chopper.

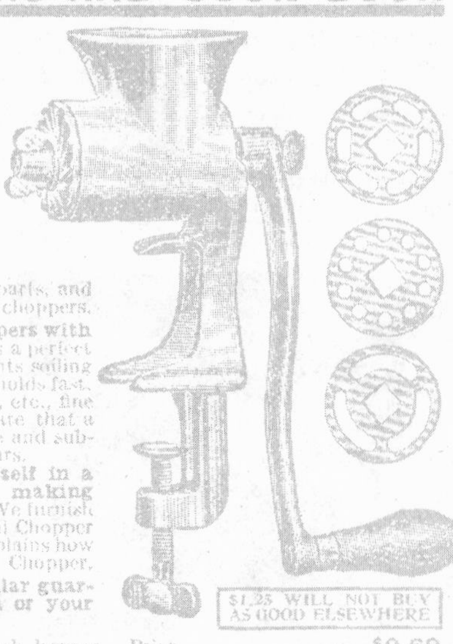

$1.25 WILL NOT BUY AS GOOD ELSEWHERE

EVERY PURITAN CHOPPER WE SELL is covered by our regular guarantee of "satisfaction or your money back." We recommend Size 1 for general family use.

No. 9K29500	Size 0, chops 1½ pounds meat per minute, 2¾x2¾-inch hopper.	Price $0.69
No. 9K29503	Size 1, chops 2 pounds meat per minute, 2½x3 -inch hopper.	Price .... .87
No. 9K29504	Size 2, chops 2½ pounds meat per minute, 3 x4 -inch hopper.	Price 1.05
No. 9K29505	Size 3, chops 3½ pounds meat per minute, 4 x5 -inch hopper.	Price 1.37

74c FOR A FAMILY SIZE JAPANNED IRON SAUSAGE STUFFER.

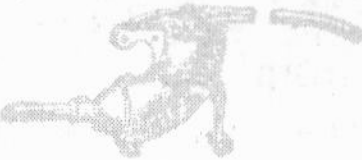

No. 9K29531 Size 1, for families. Price 74c

No. 9K29530 Size 0, for butchers. Price $1.03

96c FOR THIS RUSTPROOF SPEEDY RAILROAD SAUSAGE STUFFER.

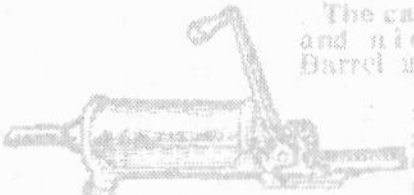

The castings are heavy and nicely japanned. Barrel is made of heavy tin plate. Suitable for family and hotel use. Capacity, 3½ pounds.

No. 9K29533 Price 96c

$1.37 FOR A 2-QUART SIZE LARD, WINE AND JELLY PRESS.

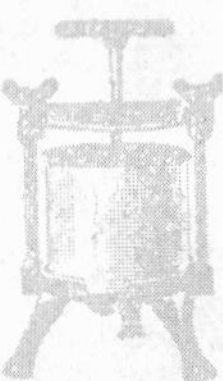

Made with special reference to strength and guaranteed against breakage under any fair usage. Cylinders are heavy tin and all parts tinned all over. Can be taken apart in a moment for cleaning. All parts are interchangeable and can be replaced.

No. 9K29538 2-quart size. Price $1.37

No. 9K29539 4-quart size. Price $2.76

No. 9K29540 10-quart size. Price $4.12

$3.04 ENTERPRISE SAUSAGE STUFFER LARD AND FRUIT PRESS.

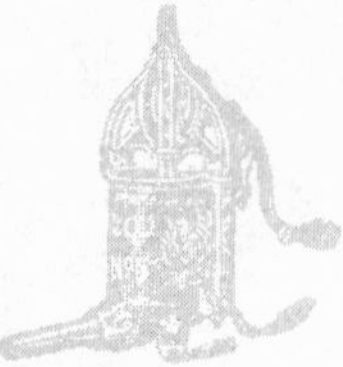

Unexcelled for butchers' or farmers' use for stuffing sausages and pressing lard. For kitchen use there is nothing like it for pressing fruit for making jellies, wine, etc. Full directions for use are sent with each press.

No. 9K29523 Two-qt. size, japanned, rack movement. Price $3.04

ENTERPRISE FOOD CHOPPERS.

Cut like a pair of scissors; do not tear, grind or squeeze the meat; impossible for any strings, sinews or gristle to pass through without being chopped. The Enterprise can be taken apart in a few seconds and is easily cleaned. All parts are interchangeable and can be replaced at small cost. Knives and plates are made of finest steel and fully warranted.

96c BRONZE BEARING EASY TURNING ENTERPRISE FOOD CHOPPER.

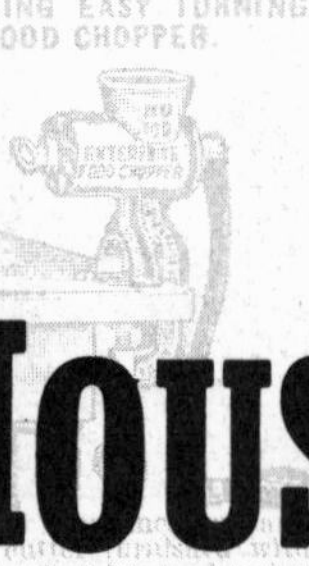

It will chop raw meat, cooked meat, vegetables of all kinds, bread and crackers, and will make peanut butter. It will chop any kind of food any size you wish for any kind of dish. Can be cleaned in a minute, is always ready and never gets out of order. Four knives, coarse, and ... each machine. The phosphor bronze bearing reduces the friction, makes the machine easier to turn and last much longer. Will chop two pounds of meat per minute.

No. 9K29502 Price 96c

$3.68 BUYS THIS HOTEL SIZE ENTERPRISE MEAT CHOPPER.

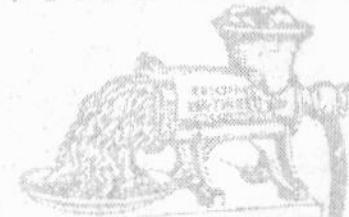

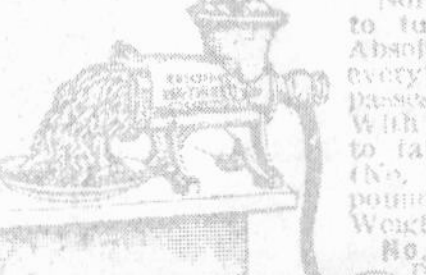

Noiseless, easy to turn, rapid. Absolutely chops everything that passes through. With legs to screw to table or bench (No. 22), chops 4 pounds per minute. Weight, 12 pounds.

No. 9K29509 Price ... $3.68

... Does not heat or discolor the meat. Is easy to turn, noiseless, and will cut any size desired. (No. 32), chops 5 lbs. per minute; weight, complete, 58 lbs.

No. 9K29512 Price $7.93

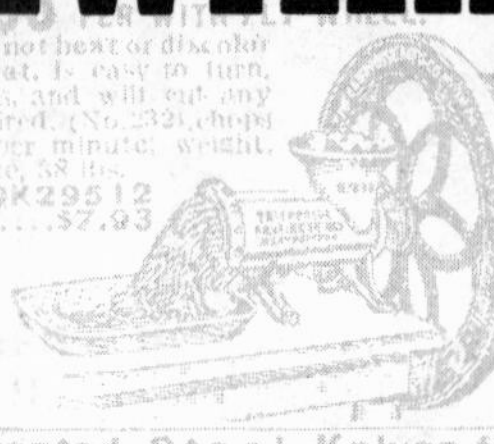

$1.65 GENUINE ENTERPRISE TINNED ROTARY KNIFE FOOD CHOPPER.

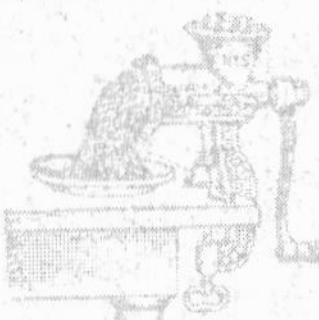

Chops exactly as shown. The meat is fed into the hopper, and by the feed screws carried forward and forced into the plate, where it is cut off by the revolving knife. Small family size, with clamp (No. 5), chops 1½ pounds per minute.

No. 9K29506 Price $1.65

$2.45 FOR A LARGE FAMILY SIZE ENTERPRISE MEAT CHOPPER.

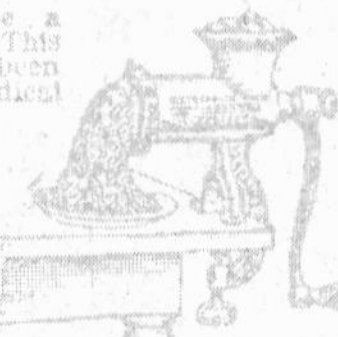

Cuts meat like a pair of scissors. This chopper has been adopted by the Medical Department of the United States army. With clamp (No. 10), chops 3 pounds per minute.

No. 9K29507 Price $2.45

Same as above except with legs to screw to bench or table (No. 12).

No. 9K29508 Price $2.24

Warranted Steel Knives for Enterprise Meat Choppers.

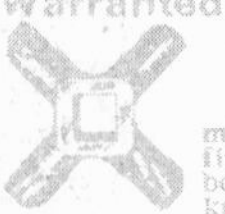

Made of best quality material, are sharp and nicely finished. Be sure to give number of chopper for which the knife is wanted.

No. 9K29517 Price, to fit chopper—

No. 5	No. 10	No. 12	No. 22	No. 32	No. 232
23c	26c	29c	43c	65c	67c

Steel Plates for Enterprise Meat Choppers.

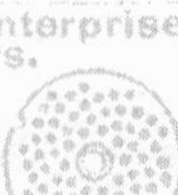

When ordering, be sure to give size holes and number of chopper for which the plate is wanted. The plate having 3-16-inch holes is most commonly used, and is what is furnished with choppers.

No. 9K29518 With 3-16, ¼, 5-16, or ⅜-inch holes. Price, to fit chopper—

No. 5	No. 10	No. 12	No. 22	No. 32	No. 232
30c	43c	45c	65c	90c	92c

Sausage Stuffing Attachments for Enterprise Meat Choppers.

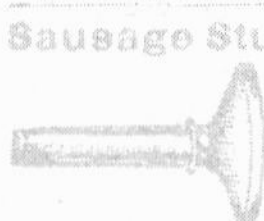

Have new patented corrugated spout, prevents air entering casing, thus preserving the sausage. Made of spun brass, nickel plated. Made in two sizes of tube, namely: ¾ inch and 1¼ inches. When ordering, be sure to give number of chopper.

No. 9K29516 Price, with ¾-inch tube. To fit Chopper—

No. 5	No. 10	No. 12	No. 22	No. 32	No. 232
40c	43c	45c	55c	63c	65c

Price, with 1¼-inch tube. To fit chopper—

No. 5	No. 10	No. 12	No. 22	No. 32	No. 232
65c	68c	72c	75c	$1.00	$1.05

LOW PRICES IN OUR LAST CATALOGUE STILL FURTHER REDUCED IN THIS BOOK ON OVER 3,000 HARDWARE ITEMS MAKE YOUR SAVING GREATER THAN EVER.

8c BRONZED 5-INCH SINGLE ARM FLOWER POT BRACKET.

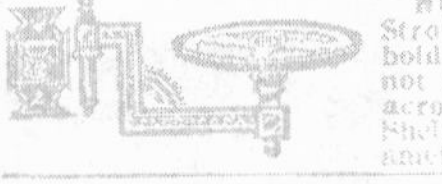

No. 9K22500 Strong enough to hold any flower pot not over 4 inches across the bottom. Shelf 4 inches in diameter. Price ... 8c

28c ENAMELED DOUBLE SHELF 12-INCH ARM FLOWER POT BRACKET.

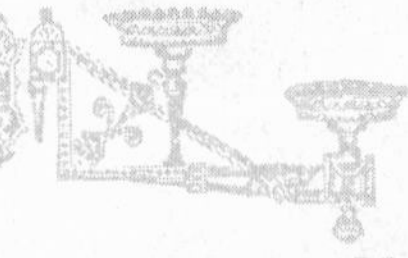

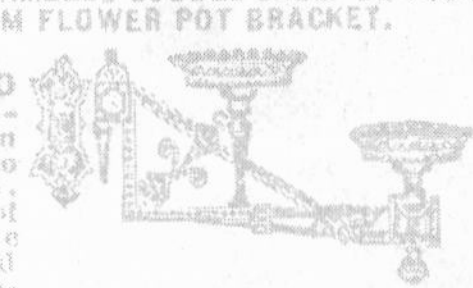

No. 9K22510 Nicely finished, an ornament to any home. Diameter of dishes, one 4 inches and one 4½ inches inside. Price 28c

...c ENAMELED 12-INCH DOUBLE ARM 4-POT BRACKET.

No. 9K22515 These brackets are well made, strong and substantial. Diameter of dishes two 4 inches and two 4½ inches inside, complete, as shown. Price 58c

$4.05 SCREW MOVEMENT ENTERPRISE STUFFER AND PRESS.

Used as a sausage stuffer, lard press, jelly press and wine press.

No. 9K29524 Four-quart size, japanned. Weight, 30 pounds. Price $4.05

No. 9K29525 Eight-quart size, japanned. Weight, 44 pounds. Price $5.69

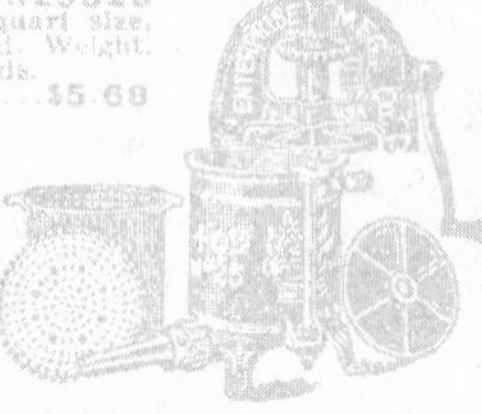

$1.74 FOR A HIGH GRADE LEADER CARPET SWEEPER.

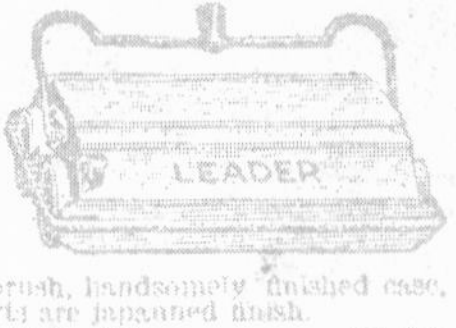

It has broom action, reversible bail, improved dumping device, the new improved braid band which never comes off, strictly pure bristle brush, handsomely finished case. The metal parts are japanned finish.

No. 9K22300 Price $1.74

$1.97 GENUINE BISSELL'S IMPROVED CHAMPION CARPET SWEEPER.

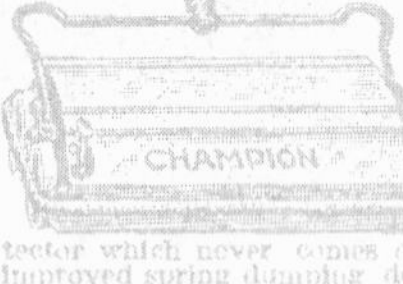

A high grade sweeper at a very low price. It has the Bissell broom action, reversible bail, new improved braid band furniture protector which never comes off, Bissell's new improved spring dumping device, pure bristle sweeping brush, handsomely finished case. All metal parts are nicely japanned.

No. 9K22305 Price $1.97

$2.46 SEROCO NOISELESS, DUSTLESS, FRICTIONLESS ROLLER BEARING CARPET SWEEPER.

IT IS IMPOSSIBLE TO MAKE A BETTER SWEEPER than our Seroco, even if we sold it for twice the price. No sweeper is superior in material, workmanship or lasting qualities and if you pay $3.00 to $5.00 for a sweeper elsewhere, you will not get as good value as you will get if you order a Seroco Sweeper.

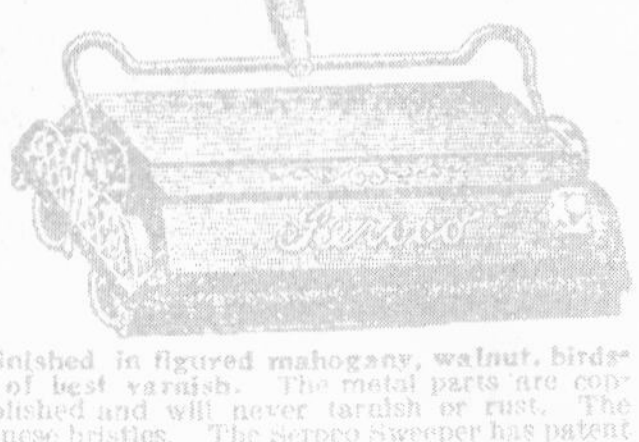

THE SWEEPER CASE is made of the finest selected hardwood 3-ply veneer, finished in figured mahogany, walnut, birdseye maple or curly birch with three coats of best varnish. The metal parts are copper plated, then triple nickel plated and polished and will never tarnish or rust. The brushes are made of the finest imported Chinese bristles. The Seroco Sweeper has patent roller bearings, shown in the illustration, which makes it run easier, take less labor to operate and do better work than any other sweeper.

THE SEROCO SWEEPER saves time and money. Costs no more than five or six good brooms and will outwear several dozen. Will follow a broom and remove more dirt and dust than the broom did and does not wear out a carpet like a broom. We fully guarantee the Seroco Sweeper. If you do not find it the finest sweeper in every respect that you ever used, return it to us and we will refund your money at once.

No. 9K22314 Seroco Carpet Sweeper. Price $2.46

VICTORIAN HARDWARE

Bob Crawford, owner of Crawford's Old House Store, knows brass. In fact, when he's discussing his replica Victorian hardware, you can hear the stuff in his voice: "These are true reproductions," he stated, "not cheap sand-cast copies which lack the perfect detail of the originals. If you're restoring or re-creating an American landmark, why use Taiwan parts?"

Crawford's catalog displays sixty-five pieces of replica hardware including hinges, doorknobs, key plates, sash lifts, and drawer pulls. These are all cast in solid bronze using the "lost wax" process to recapture the originals (circa 1885–1910) in fine detail.

Catalog available, $1.75.

CRAWFORD'S OLD HOUSE STORE

301 McCall
Waukesha, WI 53186
Tel. 414/542-0685

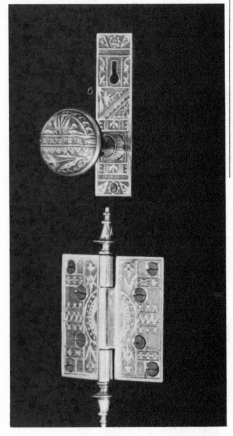

RENOVATOR'S SUPPLY VICTORIAN HARDWARE

The astounding success of the Renovator's Supply catalog places it at the point position of contemporary interest for quality Victorian reproduction. Renovator's Supply began in 1978 when, frustrated by their inability to find a source of authentically reproduced fixtures with which to restore their colonial farmhouse in western Massachusetts, Claude and Donna Jeanloz became that source, and set up a mail-order business to supply others. So great was their reception that after a single year they had to move the business into larger quarters (an old Model T garage with a restored Victorian facade). By 1982 they were posting more than three million copies of their catalog of old-style decorative items annually.

The Jeanlozes' color catalog includes solid-brass plumbing fixtures, brass and oaken bath accessories, copper weather vanes, curtains, braided rugs, fireplace accessories, and more.

Catalog of old-style decorative items available, $2.

THE RENOVATOR'S SUPPLY

182 Northfield Road
Millers Falls, MA 01349
Tel. 413/659-2211

BRASS COSTUMER

The Renovator's Supply Victorian costumer has a spiral brass shaft and makes an ideal hat or coat tree. Wall mounted, the costumer is 32 inches high and projects 8 inches.

Price: $45, ppd. (price reduced with orders of three or more).

Catalog of old-style decorative items available, $2.

THE RENOVATOR'S SUPPLY

182 Northfield Road
Millers Falls, MA 01349
Tel. 413/659-2211

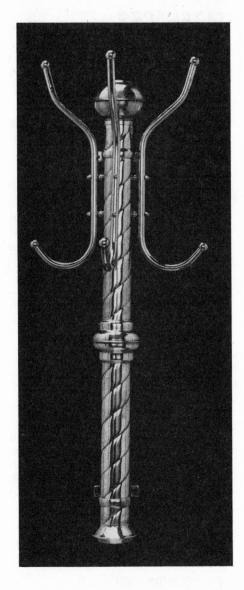

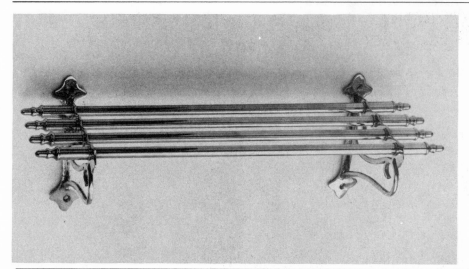

VICTORIAN TRAIN RACK

This brass rack replicates those once found in Victorian parlor cars. It comes in two sizes, both 7½ inches wide and 6¾ inches deep.

Prices: 19-inch train rack, $39, ppd.; 29-inch train rack, $49.95, ppd.

Catalog of old-style decorative items available, $2.

THE RENOVATOR'S SUPPLY

182 Northfield Road
Millers Falls, MA 01349
Tel. 413/659-2211

FIREBACKS

Although still used in parts of continental Europe, the cast-iron fireback has been virtually unknown in America since the middle of the nineteenth century. But now, thanks to the efforts of Donald Stoughton at the Country Iron Foundry, an addendum to the history of the American fireback may be written.

A fireback is a cast-iron plate which, when placed behind the fire of a hearth, absorbs the heat of the fire and further protects the rear wall of the fireplace. Lately the decorative qualities of firebacks have renewed an appreciation of their utility.

The earliest English fireback yet found was made back in 1548 and reflects the influence of the firebacks that had been popular both in Holland and Germany for the previous hundred years. In the English-speaking American colonies the use of firebacks followed the example of the mother country, and employed embossed decorative patterns based on the designs of coats-of-arms, illustrated allegories, and "loose stamps." Although the use of firebacks waned in England early in the nineteenth century, they persisted in the U.S. until around 1840, when the sealing-off of fireplaces was hastened by the invention of the airtight stove.

Country Iron is primarily an industrial foundry, but one whose president, Donald Stoughton, holds an interest in ancient casting techniques. This has resulted in the sand-cast replication of a line of beautiful firebacks that follow the originals in every detail. The illustration of the fox-mask fireback shown here was graciously provided by Mr. Stoughton as an example of a nineteenth-century American piece.

Brochure available, $1 (refundable with order).

THE COUNTRY IRON FOUNDRY

P.O. Box 600
Paoli, PA 19301
Tel. 215/296-7122

DECORATED FIREBOARDS

As the chimneys in Early American homes had no dampers, the hearths that were so cheery and warm all winter suddenly in summer provided easy access to a naturalist's compendium of insects and the birds that pursued them. So in their own defense, colonists would board up their fireplaces thereby providing themselves with another surface to decorate.

Popular designs were also cheery—flower vases, pastoral scenes, and even *trompe l'oeil* views of the hearth itself. Fireboards provided a canvas for such notable nineteenth-century American artists as Edward Hicks, whose *The Peaceable Kingdom* is well known to his modern-day countrymen. **Artist Jim Baker** has revived this traditional art form to create fireboards that may reflect a customer's special interest or quaintly glorify his or her home, farm, birthplace, business, or family history. Mr. Baker gladly accepts sketches, photographs, and verse regarding these.

Prices vary with the size and complexity of the subject desired by the customer. Shipping costs are additional.

JIM BAKER

P.O. Box 149
Worthington, OH 43085
Tel. 614/885-7040

BRASS CANDLESTICKS AND HEARTH ACCESSORIES

Using original molds and patterns, the Fancibrass Company of Pittsburgh sandcasts solid-brass candlesticks and hearth accessories from the late-nineteenth-century English open-hearth period.

Catalog and price list available, to the trade only.

FANCIBRASS

522 Parkway View Drive
Pittsburgh, PA 15205
Tel. 412/787-2499; Telex 812381

CAST-IRON DOORSTOPS

Cast-iron doorstops in the shape of various animals and other objects came into vogue beginning around 1890. Although many were used in their plain black state, they most often succumbed, in the Victorian manner, to the decorating propensities of the women of the household and were painted.

Victorian Accents' replica doorstops are available in several styles, all in white enamel and 7 to 12 inches high.
Price: $16 to $22.

Catalog of Victoriana available, $1.

WATTLE & DAUB'S VICTORIAN ACCENTS

661 West 7th Street
Plainfield, NJ 07060
Tel. 201/757-8507

OLD STURBRIDGE VILLAGE CANDLESTICKS

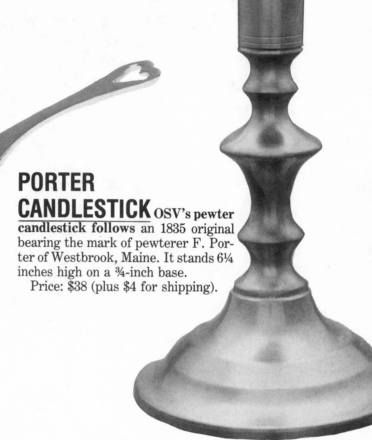

PORTER CANDLESTICK

OSV's pewter candlestick follows an 1835 original bearing the mark of pewterer F. Porter of Westbrook, Maine. It stands 6¼ inches high on a ¾-inch base.
   Price: $38 (plus $4 for shipping).

HEART-HANDLED CHAMBERSTICK

A traditional heart design has been pierced into the handle of this solid-brass chamberstick, a precise replica of a Sturbridge Village original.
   Dimensions: 2¼ inches by 8½ inches by 4½ inches.
   Price: $48 (plus $4 for shipping).

Catalog available.

OLD STURBRIDGE VILLAGE

Museum Shop
Sturbridge, MA 01566
Tel. 617/347–9843

STOW CHEST

The Crazy Crow Trading Post recommends their stow chest for the storage of gear in camp or when traveling, but it will also serve well around the house. Made of unfinished pine, the chest measures approximately 28 inches in length, 15 inches wide, and 14 inches high, with lid.

Catalog available, $2.

CRAZY CROW TRADING POST

P.O. Box 314
Denison, TX 75020
Tel. 214/463–1366

BANDBOXES

In the early part of the nineteenth-century, when travelers boarded coaches on overland journeys they carried along an item of luggage that really has no counterpart today—the bandbox. Relatively fragile containers made of pasteboard and covered with wallpaper, bandboxes were used by women when they traveled as storage for such necessaries as jewelry, scarves, combs, ribbons, and sundry bagatelles. By the second quarter of the century bandboxes were so common that even women of modest means had several in varying sizes and shapes.

But use of bandboxes was necessarily wedded to the stagecoach era. After 1850, when travels by steamboat and rail demanded stouter luggage, the bandbox gradually faded into oblivion. Originals are now so scarce as to be beyond the means of all but the wealthiest collectors. Exact replicas, however, are available.

BANDBOXES BY VICTORIAN ACCENTS

These are handcrafted bandboxes— cut, pasted, and covered in the manner of the last century. Even the papers are duplicates of nineteenth-century originals. All boxes are numbered and signed.

The bandbox set consists of an oval trinket box (4½ by 3½ by 2½ inches), a round collar box (5¾ by 3⅝ inches), and a heart-shaped box (7¾ by 7¼ by 3⅝ inches), and costs $40, plus $5 for insurance and shipping.

The oval trinket box alone, with "Damask Rose" potpourri, costs $12.95, plus $3.50 for insurance and shipping.

Catalog of Victoriana available, $1.

WATTLE & DAUB'S VICTORIAN ACCENTS

661 West 7th Street
Plainfield, NJ 07060
Tel. 201/757–8507

BANDBOXES BY OPEN CUPBOARD

The Open Cupboard's hand-sewn paste-board bandboxes come in 3½-inch ovals in three heights (1½, 2, and 2½ inches), a 3½-inch round (in the same three heights), and a 4½- by 2-inch heart shape. As was often the case during the early 1800s, all are lined with the newsprint of that period. Dealer inquiries welcome.

Price: All bandboxes, $11.95, ppd.

OPEN CUPBOARD

P.O. Box 70
Tenants Harbor, ME 04860
Tel. 207/372–8401

BANDBOXES BY LINDSAY FROST

Lindsay Frost's bandboxes are individually handcrafted, numbered and initialed in the original fashion. The seven shapes and sizes of her bandboxes have been derived from measurements made at museums and from private collections.

Price list available.

BANDBOXES

Lindsay Frost
Box A
Avella, PA 15312
Tel. 412/587–3990

NANTUCKET LIGHTSHIP BASKETS

They were called "Nantucket mink" once: "Nantucket" because they'd be about as genuine as Siberian bourbon if made anywhere else, and "mink" because women—young and old, on-island and off—coveted them so mightily.

Legend has it that the baskets were adapted from those made by local Indians who used clay and willow twigs to fashion them. Of course they weren't yet known as "lightship" baskets then—that came later, during the nineteenth century when seamen aboard the Nantucket lightships took to making them to help while away the hours spent bobbing in the North Atlantic.

Made now from white oak, Four Winds's traditional lightship basket has a rosewood top and features hand-carved elephant ivory trim. "Baskets of this quality are heirlooms," proclaims proprietress Marcia Rubin, "and are traditionally handed down to successive generations as an exquisite example of indigenous folk art."

Price: $595.

FOUR WINDS

Straight Wharf
Nantucket, MA 02554
Tel. 617/228–1597

New England Basket Works's
Cheese and Herb Drying Baskets

TRADITIONAL AMERICAN BASKETS

Diane Cummings's business began as a hobby and has since grown to the point that she now ships her product all over the country, including Puerto Rico and Alaska. These baskets—including the cheese, bread, and herb-drying shown—run the gamut of specialized Early American types. They are hand-woven following antique originals by Connecticut craftsmen, and are museum approved.

Price list available.

NEW ENGLAND BASKET WORKS

P.O. Box 645
Higganum, CT 06441

SHAKER OVAL BOXES AND "CARRIERS"

Shaker Workshops credits the work of Brother Delmar C. Wilson (1873—1961) of the Sabbathday Lake community with the inspiration for these oval boxes and carriers. They are entirely handmade by a process that steams and bends select cherry wood and secures it with copper nails to tops and bottoms made of clear pine. The Shakers used oval boxes for the storage of sewing notions and for kitchen items. I've used them as wedding gifts and know them to be of remarkably fine quality.

The oval carrier (W521) is 13¼ inches long, 9⅜ inches wide, and 2¾ inches deep, and costs $32.

There are six oval boxes made, ranging in size from 4⅜ by 2⅞ by 1½ inches and costing $22 (W310), to 13¼ by 9⅜ by 5¾ inches and costing $50 (W315).

A nested set of all six boxes (W310–W315) costs $205; a nested set of the three smallest boxes (W310–W312) costs $80.

Seasonal catalog available, 50¢.

SHAKER WORKSHOPS

P.O. Box 1028
Concord, MA 01742
Tel. 617/646-8985

FERKIN

FERKIN It's an unusual item today, but most Americans who have ever lived would quickly recognize a ferkin for the lard and butter bucket that it was. Most would have had at least one in their kitchens. Made of solid, ¾-inch pine, the Log Cabin Shop's ferkin is secured with steel bands and sealed around with wax. The outside can be finished either with stain or oil and painted, toll painted, stenciled, or otherwise decorated. It stands 9 inches high with a diameter at bottom of 8½ inches.

Log Cabin catalog #81004.

Price: $17.95 (plus postage and handling).

Catalog available, $4.

THE LOG CABIN SHOP

P.O. Box 275
Lodi, OH 44254
Tel. 216/948-1082

HAND-TIED BROOMS

HAND-TIED BROOMS Brooms, hand-tied "in the old way," are available from La Pelleterie de Fort de Chartres in Chester, Illinois.

Prices: whisk, $4; fireplace, $7; small floor, $9; medium floor, $10; large floor, $14.50 (postage and handling additional).

Catalog of historical clothing and accouterments available, $3 (refundable with purchase of $30 or more).

LA PELLETERIE DE FORT DE CHARTRES

P.O. Box 627
Chester, IL 62233
Tel. 618/826-4334

COFFEE GRINDERS

If this is coffee, bring me tea. And if this is tea, please bring me a cup of coffee.
—attributed to Abraham Lincoln

Before the revolution, Americans drank tea as avidly as any of King George's subjects. It was in fact the revenue potential created by all this colonial tea drinking that resulted in the imposition of one of George III's most despised taxes—the Townshend Acts of 1767. With these duties commenced the notion of coffee drinking as a patriotic display, leaving tea to the Tories.
With lordly indifference to this, the British Parliament passed the Tea Act in 1773, which gave a monopoly in tea to the British East India Company, resulting in even higher prices for the drink. By December the Boston Tea Party had sealed tea's fate and made coffee, despite the Great Emancipator's ambivalence, our national cup.

FROM MR. DUDLEY

FROM MR. DUDLEY The Mr. Dudley Company of Oceanside, California, carries sixteen models of replica Early American coffee grinders. These are not exact duplicates as they vary in size and detail from the originals.

For dealer information write:

DUDLEY KEBOW, INC.

2603 Industry Street
Oceanside, CA 92054
Tel. 619/439-3000

FROM THE PIONEER PLACE

This old-fashioned coffee mill is a real beauty, with both its metal and wooden parts made from original nineteenth-century patterns. I'd call this a reproduction, but the Stoll brothers of Pioneer Place have another phrase for it—to them it's a "new antique"!
   Price: $37.50, ppd.

THE PIONEER PLACE

Route 2, 9938 County Road 39
Belle Center, OH 43310

IRONWARE

The Lodge Manufacturing Company is a fourth-generation family business incorporated in 1896. The extensive selection of ironware includes skillets, old-style griddles, camp ovens, country and straight kettles, and cornstick and muffin pans.

Price list and order form available.

LODGE MANUFACTURING COMPANY

P.O. Box 380
South Pittsburgh, TN 37380
Tel. 615/837-7181

TINWARE

It is said that if new tinware be rubbed with lard and thoroughly heated in the oven before being used it will prevent it from rusting.
—*From the 1904* Farmer's Almanac

Tinware was commonly used prior to 1870 when it began to be replaced by speckled enamelware. La Pelleterie offers top-quality tinware—plates, bowls, cups, and mugs—authentically replicated and "the correct style for use in camp or rendezvous."
   Prices: 8½-inch tin plate, $3; 10-inch tin plate, $3.50; 3½- by 3-inch cup, $2.50; pint mug, $5; 4¾- by 2-inch bowl, $2.50; 5½- by 3-inch Paul Revere bowl, $4 (postage and handling additional).

Catalog available, $3 (refundable with purchase of $30 or more).

LA PELLETERIE DE FORT DE CHARTRES

P.O. Box 627
Chester, IL 62233
Tel. 618/826-4334

GRANITEWARE
First produced in 1870 by the St. Louis Stamping Company, enameled graniteware's special glaze made cooking and cleaning a lot easier. By the turn of the century there were many varieties available—some mottled, some marbled, some spattered, some speckled—and a twenty-four-piece set was advertised in the Sears catalogue for $4.37.

Although the American Graniteware Association (P.O. Box 605, Downers Grove, IL 60515) maintains that none of the currently manufactured graniteware can come even close to the original in quality, they allow that the ware manufactured by the General Housewares company is about the best available. Their "Frontier Campware" offers a nice variety of spattered enamel graniteware, including a huge twenty-serving coffee boiler.

Brochure and order form available.

GENERAL HOUSEWARES CORPORATION

Consumer Services
P.O. Box 4066
Terre Haute, IN 47804
Tel. 812/232–1000

"MISSIONARY" COOKING POT
Missionary work in Africa reached its zenith during the nineteenth century when self-sacrificing clergy packed their linen frocks and brought the Word of God to Hottentot and Zulu alike. It's a controversial matter now, but legend has it that it was the natives who sometimes did the converting: making the missionaries into brimming potfuls of rain-forest ratatouille.

Marching as to entree is passé now, but the cooking pots are back with us. They're smaller than I remember from seeing them in those old cartoons (the missionary's position would've had to have been a kind of crouch), but cast in the old molds by the firm that originally made them, they're the genuine article nonetheless.

Literature available.

THE COALBROOKDALE COMPANY

American Sales Office
RFD 1, Box 477
Stowe, VT 05672
Tel. 802/253–9727

1884 MILK BOTTLES

"Your customers will be willing to pay more for milk if delivered in sealed bottles," advised the Sears-Roebuck catalogue of 1908. Jenifer House's milk bottles are reproductions of those used by the "Thatcher Dairy" in 1884 and have the desired airtight seals. That the bottles are embossed "Absolutely Pure Milk" should not limit your imagination in putting them to use at home.

Price: set of three, $28.95, ppd. (add $1 west of the Mississippi). Specify clear, cobalt, pink, or amethyst glass.

Gift catalog available.

JENIFER HOUSE

New Marlboro Stage
Great Barrington, MA 01230
Tel. 413/528-1500

WAFFLE IRON

At the turn of the century Sears-Roebuck advertised a waffle iron that looked just like this one for 78¢. Then, of course, they were the most mundane of household items. John Wright's waffle iron has a 20-inch diameter and a single twentieth-century innovation—hollow "teeth" on the baking plates.

For dealer information contact:

JOHN WRIGHT, INC.

North Front Street
Wrightsville, PA 17368
Tel. 717/252-3661

PLANS FOR AN OAKEN ICE BOX

Well, *almost* an ice box. The Hammermark company's plans lack the tin insulation and other features that would enable the cabinet to store ice, but they do closely follow the design of iceboxes advertised in the Sears catalogue of 1904.

Product sheet available, $1 (refundable with order).

HAMMERMARK ASSOCIATES

P.O. Box 201-SC
Floral Park, NY 11002

HOUSEWARES FROM AMAZON VINEGAR & PICKLING WORKS

In Buffalo, New York, there's a fern bar named Mother's Bakery. Directly across the street stands another called The Butcher Shop. The only baked goods in the former are those little goldfish crackers, and the only meat in the latter is best left to the reader's imagination. While it's true that Anglo-Americans have traditionally given silly names to gin mills, today all sorts of "olde timey" businesses have things in their monikers as rare to them as buffalos are to Buffalo. Amazon Vinegar & Pickling sells neither.

I dunno, perhaps the mail-order outfit is housed in a former pickling plant. Maybe the pickles produced there were known as "Amazons." Let's hope so. But while we're at it, let's point out that Amazon Vinegar also puts out a wonderfully varied catalog of nineteenth-century replicas. Below is a sampling of their housewares.

BRASS INKWELL AND TWO FEATHER QUILLS

Amazon's inkwell is a small brass cylinder set on a broad base. The accompanying quills have no nibs cut into them and will require the use of a penknife.

Price: $6 (plus $3 for shipping).

BRASS PADLOCKS Each

brass padlock comes with two keys and a lock guard and drain hole. You have a choice of two sizes: the smaller to lock your camp chest, Saratoga trunk, or carpetbag; the larger for use on shipboard or boxcar doors.

Prices: small padlock $9.50; large padlock, $15 (plus $2 each for shipping and handling).

DEED BOX This unpainted tinware box

has a rounded top, a hinged lid with handle, and a hasp for a lock. The original would likely have been painted black with fine red-and-gold striping.

Dimensions: 12 inches by 9 inches by 9½ inches.

Price: $40 (plus $4 for shipping).

40-page catalog, Christmas catalog, and seasonal mailings available, $2.

AMAZON VINEGAR & PICKLING WORKS DRYGOODS

Department AH
2218 East 11th Street
Davenport, IA 52803
Tel. 319/322–6800

CUMBERLAND GENERAL STORE HOUSEWARES

From supermarkets to shopping malls, the descendants of the traditional American general store exist today in their several overly air-conditioned forms. If you still want to see the real thing though, one place you can go is Crossville, Tennessee.

Crossville lies at the heart of Eleanor Roosevelt's mid-1930s Homesteads Project, an experiment to provide rural Volunteer Staters with jobs and low-cost homes during the depression. The Cumberland General Store was something of an outgrowth of Homesteads.

More than a potbelly stove surrounded by an array of basic goods for the home and farm, Cumberland annually publishes a "Wish and Want Book"—a kind of commercial, mail-order version of this book. Below are just a sample of the housewares that Cumberland sells from among its "all new goods in an endless variety for man and beast."

ROUND DINNER PAIL

The following is reprinted from the Cumberland General Store "Wish and Want Book":

W. Smith, of Sharp Place, Tennessee, hewed out railroad ties for a living. . . . After felling a white oak and forming it to proper dimensions with a broad axe, he would hoist it on his shoulder and carry it out of the woods to a mule trail. At times, ties brought as much as 15¢ apiece. Each day, he carried a four lb. lard bucket full of pinto beans and corn bread. Now you may not have to replenish as much energy as old Smith did but you're sure to enjoy this miner's dinner pail fashioned after his old lard bucket. Made from extra-hard cold-rolled aluminum. Sanitary seamless construction. Capacity, five quarts.
Price: $14.96, F.O.B. point of origin.

HIP BATH   **During the 1830s when, in preparation for the Sabbath, the Saturday-night bath began as an American institution,** big tin washtubs were often brought before the hearth or kitchen stove. Here the

SOAPSAVER

Save soapsuds if you have a garden, for they form a very useful manure for flowers, as well as shrubs and vegetables. It is well to have a sunk tub in every garden where the soapy water can stand until required for gardening.
—"Useful Hints" from the 1900 Farmer's Almanac

Cumberland's soapsaver, a once-common device for making use of soap slivers, can help here. "Swish it in your water for lots of suds," says Cumberland.
Price: $5.06, F.O.B. Crossville, Tennessee.

---

bather sat with soap in hand, awaiting kettles full of hot water for scrubbing. **The wash tubs** were soon replaced with more formal bathtubs such as this one sold by the Cumberland General Store. This galvanized tub, which measures 30 inches high and has a width of 31 inches, provides complete back support and features both soap and armrests.
Price: $99, F.O.B. Crossville, Tennessee.

"Wish and Want Book" available, $3.75, ppd.

CUMBERLAND GENERAL STORE

Route 3
Crossville, TN 38555
Tel. 615/484-8481

LOVELL CLOTHES WRINGER

"The life of a wringer," proclaimed the Sears catalogue of 1908, "largely depends upon its rolls." Quite right, too. Pioneer Place's Lovell wringer employs semi-soft "balloon" rollers for just this reason. These, in addition to the wringer's all-steel frame, gray baked-enamel finish, rustproofing, and hard maple bearings, make for a durable appliance.
It can be attached to stationary or portable tubs (round or square), its clamps open to 1¾ inches, and it's equipped with 12- by 1⅞-inch rollers.
Price: $67.50, ppd.

KITCHEN PUMP

Cumberland's old-style kitchen pump is made of cast iron and is completely functional. Easily installed by any plumber or handyman, the pump hooks right up to the cold-water lines and will not interfere with any other faucets. It stands 15 inches high, with a shipping weight of 25 lbs.
Price: $160, F.O.B. point of origin.

PIONEER PLACE HOUSEWARES

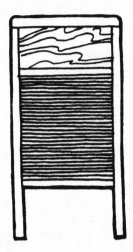

GRANDMA'S ECONOMY WASHBOARD This "labor-saving device" comes complete with
back drain and standard-size rubbing surface and is very serviceable. Its overall size is 23 by 12½ inches.
Price: $10.50, ppd.

COPPER
WASH BOILER This copper wash boiler was built for Pioneer Place by the same company that developed the original boilers a century ago. Excellent for water-bath canning, it will fit over two burners, holds almost ten imperial gallons, and comes complete with lid.
Dimensions: length 22 inches, width 12 inches, height 13 inches.
Price: $45, ppd.

Catalog available.

THE PIONEER PLACE

*Route 2, 9938 County Road 39
Belle Center, OH 43310*

HOUSEWARES FROM WHITE MOUNTAIN FREEZER COMPANY

Best known today as the only manufacturer of ice and rock salt commercial ice cream freezers, the White Mountain Freezer Company began business in 1842 and still makes several nineteenth-century products for the home.

HAND-OPERATED ICE CREAM
FREEZER In 1778, during the "Winter of our Discontent," Gen. George Washington knelt in the snow and prayed, it's not cynical to suggest, that the Continental Congress would grant his army enough money to keep it from starving.

In 1790, during a sweltering summer in New York, President Washington reputedly blew several hundred dollars on ice cream.
Somehow it's comforting to know that the light that shines on the memory of the Father of our Country isn't so blinding that it hides his weaknesses. This is particularly true of those weaknesses we all share, for ice cream is the favorite food of Americans.
Of course our beloved frozen concoction was very expensive in Washington's time, and might still be today were it not for the invention of the ice cream freezer by Nancy Johnson, a New Jersey woman, in 1846.
The design of what *Money* magazine called "the best traditional hand-operated ice cream machine" now on the market was turned out about a century ago. Made of maple-stained white pine, braced with copper wire, and emblazoned with White Mountain's forest-green Old Man of the Mountain logotype, the best available is also the handsomest imaginable.

ORIGINAL "READING-STYLE"

APPLE PARER
This Civil **War-vintage design comes from Pennsylvania.** Made of cast iron, White Mountain's "Reading-style" apple parer clamps onto any table to pare apples in one continuous motion before "kicking them off" into a bowl.

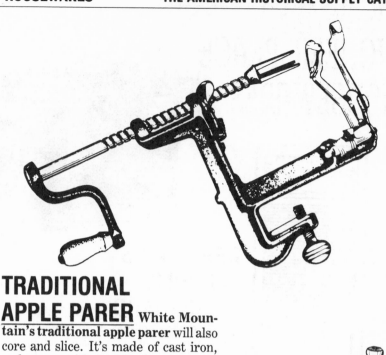

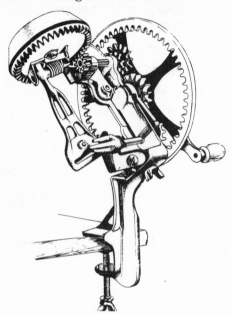

TRADITIONAL APPLE PARER
White Mountain's **traditional apple parer** will also core and slice. It's made of cast iron, and comes with a table clamp.

POPCORN POPPER
Traditional materials and design, with churn and wooden handle.

MODEL 910 HANDCRANK DOUGH MAKER
With its **traditional native** pine bucket, and a sturdy cast-iron handle and gear train, this is very similar to the ice cream freezer in its design. It makes a batch of dough for up to three loaves.

For prices and ordering information, write:

WHITE MOUNTAIN FREEZER COMPANY

Winchendon, MA 01475
Tel. 617/297–0015

HOUSEWARES FROM THE CHOP-RITE MANUFACTURING COMPANY

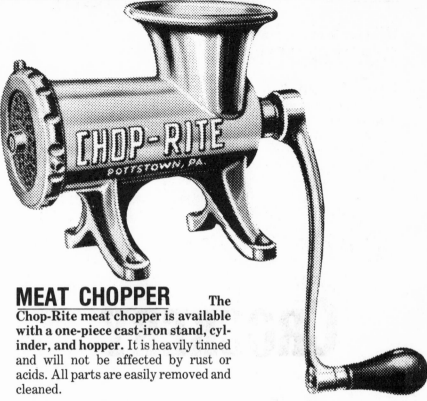

Chop-Rite of Pottstown, Pennsylvania, manufactures several traditional kitchen utensils.

CHERRY STONER
"Pits every cherry—will not miss." The Chop-Rite cherry stoner will pit the fruit without otherwise disfiguring it. The stoner cleans easily, and will not rust since it is heavily tinned.

MEAT CHOPPER
The Chop-Rite meat chopper is available with a one-piece cast-iron stand, cylinder, and hopper. It is heavily tinned and will not be affected by rust or acids. All parts are easily removed and cleaned.

SAUSAGE STUFFER, LARD OR FRUIT PRESS
This is actually three implements in one: it stuffs sausage casings, presses lard or cheese, and squeezes fruit and vegetables. It features cast-iron cylinders bored perfectly true. The tin cylinder lies within the cast cylinder to enable the operator to remove hot cracklings without inconvenience. Nontoxic black finish. Capacity: 8 quarts. Height: 22 inches.

Wholesale price list and retailer information available.

CHOP-RITE MANUFACTURING COMPANY

P.O. Box 294
Pottstown, PA 19464
Tel. 215/326–5970

Evangeline Pattern.

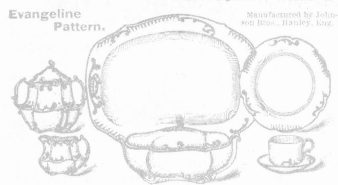

Manufactured by Johnson Bros., Hanley, Eng.

English semi-porcelain ware; thin and pure white. The glaze is burnt on and will not nick or chip with ordinary use. The shape is of the very latest design and the raised scroll work is handsomely ornamented with neat gold decorations. Pure white dinner ware of this quality with gold decoration is unusually attractive and sure to please. We shall be pleased to furnish any quantity you may desire.

Order No. 54004.

	Per doz.
1 Tea Cups and Saucers. 12 cups and 12 saucers	$1.87
2 Coffee Cups and Saucers.12 cups and 12 saucers	
3 Plates, scalloped edge, 5 inch	.18
4 Plates, scalloped edge, 6 inch	
5 Plates, scalloped edge, 7 inch	
6 Plates, scalloped edge, 8 inches	1.75
7 Soup Plates, 7 inches	1.52
8 Sauce Dishes. 4-in	.71
9 Individual Butter Plates	.47
10 Bone Dishes	$1.04
11 Bowls, 1 pt	1.87
12 Oyster Bowls, 1 pint	1.87
13 Oatmeal Bowls, 1 pint	1.87
20 Platters, 16-inch	
21 Covered Dish, 8-inch	.94

CROCKERY

	Each
22 Casserole, Square covered dish, 8-in	$1.06
Soup Tureen,Cover and Ladle no stand	3.50
24 Sauce Tureen, complete with cover, ladle and stand	1.18
30 Pitcher, 3 quarts	.71
31 Tea Pot and Cover	.63
32 Sugar Bowl and cover	.54
33 Cream Pitcher	.26
34 Cake Plate	.31

Utopian Pattern.

Manufactured by Henry Alcock & Co., Hanley, England.

Superior grade of English Royal semi-porcelain, decoration of small forget-me-not flowers, handsomely put on under the glaze; all the pieces are shapely and have richly gold trimmed edges and handles, plates are scalloped on the edge. This is a very handsome table set and can be furnished in two colors. fawn and pencil, both equally attractive. When ordering be sure to state which color you prefer.

Order No. 54005.

	Per doz.
1 Tea Cups and Saucers, handled	$2.00
2 Coffee Cups and Saucers, handled	2.35
3 After Dinner Coffee Cups and Saucers, handled	1.67
4 Plates, 5 inches	1.12
5 Plates, 6 inches	1.38
6 Plates, 7 inches	1.63
7 Plates, 8 inches	1.88
8 Soup Plates, 7 inches	1.52
9 Sauce Plates	.75
10 Individual Butters	.51
11 Bakers, 3-inch (used as side dishes)	1.75
12 Bone dishes	1.75
13 Bowls, 1 pint	$2.00
14 Oyster Bowls, 1 pint	2.00
15 Oatmeal Bowls, 1 pint	2.00
16 Platters, 8-inch	$0.22
17 Platters, 10-inch	.38
18 Platters, 12-inch	.63
19 Platters, 14-inch	.87
20 Platters, 16-inch	1.38
21 Bakers, 7-inch	.26
24 Scalloped Nappies	
25 Scalloped Nappies	.38
29 Pitchers, 1-pint	.26
30 Pitchers, 1-quart	.30
31 Pitchers 2-quart	.51
32 Pitchers 3-quart	.75
33 Covered Dishes, 9 inch	1.00
34 Casserole (square covered dish 10-inch	1.12
37 Soup Tureen and ladle (no stand)	3.75
38 Sauce Tureen with ladle and stand	1.26
39 Sauce Boat	.34
40 Pickle Dish	.26
41 Cake Plate	.34
42 Covered Butter Dish	.75
43 Teapots	.67
44 Sugar Bowls	.56
45 Cream Pitchers	.26

Columbia Pattern.

Manufactured by Johnson Bros., England.

Semi-porcelain ware, thin and very shapely; decoration consists of flowers, leaves and fine spray in neutral brown color; warranted not to wash or wear off; scalloped edge plates. This is a very desirable pattern and cannot fail to please. We will sell you as few or many pieces as you wish.

Order No. 54007.

Order No. 54007.

	Per doz.
1 Tea Cups and Saucers with handles	$1.47
3 Coffee Cups and Saucers with handles	1.71
3 Plates, scalloped edge, 5 inches	.83
4 Plates, scalloped edge, 6 inches	1.02
5 Plates, scalloped edge, 7 inches	1.19
6 Plates, scalloped edge, 8 inches	1.38
7 Plates, scalloped edge, 7-in., soup	1.19
8 Fruit Saucers, 5-in.	.55
9 Individual Butters	.38
10 Bone Dishes	1.28
11 Bakers (used for side dishes), 3-inch	1.28
12 Bowls, 1 pint	1.47

	Per doz.
13 Oyster Bowls, 1 pint	$1.47
14 Bakers, 7 inches	$0.19
15 Bakers, 8 inches	.28
16 Bakers, 9 inches	.38
17 Platters, 8 inches	.16
18 Platters, 10 inches	.28
19 Platters, 12 inches	.47
20 Platters, 14 inches	.64
21 Platters,16 inches	1.02
22 Scalloped Nappies, 7 inches	.19
23 Scalloped Nappies, 8 inches	.28
24 Scalloped Nappies, 9 inches	.38
26 Soup Tureen.with ladle and stand	3.65

	Each
27 Sauce Tureen,with ladle and stand	$0.92
28 Sauce Boat	.26
29 Pickle Dish	.19
30 Covered Butter Dish	.56
31 Covered Vegetable Dish	.74
32 Casserole (square covered dish)	.83
33 Tea Pot	.50
34 Sugar Bowl	.42
35 Cream Pitcher	.19
36 Cake Plate	.26
37 Pitcher, 3 quarts	.56
38 Pitcher, 2 quarts	.38
39 Pitcher, 1 quart	.22
40 Pitcher,1 pint	.19
41 Pitcher, ½ pint	.16

Oregon Pattern.

Manufactured by Mellor, Taylor & Co., Burslem, England.

Genuine English Semi-porcelain ware. A delicate anemone flower spray decoration in a steel gray color put on under the glaze, warranted not to wear off or to crack. The shapes are new and gracefully moulded. For a low priced pattern it is unexcelled as to finish, decoration and durability, and is a decided change from the ordinary brown prints.

Order No. 54010.

	Per doz.
1 Tea Cups and Saucers, handled	$1.40
2 Coffee Cups and Saucers, handled	1.64
3 Pie Plates. 5-inch	.78
4 Plates, 6-inch	.95
5 Plates, 7-inch	1.13
6 Plates. 8-inch	1.31
7 Soup Plates. 7-inch	1.15
8 Fruit Saucers	.50
9 Individual Butters	.35
10 Bakers, 3-inch (for side dishes)	1.23
10½ Bone dishes	1.23
11 1 pt. Bowls	1.40
12 1 pt. Oyster Bowls	1.40
Oat Meal Bowls,5-inch	1.40

	Each
13 Platters, 8-inch	$0.14
14 Platters, 10-inch	.27
15 Platters, 12-inch	.43
16 Platters, 14-inch	.61
17 Platters, 16-inch	.96
18 Bakers, 7-inch	.18
19 Bakers, 8-inch	.27
21 Scalloped Nappies, 7-inch	.18
22 Scalloped Nappies, 8-inch	.27
25 Pitchers, ½ pt.	.14
26 Pitchers, 1 pt.	.18
27 Pitchers, 1 qt.	.21
28 Pitchers, 2 qt	.35
29 Pitchers, 3 qt.	.54

	Each
30 Soup Tureen,with ladle and stand	$3.30
31 Sauce Tureen (with ladle and stand)	.88
32 Sauce Boat	.24
33 Pickle Dish	.18
34 Covered Butter Dish	.53
35 Covered Vegetable Dish	.70
36 Casserole (square covered dish)	.78
37 Teapot	.41
38 Sugar Bowl	.39
39 Cream Pitcher	.18
40 Cake Plate	.24

Lexington Pattern.

Manufactured by Johnson Brothers, Hanley, England.

English semi-porcelain, a very pretty shape, decorated with a light brown begonia leaf, enameled with blue forget-me-nots and warranted not to wash or wear off; scalloped edge plates, gold traced handles. We shall be pleased to have your order for any quantity, no matter how small.

Order No. 54011.

	Per doz.
1 Tea Cups and Saucers with handles	$1.87
2 Coffee Cups and Saucers with handles	2.18
4 Plates, scalloped edge, 5-inch	1.06
5 Plates, scalloped edge, 6-inch	1.28
6 Plates, scalloped edge, 7-inch	1.52
7 Plates, scalloped edge, 8-inch	1.75
8 Plates, scalloped edge, 7-in., soup	1.52
9 Fruit Saucers, 4-in.	.71
10 Individual Butters	.47
11 Bone Dishes	1.64

	Per doz.
12 Bakers (used for side dishes),3-in	$1.64
13 Oyster Bowls, 1 pint	1.87
14 Bakers, 7-inch	$0.26
15 Bakers, 8-in	.33
16 Platters, 8-in	.20
17 Platters, 10-in	.35
18 Platters, 12-in	.59
19 Platters, 14-in	.82
20 Platters, 16-in	1.28
21 Soup Tureen with ladle	3.50
22 Sauce Tureen with ladle and stand	1.18
23 Sauce Boat	.32

	Each
24 Pickle Dish	$0.25
25 Covered Butter Dish	.71
26 Covered Vegetable Dish, 9-inch	.84
27 Casserole (square covered dish)	1.06
28 Tea Pot	.63
29 Sugar Bowl	.54
30 Cream Pitcher	.25
31 Cake Plate	.31
32 Pitcher, ½ pt.	.20
33 Pitcher, 1 pint	.23
34 Pitcher, 1 qt.	.27
35 Pitcher, 2 qts.	.47
36 Pitcher, 3 qts.	.71

REDWARE POTTERY

Redware pottery is made from the red clay common to most of the eastern seaboard. Its workable qualities were immediately apparent to early settlers, and by 1630 American potters were fashioning it into household wares, flowerpots, pipes, roofing tiles, and the like. The distinctive charm of redware is produced by the mottled coloration of the glaze and the brushing of green and brown that are allowed to flow down the surface of the piece.

About a decade ago the production of redware pottery was begun in Woodstock, Connecticut, by Paul D. Lynn and Kathryn Woodcock-Lynn of Woodstock Pottery. Conscious of the fact that they were reviving a local tradition begun in 1793 by Thomas Bugbee of nearby Quasset, the couple based many of their designs for reproduction redware bowls, mugs, pitchers, porrigers, and jugs on Bugbee's eighteenth- and nineteenth-century examples.

Brochure available.

WOODSTOCK POTTERY

Woodstock Valley, CT 06282
Tel. 203/974–1673

STONEWARE POTTERY

Working out of his 1794 farmhouse and the rebuilt Model T garage that once belonged to his grandfather, Jeff Lalish and his cooperative of potters handcraft eighteenth- and nineteenth-century stoneware replications of Albany slipware in traditional shapes. The pieces come with white or matte oatmeal glazes and are decorated with "either traditional or folk-inspired" bird and flower designs in both cobalt blue and multicolor.

Each summer Northwood Pottery is host to the annual Northwood Craftsman's Fair on August 21 and 22. The fair is open to the public and there is free music and other entertainment. No mail-order available.

NORTHWOOD STONEWARE POTTERY

Route 4, Box 458
Northwood, NH 03261

DEDHAM POTTERY

Toward the end of the nineteenth century Hugh Robertson, a fifth generation master potter from Dedham, Massachusetts, uncovered the ancient Chinese secret of crackle glazing. Combining this process with a variety of distinctive hand-painted patterns that became his trademark, Robertson incorporated the Dedham Pottery Company.

Public acceptance of Robertson's Dedhamware was great, and before very long his pieces, often carrying the cobalt-blue rabbit motif, were well known. In the five decades that Robertson's business continued to manufacture Dedhamware, demand never caught up with supply.

Dedhamware was revived in 1975, when Chotsie Starr began redirecting her basement-based pottery hobby into fashioning reproduction Dedham pottery. She quickly found that interest in this pottery had only been lying dormant since Robertson's day, and with her two sons she founded the Potting Shed in 1977.

Like the originals, the Potting Shed's Dedham pottery is fully handcrafted, relying on a painstaking sequence of molding, painting, firing, and finishing that takes a week to complete. To distinguish reproductions from originals, the bottom of each piece is marked with the Potting Shed trademark, a star.

Catalog available, $1.50.

THE POTTING SHED

P.O. Box 1287
Concord, MA 01742
Tel. 617/369–2981

TRADITIONAL MAINE BEANPOT Although Henry David

Thoreau never laid eyes on Rowantree's handmade beanpot, a well-known admirer of his who had never been anywhere near Maine once did. Rowantree's founder, Adelaide Pearson, considered pottery making only "recreational activity" at the time she showed her work to a friend, Mahatma Gandhi, in 1936. Gandhi, who felt that the "oldest craft known to mankind" deserved greater devotion, admonished Pearson to take her work more seriously. Thus charged, Ms. Pearson began the production of earthenware the quality of which has warranted its being grouped among the Madison Chinese Export and Eisenhower Gettysburg Service shown at the Smithsonian Institution's American Presidential China Exhibit.

Rowantree's two-quart beanpot is made of a secret combination of Maine ores. It is ovenproof and has ridges for nonslip handling. The company will pack and ship earthenware to any part of the United States.

Literature available.

ROWANTREE'S POTTERY

Blue Hill, ME 04614
Tel. 207/374–5535

Genuine Rich Cut Glass.

The demand for cut glass has induced us to offer a few items of the best value to be found. The Strawberry Diamond and Fan "Cutting" is one of the most beautiful patterns, every piece splendidly cut and highly polished in the most brilliant manner. It is as useful as silverware and is more beautiful to offer for presents, wedding gifts, etc. The illustrations are not expected to do it justice, as it is beyond comparison with the ordinary pressed glassware.

54900 Cut Glass Salad Bowl, 8 inches in diameter, genuine Strawberry diamond and fan cutting. Each....$6.65

54901 Cut Glass Salad Bowl, 7 inches in diameter. Each....$5.35

54903 Cut Glass Berry or Fruit Bowl, 8 inches in diameter genuine strawberry diamond and fan cutting. Each....$5.35

54904 Cut Glass Handled Nappie Jelly or Olive Dish, genuine strawberry diamond and fan cutting. Each....$2.75

54905 Cut Glass Vinegar Bottle, genuine strawberry diamond and fan cutting. Each....$1.70

54906 Cut Glass Table Tumbler, genuine strawberry diamond and fan cutting. Each....$0.42

54907 Cut Glass, Sugar and Cream Tete-a-tete or afternoon tea size, genuine strawberry diamond and fan cutting. Per set....$5.35

55017 Genuine cut glass strawberry diamond and fan cutting. Globe shape, silver plated top, salt and pepper shakers. Each, 37 cents, per dozen....$2.70

Czarina Crystal Pattern.

An exact imitation of the celebrated strawberry diamond and fan genuine cut glass pattern, which came into prominence during the World's Fair. The shapes are very pleasing and novel. Color of glass pure crystal. We guarantee finish to be the very best obtainable. This is undoubtedly the handsomest pattern out this season and one we feel sure will please you in every respect.

55018 Table set containing four pieces as illustrated. Per set....$0.55

55019 Czarina Half Gallon pitcher. Each....$0.40
55021 Czarina Half Pint Table Tumblers. Per dozen....$0.68

55022 Czarina Oil or Vinegar Bottles. Each....$0.20
55023 Czarina Syrup Pitcher, nickel plated top. Each....$0.23

55024 Czarina Salt and Pepper Shakers, silver plated tops. Specify salt or pepper when ordering. Each....$0.10
Per dozen....1.08

55026 Czarina Berry Dishes.

Inches in diameter.	Price, each.
6 inches	$0.10
7 inches	.17
8 inches	.22
9 inches	.25

55027 Czarina Small Berry Nappies, used generally with large size nappies or dishes.

Inches in diameter.	
4 inches	
4½ inches	
5 inches	

Czarina Celery Tray. Each, $0.20

55031 Czarina Cake Salver.
9 inch, each.
10 inch, each.

55030 Czarina Footed Jelly Dish.
Each....$0.12
Per dozen....1.35

55034 Czarina Flower Vases.

	Each	Per doz.
7 inches high	$0.15	$1.62
8 inches high	.18	1.95
10 inches high	.30	3.24

Czarina Ruby and Crystal Pattern.

The shapes in this pattern are the same as our crystal czarina. We recommend this pattern above all others to lovers of colored ware. The ruby is put on in a very pleasing manner, aside from this the prices are lower than any other pattern ever produced in ruby and crystal colors.

55035 Ruby and Crystal Czarina Table Set, same number of pieces and same shape as No. 55018. Per set....$1.05

55036 Ruby and Crystal Czarina Half Gallon Pitcher, for illustration see No. 55019. Each....1.00

55038 Ruby and Crystal Czarina Half Pint Tumblers, see No. 55021 for illustration. Per dozen....1.35

55039 Ruby and Crystal Czarina Oil or Vinegar Bottles, see No. 55022 for illustration. Each....35

55040 Ruby and Crystal Czarina Salt and Pepper Shakers plated top, specify salt or pepper when ordering see No. 55024 for illustration. Each....18
Per dozen....1.95

55042 Ruby and Crystal Czarina 8-inch Berry Dishes, see No. 55026 for illustration. Each....40

55043 Ruby and Crystal Czarina 4½-inch Berry Nappie. See No. 55027 for illustration. Per dozen....1.25

55046 Ruby and Crystal Czarina Celery Tray, for illustration see No. 55030. Price....50

St. Bernard Pattern.
Crystal Engraved.

We aim at all times to offer the latest and most pleasing patterns. As a novelty the St. Bernard pattern cannot be equaled. All the covered pieces have handles. The figure, as illustrated, is the image of a St. Bernard dog. The main surface is decorated with a very attractive engraving, which with part of surface in figured relief, makes the effect a very pleasing one. All the pieces are extra large, and finished by the latest and best process known to manufacturers.

55049 St. Bernard Table Set, four pieces as illustrated. Per set....$0.75

55050 St. Bernard engraved berry bowls.

Diameter	Price.

55052 St. Bernard Engraved Covered Berry Bowls.

Diameter	Price.
7 inches	$0.50
8 inches	.62

55054 St. Bernard Engraved Half Gallon Water Pitcher. Each....$0.50

55056 St. Bernard Engraved Half Gallon Tankard. Each....$0.50

55059 St. Bernard Engraved Half Pint Tumbler. Per dozen $1.60

55060 St. Bernard Engraved Celery Holder. Each....$0.24

55061 St. Bernard Engraved 4½-inch Berry Dishes. Per dozen....$0.90

55067 St. Bernard Engraved Oil or Vinegar bottle. Each....$0.22

SAMUEL PIERCE TANKARD

The original pewter tankard was made circa 1820 in Greenfield, Massachusetts. It stands 4⅜ inches tall by 3½ inches wide at the base.

Price: $58 (plus $4 for shipping).

Color catalog available.

OLD STURBRIDGE VILLAGE MUSEUM SHOP

Sturbridge, MA 01566
Tel. 617/347-9843

MINT JULEP CUPS

The inhabitants of Maryland . . . were notoriously prone to get fuddled and make merry with mint julep and apple toddy.
—*Washington Irving,* A History of New York, *1809*

Copying an original made in Shelbyville in 1795, the Wakefield-Scearce Galleries produces the only authentic Kentucky mint julep cup available. The following information came from the firm's president, Mark J. Scearce:

Mint Julep cups got their name in Kentucky in the latter part of the eighteenth century. . . . The Julep cups have long been associated with horse racing and shows, and often were awarded as racing trophies in lieu of a purse.

Our cup is unusual in that it is hand-beaded both on top and at bottom and is marked "Shelbyville, Ky." It also bears a little American eagle mark, underneath which the current president's initials are engraved. We change these with each new administration and the old ones are never made again, so the cups become collector's items.

Catalog of fine imported antiques available.

WAKEFIELD-SCEARCE GALLERIES

Historic Science Hill
Shelbyville, KY 40065
Tel. 502/633-4382

BEEHIVE HONEYPOT

The original from which this honeypot was copied was one created in 1800 by Paul Storr, a London silversmith. One of the rarest of the naturalistic themes then popular, the "beehive" is eagerly sought after by collectors of fine and unique silver. The last such honeypot of note, reports Victorian Accents' Dan Damon, was sold at auction by Sotheby's of London on October 14, 1976, for $4,500.

Victorian Accents' replica is made with tarnish-proof silverplate. It has a glass liner and a spoon is included. It measures 5 inches tall by 5¼ inches wide.

Price: $39.95 (plus $5 for insurance and shipping).

1848 SERVING TROWEL

Victorian Accents' ornately scrolled serving trowel is a reproduction of a piece by Barnard's of London made in 1848. The trowel's silver-plated blade ends in a richly embossed shaft and crown, with a *faux ivoire* handle.

Price: $49.95 (plus $6.50 for insurance and shipping).

Catalog of Victoriana available, $1.

WATTLE & DAUB'S VICTORIAN ACCENTS

661 West 7th Street
Plainfield, NJ 07060
Tel. 201/757-8507

OLD STURBRIDGE VILLAGE CRYSTAL REPRODUCTIONS

Following a technique practiced in Europe for centuries, blown glass involves gathering a mass of molten glass at the end of a hollow rod and inflating the glass while rotating the rod to effect the piece's final shape. Brought here by men such as Caspar Wistar (a German immigrant who established the colonies' first glass manufactory in 1739), blown glass was virtually universal until well into the nineteenth century.

Glassmaking was revolutionized in 1830 by Deming Jarvis who, at his factory in Sandwich, Massachusetts, produced the first pressed-glass drinking vessel. Glass-pressing eliminated the need to blow glass, and Jarvis's employees nearly struck over the prospect of being thrown out of work.

Marked by the "OSV" logotype to distinguish them from the originals in its collections, Old Sturbridge Village's crystal reproductions use the pressed-glass method exclusively.

RIBBED PALM GOBLET

OSV's ribbed palm goblet has been replicated from an early pressed-glass design. It stands 6¼ inches high with a rim width of 3¼ inches.

Price: $12.50 (plus $3 for shipping).

BARREL DECANTER

Like the tumbler it accompanies, Old Sturbridge Village's barrel decanter translates the design of a mundane object into an elegant piece of crystal. It stands 11 inches high and has a capacity of 40 ounces.

Prices: barrel decanter, $38 (plus $4 for shipping); barrel decanter and a set of six tumblers, $65 (plus $5 for shipping).

BARREL TUMBLER

After pressed glass came into vogue, drinking glasses were produced in hundreds of patterns. Popular themes among these were the bull's-eye, the frosted leaf, the honeycomb, and the horn-of-plenty. OSV's barrel-design tumbler is not as ornate as these, but with its irregular texture, has the same naturalist beauty.

It comes in a 10-ounce, double "old-fashioned" size.

Price: $6.75 (plus $3 for shipping).

SHEAF O' WHEAT

PLATE This crystal plate is 10 inches in diameter, and bears the legend "Give Us This Day Our Daily Bread."

Price: $18 (plus $3 for shipping).

Color catalog available.

OLD STURBRIDGE VILLAGE

Museum Shop
Sturbridge, MA 01566
Tel. 617/347–9843

LIGHTING SUPPLIES

Zenith Hall Lamp.

No. 2R816 Zenith Hall Lamp. Just the thing for a small hall. Ruby, opal or pink globe. This is the cheapest and best hall lamp in the market. In ordering state which color globe you prefer. Shipping weight. 25 pounds.

Price.......... $1.49

Square Hall Lamp.

No. 2R819 Square Hall Lamp. This is a larger and better lamp than the Zenith and costs very little more. In two colors, crystal etched or ruby etched glass as desired. Be sure to state color desired. This hall lamp is handsome enough for any dwelling. It is an exact reproduction of the high priced gas lamp that has always been so popular. Length, 36 inches. Complete with burner and chimney. Shipping weight, 25 pounds.

No. 2R816 Our price...... $2.49 No. 2R819

Store Lamps.

No. 2R825 Store Lamp. The best and cheapest in the market. For large areas and where good light is required only the best lamps should be procured. We keep them and guarantee every lamp we sell to give perfect satisfaction. The Juno gives a steady and white light. Just the thing to throw light on a window display. Complete as illustrated. 15-inch tin shade, suitable for store or window lights. 85-candle power. Shipping weight, 40 lbs. Price, brass finish. $2.00 Price, nickel finish, $2.25

No. 2R830 Same lamp as No. 2R825 only trimmed with 10-inch white porcelain dome shade which makes a much neater lamp without much greater cost. Shipping weight, 50 pounds.

Price, brass finish........ $2.45
Price, nickel finish........ 2.75

The Juno Mammoth Store and Hall Lamps.

No. 2R834 Juno Mammoth Store and Hall Lamp, 400-candle power. The strongest and best finished lamp on the market. The wick movement is perfect and so simple that a child can rewick the lamp. Patent lock ring to hold fount in ring obviates all danger of fount jarring out of frame. Fount taken out from below for filling. You are taking no chances with this lamp as we guarantee every one to give perfect satisfaction, or we will replace them and pay all expenses. The lock ring used to hold the Juno is a great convenience. The fount can easily be taken out from below for refilling. Complete, as illustrated, 14-inch plain dome shade, suitable for churches, halls, stores, etc. Each lamp is carefully packed in a barrel to insure safe delivery. Shipping weight, 40 pounds.

Price, complete, brass finish........ $3.69
Price, complete, nickel finish........ 4.25

No. 2R836 Same lamp as above only it is trimmed with a 20-inch tin shade, making a cheaper and more suitable lamp for saw mills, factories, etc.
Price, complete, brass finish........ $3.25
Price, complete, nickel finish........ 3.50

No. 2R838 Same lamp as above, trimmed with 14-inch white dome shade and fitted with an automatic spring extension so it can be lowered for cleaning or lighting without the use of step ladder or chairs. Length of lamp, closed, 42 inches; fully extended, 78 inches. Money cannot buy a finer constructed lamp. This makes an ideal lamp for churches, halls and fine stores. Very handsome in appearance. Shipping weight, 50 pounds.

Price, complete, brass finish........ $5.98
Price, complete, nickel finish........ 6.75

Our $7.15 Chandelier

Chandelier, with patent automatic extension for raising and lowering. A handsome chandelier at a price that puts it within the reach of all. This beautiful parlor fixture, useful as well as ornamental, is finished in rich gold bronze, and completed with etched globes of a very popular shape. The burner is of a new design that can be lighted and trimmed without removing the globe or chimney, thus avoiding the possibility of breakage in handling them. We furnish this fixture in the following sizes: Shipping weight, 50 to 75 pounds.

No. 2R867 Two-light, complete... $ 7.15
No. 2R868 Three-light, complete, as shown 9.10
No. 2R869 Four-light, complete... 11.70

Polished Bronze Chandelier.

Chandelier, Polished Bronze, rich gold finish. The metal ball in center of chandelier is finished in rich enamel, either ruby or green. Length of chandelier, 36 inches; has patent extension, which extends 21 inches, making length of chandelier fully opened 57 in. ... and trimmed without removing globes ... chimney ...

No. 2R874 Price, complete, four lights..... 13.60
Shipping weight, 90 pounds.

Patent Extension Chandelier.

Patent Extension Chandelier. Length, closed, 36 inches; extended, 57 inches. This chandelier is elegantly finished in rich gold, has colored metal center; trimmed with unique burners, which can be trimmed and lighted without removing chimney or globes. Trimmed with fine etched crystal globes. Shipping weight of three-light chandeliers, about 75 pounds; the four light, 90 pounds.

No. 2R878 Price, complete, three lights... $13.65
No. 2R879 Price, complete, four lights... 16.25
Church or Hall Chandelier. Same chandelier as above, except burners. This fixture is trimmed with the celebrated B. & H. No. 1 center draft burners, each light 50-candle power.
No. 2R882 Price, complete, three lights... $16.35
No. 2R883 Price, complete, four lights... 18.85

Our 98c Banquet Lamp.

No. 2R890 We have reduced the price of this beautiful banquet lamp from $1.55 to 98 cents, bringing the price within the reach of all, so that there is no reason why any family should not have a banquet lamp to help decorate their home. This lamp is 21 inches high, and has a tinted globe and bowl, shading from white to green, with beautiful floral decorations, as illustrated. It is furnished with a No. 2 brass burner and rests upon a cast brass base. When securely packed in a box this lamp will weigh about 25 pounds, and we hope that you will include one of these lamps in your next order which is to go forward by freight, thus reducing the charges to a minimum.

Our special price... 98c

Our Very Finest Lamp for $6.95.

No. 2R900 For $6.95 we offer you one of the largest, handsomest, and best banquet lamps made, a lamp equal to those that retail at double our price. It stands 25 inches high, has a 12-inch globe and 15-inch bowl, resting on a gold plated stand. Both globe and bowl are delicately tinted and the decoration consists of natural color flowers, put on the globe before the last firing by free hand work so that it will not fade or rub off. The fount is removable and made of bright pressed brass. The lamp is equipped with the best large No. 2 Royal 100-candle power center draft burner. This lamp is so large and handsome that no illustration can do it justice. It is securely packed in a barrel and weighs 40 pounds.

Our special price...... $6.95

Our $5.90 Cerise Banquet Lamp.

No. 2R902 This is the celebrated Cottage Cerise Lamp, which is only manufactured by one factory in the United States. Both globe and bowl are of the one dark red shade with the velvet finish, making a very soft light at night. This cerise color is not on the outside of the globe or bowl, but is in the glass itself, giving a much better light than those which are tinted on the outside of glass and hand decorated. It is an ornament to any parlor either day or night. It is 25 inches high with a 12-inch globe and 14-inch bowl. It has a No. 2 Royal center draft burner and removable brass oil fount. Packed securely in a barrel, weighing 40 pounds.

Our special price..... $5.90

Our Big $5.65 Vase Banquet Lamp.

No. 2R904 This handsome lamp is nearly the same pattern as No. 2R900, but slightly smaller in size and different decoration. It has the popular tinted globe and bowl with the distinct free hand decoration, making it an ornament to any home. It has the cast brass gold plated base, and a brass oil fount with No. 2 center draft burner. It stands 24 inches high, with a 10½-inch globe and 12½-inch bowl. The burners of all our center draft lamps are easily taken apart and cleaned so that you will experience no trouble along this line. Our $5.65 price means a saving of fully 50 per cent on this particular lamp. Securely packed in a barrel weighing 40 pounds.

Our special price..... $5.65

The New Orleans electric lights were more numerous than those of New York, and very much better. One had this modified noonday not only in Canal and some neighboring chief streets, but all along a stretch of five miles of river frontage.

—Mark Twain,
Life on the Mississippi, *1883*

WHALE OIL

LAMPS The whale oil may be **hard to come by,** but the elegant solid-brass lamps from the Mystic Seaport Museum Store can get by on either lamp oil or kerosene.

Prices: 5-inch-high lamp, $17; 7-inch-high lamp, $22.

Color gift catalog available.

MYSTIC SEAPORT MUSEUM STORE

Mystic, CT 06355
Tel. 203/536–9957

LAMP POST   The National

Trust for Historic Preservation offers a reproduction of one of the lamp posts that line the curving drive at Lyndhurst, a Gothic Revival mansion overlooking the Hudson River at Tarrytown, New York. The cast-iron lamp posts, with their handsome Corinthian capitals, were originally manufactured around 1900. The National Trust's 8-foot 10-inch reproduction is also made of cast iron and has a finish of alkyd enamel in gray, black, or antique verdigris.

Price: $2,995 (plus $45 for shipping and handling).

Catalog available, $1.

PRESERVATION SHOPS

Department AH
National Trust for Historic
Preservation
1600 H Street NW
Washington, DC 20006
Tel. 202/673–4200

LEADED-GLASS LAMPS

Nostalgia Decorating's leaded-glass lamps are hand-cast and give a period accent to the Victorian room. They are available in 19-, 20-, and 22-inch heights, and with either red, blue, green, or caramel stained-glass panels.

Color brochure of Tiffany-style lamps and other decorating items available, $1.50 (refundable with order).

NOSTALGIA DECORATING COMPANY

P.O. Box 1312
Kingston, PA 18704
Tel. 717/288–1795

CUMBERLAND GENERAL STORE KEROSENE OIL LAMPS

KEROSENE LAMP WITH HANDLE

WALL BRACKET

"Nothing fancy about it," avers the Cumberland catalog, "just good old-fashioned utility." This lamp's handle wall bracket is made of nickel-plated steel, and hooks on two screws or nails to any wall. The reflector is made of tin-plated steel. The lamp burns for approximately 22 hours on a single filling. Its overall height is 12½ inches and its reflector is 7½ inches in diameter. Shipping weight: 4 lbs.
    Price: $10.64.

OLD-FASHIONED WALL BRACKET

LAMP

Complete with a no. 2 burner, wick, chimney, cast-iron wall bracket, and Mercury Mirror reflector. Shipping weight: 15 lbs.
    Price: $49.50.

MARLE REPLICA LIGHTING

FIXTURES

After the Second World War, the Marle Company's use of New England craftsmen to produce period lanterns in copper and brass was restarted with a Yankee foreman who began working with the firm in his seventieth year and retired in his eightieth. This legacy of devotion to small-scale craftsmanship and attention to detail has resulted in the Marle Company's "hundreds and hundreds" of lanterns to be seen in historic buildings, fine residences, office buildings, and shops.

Among the nineteenth-century replicas produced by Marle's craftsmen is a whale-oil lantern of copper and brass, a hall lantern, and a turn-of-the-century gas light with leaded glass.

Catalog and price list available; showroom visits encouraged.

MARLE COMPANY

170 Summer Street
Stamford, CT 06901
Tel. 203/348–2645

SEWING LAMP

An original-pattern sewing lamp of the type once found in every home. It holds 26 ounces of fuel, stands 14 inches tall, and has a shipping weight of 6 lbs.
    Price: $11.34.

All lamps are shipped F.O.B. Crossville, Tennessee.

"Wish and Want Book" available, $3.75.

CUMBERLAND GENERAL STORE

Route 3
Crossville, TN 38555
Tel. 615/484–8481

R. E. DIETZ LANTERNS

The citation for "Dietz Celebrated Tubular Lanterns" in the Sears catalogue of 1908 attests to the company's boast of manufacturing the lanterns that "lit America's history."

The Dietz company was founded in 1840 by Robert E. Dietz, who gave up his job in a hardware store at the age of twenty-two to buy a small lamp and oil business in Brooklyn, New York. Until the mid-1850s, when kerosene was first produced as a distillate of petroleum, Dietz manufactured whale-oil lamps and wall-lamp fixtures.

Around 1867, R. E. Dietz acquired the patents and rights to manufacture a tubular lantern, which the Original #76 described below reproduces. Used by Yankee seamen and Confederate guerrillas, on Mississippi riverboats and beside California prospectors, these lanterns are surviving standard-issue nineteenth-century Americana.

THE ORIGINAL #76 KEROSENE LANTERN

A reproduction of the nineteenth-century tubular model, the Original #76 is flat black with brass trim and stands 10 inches high
Price: $9.

PIONEER ESTATE POST LANTERN
A "true replica" of the Dietz street and railway platform lamp of the late 1800s, this post lantern has been converted from kerosene to electricity. Constructed of steel, with a black enamel finish, it stands 22 inches high and 15 inches wide.
Price: $121.

BRASS HURRICANE KEROSENE LAMP
A reproduction from Dietz's 1840 dies in a solid-brass special edition, each lamp is serially numbered.
Price: $85.

Literature and order forms available.

R. E. DIETZ COMPANY
225 Wilkinson Street
Syracuse, NY 13204
Tel. 315/424-7400

PROGRESS VICTORIAN LIGHTING

The Victorian era, which takes its name from the long reign of Queen Victoria (1837–1901) encompasses a period of remarkable social advance and technological change.

During this time in America the Civil War was fought and slavery abolished, twenty-eight states came into the Union, mass production introduced inexpensive machine-made items to a burgeoning middle class, and magnificent steamships and railroads expanded the possibilities for travel.

This rapid transformation of society brought about a concomitant nostalgia for the past, and interest in such designs as Greek and Roman classicism, American colonial revival, rococo, and Oriental and Italianate was reflected in much of what was produced. Although the Victorian era is remembered as one with excessively ornate design, its truly "eclectic" nature included many spare, linear forms.

This wide range of Victorian design is fully represented in Progress Lighting's collection of gas and electric fixtures. Emphasizing the company's commitment to absolute authenticity (which relies on the use of old dies and molds), its products are accompanied by a testimonial by Dr. Roger Moss, executive director of Philadelphia's Athenaeum, an independent research library established in 1814 to collect materials "connected with the history and antiquities of America."

The Classical Revival chandelier illustrated here is based on an original manufactured by the Victorian era's leading producer of lighting fixtures, Cornelius & Company of Philadelphia. This was the same firm that supplied fixtures to the U.S. Capitol when it was refurbished during the Civil War.

Dimensions: body height, 32 inches; diameter, 29 inches.

Catalog of Victorian lighting fixtures available, $1.

PROGRESS LIGHTING

Erie Avenue and G Street
Philadelphia, PA 19134

NOWELL'S LIGHTING FIXTURES

Nowell's manufacture of reproduction Victorian lighting fixtures started out in the parts bin. In 1954 Nowell's began restoring old lamps and fixtures ("in San Francisco," says Nowell's Barbara Mendenhall, "we mean Victorian when we say 'old,' because everything here was built after the Gold Rush"—not to mention the earthquake), undertaking projects for the M. H. de Young Museum and the Haas-Lilienthal Mansion, among others. As these contracts required the use of old techniques to refabricate parts from original materials, before long Nowell's was making Victorian fixtures from scratch. "A few dozen projects like this," as they put it, "and we had enough jigs and patterns and molds and sources for obscure parts to make the San Francisco Line."

The San Francisco Line numbers forty-four fixtures in all, and Nowell's has graciously sent us ten representatives.

THE EMBARCADERO The Embarcadero is a twelve-light gas fixture with etched floral ball shades. It is suitable for the grand entry or the ballroom.

Dimensions: width (with glass), 70 inches; standard height, 60 inches.

THE POLK GULCH This is **described as a** small gas-type hall light designed for low ceilings. Finished in polished or antique brass.

Dimensions: width, 10 inches; standard height, 16 inches.

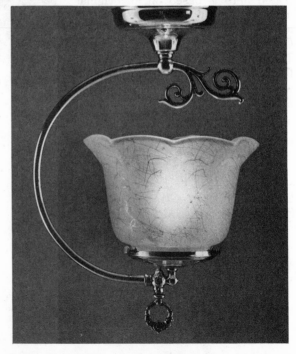

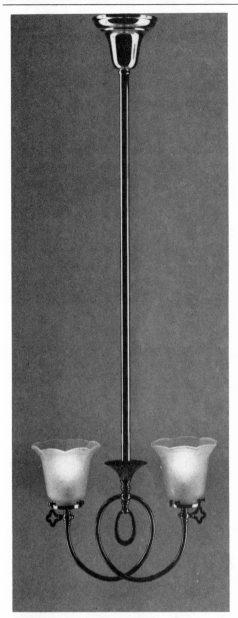

THE EMPEROR NORTON
This twelve-light gas or electric fixture comes in polished or antique brass.

Dimensions: width (with glass), 50 inches; standard height, 72 inches.

RINCON HILL
This was re-created from a hall light, casting the gas cocks from the original and using the same hand-assembly techniques.

Dimensions: width (with glass), 14 inches; standard height, 42 inches.

THE MEIGGS WHARF
A good gift for anyone who considers Victorian design a lot of overly ornate folderol, the Meiggs Wharf is a gas-style fixture for a small parlor or entry.

Dimensions: width (with glass), 40 inches; standard height, 40 inches.

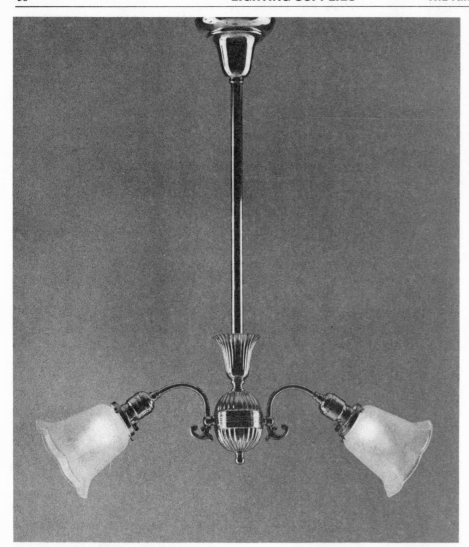

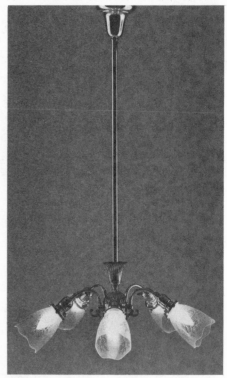

THE OLD WALDORF
A five-light electric parlor fixture with optional full-ribbed or half-ribbed body, the Old Waldorf is finished in polished or antique brass.

Dimensions: width (with glass), 22 inches; standard height, 39 inches.

THE NATIONAL HOTEL
Recommended as a hall, bath, kitchen, or pantry fixture, the National Hotel is finished in polished or antique brass.

Dimensions: width (with glass), 22 inches; standard height, 39 inches.

THE TIVOLI
A five-light fixture with heavy crystal prisms, the Tivoli is "about as Victorian as you can get," says Nowell's. It comes in polished or antique brass.

Dimensions: width (with glass), 40 inches; standard height, 42 inches.

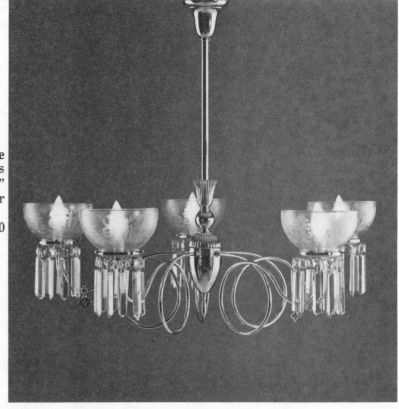

THE PACIFIC

CLUB **An adaptation of a period** ballroom gas and electric fixture, the Pacific Club is assembled by hand and comes in polished or antique brass.

Dimensions: width (with glass), 36 inches; standard height, 42 inches.

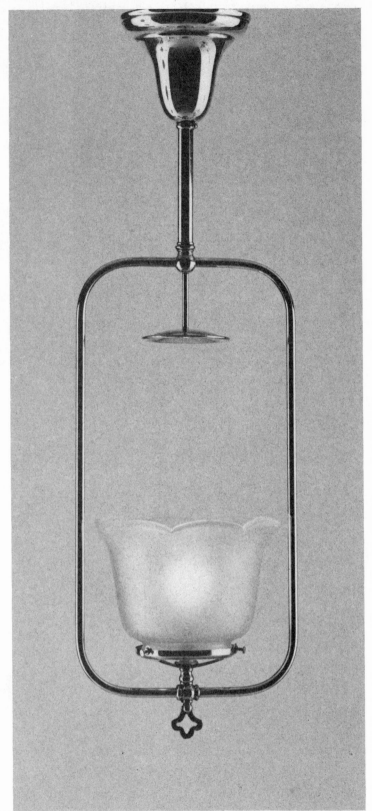

THE NATOMA **A single-light** Victorian hall fixture, the Natoma's small smoke bell originally shielded the ceiling from the flame of the gas jet.

Dimensions: width, 9 inches; standard height, 42 inches.

Catalog available, $3.50. Brochure available free.

NOWELL'S, INC.

P.O. Box 164
Sausalito, CA 94965
Tel. 415/332-4933

RENOVATOR'S SUPPLY VICTORIAN LIGHTING

SINGLE VICTORIAN BRACKET LAMP

A solid-brass reproduction with frosted white glass, the lamp projects 8 inches, is 10 inches high and about 5 inches wide.

Renovator's Supply catalog #23197.
Price: $42.85.

DESK LAMPS

Extremely popular, these elegant brass lamps are virtually the symbol of the Victorian revival. In addition to the adjustable lamp illustrated, an upright model is available.

Dimensions: base width, 6½ inches; height, 14 inches.

Renovator's Supply catalog #30500 (upright).
Price: $99.
Renovator's Supply catalog #30501 (adjustable).
Price: $99.

Renovator's Supply imposes a $2 handling charge on orders.

Color catalog of old-style decorative items available, $2.

THE RENOVATOR'S SUPPLY

182 Northfield Road
Millers Falls, MA 01349
Tel. 413/659–2211

DOUBLE-ARM BRAKET LAMP

Painted over and dark since Hector was a pup, lamps just like this one graced the old windows of an apartment I rented on New York's Lexington Avenue the same year that The Renovator's Supply was founded. Once excavated from their several layers of paint, these burnished bits of low-rent archeology added considerable charm to the place.

Renovator's replica, in a rope motif and with a frosted-glass shade, has arms capable of infinite adjustment up to 25¾ inches from the wall. The brass base is 5½ inches in diameter.

Renovator's Supply catalog #23198.
Price: $45 (price reduced with orders of three or more).

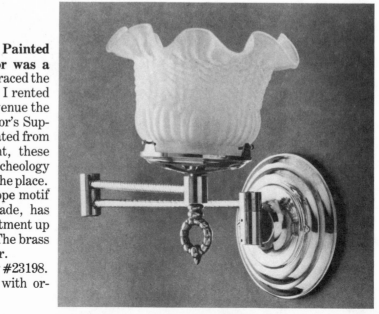

PHOENIX CARBON-LOOP LIGHT BULBS

In 1880 Thomas Alva Edison's first commercially practical light bulbs had filaments made from *bamboo*. In time, however, the man who said "Show me a thoroughly satisfied man and I'll show you a failure" replaced these with a carbon-loop filament that emitted a soft, yellow light.

In its series of Phoenix Historic Light Bulbs, Bradford Consultants of Collingswood, New Jersey, replicates three of Edison's carbon-loop bulbs. From the dainty Bijou to the very bulbous Majestic, all use 120 volts and fit a standard medium base.

Also duplicated by Bradford is the famous Mazda bulb, Edison's next (1909) improvement, which employed a tungsten metal filament. The Mazda shined with a *white* light and lit "the *Titanic* on her fateful maiden voyage," as Bradford's brochure intones. "Behind heavy drapes it helped relieve the gloom cast by World War I."

Price: $4.80 apiece (unit price reduced on orders of twelve or more).

Brochure available.

BRADFORD CONSULTANTS

16 East Homestead Avenue
Collingswood, NJ 08108
Tel. 609/854-1404

PLAIN AND PRINTED CALICOS OF ALL DESCRIPTIONS. | FIGURED SILKOLINES AND SATEENS FOR COMFORTERS

6½c DRESS AND SHIRTING PRINTS, FULL STANDARD GOODS.

EVERYTHING KNOWN IN PRINTED CALICO. We have included under this one number our entire line of staple and fancy shirting and dress prints. This enable you to make your selections with greater convenience. Simply state catalogue number and style of print you want and we will please you in the goods you receive, as well as save you money on the purchase.

No. 36K3711 Shirting or Dress Prints. All full standard goods in weight, count, and finish. You may frequently be able to buy printed calicos at as low a price as our full standard goods at this special price of 6½ cents. Don't do it. Save your money by purchasing high grade goods originally. These calicos will last so much longer and always look so much better—in short you'll get so much more real satisfaction out of the use of our goods that the economy of your investment is at once apparent. We are constantly adding new styles, so that the different our calicos have created wherever they go may not be lessened. New choice styles, embracing everything that is good in dots, figures, checks and stripes. White grounds with red, blue or black figures, pinks, light blues, Garibaldi red and blacks, black and reds, red and whites, wines, cadets, grays, black and whites, indigo blues, browns, shepherd checks in black and white, pink, blue, green and brown, chambrays, chocolates madders, beige effects, tans and a full line of plaids, etc. Be sure to state color wanted. Width, 25 inches.

Price, per yard 6½c
Full piece of about 50 yards, per yard, 6¼c

11c HEAVY GERMAN CALICO, INDIGO BLUE DRESS PATTERNS.

No. 36K3783 Wide and heavy Pure German Indigo Dress Print. The real old fashioned heavy calico that has been the standby for so many years. Very few manufacturers beside our own have maintained the original quality, and although print cloths have advanced sharply we are still away below all competition on prints as well as all other lines of merchandise. Neat styles, figures, dots and stripes. Mention style wanted. Width, 31 inches.

Price, per yard 11c
Full piece of about 45 yards, per yard .. 10½c

7c OIL BOILED CALICO, RED, BLUE OR BLACK

No. 36K3813 Guaranteed oil boiled and fast color Plain Calico. Handard goods. Comes in turkey red, indigo blue or black. Be sure to state color wanted. Width, 25 inches.

Price, per yard 7c
Full piece of about 50 yards, per yard ... 6½c

9½c WIDE RED CALICO, OILBOILED COLOR.

No. 36K3817 A nice soft Turkey Red Calico, oil boiled and guaranteed color. A wide cloth at a price usually asked for the narrow goods. Width, 31 inches.

Price, per yard ... 9½c
Full piece of about 40 yards, per yard 9c

FIGURED SILKOLINES AND SATEENS FOR COMFORTERS

Comforter Prints.

6½c FANCY COMFORTER PRINTS, HIGH GRADE GOODS, NEW DESIGNS.

No. 36K3835 No better Fancy Comforter Print made than this number. Handsome scroll patchwork, floral and oriental patterns in a full line of colors. As a rule, one does not expect much of anything in the way of style in a low priced print, but we have selected the very best patterns for our line this fall, and really never saw better work in those goods. Width, 24 inches.

Price, per yard 6½c
Full piece of about 50 yards, per yard ... 6½c

11c NEW COMFORTER SILKOLINES, BEAUTIFUL PATTERNS.

No. 36K3847 Handsome Figured Silkoline in a choice selection of new and up to date patterns. No better goods made than these and we stand back of every yard for attractiveness and service. Colors are all fast shades and most beautiful tones, full and deep. The patterns are really artistic. Comes in light green, dark green, red, rose pink, light blue or cream grounds with appropriately tinted patterns. Be sure to state color wanted. Width, 36 inches.

Price, per yard 11c
By the piece of about 42 yards, per yd. 10½c

THE leading paper pattern distributors are now bringing out current patterns especially designed for 24-inch goods. Printed calicos will, therefore, have an increased demand. See our Standard Calico No. 36K3711 on this page.

6½c RED AND BLACK FINE COMFORTER PRINTS GUARANTEED OIL RED.

No. 36K3843 Genuine Oil Boiled Comforter Prints. Red grounds with black scroll and other tasty designs. Those who have once used these red and blacks may be counted on for repeated orders. They make friends everywhere. We are showing a variety of new designs this fall, including patchwork patterns. Full standard goods in every respect. Color warranted. Width, 24 inches.

Price, per yard 6½c
Full piece of about 50 yards, per yard .. 6¾c

16c Fancy Comforter Sateens, Handsome Patterns.

No. 36K3849 For those who feel that they must have something heavier and better than the SILKOLINES for COMFORTER USE, we have added this fine and beautiful figured SATEEN. We always invite comparison and before buying comforter sateens which may seem as low as ours, do yourself justice by sending for our samples. We have gone over the comforter sateen market thoroughly and after examining the lines of every first class manufacturer, base placed our contracts on these goods on a basis that shows you a saving of 25 to 50 cents on a comforter length. The patterns are all new and especially designed for comforter work. They will appeal to you the moment you see them. Illustration in black and white cannot do them justice. The colors are dark green, light green, rose pink, light blue, cream, red or white ground with appropriately tinted floral patterns like illustration. Be sure to state color wanted. Samples free on request if necessary. Width, 36 inches.

Price, per yard 16c
By the piece of about 40 yards, per yd. 15c

FLANNELS AND FLANNELETTES

Buffalo Shirting Flannels. California Shirting Flannels. Canton Flannels. Domet or Shaker Flannels. Eiderdowns. Embroidered Flannels. Fleeced Back Flannelettes.
Hen Mottled Flannels. Mixing Flannels. Outing Flannels, Plain and Fancy. Shirt Patterns, Flannel and Flannelette. White Wool Flannels.

WE WILL ___ ___TED ___ ___ AT LEAST ___ ___ THE MO___ ___
for a minute ___ ___ great deal ___ ___ flannels selected and ___ ___ possible to ___ carefully percentage ___ ___ them. ___ Small

FURTHERMORE, WE KNOW OUR GOODS. We sell many thousands of cases of cotton and wool flannels every season, and each yard of goods must pass a rigid examination, and it any are found to be below our specification we turn them back. We have no more loyal customers today on these goods than those who, following up their satisfaction with their first order, have favored us, season after season, with their own orders and their recommendation to friends and neighbors.

DRY GOODS

IT WOULD BE IMPOSSIBLE FOR US TO DOUBLE OUR FLANNEL BUSINESS AS WE HAVE DONE without the support of our customers of seasons back in continuing to send us their orders, and it would be out of the question for us to expect their staunch loyalty unless we stood pat on the quality and satisfaction question and gave them better goods for the same money or less, or the same high quality at lower prices than it is possible for them to obtain anywhere else.

TO THOSE WHO HAVE NEVER TRIED THESE GOODS we say that only reliable fabrics of known value will be sent out by us, and we stand ready at all times to cheerfully refund the purchase price plus the transportation charges you may have paid on any merchandise with which you are not thoroughly satisfied. If this is fair let us fill your order and start you on Economy Road.

7½c FANCY OUTING FLANNELS, CHECKS, PLAIDS, STRIPES. GOOD NAP.

No. 36K3862 Fancy Outing Flannels. Good weight and nicely napped. We could not buy this cloth from the mill today in one hundred case lots at the price we quote you. This only serves to show how we benefit by our anticipation of the market advances. A tasty assortment of pretty checks, plaids and stripes, both light and dark, as well as plain pink, light blue and cream. Be sure to state color wanted. Width, 27 inches.

Price, per yard...... 7½c
By the piece of about 50 yards, per yard.....7¼c

9c FANCY OUTING FLANNELS, PRETTY CHECKS, PLAIDS AND STRIPES.

No. 36K3865 Extra Weight Fancy Outing Flannel, well napped. Will give excellent service. The cloth is close and nicely finished. The styles are very pleasing, coming in both light and dark in a good variety of checks, plaids and stripes. There are also several tasty bourrette styles which are worthy of production in much higher priced qualities. We recommend the purchase of a full piece of these goods which shows you an additional saving of 20 cents on your purchase. Width, 28 inches.

Price, per yard...... 9c
By the piece of about 40 yards, per yard.....8½c

10½c FANCY OUTING FLANNELS, OUR HEAVIEST AND BEST QUALITY.

No. 36K3872 Our Heaviest and Best Fancy Outing Flannel. This is a cloth that retails ordinarily for 15 cents per yard, and considered good value at that price. The very newest styles in both staple and fancy checks, plaids and stripes are to be found in the assortment, which covers a handsome variety of colorings, light and dark. Many of the styles shown are copied from dress goods patterns. A very warm and durable outing flannel. No better made. Be sure to mention whether light or dark color is wanted. Width, 27 inches.

Price, per yard...... 10½c
By the piece of about 40 yards, per yard.....10c

9½c PLAIN OUTING FLANNELS, DARK, SOLID COLORS. SERVICEABLE.

No. 36K3887 Firm Fast Colored Outing Flannels in plain dark colors only. Well napped and a cloth that will give excellent service. This is a flannel that will thoroughly please you, not only in appearance, which is fully equal to outing flannels quoted by any other dealer at 12½ cents per yard, in depth of color and natural warmth, which pronounce it a household favorite everywhere. Looks and feels like a piece of the French flannels that have been so much in demand. Colors are wine, medium gray mixed, dark gray mixed, navy, dark brown or black. Be sure to state color wanted. Width, 27 inches. Price, per yard.. 9½c
By the piece of about 50 yards, per yd.....9c

9½c DAISY CLOTH OR BABY FLANNEL, PINK, BLUE, CREAM OR WHITE.

No. 36K3890 Baby Flannel, medium heavy weight, of beautiful soft texture. Has a well denned flannel twill, with pretty soft nap on both sides. Comes in solid colors only. Cardinal, pink, light blue, pure white or cream color. It is much used for babies' wear, as well as for ladies' dressing sacques, kimonos, tea gowns, night dresses, etc. At 10 cents per yard this is really an exceptional value. Be sure to give color wanted. Width, 28 inches.

Price, per yard...... 9½c
By the piece of about 50 yards, per yard....9c

Fancy Figured Flannelettes.

Samples free on request if necessary.

10c HANDSOME DRESS FLANNELETTES, ALL THE POPULAR NEW STYLES.

No. 36K3930 An elegant assortment of stylish Dress Flannelettes at a very low price. The cloth is firm, well woven and will give extra wear. Has a nice dressy appearance. Back of fabric is lightly napped. Among the many new styles shown will be found several appropriate kimono ideas as well as others adapted for wrappers, waists and children's wear. Colors are navy, wine, cardinal, reseda green, tan, mist, light blue, brown, gray or black. Figures, stripes or dots, as desired. We also have tasty plaids in red, blue, green or brown. Width, 28 inches.

Price, per yard...... 10c
By the piece of about 40 yds., per yd....9½c

7c GUINEA HEN FLANNEL, NICE MOTTLED EFFECTS. GOOD WEIGHT.

No. 36K3900 Choice Guinea Hen Flannel. Good black cloth. Well napped, soft and warm. Wears splendidly. Our Guinea Hen Mottled Flannels are flushed on both sides, making a much more desirable cloth than the general run of these goods. Colors are mottled pink, blue, gray or brown. Be sure to state color wanted. Width, 27 inches.

Price, per yard...... 7c
By the piece of about 60 yards, per yard....6½c

10c GUINEA HEN FLANNEL, EXTRA WARM CLOTH. FOUR COLORS.

No. 36K3925 Our Best and Heaviest Mottled Flannel, or Guinea Hen, as it is commonly called. This is a stout cotton flannel, having a delightfully soft fleece and is wonderfully warm. Gives the greatest service imaginable. Comes in mottled pink, blue, gray or brown. Be sure to state color wanted. Width, 28 inches.

Price, per yard...... 10c
By the piece of about 55 yards, per yd. 9½c

13c FANCY DRESS FLANNELETTES, EXTRA FINE AND WIDE.

No. 36K3960 Our Best and Widest Fine Dress Flannelette. We have pink, light blue, tan, cardinal, navy, brown or black in figures like illustration, also some very handsome plaids in red, green, blue and brown combinations, black and white shepherd checks, as well as staple dots and a few choice fancy stripes. Be sure to state color wanted. Width, 34½ inches.

Price, per yard...... 13c
By the piece of about 40 yds., per yd. 12½c

HUDSON'S BAY POINT BLANKETS

By the third week in December [1865] everything was in readiness, and about two thousand warriors began moving south . . . along the Tongue. The weather was very cold, and they wore Buffalo robes with the hair turned in, leggings of dark woolen cloth, high-topped Buffalo fur moccasins, and carried red Hudson's Bay blankets strapped to their saddles.
—Dee Brown, Bury My Heart at Wounded Knee, *1971*

By the time these Sioux embarked on what became known as Red Cloud's War, the Indians of North America were long familiar with the Hudson's Bay point blanket. Introduced into trade in 1779, it was used to barter with natives all across the American and Canadian wilderness, the "points" (indicated by parallel black bars woven into the fabric) denoting the number of pelts required to equal the blanket's value. Continuously manufactured in England for two centuries, the Hudson's Bay point blanket has never slackened in either its usefulness or appeal.

Made of 100 percent pure virgin wool, it is available in two sizes, four point (regular) and six point (queen), and comes in six colors: candy-stripe, sky blue, reseda, gold, green, and red.

Contact:

L. L. BEAN, INC.

Freeport, ME 04033

or Hudson's Bay's exclusive agents in the United States:

PEARCE WOOLEN MILLS

Woolrich, PA 17779

THE NEW HAMPSHIRE BLANKET

The story of the New Hampshire blanket is one of many that can be told which show that the simple logic of nineteenth-century industrial organization has much to offer in the way of contemporary economic value.

In 1975 Bruce Clement, the Cheshire County, New Hampshire, agricultural agent, and John Colony III, the proprietor of Harrisville Designers were trying to find a way to increase the return on wool to New Hampshire's sheep breeders. They arrived at the idea of taking the sheared Granite State wool and turning it into a finished product right within the state's borders. Thus the New Hampshire blanket, spun by Harrisville from the finest Dorset and Corriedal fleeces, and woven at the Homestead Woolen Mills in West Swanzey, was born.

"Made to last at least 200 years," the 100 percent wool New Hampshire blanket is a limited-edition item. It uses the traditional indigo blue and cochineal red colors of the eighteenth century and weaves them into a classic windowpane pattern (the middle pattern in the illustration is the only one currently available).

Literature obtainable.

HARRISVILLE DESIGNS

Main Street
Harrisville, NH 03450
Tel. 603/827–3333

NATIONAL TRUST FLOOR CLOTH

As a substitute for expensive carpeting, American floor cloths reached the height of their popularity during the early part of the nineteenth century. The National Trust for Historic Preservation's floor cloth replica shows a country scene from that time, complete with houses, barns, fields, and a horse and carriage.

Made of heavy cotton duck, the National Trust's 3- by 4-foot replica is hand-painted and sealed.

Price: $160 (plus $5 for shipping and handling).

Catalog available, $1.

PRESERVATION SHOPS

Department AH
National Trust for
Historic Preservation
1600 H Street NW
Washington, DC 20006
Tel. 202/673–4200

AMISH AND MENNONITE

QUILTS **Like the husking bees, spinning bees, and road- and church-building bees that came before,** the quilting bees that began in the early 1800s were happy social gatherings for the purpose of getting a particular kind of work done.

The Old Country Store of Intercourse, Pennsylvania, purveys traditional Amish and Mennonite quilts still handmade at quilting bees by Lancaster County craftswomen. These quilts are made from new fabric (not pieced together from worn-out clothing as quilts once were), but the technique and designs—including the dramatic Lone Star, the Oriental-influenced Fan, and the Colonial Star (depicted)—are ancient.

"Quiltalog" available, $1.

THE QUILT ROOM

Old Country Store
Intercourse. PA 17534

PERIOD TEXTILE FURNISHINGS

FURNISHINGS Nancy Bogdonoff Borden's display of **eighteenth- and early-nineteenth-century fabrics in the window of her Portsmouth shop is always changing,** but only a fraction of her large line of textile furnishings can ever be shown—copperplates, Indian palampores, calicos, moreens, worsteds, and more. Her selection of museum-documented fabrics has been derived from those at textile collections at Winterthur, Williamsburg, Sleepy Hollow, Historic Charleston, South Street Seaport, Historic Newport, Greenfield Village, Old Sturbridge Village, and the Victoria and Albert Museum. These fabrics are meticulously hand-sewn according to traditional techniques.

Consultation for custom-made period window curtains, bed hangings, furniture casings, and upholstery may be arranged throughout New England by appointment.

Brochure available.

NANCY BORDEN

P.O. Box 4381
Portsmouth, NH 03801
Tel. 603/436-4284 or 431-8733

RAG RUGS

Because of their folksy charm, most people wrongly associate rag rugs with the eighteenth century. In point of fact this type of floor covering was a kind of *postindustrial* furnishing that followed the availability of machine-made yarns in the 1830s. This lowered the cost of materials while providing a good source of scraps for homemakers to weave into small rugs for hearth and bedside.

SHAKER WORKSHOPS' RUGS

Shaker Workshops' rag rugs duplicate those made in nineteenth-century Shaker communities. Hand-woven in New England of fine-quality wool rags on 100 percent linen warps, they are intended for a lifetime of wear.

The rugs come in four predominant colors—browns, blues, red/gray, and green—and in two standard sizes (not including a 3-inch colored linen fringe at either end): 3 by 5 feet at $90, and 6 by 9 feet at $325. Runners are also available in 24-inch widths, at $12 a foot. (Shipping and handling charges are extra.)

Seasonal catalog available, 50¢.

SHAKER WORKSHOPS

P.O. Box 1028
Concord, MA 01742
Tel. 617/646-8985

HERITAGE RUGS

This Bucks County outfit weaves its rag rugs on an antique hand-built loom that permits widths up to 15 feet and lengths up to 35 feet. As all the rugs are custom made, each is assigned a number and is "registered as a Heritage original."

Heritage Rugs suggests that you send along a sample (paint colors, wallpaper, or fabric) of the colors you'd like woven into your rug.

Rug sizes in feet (and costs): 4 × 6 ($145), 5 × 7 ($215), 6 × 9 ($330), 8 × 10 ($490), 9 × 12 ($660), 10 × 15 ($915), 12 × 15 ($1,100), 15 × 15 ($1,375)—plus shipping and handling charges.

Brochure available, 50¢.

HERITAGE RUGS

Kay and Ron Loch
Lahaska, PA 18931
Tel. 215/794-7229

CARPETBAGS

CARPETBAGS Long before the business and political opportunists from the North known as "carpetbaggers" headed south to exploit the situation created there by the Reconstruction Act of 1867, carpetbags were a common sight.

They began to appear in 1840, six years following the U.S. patent for an in-grain-carpet power loom was issued. But by the 1870s Reconstruction had so tarnished the carpetbag's reputation that its popularity waned. In time the word "carpetbag" became so kindred to "scoundrel" that in 1884 the Kingston, New Mexico, *Clipper* would remark: "An effort is being made to remove more of the jobbers, bloodsucks, and renegade carpet-bag scrubs from our territory."

If after that characterization you still want one, the Smithsonian Institution offers carpetbags in two sizes, each patterned after originals in its collection and made from power-woven Brussels carpet, one of the most popular mid-nineteenth-century types.

Prices: 7 by 12 inches, $110 (plus $2.60 for shipping); 16 by 21 inches, $165 (plus $3.50 for shipping).

Gift catalog available, $2.

THE SMITHSONIAN INSTITUTION

P.O. Box 2456
Washington, DC 20013
Tel. 202/357–1826

Stamped Muslin Pillow Shams.

	Per pair.	Per doz. pair.
16707 Stamped Muslin Pillow Sham, not hemmed. Assorted patterns, 28x 25	$0.20	$2.00

16710 Hemstitched Stamped Muslin Pillow Shams, assorted patterns. Per pair...$0.35 and .50

Embroidered Pillow Shams.

16735—43

16735 White Muslin Pillow Shams, 30x30. Embroidered in fast dyed red, with Good Night on one and Good Morning on the other. Per pair, $0.38

16743 White Muslin Pillow Shams, 30x30. Embroidered in white, with Good Night on one and Good Morning on the other. Per pair, $0.35

16748 White Muslin Pillow Shams, 30x30. Embroidered in fast dye red. Per pair, $0.43

16752 White Muslin Pillow Shams, 30x30. Embroidered in fast dye red. Per pair, $0.60

Muslin Pillow Cases.

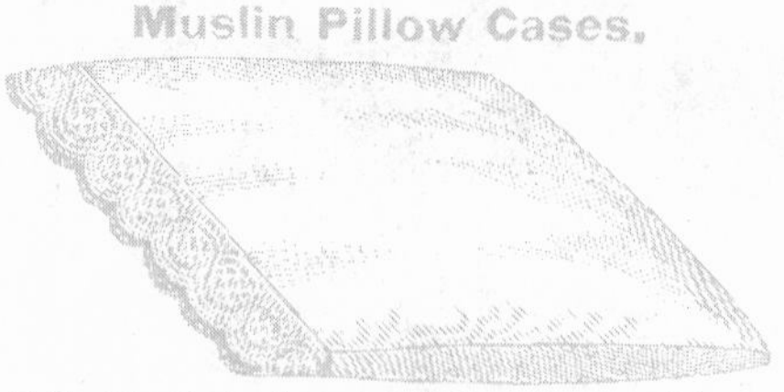

16763 Bleached Hemmed Pillow Cases, with American lace. Size, 22x35. Per pair..........$0.40
Per dozen pairs.......... 4.35

Plain Muslin Pillow Cases.

16768 Bleached, Hemmed Pillow Cases, same as above, 16763, without lace. Per pair...$0.30
Per dozen pairs.......... 3.40

Pepperell Bleached Bed Sheets.

16774 Bed Sheets, $2\frac{1}{2}$ yards long by 2 yards wide, made from good bleached sheeting, hemmed.
Each.......... $0.50
Per one dozen sheets.......... 5.75

16788 Bleached Muslin Sheets, $2\frac{1}{2}$ yards long by $2\frac{1}{4}$ yards wide. Each.......... .60
Per one dozen sheets.......... 6.75

Ottoman Burlap Patterns.

16808

16795 Ottoman. Dog's head in center, handsome border, size, 20x20 inches.
Each..........$0.12

16801 Ottoman. Cat's Head in center, octagon border in two colors. Size 20x20 inches.
Each..........$0.12

16805 Ottoman. Branch of Roses in center, oval border. Size, 14x20 inches.
Each..........$0.10

16808 Ottoman. Floral Center of Roses, Pansies, and Bell Flowers, octagon border. Size 20x20 inches. See cut. Each..........$0.[illegible]

Burlap Rug Patterns.

Turkish and Assorted Patterns. We show two patterns only, but quote 15 patterns, as per quotations below.

The above cut represents the manner of placing our patterns in the frames for working. Take 4 slats similar to bed slats. Place them as shown in cut; then fasten corners together, leaving the inside large enough to hold the pattern and about two inches between pattern and frame, so as to stretch the pattern. Then, after hemming the pattern, sew it into frame as shown in the cut, stretching tightly and square. Then proceed to work the pattern by following the lines with the various colors designated.

16815 Turkish Design. Size 18 in. by 1 yard; price, 23 cents. Similar to cut (136).

16820 Bouquet of Roses in center, surrounded by scroll in old gold and brown; geometric border, with roses in corners. Size, $\frac{1}{2}$x1 yd. (40).
Price.......... $0.23

16823 Spaniel Dog lying on center panel; spray of roses at each end, scroll border. This pattern is an unusual favorite. Size, $\frac{1}{2}$x1 yard (19).
Price.......... .23

16825 Lilies, Rosebuds and Pansies in center surrounded by scroll of old gold and brown combined with Mosaic border. Size, $\frac{2}{3}$x$1\frac{1}{3}$ yards (43). Price.......... .27

16827 Oval Panel, with fine Stag's Head in center [illegible]

DECORATION

[illegible] Size, $\frac{3}{4}$x$1\frac{1}{4}$ yards (96). Price.......... .35

16840 Spaniel Dog lying on Mosaic carpet, surrounded with a unique oval, with twined ash leaves, scroll in corners of plain border. Size, $\frac{3}{4}$x$1\frac{1}{4}$ yards (36). Price.......... .35

16841 Turkish Design, similar to 16815. Size, $\frac{3}{4}$x$1\frac{1}{4}$ yards (150). Price.......... .37

16843 Stag by the Lake; heavy rich border of scroll work; beautiful landscape in center. Size, $\frac{3}{4}$x$1\frac{1}{2}$ yards (22). Price.......... .42

16844

16844—Large, intelligent-looking dog lying on a lawn, lake and mountain in the distance. Grecian border. Size $\frac{3}{4}$ x $1\frac{1}{2}$ yards (91.)
Price.......... $0.42

16849 Cat and Three Playful Kittens, with handsome scroll border. Size $\frac{3}{4}$x$1\frac{1}{2}$ yards (59).
Price.......... .42

16853 Bouquet of Morning Glories, Lilies, etc., in center; Grecian border. Size $\frac{3}{4}$x$1\frac{1}{2}$ yards (90). Price.......... .42

16868 Large Lion lying in the foreground with another in distance. Landscape with luxurious tropical plants. Size $\frac{3}{4}$x$1\frac{3}{4}$ yards (7). Price.... .50

16877 Turkish Design. Size $\frac{3}{4}$x$1\frac{3}{4}$ yards (170).
Price.......... .60

Material Used in Working the Patterns.

Every household has its supply of odds and ends, rags and ravelings, which can be woven into articles of beauty and utility. Rags worked into the proper patterns with the improved rag machine produce very rich and handsome rugs and ottomans, having a tapestry effect which gives no suggestion of the cheapness of the material.

Some prefer to work colored yarn with their rags, others use fancy yarns altogether. In the latter case it may be estimated that it will require from one-quarter to one-half pound of yarn to every square foot of canvas worked, according as you want the article, light or heavier. One-half pound of good yarn to the square foot will make a rug nearly three-quarters of an inch thick.

Colored Rug Yarn.

Order No. 16881.

Yarn especially manufactured for this purpose and kept in stock by us can be supplied in any quantity.

The average amount of yarn required to fill our patterns is shown in the following list, but for the weight of each separate color we refer you to our yarn list which we will send when asked for.

	Pounds.	
No. 136	$1\frac{3}{4}$	"
" 19, 40	2	"
" 24, 43, 80	$2\frac{2}{3}$	"
" 36, 96, 150	$3\frac{1}{2}$	"
" 39, 90, 91	$4\frac{1}{2}$	"
" 22	$4\frac{3}{4}$	"
" 7, 170	$5\frac{1}{2}$	"
Ottomans, 6, 7, 8	$\frac{3}{4}$	"
Ottomans, 2	$\frac{3}{4}$	"

The above ingrain carpet yarn, assorted colors, 4 skeins to pound. Per skein..........$0.20
Per pound.......... .75

The Gem Tufting and Embroidery Machine.

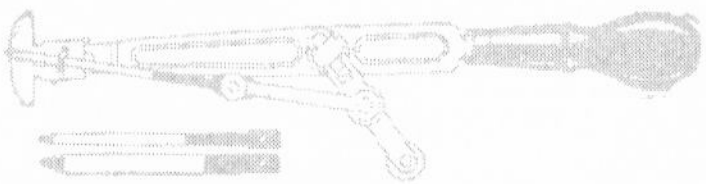

16888 Has four needles. Will work rags, yarn, zephyr and silk. A machine for $1.40 that makes Turkish Rugs, Ottomans, Curtains, Stair Carpets, Hoods, Mittens, Slippers, Quilts, Piano Spreads or Table Covers, which have all the gorgeous appearance of the genuine Turkish or Persian design. So simple that a ten year old child can operate it. With this machine you can beautify your homes and teach your children to be industrious. Special instructions with each machine. Postage 7 cents.
Each.......... $1.40

Canvas.

16890 Java Canvas, white, 18 in. Per yard.....$0.20
16892 Penelope Canvas, 27 in. Per yard.......... .25

Ladies' Gingham Aprons.

16895 Ladies' Good Gingham Aprons, assorted checks, in brown, green and blue, 38 inches long, 45 inches wide. See cut. Each..........$0.25
Per dozen.......... 2.75

Ladies' White Aprons.

16900 Ladies' White Muslin Aprons, good quality, trimmed with lace and strings. See cut (1625).
Each..........$0.15
Per dozen.......... 1.65

Aluminum Cooking Utensils

Are Fast Displacing Tin and Iron—so Light and Clean.

CUSTOM-PAINTED FOLK PORTRAITS

During the period following the Revolutionary War the limner artist, an itinerant, usually untrained painter of portraits, answered the need of the growing middle class for likenesses of their families. Well into the nineteenth century, limners were to be found traveling from village to town, staying with a family and painting them for room and board before moving on.

Although she insists on staying put in her Quitman, Mississippi, home, Barbara Phillips will do custom portraiture in the folksy limner style. Mrs. Phillips's paintings are executed on stretched canvas and require an unsmiling photo of the subject (with the eye color specified). As this type of folk portraiture often included the use of props, Mrs. Phillips also invites information regarding the subject's profession, interests, or hobbies.

Prices are for one subject (additional persons are $50 each): 12 by 16 inches at $150, 16 by 20 inches at $200, 18 by 24 inches at $250, and 24 by 36 inches at $350.

Profiles (of one subject only) are also available: 5 by 7 inches at $35, 8 by 10 inches at $50, 9 by 12 inches at $75, and 11 by 14 inches at $100.

THE BATTERED BRUSH

Barbara F. Phillips
228 Dogwood Avenue
Quitman, MS 39355
Tel. 601/776-3180

THE REPLICA ELIZA SEAMAN SAMPLER

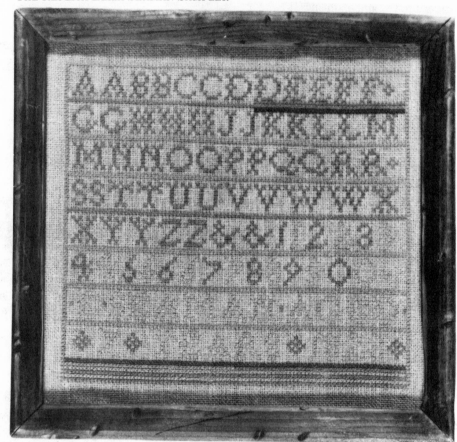

SAMPLER KITS The Early
American "examplar," or sampler—an article of linen embroidered to show the alphabet or a verse—has been replicated into kits for needleworkers by the Examplarery of Dearborn, Michigan.

Using antique samplers, many with historic significance, the Examplarery reproduces them with an exactitude that extends to the use of imported hand-dyed linens and naturally dyed floss. All of the Examplarery's samplers are authorized museum reproductions, and even the errors in the originals—which were often created by girls as young as eight years—are faithfully included as first wrought.

The sampler depicted is a replica of one made in 1823 by eight-year-old Eliza Seaman. Miss Seaman, whose original sampler is part of the Detroit Historical Museum's textile collection, was to achieve wide reknown as an abolitionist and suffragette. Married in 1836 to Augustus Leggett, the couple included Walt Whitman, Ralph Waldo Emerson, and Louisa May Alcott among their friends.

Kit catalog available, $1.25.

THE EXAMPLARERY

P.O. Box 2554
Dearborn, MI 48123
Tel. 313/278-3282

ELIZA SEAMAN LEGGETT

BRASS ACCESSORIES

Fancibrass's decorative brass accessories have been sand-cast from original molds and patterns of one of England's largest and oldest brass foundries. The pattern for the ship's cannon depicted here was laid down in 1880; other items shown are (from top to bottom) mortice key, butcher's weights, gavel, and paper knife. These and other Fancibrass decorative appointments are handcrafted as they were in the nineteenth century.

Catalog and price list available to all trade customers.

FANCIBRASS

522 Parkway View Drive
Pittsburgh, PA 15205
Tel. 412/787-2499; Telex: 812381

DECORATIVE IRON PLAQUES

The Darby Family, whose patriarch Abraham founded England's Coalbrookdale Company early in the eighteenth century, has a history intimately intertwined with that of the Industrial Revolution itself. In 1709 Abraham Darby became the first man to successfully smelt iron with coke, and more than a century later his descendant Francis would become a major force in diversifying the ways in which iron could be used.

Francis shared in the management of Coalbrookdale from 1827 to 1850, and was a great lover of music and art. He was responsible for the production of Coalbrookdale's first decorative cast-iron products, an area that became known as one of the company's specialties toward the end of the nineteenth century.

The Longfellow Plaques are ornamental castings derived from the American poet's famous "Village Blacksmith." The intricately detailed plaques were originally cast in the 1840s and are still available from Coalbrookdale today.

Dimensions: 18½ by 10¼ inches. Weight: 17 lbs., with bracket for mounting. 1840 Last Supper Plaque also available.

Literature obtainable.

THE COALBROOKDALE COMPANY

American Sales Office
RFD 1, Box 477
Stowe, VT 05672
Tel. 802/253-9727

SHAKER "TREE OF LIFE" PRINT

Shaker "spirit drawings" were detailed renderings of heavenly visions. The "Tree of Life" was "seen and painted" during the summer of 1854 by Sister Hannah Cohoon of the Hancock (Massachusetts) Community. Shaker Workshops' replica print reproduces the vivid greens and orange of the original on 18¼-by 23¼-inch parchment paper.
  Price: $30, ppd.

Color catalog of Shaker crafts available, 50¢.

SHAKER WORKSHOPS

P.O. Box 1028
Concord, MA 01742
Tel. 617/646–8985

TURN-OF-THE-CENTURY ADVERTISING PRINTS

As early as the 1840s root beer was a drink highly favored by children and temperate adults alike. Young men grew up, stayed sober, and got old sipping the carbonated concoction before the Hire's Root Beer ad that Nostalgia Decorating so faithfully duplicates appeared on the scene. Accompanying Hire's are more than fifty other full-color prints extolling Burpee's Seeds, making chauvinistic appeals for Beals-Torrye Shoes, quoting Cream of Wheat's "sambo" chef, and displaying theatrical broadsides, magazine covers, and Victorian beer company pin-ups. Nostalgia Decorating also has replica antique advertising signs in tin and porcelain available.

Price: $3.50 per print (plus $2 for shipping and handling).

Full-color brochure available, $1.50 (refundable with purchase).

NOSTALGIA DECORATING COMPANY

P.O. Box 1312
Kingston, PA 18704
Tel. 717/288–1795

CUSTOM-MADE TRADITIONAL FRAMES

John Morgan Baker, son of the artist Jim Baker (whose fireboards are described above in the "Housewares" section), uses solid curly maple to handcraft frames in the old way. The wood is selected for the beauty of its grain, and all corners are mitred for joint strength. The result is a handsome article, the deep-brown rubbed finish of which suggests early rifle stocks. A lighter honey tone, also considered ideal for portraits, samplers, crewel work, folk art, and mirrors, is available.

Mr. Baker's frames are obtainable with either flat or beveled surfaces (the flat frame is considered to be the more authentic Early American type) in three widths: 1½, 2¼, and 3 inches. Respectively, these sell for $1.25, $1.50, and $1.75 *per united inch* (meaning the number of inches in the width plus the length of the item to be framed). The frames are shipped assembled, without glass or hardware.

Literature and order blank available.

JOHN MORGAN BAKER

P.O. Box 149
Worthington, OH 43085
Tel. 614/885–7040

CURTAIN POLE FINIALS

The Ground Floor of Charleston, South Carolina, offers period curtain-pole finials in motifs such as bursting seed pods, pineapples, or the thistle pictured.

Price: $40 each pair, brackets and rings not included.

THE GROUND FLOOR

95½ Broad Street
Charleston, SC 29401
Tel. 803/722–3576

DECOYS

DECOYS No one knows when decoys were first used, but the earliest ones now to be found date from around the time of the Civil War. The surprising newness of the decoy has condensed the period required to romanticize the old ones, and today any old "block" (so called because they were carved from blocks of wood) made before 1950 is considered an antique. This means that there are still plenty of the oldtime carvers around who are prepared to laugh at you for looking on them as folk artists, even though their body of work has almost entirely been replaced by plastic factory-mades.

Dan O'Donnell, Sr., and Jim Tooker have a different view of the matter: even the new decoy makers, they claim, "will someday find themselves a part of American history too." Tooker, who has devoted five years to studying the techniques of the old carvers, shared with O'Donnell an interest in recreating the decoys made early in this century. They founded the Decoy Works, happily, just at the time when an interest in antique decoys as decorative items was building.

Tooker and O'Donnell offer a variety of shorebirds patterned after the famous makers and painted in the old style. Jim's nine-step antiquing process is so effective in making the blocks seem old and worn that he must sign and date each one.

Catalog sheet available, $1.

THE DECOY WORKS

2601 S.W. 122nd Avenue
Davie, FL 33330
Tel. 305/472–7910

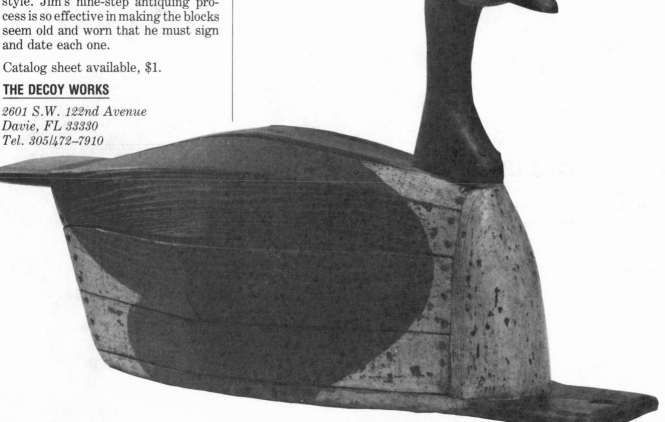

SILENT COMPANION

Chartered by Congress in 1949 to encourage public participation in the "preservation of districts, sites, buildings, and objects significant to American history and culture," the National Trust for Historic Preservation not only provides advisory, financial, and educational assistance to appropriate organizations and individuals, but owns many historic properties as well. Membership in the National Trust and the purchase of the item below (and others of theirs listed elsewhere in this book) aids the organization with its efforts on behalf of our national heritage.

Silent companions, the life-size depictions of adults, children, and pets copied from portraits, was brought over to America from the Netherlands during the seventeenth century. They were considered cheering room decorations, and usually pulled duty brightening a dismal corner or standing sentinel before the hearth. The National Trust's wooden companion was adopted by Abbie Cutter from an American primitive painting entitled *Young Boy Seated With Dog*. The original is on display at the Woodlawn Plantation in Mount Vernon, Virginia.

Hand-painted wood, 41 by 23½ inches.

Price: $170 (plus $9.85 for shipping and handling).

Catalog available, $1.

PRESERVATION SHOPS

Department AH
National Trust for Historic
   Preservation
1600 H Street NW
Washington, DC 20006
Tel. 202/673–4200

76

SEARS, ROEBUCK & CO., Cheapest Supply House on Earth, Chicago. CATALOGUE No. III.

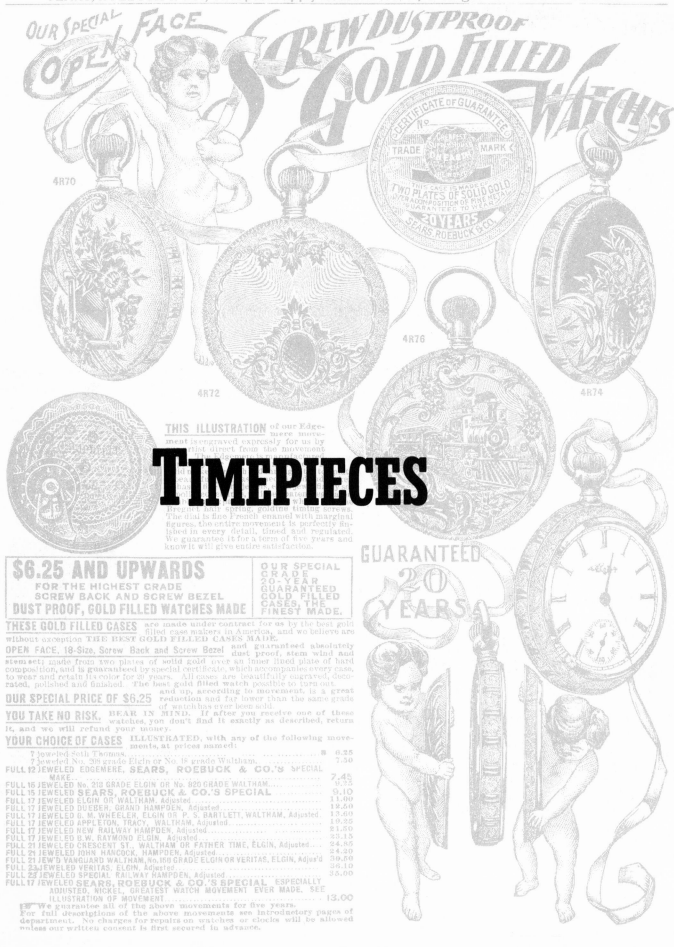

OUR SPECIAL OPEN FACE SCREW DUSTPROOF GOLD FILLED WATCHES

4R70 · 4R72 · 4R76 · 4R74

Timepieces

THIS ILLUSTRATION of our Edgemere movement is engraved expressly for us by artist direct from the movement. The Edgemere is manufactured. The dial is fine French enamel with marginal figures, the entire movement is perfectly finished in every detail, timed and regulated. We guarantee it for a term of five years and know it will give entire satisfaction.

CERTIFICATE OF GUARANTEE No. TRADE MARK THIS CASE IS MADE OF TWO PLATES OF SOLID GOLD OVER A COMPOSITION OF FINE METAL GUARANTEED TO WEAR 20 YEARS. SEARS, ROEBUCK & CO.

GUARANTEED 20 YEARS

$6.25 AND UPWARDS
FOR THE HIGHEST GRADE
SCREW BACK AND SCREW BEZEL
DUST PROOF, GOLD FILLED WATCHES MADE

OUR SPECIAL GRADE 20-YEAR GUARANTEED GOLD FILLED CASES, THE FINEST MADE.

THESE GOLD FILLED CASES are made under contract for us by the best gold filled case makers in America, and we believe are without exception THE BEST GOLD FILLED CASES MADE.

OPEN FACE, 18-Size, Screw Back and Screw Bezel and guaranteed absolutely dust proof, stem wind and stem set; made from two plates of solid gold over an inner lined plate of hard composition, and is guaranteed by special certificate, which accompanies every case, to wear and retain its color for 20 years. All cases are beautifully engraved, decorated, polished and finished. The best gold filled watch possible to turn out.

OUR SPECIAL PRICE OF $6.25 and up, according to movement, is a great reduction and far lower than the same grade of watches has ever been sold.

YOU TAKE NO RISK. BEAR IN MIND. If after you receive one of these watches, you don't find it exactly as described, return it, and we will refund your money.

YOUR CHOICE OF CASES ILLUSTRATED, with any of the following movements, at prices named:

7 jeweled Seth Thomas	$ 6.25
7 jeweled No. 298 grade Elgin or No. 18 grade Waltham	7.50
FULL 12 JEWELED EDGEMERE, SEARS, ROEBUCK & CO.'S SPECIAL MAKE	7.45
FULL 15 JEWELED No. 218 GRADE ELGIN OR No. 820 GRADE WALTHAM	9.25
FULL 15 JEWELED SEARS, ROEBUCK & CO.'S SPECIAL	9.10
FULL 17 JEWELED ELGIN OR WALTHAM, Adjusted	11.00
FULL 17 JEWELED DUEBER, GRAND HAMPDEN, Adjusted	12.50
FULL 17 JEWELED G. M. WHEELER, ELGIN OR P. S. BARTLETT, WALTHAM, Adjusted	13.60
FULL 17 JEWELED APPLETON, TRACY, WALTHAM, Adjusted	19.25
FULL 17 JEWELED NEW RAILWAY HAMPDEN, Adjusted	21.50
FULL 17 JEWELED B.W. RAYMOND ELGIN, Adjusted	23.15
FULL 21 JEWELED CRESCENT ST., WALTHAM OR FATHER TIME, ELGIN, Adjusted	24.85
FULL 21 JEWELED JOHN HANCOCK, HAMPDEN, Adjusted	24.20
FULL 21 JEW'D VANGUARD WALTHAM, No.150 GRADE ELGIN OR VERITAS, ELGIN, Adjus'd	30.50
FULL 23 JEWELED VERITAS, ELGIN, Adjusted	36.10
FULL 23 JEWELED SPECIAL RAILWAY HAMPDEN, Adjusted	35.00
FULL 17 JEWELED SEARS, ROEBUCK & CO.'S SPECIAL, ESPECIALLY ADJUSTED, NICKEL, GREATEST WATCH MOVEMENT EVER MADE. SEE ILLUSTRATION OF MOVEMENT	13.00

We guarantee all of the above movements for five years. For full descriptions of the above movements see introductory pages of department. No charges for repairs on watches or clocks will be allowed unless our written consent is first secured in advance.

AARON WILLARD

CLOCK KIT Aaron Willard and his brother Simon were among the most renowned and prolific clock makers of the turn of the nineteenth century. Their "coffin clock" (circa 1800) reflects the clean lines of its grim namesake.

The coffin clock comes with a completely assembled eight-day movement and sounds a cheery "gong" (no, not a death knell) on the hour. The pine case, with glass-covered dial and pendulum window, is 36 inches high, 10 inches wide, and 5 inches deep, and assembles in four hours.

   Price: $229.

Catalog of reproduction furniture kits available, $1.

COHASSET COLONIALS

834 X Ship Street
Cohasset, MA 02025

SHARP STEEPLE CLOCK

Dan Damon of Victorian Accents writes that the "Sharp Steeple clocks that enjoyed a tremendous vogue during the 1840s and 1850s reflected Gothic Revival architecture, then in its heyday."

Mr. Damon's handcrafted clock, with its rich hand-rubbed walnut finish and mitred construction, "faithfully echoes the originals in its details." The lower panel of the hinged glass door is painted in a floral motif with gold trim. An adjustable brass pendulum regulates the hands, and chimes count the hour and strike the half hour.

   Battery operated, it stands 26½ inches high, 18½ inches wide, and 8 inches deep.

   Price: $175, ppd.

Catalog of Victoriana available, $1.

WATTLE & DAUB'S VICTORIAN ACCENTS

661 West 7th Street
Plainfield, NJ 07060
Tel. 201/757–8507

VICTORIAN STREET CLOCKS

The Victorian street clock is an idyllic fixture in the urban landscape. Black and ornate, it has a great harvest-moon face to tell the time cordially on summer nights and steadfastly through winter storms. Because elegant examples of these timepieces are still manufactured by the venerable New England firm of Kenneth Lynch & Sons, the Victorian clock that stands downtown needn't be a relic.

Renowned for their special work in architectural sheet-metal ornamentation, Lynch's street clock rises 20 feet to a 4-foot-diameter face. It has a wrought-iron steel base and a steel-reinforced column. The clock is electrically lit and offers several types of Victorian ornamentation for use around its dial.

Catalog of architectural and decorative sheet-metal ornaments available, $2.50.

KENNETH LYNCH & SONS

P.O. Box 488
Wilton, CT 06897
Tel. 203/762-8363

NINETEENTH-CENTURY CLOCK ITEMS

The firm of Mason & Sullivan of Cape Cod has been manufacturing replica clocks (both in kit form and with fully finished cases) for thirty-seven years. They have an excellent reputation for quality that has resulted from their high standards in wood, joinery, movements, and detailing. The following is a sample of their replica nineteenth-century clocks:

NO. 2 REGULATOR CLOCK

Seth Thomas (1785–1859) was one of this country's best known clock makers. In 1807 Thomas co-founded the Connecticut firm of Terry, Thomas, and Hoadley to manufacture clocks by mass production, an important step in making them available to the common man. Mason & Sullivan's No. 2 Regulator is modeled after a Seth Thomas original, obtainable during the 1860s and 1870s.

Dimensions: 36 inches high, 15 inches wide, and 6 inches deep.

RAILROAD REGULATOR

The Regulator clock was used by the railroads to regulate the profusion of time zones to be found in America during the nineteenth century (as many as fifty-six in 1883). Mason & Sullivan's Railroad Regulator duplicates one that could have been found in many of the railway stations of the late 1800s.

Dimensions: 32 inches high, 18 inches wide, and 7 inches deep.

SHAKER TALL CLOCK

Inspired by a "rare and important" clock case made by Erastus Rude (1774–1820) and now at the Shaker Museum in Old Chatham, New York, Mason & Sullivan's replica is true to the original in all but size: theirs is 71 inches high, 18 inches wide, and 10 inches deep.

VIENNA REGULATOR CLOCK

The clocks that were popularly known in America as "Vienna Regulators" were derived from nineteenth-century German and Austrian clocks that were highly valued for their craftsmanship. Mason & Sullivan's version replicates a Vienna Regulator at midcentury—its movement not yet overpowered by scroll-work.

Dimensions: 42 inches high, 12¾ inches wide, and 8 inches deep.

ENGLISH CARRIAGE CLOCK

Shown in mahogany with moving moon dial, the carriage clock is 15½ inches high, 10⅞ inches wide, and 6⅛ inches deep.

Prices vary with the kit's level of difficulty.

Seasonal catalog of replica clocks available.

MASON & SULLIVAN COMPANY

586 Higgins Crowell Road
West Yarmouth, MA 02673
Tel. 617/778–1056

CUMBERLAND GENERAL STORE TIMEPIECES

RAILROAD POCKET WATCH

The face of Cumberland's railroad pocket watch has large and plain black numerals against a white background. Engraved into the case back is the image of a steam locomotive. It comes in a nickel finish with matching chain.

Dimensions: 2⅞ by 2⅝ inches.
Price: $36.95.

1870 MANTLE CLOCK

The classic Seth Thomas mantle clock of 1870 has been re-created in solid walnut with a heavy scroll-and-leaf design hand-carved into a pediment base with intricately detailed side finials and a turned-wood bezel.

Price: $238. All goods F.O.B. Crossville, Tennessee.

"Wish and Want Book" available, $3.75

CUMBERLAND GENERAL STORE

Route 3
Crossville, TN 38555
Tel. 615/484–8481

COLLECTOR'S CLASSIC EDITION SOCIETY, LTD.

Back in 1982 I spent some time out in southern California, and during one of their annual seasons, passed the day at a desert health resort just then enjoying its brief period of breaking chic.

I was there at the invitation of a staff member who was trying to sell me her battered 1967 Volkswagen Squareback, still laden with all sorts of totems from that year's Summer of Love, including a "God's-Eye" decal that peered out the rear window. As the staff member sensed that this sale was going to require some buttering up, I was further invited to bathe in the mineral spring that ran through the property. And so, with a borrowed bathing suit and my new L.L. Bean Hamilton watch, I parked myself on a flat rock in a pleasantly sulfurous eddy. Soon after, a fellow floated over whom I recognized as the actor who played Starsky in the old "Starsky and Hutch" television series. Starsky introduced himself warmly, but seemed to lose interest in our conversation after I pointed out my reason for being there, which stood in a nearby parking lot. "Must prefer," I thought, "shaker-hooded pony cars with those nifty red transfer graphics."

After I left the spring I noticed that a delicate haze had formed on the inside of the Hamilton's crystal. It clouded the words "water resistant" written on the dial, but clearly distinguished their meaning from "waterproof."

Now this watch was Hamilton's reproduction of its old World War II military watch, but it cost only $60 new, so the moisture (which began to form repeatedly into three droplets on the Hamilton's hands in the realization of its own little atmospheric cycle) didn't much bother me. Still, I thought I'd get it repaired first thing Monday.

The Orange County jeweler was impressed with the $60 Hamilton and thought it best to send it up to Los Angeles for repair. An estimate, he said, would come to me later by mail. What arrived was either plain knavery or a great testimonial to the watch as a reproduction: "This is a valuable antique," the estimate read, "and must be preserved. $120 for repair."

It may have been the heat of my response that did it, but the haze suddenly evaporated forever. The Hamilton's running a bit slow now, but it still impresses vets. (That's more than I can say for the VW.)

The Collector's Classic Society was set up by the Hamilton Watch Company to periodically market limited-edition reproductions of their "magnificent historic timepieces." These are superior-quality watches, all far more expensive than my World War II repro. In 1982, for example, the Collector's Classics included a replica Lady Hamilton gold pendant watch from the 1890s that sold for $348.

Direct inquiries to:

THE HAMILTON WATCH COMPANY

1817 William Penn Way
Lancaster, PA 17603
Tel. 1-800/233-0281

YOUR MONEY WILL BE IMMEDIATELY RETURNED TO YOU FOR ANY GOODS NOT PERFECTLY SATISFACTORY.

$15.58 FOR OUR NEW 1908 ACME PROGRESS FOUR-HOLE STEEL COOK STOVE

BURNS ANY KIND OF FUEL, HARD OR SOFT COAL, WOOD, COKE OR CORN COBS.

A REDUCED PRICE. We offer this wonderful new 1908 pattern Acme Progress Steel Cook Stove as the very latest and very highest grade steel cook stove offered on the market, the equal of any steel cook stove you can buy at double our price. It will burn hard or soft coal, coke, wood, or any other fuel; it will be found to be the most adaptable steel cook stove you can buy, and

IT IS SOLD TO YOU UNDER OUR POSITIVE BINDING GUARANTEE OF SATISFACTION OR YOUR MONEY BACK.

THE BODY of the Acme Progress Steel Cook Stove is made of heavier steel than is used by other makers. The heavy steel plates are accurately cut and punched for riveting and they are carefully milled and fitted together; they are securely hand riveted, thoroughly braced, and so thoroughly are they designed and so carefully are they made that an Acme Progress Steel Cook Stove will be in better condition after five years of constant use than the ordinary light weight or cast iron cook stove would be after but one year's use.

THE MAIN TOP. The main top, cover and centers are made of the very finest cast stove plate from the purest pig iron, and should not be confused with malleable top ranges which other manufacturers sometimes call "steel" with the deliberate purpose to deceive you. No malleable iron top ever made can compare in lasting quality with the cast stove plate tops used in the manufacture of our stoves and ranges.

THE FIRE BOX is well constructed of proper depth and width to provide enough heat for the oven without waste of fuel. With the two end pieces removed and the cast iron extension attached, the fire box is easily prepared for burning wood, making the length of fire box for wood 23½ inches. We equip the Acme Progress with duplex grate, which can be used for hard or soft coal, wood, or any other fuel, as shown on page 637.

THE PERFECT OVEN of the Acme Progress Steel Cook Stove is made from extra heavy cut steel plate, hand riveted with wrought rivets, carefully reinforced throughout, and with our arrangement of flues and airtight construction it is a very quick, fine and satisfactory baker. It is of very generous proportions, being 17½x20x12 inches in size, and it has one steel spring counterbalanced drop oven door on the right side, with rococo cast frame and handsomely nickeled medallion center plate and handle. The oven bottom of our Progress Steel Cook Stove is made of the highest grade selected stock sheet steel, so constructed, bolted, braced, and reinforced that it will always remain level, and there is absolutely no possibility of it buckling, warping, or sagging. The oven top is protected with a heavy corrugated cast plate which also serves to distribute the heat to all parts of the oven. The oven door is on the right side (the left side left blank). The door opens downward the same as on our steel ranges, forming a large, commodious shelf. The oven door frame is very strong and ornamented with a beautifully nickel plated handle and panel.

THIS STOVE is furnished in numbers 8-20 or 9-20 sizes. Its cooking surface has four holes and the size of the top, including extension reservoir, is 42½x25 inches. The height from floor to main top is 30½ inches. Length of fire box for wood, 23½ inches; size pipe to fit collar, 7 inches. This stove is furnished complete with lifter, shaker and scraper for removing the soot from under the oven.

Prices, strongly crated and delivered on cars at our foundry at Newark, Ohio:

No. 22K205 Price, No. 8-20, with reservoir and 8-inch lids......................$15.58
On this stove the fire box is 8½ inches wide and 5½ inches deep, its length for coal is 18 inches and for wood 23½ inches. Capacity of reservoir, 17 quarts. Shipping weight, 340 pounds.
No. 22K206 Price, No. 9-20, with reservoir and 9-inch lids......................$15.88
Prices do not include pipe or cooking utensils. For cooking utensils see pages 461 to 466.

THE LARGE RESERVOIR TANK is made of the best grade of cast iron, white porcelain lined to prevent rusting. Easily kept clean and returnable. It has a capacity of 17 quarts. DAMPERS are convenient to reach and so placed that they are easily regulated. POUCH FEED—The Progress Steel Cook Stove has a large poucheed for feeding coal or coke and will also permit of the insertion of a broiler over the fire.

WOOD FEED DOOR swings to the left and is constructed to prevent ashes from piling against the inside and falling to the floor when the door is opened. THE ASH DOOR is extra large, the ash pan is made of the highest standard grade refined steel, fits the large, roomy hearth under the ash door, which prevents the ashes from spilling on the floor when being removed. The bottom edge is reinforced with heavy steel, which is run around the entire body of the stove and strongly riveted to the steel plates of the body.

THE HEAVY CAST BASE, as will be seen by referring to the illustration of our Acme Progress Four-Hole Steel Cook Stove, is fitted with a very heavy cast iron base of the very newest rococo pattern.

IF DESIRED WITHOUT RESERVOIR BUT WITH END SHELF

STOVES AND RANGES

ACME ROVER GENUINE STEEL FOUR-HOLE COAL AND WOOD COOK STOVE

A REDUCED PRICE.
WITH RESERVOIR $6.75 AND UPWARD

MODEL OF 1908

Three found $7.75 to size

COMPARED ... in either ... will find the price we are offering on this reservoir steel cook stove less than one half what others charge, and it is positively THE GREATEST STOVE VALUE THE WORLD HAS EVER SEEN.

COMPARED WITH THE LOWEST PRICES we could possibly make you on any of our cast iron reservoir cook stoves we save you easily from $4.00 to $7.00, and compared with any other steel cook stove we could sell you we show you a saving of from $6.00 to $8.00; and compared with any price any other maker or dealer could offer you we show you a saving in cost on this, OUR ACME ROVER STEEL COOK STOVE WITH RESERVOIR, of easily $7.00 to $15.00.

THE BODY is made of the highest grade sheet steel, thoroughly bolted, braced, reinforced throughout, the very best oven construction; our new special flue, draft damper and circulating system, made to burn hard coal, soft coal, or wood. With each stove we furnish a special grate for wood. Has a cast top—the exact same grade of top that we use in our highest grade stoves and ranges; four lids, cut centers, supported by our own special system of construction. At the special price named, the stove is furnished with a detachable or removable reservoir, as shown in illustration. In shipping the stove we pack the reservoir inside of the oven, and the stove is crated in a way that there is no chance of its reaching you in bad condition—in fact the stove is unbreakable.

WE HAVE A LARGE STOCK OF these stoves on hand, ready for immediate shipment. It will just take a few days for your order to reach us and the stove to reach you. The stove being made of sheet steel is comparatively light and the freight charges will amount to next to nothing. This stove can be shipped from 100 to 500 miles at from 35 cents to 75 cents; from 500 to 1,000 miles at from 50 cents to $1.00; greater or lesser distances in proportion.

REPAIR PARTS.

We will always carry a complete stock of repairs and repair parts in years to come; even ten years hence we will be able to deliver you any piece or part to replace or repair any defective part and this at actual cost, a mere fraction of what other stove dealers charge.

NOTE OUR REDUCTION IN PRICE

THIS ILLUSTRATION, engraved by our artist from a photograph, showing our new 1908 model Acme Rover, four-hole, reservoir, all steel cook stove, which we offer at $6.75, $7.75 and $8.75, will give you a good general idea of the appearance of this stove.

DETAILED DESCRIPTION

THE BODY is built of heavy smooth steel plate, is substantially put together, riveted with wrought iron rivets, strongly reinforced and braced in every part. The heavy plates are well riveted and jointed.

THE MAIN TOP. In manufacturing this, our Acme Rover, we have constructed the main top and covers of good stove plate. It has four cooking holes and with ordinary care and usage the main top and covers will last years. All parts of the main top are carefully fitted, with sufficient allowance for heat expansion.

THE LARGE FIRE BOX. It has an extra large fire box, provided with practical cast iron linings, with shaking and dumping grate. With every stove we include, free of cost, an extra grate for wood, so you can burn hard coal, soft coal or wood.

THE FIRE DOOR is beautifully designed and swings to the left.

THE ASH PIT is large and roomy and is provided with a large ash pan.

THE DRAFT SLIDE is in front, of more than usual capacity.

THE OVEN is of very generous proportions, perfectly square, is a very satisfactory, quick and even baker, and is furnished with a steel wire oven rack.

THE OVEN DOOR is on the right side (the left side left blank). It is our latest swing pattern, attractive rococo design, steel lined, perfectly square, and fits snug to the body of the stove, thus retaining all the heat in the oven.

THE FLUES are ample and provided with cleanout in rear of ash pit, which is reached from the front of the stove.

THE RESERVOIR is made of galvanized iron, heats by direct contact with the side of the stove, is removable and can be used on either end or rear side at pleasure, or can be used on top of stove as occasion requires.

GOOD SERVICE. The long looked for steel cook stove for practical people, neat, compact, serviceable and cheap. No such value in a cook stove ever offered before. This, our Acme Rover Steel Cook Stove, is shipped ready to set up, the four legs and all other loose parts packed inside. When received you have only to put on the legs, pipe and other loose parts, when it is ready to fire, the same as if you were moving an old stove from one room to another.

PRICES FOR OUR ACME ROVER STEEL COOK STOVE, FOR COAL AND WOOD, WITH RESERVOIR, FOUR COOKING HOLES, DUMPING GRATE, LARGE ASH PAN, STEEL OVEN RACK, GALVANIZED RESERVOIR ADJUSTABLE TO EITHER END, SIDE OR BACK.

Catalogue Number	Range Number	Size of Lids	Size of Oven, inches	Main Top, Including Reservoir	Height of Main Top, inches	Size of Pipe to Fit Collar, inches	Size of Fire Box, inches			Capacity of Reservoir	Weight, Pounds	Price
							Length	Width	Depth			
22K210	7-12	No. 7	12x10x10	35 x19 inches	25	6	16½	6½	4	14 quarts	127	$6.75
22K211	8-14	No. 7	14x18x10½	37½x21 inches	23½	6	17	6½	4½	18 quarts	147	7.75
22K212	8-16	No. 8	16x18x11	40½x21½ inches	28½	6	17½	7	5	21 quarts	169	8.75

RESTORED ANTIQUE RANGES AND STOVES Good

Time Stove, Richard "Stove Black" Richardson's twelve-year-old operation, is just off the main road leading into Goshen, Massachusetts—not far from where the first parlor cookstove was built in 1845. The stoves that emerge from Good Time's barn-red shop there—restored nineteenth-century parlor stoves, kitchen ranges, potbellies, and others—are daunting in their intricate beauty. The evidently old-fashioned workmanship and gauge, the (often) magnificent rise and monumental heft of such as the Glenwood Oak (1898), Railway King (1885), and Base Burner Six Door (1896) makes Richardson's showroom something of a Smithsonian of wood and coal burners. It is the rarity of antiques such as these that usually gives them their value, but Good Time's restored stoves and ranges are here to do a job. Thus quaint patina is unceremoniously discarded and resurrection comes in a glitter of renickeled newness that can transport you right back to the loading dock of some late-nineteenth-century foundry.

Richardson claims that his restored antiques go their modern counterparts better in more than workmanship and looks: "After all," he says, "these stoves were produced in an era when wood was split by hand and hauled by horse. There were no gas-powered chain saws, hydraulic lifters, or even backup heating systems. The stoves had to use precious fuel as efficiently as possible."

Catalog available. Visitors welcome.

GOOD TIME STOVE COMPANY

Route 112
Goshen, MA 01032
Tel. 413/268–3677

CONESTOGA WAGON WOOD STOVE The Esse

Queen, a small mid-nineteenth-century woodburner that was often used to warm the interiors of prairie schooners, is still manufactured by Smith & Wellstood, Ltd., a British firm with an American heritage.

James Smith, a founder of the company, was a colorful and enterprising Scot who emigrated to America in 1832 under the "guardianship" of Stephen Wellstood. Smith eventually settled in Jackson, Mississippi, where he opened a store that sold stoves, ranges, and hardware.

Owing to his Scottish wife's ill health, James Smith returned to Edinburgh in 1853 an ardent secessionist who would include Jefferson Davis and Robert E. Lee (as well as Garibaldi) among his friends. He turned his store over to his brother Robert and set up a foundry at Bonnybridge in 1860. A park in the center of Jackson now bears James Smith's name and a monument in the

cemetery there memorializes Robert, a Confederate colonel who was killed while leading a cavalry charge at the Battle of Mumfordsville.

Dimensions: width, 20½ inches; depth, 15¾ inches; height, 23 inches.

GREYFRIAR'S IMPORTS, LTD.

65 Broadway
Greenlawn, NY 11740
Tel. 516/754–1831

SOAPSTONE

STOVE In addition to its subtle beauty, soapstone has the remarkable ability to store (and slowly release) twice as much heat as either cast iron or steel. But building stoves made of soapstone requires a degree of patience and attention to detail that precludes mass production. For this reason, soapstone stoves were manufactured in small quantities even during their mid-nineteenth-century heyday, receiving heirloom status the moment they left the gate.

In its revitalization of soapstone manufacture, the Woodstock Soapstone Stove Company maintains a reverential approach to this tradition. Patterned after a stove made in northern New England in the 1860s, these stoves are authentically detailed and built one at a time by a single craftsman.

The Woodstock Soapstone Stove is a 28- by 26- by 20-inch woodburner providing a maximum heat output of 45,000 BTUs per hour over a ten- to twelve-hour period. It has airtight construction and can heat an area of more than 7,000 cubic feet.

Price: $995.

WOODSTOCK SOAPSTONE STOVE COMPANY

Route 4, Box 223
Woodstock, VT 05091
Tel. 802/672–5133

TRANSOCEAN LTD.'S UNUSUAL STOVES

AIR TITE PARLOR STOVE

Right down to its mica windows, Transocean's parlor stove has been replicated from a nineteenth-century original. It features double-bottom construction, a built-in cast-iron top, and side and back baffles. Its flat surface (under the swing-mounted, nickel-plated top) allows for supplemental cooking. The Air Tite's large front door has two spin-type draft controls. It requires a 6-inch pipe, and should be installed in a noncombustible hearth.

Dimensions: height, 33¾ inches; width, 26 inches; depth, 23½ inches. Weight: 286 lbs. (shipping weight 303 lbs).

Price: $359, F.O.B. Salt Lake City, Utah. Brass trim optional.

TRANSOCEAN LIMITED

2290 Panorama Drive
Holliday, UT 84117
Tel. 801/278–3635

Transocean, Ltd., imports, exports, and manufactures a wide variety of wood- and coal-burning stoves, specializing, as they say, "in the unusual."

THE SHEEPHERDER

Transocean reproduces the Sheepherder from the turn-of-the-century "Handy." Here's the Sheepherder's story, as told by Nancy Olsen of Transocean:

My favorite model of all is the Sheepherder, because I had a direct hand in seeing it remanufactured. My husband and I were visiting his relatives at their sheep ranch in Kemmerer, Wyoming. Browsing around their place, we came upon one of their sheep camp wagons that had this stove named "Handy" inside. I fell right in love with it and was told by Uncle Don that it had been produced many years ago at the Fort Leavenworth, Kansas, prison foundry. He told us that it was a very efficient stove, and that he wished it were still produced! The stove had all of its original parts, so we asked Uncle Don if he could do without it for six months or so while we made a mold from it. He agreed, and we returned the original to him some months later. After we placed the first ads for the stove in the National Wool Grower, we had folks calling from all over the country saying that they had one just like it that needed parts. We sent them these and they wrote back just to tell us how delighted they were to get their stoves working again.

The Sheepherder is a 100 percent cast-iron woodburner with built-in draft controls and a front-loading firebox. These features, plus the four 7-inch cook lids and the 6-inch-diameter stovepipe, allow for a cookstove capable of producing a good volume of radiant heat.

Dimensions: height, 25 inches; width, 18½ inches; and depth 23 inches. Weight: 176 lbs. (shipping weight 196 lbs.). Price: $198.50, F.O.B. Salt Lake City, Utah.

THE QUEEN AND PRINCESS ATLANTIC KITCHEN RANGES

At the center of every home during the turn of the century was the wood- or coal burning kitchen range. The stove was used not only for cooking and baking, but also to provide the household with hot water and to heat adjoining rooms. By the early part of the twentieth century full-size kitchen ranges were being built by the hundreds of thousands all across the country.

Portland Stove's Queen Atlantic has been in continuous production since its introduction in 1906. From among such royalty of the time as the Star Kineo, the Home Comfort, the Crown Acorn, and the Glenwood, only she still reigns. Like her slightly smaller (but more ornate) sibling, the Princess Atlantic, the Queen is 100 percent cast iron, available as either a wood- or coal-burner, and has long and deep fireboxes to accommodate long-burning loads. Both ranges also have six-lid tops, deep ash pits, optional hot-water reservoirs, and warming ovens. The Queen Atlantic is the largest cast-iron kitchen range now made.

Dimensions: Queen Atlantic—32¼ inches high (to range top), 30 inches deep, and 57 inches wide (including end shelf); Princess Atlantic—31½ inches high (to range top), 30 inches deep, and 54 inches wide (including end shelf).

Prices: Queen Atlantic, $2,091; Princess Atlantic, $1,795. Additional costs: installed water jacket, $97; hot-water reservoir, $375; warming oven, $275.

PORTLAND STOVE'S RANGES AND STOVES

THE ST. NICHOLAS PARLOR STOVE

The versatile parlor stoves built from 1800 through the turn of the century were by far the most popular cast-iron stoves of their time. The St. Nicholas was and is "King of the Parlor Stoves," having been in continuous production since it was first introduced. The St. Nicholas is coal-burning only, holds about 35 lbs. of coal, burning about twenty-four hours in spring and fall (twelve to eighteen hours in winter), and is capable of heating 12,000–15,000 cubic feet. It requires a 6-inch stovepipe.

Dimensions: height to top of smoke collar, 25 inches; overall height, 60 inches; width, 23 inches; and depth, 28 inches. Weight: 280 lbs. (shipping weight 300 lbs.).

B&M STATION AGENT STOVES

Portland Stove is one of the last remaining manufacturers of top-quality pot-belly stoves. Their B&M Station Agent series offers two sizes:

No. 1 Station Agent dimensions: height, 30½ inches; outside diameter, 14½ inches; firepot diameter, 12 inches; lid size, 8½ inches. Coal burn time is eight to ten hours, and the stove requires a 5-inch stovepipe. Weight: 104 lbs.

No. 3 Station Agent dimensions: height, 42 inches; outside diameter, 22½ inches; firepot diameter, 15 inches; lid size, 10 inches. Coal burn time is sixteen to twenty-four hours, and the stove requires a 6-inch stovepipe. Weight: 234 lbs. Prices: No. 1 Station Agent, $329; No. 3 Station Agent, $749.

PORTLAND STOVE COMPANY

P.O. Box 377
Fickett Road
North Pownall, ME 04069
Tel. 207/688-2254

GODIN STOVES

GODIN STOVES With only slight modifications in the original molds, the stoves built today by France's Godin Foundry are the same as those it first built in 1889. These stoves—the Oval, the Large Round, and the Small Round (or Petit Godin)—have been repeatedly applauded by critics of industrial design since their late-nineteenth-century introduction. In true 1800s fashion, the Godins are made from 100 percent pig iron and have mica windows.

The Godin stoves all burn either wood or coal and are airtight. Because of their upright design and use of more firebrick per cubic inch of firebox than any other stove, the Godin stoves demonstrate the enduring value of de-

signs created back when stoves were the primary source of home heating.

France's "Belle Époch" began with the new century. Marked by an independence from earlier modes of thought and design, the Belle Époch introduced art nouveau, a design characterized by semi-naturalistic forms arranged assymetrically, with swaying, aquatic lines. Celebrated at the Paris Exposition of 1900, the art nouveau style is still to be seen in the signs of the Paris Métro, the first line of which was built then.

The Godin Belle Époch Stove first appeared in the company's 1903 catalog.

With its cast-iron open scrollwork, vitreous enameling, and reversible ceramic decorated panels, the Belle Époch is still available more than eighty years later.

Prices: Oval, $695; Large Round, $795; Petit, $575; Belle Époch, $950 (not including ceramic tiles).

For literature and dealer information, contact:

STONE LEDGE COMPANY
170 Washington Street
Marblehead, MA 01945
Tel. 617/631–8417

THE GODIN OVAL, LARGE ROUND, AND SMALL ROUND (PETIT GODIN)

THE COALBROOKDALE

DARBY

The accomplishments of the Darby family—whose forebearer Abraham founded the Coalbrookdale Company in 1709—are landmarks in the progress of nineteenth-century British industrialism. Abraham himself was the first in history to successfully smelt iron with coke, and by the middle of the eighteenth century Abraham's company would become the first in the world to manufacture iron wheels and rails.

Throughout the two hundred years that the Darbys were to manage the Coalbrookdale foundry their accomplishments mounted impressively: the assembly and testing of the world's first steam railway (1742); and production of the wrought-iron plates for the legendary steamship *Great Britain*, the first all-steel propeller-driven ship (1843). But the Darby family is likely best remembered for building a symbol—the Iron Bridge.

When Abraham Darby III took over his family's empire in the 1770s he observed that the Severn River, while an effective link to world markets, split his company in two. The people and materials necessary to run his business on a daily basis had to be ferried back and forth across the river by boat. To improve this situation he decided to build a bridge, a bridge that for the first time in history would be made of iron.

In the summer of 1779 work commenced. Massive stone abutments were constructed on each side of the river as bridge supports. The ribs, 50 feet long and weighing 6 tons apiece, were poured at Coalbrookdale in huge sand molds. When finished, the bridge required 370 tons of iron and had an arch spanning 100 feet.

Quaint as it appears today, the Iron Bridge was representative of the industrialization of the western landscape. Restored at the time of its bicentennial in 1979, the bridge has become emblematic of the Industrial Revolution itself.

During the nineteenth century, stoves emerged as an important part of Coalbrookdale's diverse line of iron manufacture. But unlike others of their products described in this book, the Coalbrookdale Darby is not a reproduction, or even a replica. The Darby is rather a twentieth-century stove designed with classical themes evocative of the nineteenth. Yet with the grand history of the Coalbrookdale

Company behind it, the Darby could hardly be left out.

The Darby features all-cast-iron construction with double-skinned walls (the inner lined with firebrick), and produces both radiant and convected heat from wood and coal—55,000 BTUs per hour for up to twenty-four hours (coal).

Dimensions: 29 inches high, 32¾ inches wide, and 17¼ inches deep. Weight: 560 lbs.

Price: $1,250, F.O.B. Pittsburgh, Pennsylvania.

Literature available.

THE COALBROOKDALE COMPANY

American Sales Office
RFD 1, Box 477
Stowe, VT 05672
Tel. 802/253-9727

THE ELMIRA OVAL COOKSTOVE

The Elmira Oval is an airtight replication of the Findlay Oval stove, first introduced in 1908 by the Findlay Brothers Foundry near Ottawa, Ontario. Until its demise in 1956, the Findlay Oval was sold as the "Queen of the Cookstoves" to three generations of Canadian Mennonites. It was, in fact, their devotion to the Oval cookstove that brought about its remanufacture.

In the early 1970s Tom Hendrick, a hardware dealer from Elmira, Ontario, was doing all he could to scrounge old Findlay Oval replacement parts for stoves owned by area Mennonites. Hardly a day would pass when an Amish customer wouldn't pull his horse and buggy up to Hendrick's place to inquire after these parts and then extoll the old Oval's virtues.

So with the idea of having parts remanufactured, Hendrick went over to the Findlay foundry one day in 1976 to find the stove's original castings turning red behind the plant. The wood stove revival of the late 1970s was only an ember

then, undetected by the Findlay people, and they were uninterested in Hendrick's suggestion that they bring the stove back. So after mulling the idea over for a while, he decided that he'd go it alone. Hendrick slapped down the money for parts for about fifty stoves, and the Elmira Stove Works was born.

Today the Elmira operation is housed in a 35,000-square-foot factory and employs more than a hundred people. The requirements of the local Mennonites that made this all possible haven't been forgotten, but the "buxom-beauty" Oval and her more modest newly designed sisters, the Julia and the Sweetheart, now enjoy accolades from throughout the world.

In the course of remanufacturing the old Findlay Oval, Elmira has made several modifications to eliminate faults and otherwise provide improvements: the new Oval is airtight and provides a 25 percent longer burn; areas of wear discovered in the original have been reinforced; and many parts that were originally painted-over steel have now been porcelainized.

Also, the stove top has been thickened for better heat retention and the grates now have a summer and winter level. An optional water jacket that replaces a portion of the firebox can now heat from eight to ten gallons of

water an hour. A coal-burning conversion package, and almond and gold porcelain colors are available.

The basic black Oval cookstove weighs 500 lbs. and costs $2,095 (with almond or gold porcelain, $2,165). The black Oval with the water reservoir weighs 550 lbs. and costs $2,295 (with almond or gold porcelain, $2,365). The coal-grate package costs $100 and the water jacket costs $99, both additional. All prices are F.O.B. Buffalo, New York.

Literature available.

ELMIRA STOVE WORKS

22 Church Street West
Elmira, ON
Canada N3B 1M3
Tel. 519/669-5103

YOU CANNOT AFFORD TO OVERLOOK THE

WONDER VALUES ON THIS PAGE

OUR WONDER VALUE DISC HARROWS.

$14⁵⁵

ALL STEEL FRAME AND WEIGHT BOXES.

We offer these high grade up to date Double Lever Disc Harrows at prices lower than have ever been attempted upon discs of even most inferior quality. There are no more durable or perfect working disc harrows on the market and at our prices they are value which no other house can duplicate.

No. 32K435 8-16-Inch Disc Harrow. Wt. 400 lbs. Price............$14.55
No. 32K436 10-16-Inch Disc Harrow. Wt. 430 lbs. Price............$15.95
No. 32K437 12-16-Inch Disc Harrow. Wt. 500 lbs. Price............$17.35
No. 32K438 14-16-Inch Disc Harrow. Wt. 515 lbs. Price............$18.95
No. 32K439 16-16-Inch Disc Harrow. Wt. 530 lbs. Price............$20.65

OUR WONDER VALUE PONY GANG PLOWS

$12⁸⁷

These Walking Gang Plows are old time favorites. Perfectly adapted for all kinds of shallow plowing and especially desirable for orchard cultivation.

No. 32K430 Chilled Pony Gang Plow. Wt. 295 lbs. Price......$12.87
No. 32K431 Combination Pony Gang Plow. Wt. 295 lbs. Price......$14.55
No. 32K432 Steel Pony Gang Plow. Wt. 295 lbs. Price......$17.65

OUR WONDER VALUE BRUSH AND GENERAL PURPOSE PLOWS.

$7³⁵

This is one of the most popular styles of plows on the market, as it serves the purpose of a brush plow and its shape also makes it possible to use it for tame sod or stubble plowing.

No. 32K415 12-Inch Brush Plow. Wt. 85 lbs. Price......$7.35
No. 32K416 14-Inch Brush Plow. Wt. 90 lbs. Price......$7.70

OUR WONDER VALUE ROD BREAKING PLOWS.

$5⁷⁵

These are the highest grade and best built plows of their type.

No. 32K420 12-Inch Rod Breaking Plow. Wt. 61 lbs. Price......$5.75
No. 32K421 14-Inch Rod Breaking Plow. Wt. 64 lbs. Price......$5.95
No. 32K422 16-Inch Rod Breaking Plow. Wt. 67 lbs. Price......$6.15

OUR WONDER VALUE PRAIRIE BREAKING PLOWS.

$7³⁷

This is the most popular style of Prairie Breaking Plow on the market and is too well known to need further description.

No. 32K425 12-Inch Prairie Breaking Plow. Wt. 133 lbs. Price......$7.37
No. 32K426 14-Inch Prairie Breaking Plow. Wt. 137 lbs. Price......$7.65
No. 32K427 16-Inch Prairie Breaking Plow. Wt. 140 lbs. Price......$7.85

NOW IS THE TIME FOR YOU TO BUY. We can save you big money on farm implements and machinery of all kinds.

WHILE OUR PRICES ARE ABOUT ONE-HALF WHAT OTHERS ASK,

no one can furnish you with a superior quality of goods.

WE GUARANTEE TO SATISFY YOU or you get every cent of your money back and freight charges both ways.

OUR WONDER VALUE STEEL WALKING PLOWS

OTHERS ASK $12.00 TO $15.00 FOR NO BETTER.

$7⁷³

SHARE, MOLD-BOARD AND LANDSIDE MADE OF SOFT CENTER STEEL.

No. 32K401 12-Inch Walking Plow.
No. 32K402 14-Inch Walking Plow.
No. 32K403 16-Inch Walking Plow.

OUR WONDER VALUE STEEL SULKY PLOWS

$24⁷⁵

HIGH LIFT

SOFT CENTER STEEL MOLD-BOARD, LANDSIDE AND SHARE.

BEAM

No. 32K405 14-Inch Sulky Plow. Wt. 455 lbs. Price............$24.75
No. 32K406 16-Inch Sulky Plow. Wt. 460 lbs. Price............$25.65

OUR WONDER VALUE STEEL GANG PLOWS

$39⁹⁵

EQUAL IN EVERY WAY TO GANG PLOWS WHICH OTHERS SELL FOR FROM $50.00 TO $60.00

HIGH LIFT

SOFT CENTER STEEL MOLDBOARD, LANDSIDE AND SHARE

BEAM HITCH

PRICE INCLUDES TWO ROLLING COULTERS

No. 32K410 12-Inch Gang Plow. Wt. 675 lbs. Price............$39.95
No. 32K411 14-Inch Gang Plow. Wt. 680 lbs. Price............$40.85

OUR WONDER VALUE CULTIVATORS.

$17⁶⁵

This is one of the most desirable combined Riding and Walking Cultivators on the market.

No. 32K450 6-Shovel Break Pin Cultivator. Wt. 410 lbs. Price......$17.65
No. 32K451 8-Shovel Break Pin Cultivator. Wt. 425 lbs. Price......$18.15
No. 32K452 8-Shovel Break Pin Cultivator. Wt. 435 lbs. Price......$18.70
No. 32K453 8-Shovel Spring Trip Cultivator. Wt. 435 lbs. Price......$19.25
No. 32K454 6-Shovel Spring Trip Cultivator. Wt. 495 lbs. Price......$20.65

OUR WONDER VALUE ANGLE BAR HARROWS

This is one of the most satisfactory wood plows made.

No. 32K440 48-Tooth Angle Bar Harrow. Wt. 125 lbs. Price......$3.43
No. 32K441 60-Tooth Angle Bar Harrow. Wt. 150 lbs. Price......$4.29
No. 32K442 72-Tooth Angle Bar Harrow. Wt. 190 lbs. Price......$5.15
No. 32K443 90-Tooth Angle Bar Harrow. Wt. 210 lbs. Price......$6.43

OUR WONDER VALUE SPRING TOOTH HARROWS

No. 32K445 16-Tooth Harrow. Wt. 160 lbs. Price......
No. 32K446 18-Tooth Harrow. Wt. 170 lbs. Price......$6.68
No. 32K447 20-Tooth Harrow. Wt. 180 lbs. Price......$7.45

OUR WONDER VALUE COMBINED FEED CUTTER AND SHREDDER.

$18⁹⁵

You cannot buy the equal of this machine elsewhere for less than $30.00.

No. 32K460 Feed Cutter and Shredder. Wt. 325 lbs. Price......$18.95

OUR WONDER VALUE SWEEP HORSE POWERS.

These powers are of standard design.

No. 32K465 Two-Horse Power. Wt. 795 lbs. Price......$20.75
No. 32K466 Four-Horse Power. Wt. 1,015 lbs. Price......$28.15
No. 32K467 Six-Horse Power. Wt. 1,050 lbs. Price......$30.75

$20⁷⁵

FARM AND GARDEN

> The log at the wood pile, the axe supported by it;
> The sylvan hut, the vine over the doorway, the space cleared for a garden,
> The irregular tapping of rain down on the leaves, after the storm is lulled.
> ..... The sentiment of the huge timbers of the old fashion'd houses and barns.
>
> —Walt Whitman

THE BAKER RUN-IN-OIL WINDMILLS AND TOWERS The following has been reproduced from the Heller-Aller catalog:

THE HELLER-ALLER CO., NAPOLEON, OHIO, U.S.A.

Satisfaction

Baker Windmills are backed by nearly a half century of windmill building experience. A proven and perfected product. All parts running in a bath of oil. Requires attention but once a year. More sails to the wheel. Easy and quiet running. Will fit on any make tower.

For Sale By

"Old Reliable"

Thousands of users have nicknamed the Baker Windmills. W h y? Because they have proven themselves capable of giving a life time of economical and dependable water pumping service. All working parts are running in a bath of oil. Requires oiling but once a year. More sails to the wheel. Simple and sturdy throughout. Will fit any make tower.

For Sale By

BACK GEAR BAKER RUN-IN-OIL WINDMILLS

Fig. 906
6, 8, 10, 12 Foot Sizes

Phantom View

Entire Mechanism

The "Baker" Windmill is a powerful and sturdy mill with smooth and easy running qualities.

The wheel is designed with a multiplicity of blades correctly curved and pitched to convert the maximum amount of energy from the prevailing winds to pumping power. Through the back gear arrangement, the wheel makes three revolutions to produce one complete pumping stroke.

The back gear design provides two pinion gears pinned to the main shaft against the interior sides of the oil bowl. The pinion gears drive the two large gears mounted on the stud shafts which project into the bowl from the hubs on either side of the bowl. The use of two sets of gears, one on either side of the bowl, distributes the load evenly assuring less wear and longer life of the mechanism. The pitman is connected from the offset hub of the large gears to the center of the rocker arm. The rocker arm, which is connected to boss provided at the back end and is an intergral part of the bowl, carries the side straps which run upward and are secured to the pump rod casting. As the wheel turns the main shaft, the train of the mechanism produces the up and down stroke of the pump rod.

The vane made of high grade galvanized steel, is of larger area and long so as to serve postively as a rudder to keep the wheel into the wind.

DISTINCTIVE FEATURES OF THE BACK GEARED BAKER WINDMILL

1. A Perfect Product - Over 80 years experience in windmill production results in the finest. Simple in design and use of the best materials available.

2. Gray iron castings and cold rolled shafting team up to provide the most rigid construction, and the best wearing surfaces in this windmill.

3. The complete operating mechanism runs in the pool of oil contained in the bottom of the one piece cast iron bowl, lubricating all moving parts and bearing surfaces. There are no parts above the bowl to become dry. This is POSITIVE OILING.

4. Leverage Advantage - The underslung rocker arm gives the Baker Windmill direct upward lifting motion providing the greatest power transferal and resulting in an easy operating windmill.

5. Two pinions and 2 large gears on either side of the pump rod distributes the load, giving smoother action and longer life.

6. Compact and Simple Design - A minimum of working parts, all brought together within the bowl, produce the most compact train of power transmission.

7. Bearings - All bearings are made of the best grade of cast iron and because of the graphitic content of gray iron, an excellent bearing surface is created in this useage. The main removeable bearing is provided with an oil grove the full length of the bearing surface permitting the oil which is picked up by the pinion gear, to move through the bearing to the oil seal at the far end where the oil is trapped and dropped into an oil return channel taking the oil back to the bowl.

8. The Baker Wheel - After many years of experience and thorough testing, this wheel was developed to capture the maximum amount of energy from the wind and transform it into pumping power. The result is a windmill easily able to activate a pump in a slight wind.

9. The Baker Vane - Extra long and with Maximum area of galvanized steel to serve as a rudder to keep the wheel into the wind under variable conditions. The vane is "Automatically Self Governing" so that when the wind reaches a high velocity, it will take the windmill out of gear to avoid damage.

10. Ball Bearing Turntable - Two iron castings with chilled ball bearing races are provided to accept a complete ring of ¼" ball bearings. The main casting is secured to the top of the tower and the second casting rides on the ring of ball bearings. The mast pipe of the windmill goes through the center of the two castings and is thereby free to revolve easily on the tower so that the wheel may always face the wind.

11. Will Fit Any Make of Existing Tower - Different styles of turntables and truing centers are available to fit many towers. If the Baker turntable cannot be adapted to the existing tower we can furnish, at small additional cost, stub towers which can be added to any tower and which will accommodate our equipment.

12. Easily Erected - Baker windmills are simple to assemble and erect.

Price list and literature
available, $1.50.

THE HELLER-ALLER COMPANY, INC.

Corner Perry & Oakwood
Napoleon, OH 43545
Tel. 419/592-1856 or 592-3216

THE HELLER-ALLER CO.. NAPOLEON. OHIO. U.S.A.

Four Post Galvanized Steel Towers

Heller-Aller Towers are extra well braced and banded, thus giving added strength and security. All tension is taken care of at our factory and so no adjustment or alignment is left to the erector who may be inexperienced. We use flat steel bands for braces, which once erected, draw the tower firm and rigid. There is nothing to work loose or cause the tower to lose alignment.

Select a tower high enough to carry the mill 8 to 10 feet above all surrounding houses, barns, trees or wind obstructions within a 300 foot radius. This permits a clean sweep of the wind from all directions to the mill, giving greatest efficiency. A high tower also protects the mill from damaging swirling winds coming off close surrounding objects.

The tower illustration shows the type of construction used in the Heller-Aller Co. towers. Corner posts are fabricated from heavy galvanized angles, 2 inch angles in the No. 1 tower and 2½ inch angles in the No. 3 towers. The bands, horizontal pieces, are fabricated of either 1 inch or 1¼ inch galvanized angles. The braces are fabricated of 7/8 inch flat galvanized steel. For Pull-Out details, see page 18.

At figure No. 2 you will note how the pump rod guides are installed. The purpose of these guides is to keep the wood pump rod straight and in the center of the tower.

No. 1 Towers—For 8-Foot Mills and smaller. Corner posts are built of 2 inch angle.
* No. 4 Towers—For 12-Foot Mills and smaller. Corner posts are 2½ inch angle.

2

1

2

2

Fig. 578

Tower Height Feet	No. 1 TOWERS			No. 4 TOWERS		
	Weight Pounds		List Price	Weight Pounds		List Price
15	320		$	420		$
20	390			520		
30	500			690		
35	570			780		
40	600			860		
50				1,030		
60				1,235		

Anchor posts, anchor plates, wood pump rods, pullout lever, and wood platform are always shipped with the tower. In ordering, always give the number of tower and height.

For repairs see page 39

Steel Stub Tower

For erecting windmills on top of other make towers and buildings consisting of four top corner angles.

* NO. 4 – HEAVY DUTY – TOWERS

For use in extremely windy situations. Also recommended for use with electric generating units. Heavy corner post angles (3/16'' x 2½'' x 2½'') to the top.

Fig. Number	Article		List Price
ST65	6½-ft. Stub with Platform		$
ST5	5 -ft. Stub with Platform		
ST4	4 -ft. Stub, less Platform		
ST3	3 -ft. Stub, less Platform		
WP	Wood Platform only, Painted		
575	Wood Pull-out Lever with Spring		

In ordering give number and height of tower.

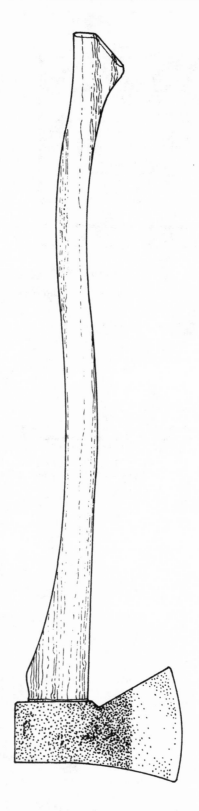

HUDSON BAY

AXE The best lore regarding the Hudson Bay axe was written by Paul Hawken (of the Smith & Hawken Tool Company) himself in his firm's Summer 1983 mail-order catalog:

There are two theories about the origin of the Hudson Bay Axe. The most popular is that it was developed from the tomahawk for use in the fur trade with the native Indian population in northern Canada. It was unquestionably a trade axe, but some scholars, including Henry Kauffman, author of American Axes, *believes that the trade axe itself evolved from earlier European axes. Dave Orchard, our customer from Washington, writes that the camp or "squaw" axes were derived from the Iberian axe of medieval times. He thinks that the shape was a result of the construction, a piece of iron wrapped around a mandrel to which was sometimes attached a cutting edge of steel. Steve Litchyarn of Texas tells of its use as a weapon, as well as a driving tool since earlier axes had a tempered poll to pound tent poles and stakes with. . . . Whatever its exact origin, the fact remains that its design gives it the greatest amount of blade area for the lowest weight, making it a good axe for softwoods.*

Hudson Bay axes have tempered-steel heads and stout hickory handles. They come in three sizes: 28 inches, weighing 2½ lbs. ($20.50); 32 inches, weighing 3 lbs. ($22); and 26 inches, weighing 3½ lbs. ($24.90). Shipping and handling charges are extra.

Tool catalog available.

SMITH & HAWKEN TOOL COMPANY

25 Corte Madera
Mill Valley, CA 94941
Tel. 415/383–4415

THE RUSTIC RELIANT WHEELBARROW

With an overall length of 60½ inches, the Rustic Reliant Wheelbarrow has been fabricated by Maine craftsmen to replicate nineteenth-century originals in proportion, material, and scale. With a frame of either Maine oak or ash (depending on availability) the Rustic Reliant sports handcrafted curved handles and a removable bed of half-inch pine. All wooden parts are protected with a linseed-oil finish. Assembly necessary.

SPRUCE HEAD WOOD PRODUCTS COMPANY

P.O. Box 14
Spruce Head, ME 04859
Tel. 207/594–2401

WOODCRAFT SUPPLY COMPANY TOOLS

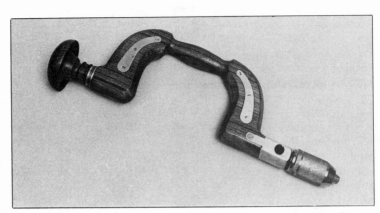

BIT BRACE The Early American bistock or brace was made of native seasoned hardwood. Woodcraft Supply's teak and brass tool is a replica of one widely collected and "found in every tool chest in the last century." The only difference: a modern drill chuck.

   Price: $102.95, ppd.

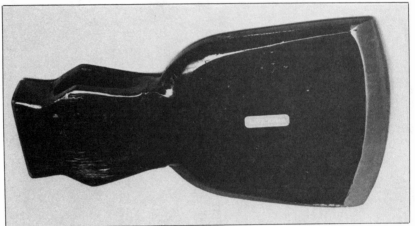

KENT BROADAXE Although often mistaken for a big and clumsy felling axe, the Kent broadaxe (also described in the entry for the Broad-Axe Beam Co., page 8) was actually used as a striking chisel for hewing square beams from round logs. Woodcraft Supply's Kent broadaxe has an offset eye, permitting the hewer to cut flat strikes on surfaces with ample clearance. The head has a 6-inch cutting edge and weighs 5 lbs.

   Price: (with 34-inch handle) $34.25, ppd.

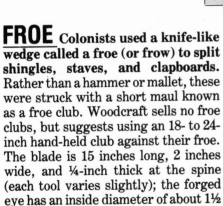

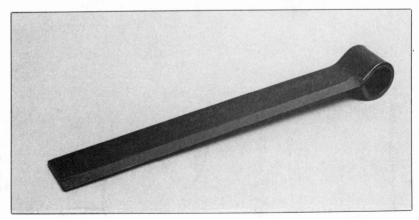

FROE Colonists used a knife-like wedge called a froe (or frow) to split shingles, staves, and clapboards. Rather than a hammer or mallet, these were struck with a short maul known as a froe club. Woodcraft sells no froe clubs, but suggests using an 18- to 24-inch hand-held club against their froe. The blade is 15 inches long, 2 inches wide, and ¼-inch thick at the spine (each tool varies slightly); the forged eye has an inside diameter of about 1½ inches.

   Price: $31.40, ppd.

TWO-MAN CROSS-CUT SAW From
Woodcraft Supply's catalog:

This American-made, quality saw is the pride of woodchoppers today just as it was a hundred years ago. It is ground for uniform thickness along the entire toothed edge. The back of the saw is thick at the ends and thin at the center to give stiffness to the saw, to prevent binding, and to allow the saw to have a minimum of set. The blade is high-grade, oil-hardened steel, with a cutting edge of four teeth to each raker in a wide, perforated lance-tooth pattern.

   Dimensions: select hardwood handle, 13 inches; blade length, 5 feet; width at center, 5⅛ inches; blade thickness, 14–16 gauge. Price: $90.75, ppd. (cannot be shipped to Alaska, Hawaii, or Canada).

Color tool catalog available, $3.

WOODCRAFT SUPPLY CORPORATION

41 Atlantic Avenue
P.O. Box 4000
Woburn, MA 01888
Tel. toll free 800/225–1153, for orders only

CUT NAILS

CUT NAILS In Wareham, Massachusetts, on the site of a mill burned by a British raiding party during the War of 1812, the world's oldest nail factory is still turning them out.

Founded in 1819, the Tremont Nail Company is a survivor of the iron industry that once flourished in and around Wareham. All during the nineteenth century local bog iron (still to be seen in the reddish soil around the town's cranberry bogs and the great heap of slag that forms an embankment beside the Wareham River) provided the basic resource for small, water-powered industries. In addition to nails, Tremont likewise produced pots, pans, wagon treads, and ship's fittings back then.

Although not intentionally archaic, the Tremont factory's old wooden buildings—with their huge foundation stones, hand-hewn beams, and array of overhead belts and drives—evoke a feeling for the kind of American industriousness that itself has grown musty. It's the modern value of its old cut nails that sustains Tremont.

Cut nails are made by a process whereby a machine-driven knife blade slices them from a flat piece of steel, resulting in a four-sided nail that tapers toward the head. Such nails were common during colonial times, but because of their superior fastening ability they are still indispensable to working masonry and (when galvanized) to shipbuilding.

Inevitably, Tremont's cut nails have not been overlooked by folks who restore antiques and old buildings. The company's fasteners have been driven into projects at Old Sturbridge Village, Colonial Williamsburg, the Harpers Ferry National Monument, Old Bethpage Village Restoration, and other historic sites. Several types of nails are available for every type of restoration.

TREMONT NAIL COMPANY

21 Elm Street
P.O. Box 111
Wareham, MA 02571
Tel. 617/295-0038

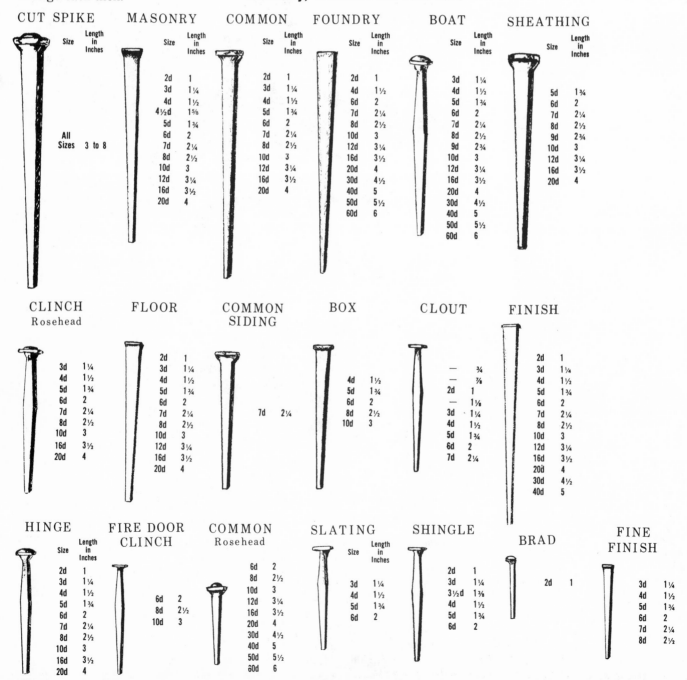

CUT SPIKE

Size	Length in Inches
All Sizes	3 to 8

MASONRY

Size	Length in Inches
2d	1
3d	1¼
4d	1½
4½d	1⅝
5d	1¾
6d	2
7d	2¼
8d	2½
10d	3
12d	3¼
16d	3½
20d	4

COMMON

Size	Length in Inches
2d	1
3d	1¼
4d	1½
5d	1¾
6d	2
7d	2¼
8d	2½
10d	3
12d	3¼
16d	3½
20d	4

FOUNDRY

Size	Length in Inches
2d	1
4d	1½
6d	2
7d	2¼
8d	2½
10d	3
12d	3¼
16d	3½
20d	4
30d	4½
40d	5
50d	5½
60d	6

BOAT

Size	Length in Inches
3d	1¼
4d	1½
5d	1¾
6d	2
7d	2¼
8d	2½
9d	2¾
10d	3
12d	3¼
16d	3½
20d	4
30d	4½
40d	5
50d	5½
60d	6

SHEATHING

Size	Length in Inches
5d	1¾
6d	2
7d	2¼
8d	2½
9d	2¾
10d	3
12d	3¼
16d	3½
20d	4

CLINCH Rosehead

3d	1¼
4d	1½
5d	1¾
6d	2
7d	2¼
8d	2½
10d	3
16d	3½
20d	4

FLOOR

2d	1
3d	1¼
4d	1½
5d	1¾
6d	2
7d	2¼
8d	2½
10d	3
12d	3¼
16d	3½
20d	4

COMMON SIDING

7d	2¼

BOX

4d	1½
5d	1¾
6d	2
8d	2½
10d	3

CLOUT

—	¾
—	⅞
2d	1
—	1⅛
3d	1¼
4d	1½
5d	1¾
6d	2
7d	2¼

FINISH

2d	1
3d	1¼
4d	1½
5d	1¾
6d	2
7d	2¼
8d	2½
10d	3
12d	3¼
16d	3½
20d	4
30d	4½
40d	5

HINGE

Size	Length in Inches
2d	1
3d	1¼
4d	1½
5d	1¾
6d	2
7d	2¼
8d	2½
10d	3
16d	3½
20d	4

FIRE DOOR CLINCH

6d	2
8d	2½
10d	3

COMMON Rosehead

6d	2
8d	2½
10d	3
12d	3¼
16d	3½
20d	4
30d	4½
40d	5
50d	5½
60d	6

SLATING

Size	Length in Inches
3d	1¼
4d	1½
5d	1¾
6d	2

SHINGLE

2d	1
3d	1¼
3½d	1⅜
4d	1½
5d	1¾
6d	2

BRAD

2d	1

FINE FINISH

3d	1¼
4d	1½
5d	1¾
6d	2
7d	2¼
8d	2½

PIONEER PLACE FARM ITEMS

GEM WATER ELEVATOR CHAIN PUMP

The Gem chain pump is made of galvanized steel, painted gray, varnished, lettered, and trimmed in black. It has malleable iron castings, a round iron sprocket, and a wooden handle, black. The Gem measures 8 by 16 inches at its outside base and is 36½ inches high. Shipping weight: 25 lbs.

Cumberland catalog #5162. Price: $116.38.

OLD COUNTRY HOES

"For all hoed crops," advises the *Farmer's Almanac* of 1881, "plant in such a way that you can reach every hill, plant or vine with the cultivator, and use this tool early and often."

Pioneer Place's old country hoes are imported and have the heft and feel of old-fashioned tools.

Price: $10, ppd.

CUMBERLAND GENERAL STORE FARM IMPLEMENTS

HEAVY-DUTY MILK CANS

These ten-gallon milk cans have been used and have worn finishes, so Cumberland sells them "as is." The store requests that you state your preference for either the recessed- or umbrella-lidded can, but must ship what is available nonetheless. Shipping weight: 28 lbs.

Cumberland catalog #5387. Price: $24.95 each.

FOUR-TINE WHITE OAK PITCHFORK

The style of these pitchforks antedates the mass-produced iron pitchforks of the late nineteenth century. Crafted according to a centuries-old method that begins with selecting the right tree, felling it, and skidding it home, Cumberland claims that their oak pitchforks are highly valued by collectors. Shipping weight: 8 lbs.

Cumberland catalog #0537. Price: $36.

FARM BELL

"Our bell is all cast iron," says Pioneer Place's mail-order catalog, "so it has an old-fashioned ring. This is not a machine-made product. Each bell is cast from individual sand molds, so bells vary somewhat in height and measurement. The ring of this bell can be heard for a mile or two."

Diameter: 15 inches. Weight: 50 lbs.
Price: $80, ppd.

Mail-order catalog available.

THE PIONEER PLACE

Route 2, 9938 County Road 39
Belle Center, OH 43310

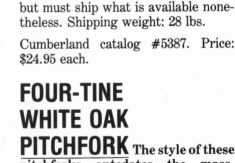

THE VULCAN HILLSIDE PLOW

This plough is so constructed that the mouldboard may be easily changed from one side to the other while the team is turning, which admirably adapts to ploughing on hill sides, as all the furrows are turned down hill.
—New England Farmer, *February 1850*

The Vulcan hillside plow is built for the hard service required by hill and mountain plowing. Simple in construction, it is strongly built and handles easily. The plow's shoe extends to the full length of the bottom standard and may readily be replaced when necessary. The beam is made of two pieces of high-carbon steel, and will not bend under the strains of plowing.

Cumberland catalog #8085(8). Weight: 73 lbs. Price: $169.59.
Cumberland catalog #8086(10). Weight: 112 lbs. Price: $233.06.

FERGUSON

PLANTER "An exceedingly substantial and desirable planter," the Ferguson is an old-style hill-type planter. This means that it drops corn every 24 inches and beans every 21 inches for a "hill" or grouping of the corn and beans planted together. One-row team or horse model. Shipping weight: 120 lbs.

WOODEN

BUCKSAW Selected Cumberland County hardwood makes an old-fashioned bucksaw with **perfect balance and feel.** Its 1-inch by 30-inch blade is made of Swedish steel, hardened, tempered, and precision filed to a razor sharpness. Mortise and tenon joints are throughout the frame. Shipping weight: 4 lbs.

Cumberland catalog #3748. Price: $29.95.

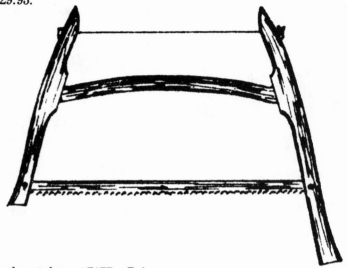

Cumberland catalog #7177. Price: $189. Prices do not include transportation or postage costs.

"Wish and Want Book" available, $3.75.

CUMBERLAND GENERAL STORE

*Route 3
Crossville, TN 38555
Tel. 615/484-8481*

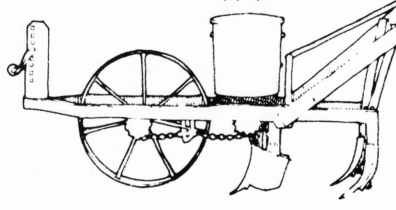

MILLS FROM THE PHOENIX FOUNDRY

The following information was supplied by the Phoenix Foundry's sole proprietor, William S. Courtis:

The Phoenix Foundry, located in northeastern Washington state, is a small foundry and light machine shop. As such we can maintain high standards of quality throughout our entire process—from the metal charged into the melting furnace to the completed product ready for sale. In contrast to today's "throw-away economy," our foundry's handcrafted products are shaped by the oldtime philosophies of quality, durability, and craftsmanship. Our products are designed and built to provide long, trouble-free service.

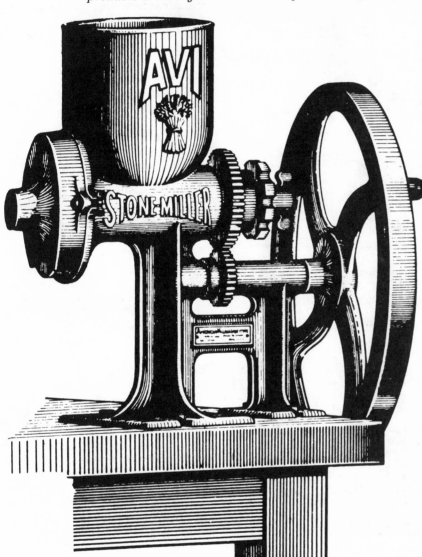

STONE-MILLER FLOUR MILL

The Stone-Miller is a ruggedly built flour mill designed to reduce the effort needed to grind wheat into fine flour. Although primarily designed for hand operation, this mill is also very efficient when driven by a mechanical power source, such as an electric motor.

The mill is of heavy cast-iron construction. Machine-cut steel gears for smooth, noise-free operation provide a 2 : 1 reduction for easy grinding. Stones are 5 inches in diameter, fed by a cast auger. The auger shaft is supported by a ¾-inch tapered roller bearing for a long, trouble-free life. Adjustment from course to fine is made with a positive lock control. Each "click-stop" changes the distance between stones by 0.005 inch.

The hopper holds 8 cups of grain. Output of fine flour from whole grain by hand power is about 10 cups per hour, and 32 cups per hour using an electric motor with a 1-inch pulley.

Height above a table is 15 inches. Total weight is about 55 lbs.

Price: $185 for the no-frills model, $237 with a stone cover and V-belt grooved flywheel.

AMERICAN HARVESTER CIDER MILL

The American Harvester double-tub cider mill combines the best features found in many different presses manufactured around the turn of the century. The Harvester is a hand-operated mill, capable of producing the most cider from the fewest apples with a minimum of effort. The double-tub feature makes it possible to grind and press at the same time. This is a practical advantage when processing large quantities of apples.

The quantity of apples that this mill will process depends on the kind used, and the speed and endurance of the operators. On the average, two people working at a steady pace shouldn't expect to produce more than 80 gallons a day.

The frame is of laminated construction for overall strength and to prevent twisting with age. All joints are dadoed and cross-bolted for strength and structural rigidity. The 12-inch-high by 13½-inch-diameter tubs have beveled hardwood staves for easy cleaning.

The 1½-inch-diameter press screw is Acme thread and passes through the cast-iron cross arm. A cast-iron foot distributes the pressure on a wooden press plate that fits inside the tub. The grinder housing is all cast iron, with a laminated-wood grinding cylinder provided with stainless-steel teeth. The 1 : 3 gear ratio is complemented by a heavy cast-iron flywheel which can store a significant amount of energy, making grinding smooth and fast.

Dimensions: overall size: about 22 inches wide, 36 inches long, and 45 inches high. Shipping weight: about 200 lbs.

Price: $357.50 to $550, depending on hardware and wood options; for hardware kits only (*no* wooden parts), $209 to $275, depending on options chosen.

THE PHOENIX FOUNDRY

P.O. Box 68
Marcus, WA 99151
Tel. 509/684-5434

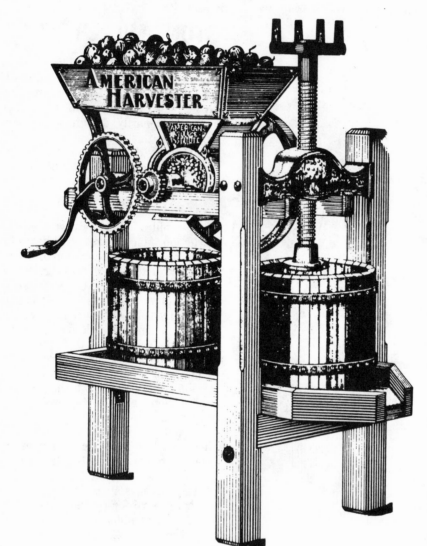

OLD-STYLE DAIRY TINWARE

The season has its effects on milk and cream. Milk in spring is supposed to be the best for drinking, and hence it would be best suited for cheese; and, in autumn, —the butter keeping better than that of summer, —the cows, less frequently milked, give richer milk, and, consequently, more butter. The morning's milk is richer than the evening's. The last-drawn milk of each milking, at all times and seasons, is richer than the first-drawn, which is poorest.

—*From the 1850* Farmer's Almanac

LOUISVILLE TIN & STOVE COMPANY

TIN WARE

IX HEAVY CREAM CANS

APPROVED

MEETS RIGID SANITARY REQUIREMENTS OF STATE HEALTH AUTHORITIES

Made of IX bright tin, seamed and full soldered. Plain body. Heavy tinned ears—riveted on. Tinned wire bail, with black enameled bailwood handle. SOLDER HEAVILY FLOWED OVER ALL SEAMS AND RIVETS making it easily cleaned and eliminating the usual cracks and crevices which harbor bacteria. Heavy drawn cover, made in one piece, with well rounded corners and deep crown that insures a tight fit. Rolled edge on wide flange extends well over rolled edge on top of can, preventing dirt and other particles from getting between the cover and body.

Nos.	96	98	912	916	920
Actual Capacity, Qts........	6	8	12	16	18
Height of body, ins..........	7	9	13	17	19
Diameter inside, ins........	8⅝	8⅝	8⅝	8⅝	8⅝
Weight, per dozen	29	32	39	46	49

Packed one-half dozen in carton

DAIRY PAILS

Made of bright coke tinplate. Raised dome bottom. Heavy wired top rim. Heavy ears riveted to body. No. 4 sanitary tinned wire bail. All seams neatly soldered. 12 quart capacity. Furnished in both IX (135 lb.) and IC (107 lb.) quality coke tinplate.

LIPPED DAIRY PAILS

Specially designed lip for easy pouring. Holds 12 quarts. All seams soldered. Top rim reinforced with heavy gauge wire. No. 4 sanitary tinned wire bail. Body made of bright coke tinplate. Ears riveted to body. Raised dome bottom. Furnished in both IX (135 lb.) and IC (107 lb.) quality coke tinplate.

IX STRAINERS

SANITARY

IX bright tin. Foot easily removed for cleaning strainer disc, making it thoroughly sanitary. Size of strainer disc gives ready flow to milk assuring far greater straining capacity than ordinary strainers. As the strainer cloth is always the first part of a strainer to give way the Sanitary is in the end the most economical since new discs can be had for a fraction of the price of a new strainer.

No. S50—Diam. top 10 ins.; height 4½ ins.; diam. bottom 3¾ ins.

1 dozen in carton; weight per carton, 8 pounds

EXTRA STRAINER DISCS

No. DS50—For No. S50 sanitary strainers.

STOVE PIPE COLLARS

PLAIN

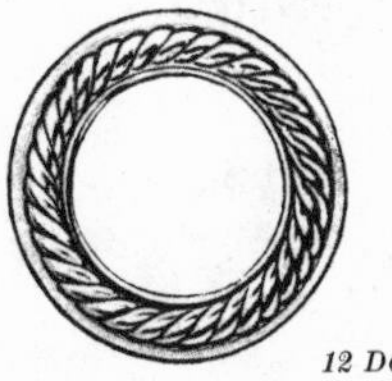

Made of Bright Tinplate

Nos.	6	7
Pipe, ins.	6	7
Price Each ....$.......... $.........		
Wt., per grs.	20	29

12 Dozen in carton

WIDE FLANGE
Made of Bright Tinplate with extra wide flange

Nos.	023	024	025	026
Diameter, ins...	9¼	9¼	9¼	10⅜
For Pipe, ins...	3	4	5	6
Wt., per gross..	30	27	25	32

For dealer information contact:

LOUISVILLE TIN & STOVE COMPANY

P.O. Box 1019
Louisville, KY 40201

HANDMADE TALL WOODEN BUTTER CHURNS

Butter nowadays is often sent to distant markets, and it becomes a matter of the first importance to pack it properly. The readiness of a sale will depend very much upon it. The utmost care should be taken in the first place to free the butter entirely from milk by washing and working it after churning, at a temperature so low as to prevent it from losing its granular texture and becoming greasy. Of course every good butter maker knows that the quality of the product will depend, in a great measure, on the temperature at which the milk or cream is churned . . . which should be from 60 to 65 degrees of Fahr.

—From the 1889 Farmer's Almanac

Capt. James Dassatti's Early American tall butter churns are available with either smooth or rough finishes.

Prices: smooth finish $45.50, and rough finish $38.50 (plus $2.50 for shipping and handling).

Catalog of military and camp items available, $1.

PRODUCTS OF THE PAST

P.O. Box 12
Wilmington, VT 05363
Tel. 802/464-5569

BAG BALM **Bag Balm was developed at the turn of the century as a lanolin-based salve for cows' udders.** Its success in this humble role has been attested to by scores of farmers over the years in letters sent to the Dairy Association Company of Lyndonville, Vermont. Among these is one written in 1936 by Edgar Cox, who held the select and unusual title "Herdsman for Admiral Byrd." Wrote the polar cowherd:

> *I know that your company knew that Admiral Byrd took cattle with him on his last expedition to the Antarctic, but I am sure that you were not aware that Bag Balm was along. I chose Bag Balm because I wanted something that I could depend upon.*

Shortly after its development it was discovered that Bag Balm's usefulness extended far beyond bovine girth galls and chapped teats. Well before the First World War, Bag Balm devotees had made it the panacea of country life, slathering it over everything from human cow licks to squeaking barn hinges. In rural areas today Bag Balm is a popular and accessible item, and children and animals alike submit to its administration with the same grudging tolerance that they showed generations ago.

DAIRY ASSOCIATION COMPANY, INC.

Lyndonville, VT 05851

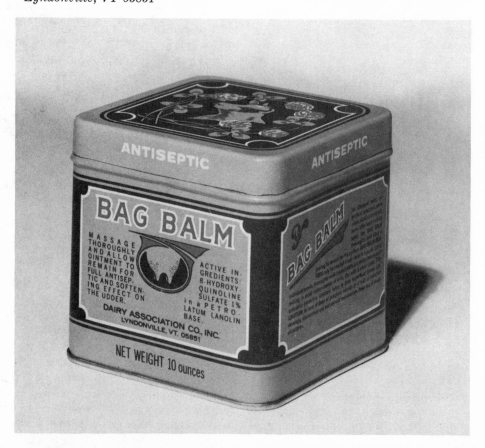

SHAKER SEED BOX

"Your gardening seeds is fine, and if I should sow 'em on the Rock of Gibraltar probably I should raise a good mess of gardening sass." Thus Artemus Ward, during an 1866 visit to the New Lebanon, New York, Shaker community, placed his benediction on nearly four-score years of Shaker seed production and marketing.

It was in the communities of New Lebanon and Watervliet, New York, that the Shakers began the first commercial seed nursery in the United States during 1789. By 1795 the New Lebanon community was actively growing seeds for sale to the "world's people," a business that increased steadily into the next century. By innovatively marketing the seeds in small paper packets and distributing them by wagon to general stores throughout the country, in time the Shakers would have this "lucrative and agreeable employment" accounting for a large portion of their revenues.

Shaker seed boxes were made to serve several functions—as a container for seed packets, as an accounting system for sales, and as a counter display. At first somberly colored, by the late 1800s the seed boxes bowed to the demands of the worldly marketplace and sported bright plumage.

With "hands to work and hearts to God," Steve Kistler (the name means "box-ler," a maker of boxes) started the Shaker Seed Box Company in Cincinnati, Ohio. With his partner William Badgley, a local artist, Kistler sells (among other Shaker furniture reproductions) a replica Shaker seed box built by an expert cabinetmaker. Crafted from high-grade pine, the limited-edition seed boxes are stained "western Shaker green," have adjustable wood partitions, and utilize dovetail construction on the box and breadboard ends on its lid. Dated, numbered, and signed ("to protect collectors of original boxes"), the interior and exterior seed box labels have been replicated from Kistler's private collection and are from the Mount Lebanon Shaker community, circa 1880.

Dimensions: 33¾ inches long, 10½ inches wide, 3½ inches deep.

Price: $120 (plus $6.50 UPS delivery charge; allow three to six weeks for delivery).

Seed box brochure available, $1.

THE SHAKER SEED BOX COMPANY

Steve S. Kistler, Proprietor
6656 Chestnut Street
In The Little Town Center
Mariemont, OH 45227
Tel. 513/271-7100

CHESTERWOOD JARDINIÈRES

Made on the premises of Chesterwood, sculptor William Chester French's summer home in Stockbridge, Massachusetts, these are hand-cast reproductions of the jardinières originally used there. They are terracotta, with cement and marble chips, and are available in two sizes: 12 inches square by 8¾ inches deep, costing $26.50 (plus $16 for shipping), and 7⅝ inches by 17¼ inches by 9¾ inches deep, costing $29.50 (plus $16 for shipping).

Catalog available, $1.

PRESERVATION SHOPS

Department AH
National Trust for Historic
*   Preservation*
1600 H Street NW
Washington, DC 20006
Tel. 202/673-4200

HAWS WATERING CAN

"The New Invention," as described by John Haws's 1885 patent, "forms a Watering Pot that is much easier to carry and tip, and at the same time being much cleaner and more adapted for use than any other put before the Public."

Haws's patent coincided with the tremendous rise in English professional gardening; in fact, throughout the reign of Queen Victoria, large glasshouse nurseries were being established in and around London in record numbers. This, combined with the perfect balance and improved watering rose offered by the Haws can, ensured its success.

Tool catalog available.

SMITH & HAWKIN TOOL COMPANY

25 Corte Madera
Mill Valley, CA 94941
Tel. 415/383-4415

FOR COMPLETE INDEX REFER TO PINK PAGES IN MIDDLE OF BOOK.

VEHICLES AND HARNESS

AMERICAN BEAUTIES

GUARANTEED TWO YEARS.

THE QUEEN OF OUR AMERICAN BEAUTIES, THE GREATEST SELLING BUGGY OF OUR AMERICAN BEAUTY LINE, IS CARRIED IN WAREHOUSES AT DIFFERENT POINTS FOR IMMEDIATE SHIPMENT, AS FULLY EXPLAINED ON PAGE 98 AND 99. DON'T FAIL TO READ ABOUT OUR WONDERFUL AMERICAN QUEEN, ILLUSTRATED AND DESCRIBED ON PAGE 99, THE MOST POPULAR BUGGY OF OUR AMERICAN BEAUTY LINE, THE GREATEST SELLER OF THEM ALL.

This line of American Beauties represents great value, and the leader of them all, the largest seller, the greatest buggy ever built outside of our highest grade Solid Comfort Buggies, is fully illustrated and described on page 99; we carry it in warehouses, as fully explained on pages 98 and 99; we sell such a large number of this one American Queen Top Buggy, the one illustrated and described on page 99, that we carry it on hand at different warehouses, so as to serve our customers promptly and save them freight charges.

$44.95

DESCRIPTION OF No. 11K610

SEAT—29½ inches; panel spring back and box spring cushion; seat ends padded and lined; upholstered in heavy dark green body cloth or extra grade moroccoline leather. BODY—Piano box style; 23 inches wide by 55 inches long; hardwood frame; boot on rear of body [illegible] toe carpet on front panel; leather dash, [illegible] TOP—Three-bow genu[illegible] ded and lined back s[illegible] rubber back curtain; [illegible] curtain fasteners; heav[illegible] nickel top propnuts; st[illegible] inch drop axles; long di[illegible] spindles; hickory axle ca[illegible] braced; full bearing fifth wheel; three and four-plate elliptic oil tempered springs; new style center bearing body loops. WHEELS—Sarven's patent style; ⅞-inch screwed rims; full ⅞-inch oval edge steel tires; 38 inches front and 42 inch[illegible] SHAFTS—Hickory shafts, trimmed with [illegible] back from tip, flat straps; doub[illegible] shifting shaft couplers. PAINTING[illegible] striped, fancy design on seat risers[illegible] shafts, rich blood carmine, striped[illegible] 8 inches or 5 feet 2 inches. State [illegible]

No. 11K610 Price, comp[illegible] braced shafts and steel tires.... [illegible]

Shipped from Evansville, Indiana.

$46.75

DESCRIPTION OF No. 11K612

BODY—Deep side panel phaeton seat; 29½ inches; solid spring overstuffed panel back and spring cushion; seat ends padded and lined; handsome seat handles; upholstered with dark green body cloth or extra grade moroccoline leather. BODY—23 inches wide by 55 inches long; piano box style; 8-inch panels; hardwood frame; drill fiber boot on rear of body; carpet; leather dash. TOP—Three-bow leather quarters and leather back stays; wool faced head lining; back stays padded and lined; lined back curtain; heavy side curtains; stitched valance; two roll-up straps; patent curtain fasteners; storm apron. GEAR—Arched axles, 15-16-inch; hickory axle caps; long distance dust and mudproof bell collar spindles; double reach, ironed; oil tempered, easy riding, three and four-plate springs; new style center bearing body loops. WHEELS—⅞-inch screwed rims, fitted with ⅞-inch oval edge steel tires; full bolted; Sarven's patent style; 38 inches front and 42 inches rear. SHAFTS—Double braced hickory shafts; trimmed with leather 22 inches back from the point, flat straps; quick shifting shaft couplers. PAINTING—Body, plain black; gear, wheels and shafts, dark Brewster green, striped. TRACK—4 feet 8 inches or 5 feet 2 inches. State width desired.

No. 11K612 Price, complete with double braced shafts and steel tires.............................$46.75

Shipped from Evansville, Indiana.

$47.85

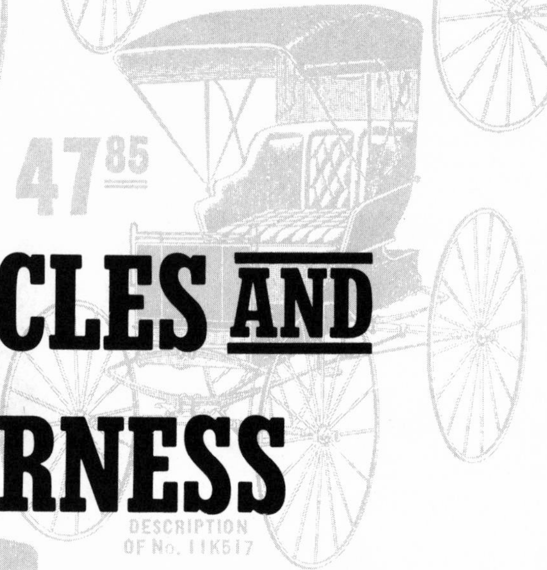

DESCRIPTION OF No. 11K517

SEAT—New style auto seat; 29½ inches; fancy back and cushion, fitted with plenty of springs; upholstered with heavy dark green body cloth or extra grade moroccoline leather. BODY—Piano box style; 23x55 inches; hardwood frame; boot on rear of body; carpet; toe carpet on front panel; leather dash, fitted with nickel dash rail. TOP—Genuine leather quarters and back stays; rubber roof and back curtain; back stays padded and lined; wool faced head lining; lined back curtain; two roll-up straps; heavy side curtains; patent curtain fasteners; storm apron; nickel top propnuts; three bows. GEAR—15-16-inch steel axles; long distance, dust and mudproof bell collar; hickory axle caps; special fifth wheel; elliptic end springs; center bearing body loops; double reaches, ironed full length. WHEELS—Sarven's patent; ⅞-inch screwed rim; full ⅞-inch oval edge steel tires; 38 inches front and 42 inches rear. SHAFTS—Hickory shafts; double braced; trimmed with leather 22 inches back from the tip, flat straps; quick shifting shaft couplers. PAINTING—Body, black, striped and decorated; fancy seat risers; gear, wheels and shafts, blood carmine, striped with black. TRACK—4 feet 8 inches narrow or 5 feet 2 inches wide. State width desired.

No. 11K517 Price, complete with double braced shafts and steel tires.............................$47.85

Shipped from Evansville, Indiana.

$45.75

DESCRIPTION OF No. 11K514

SEAT—29½ inches; solid panel overstuffed spring back and box frame spring cushion; padded and lined seat ends; upholstered in heavy dark green body cloth or extra grade moroccoline leather. BODY—23x55 inches; piano box style; hardwood frame; 8-inch panels; boot on rear of body; carpet; leather dash. TOP—Leather quarter top and back stays; back stays padded and lined, fancy stitched; heavy waterproof side curtains and lined back curtain, wool faced head lining, raised, stitched valance; two roll-up straps; patent curtain fasteners; three bows; waterproof storm apron. GEAR—15-16-inch arched axles; dust and mudproof bell collars; long distance spindles; hickory axle caps; double reach, ironed; three and four-plate oil tempered elliptic springs; new style center bearing body loops. WHEELS—Sarven's patent; ⅞-inch screwed rims, fitted with ⅞-inch oval edge steel tires; 38 inches front and 42 inches rear. SHAFTS—Double braced hickory shafts; trimmed with leather 22 inches from the tip, flat straps, quick shifting shaft couplers. PAINTING—Body plain black; gear wheels and shafts blood carmine, striped. TRACK—4 feet 8 inches or 5 feet 2 inches. State width desired.

No. 11K514 Price, complete with double braced shafts and steel tires.............................$45.75

Shipped from Evansville, Indiana.

TWO-YEAR GUARANTEE against defect in material or workmanship furnished with each American Beauty.

EACH AMERICAN BEAUTY IS CRATED UNDER 30 INCHES.

Rubber tires can be furnished on any of the buggies. See prices of rubber tires on page 92.

$43.95

DESCRIPTION OF No. 11K619

SEAT—Georgia drop back; spring cushion, 25½ inches; padded and lined seat ends; double bar nickel arm rails; upholstered in heavy dark green body cloth or extra grade moroccoline leather. BODY—20 inches wide by 55 inches long; hardwood frame; piano box style; boot on rear of body; carpet; toe carpet on front panel; patent leather dash. TOP—Two and one-half-bow; leather quarters and back stays; back curtain lined; heavy side curtains; wool faced head lining; patent curtain fasteners; two roll-up straps; storm apron. GEARS—15-16-inch axles; long distance dust and mudproof bell collar; hickory axle caps; long easy riding side springs; no reaches. WHEELS—38 inches front and 42 inches rear; Sarven's patent style; ⅞-inch screwed rims; ⅞-inch oval edge steel tires, full bolted. SHAFTS—Hickory shafts, trimmed with leather 22 inches back from tip, flat straps; double braced; quick shifting shaft couplers. PAINTING—Body plain black; gear, wheels and shafts, Brewster gear green, striped. TRACK—4 feet 8 inches or 5 feet inches. State width desired.

No. 11K619 Price, complete with double braced shafts and steel tires.............................$43.95

Shipped from Evansville, Indiana.

She returned to the main street and bent her thoughtful steps towards the center of the village. A string of wagons drawn by oxen was lumbering along. These "stage freighters" as they were called, hauled grain and flour and merchandise from Sterling.

—*Zane Grey,*
Riders of the Purple Sage

"Yes," said Harper, "Jarrette would kill him. But, Doctor"—looking at his watch as the carriage passed a gas lamp—"it is nearly four o'clock at last."

—*Ambrose Bierce,*
"A Watcher By The Dead"

PHAETON CARRIAGES
Working on his 200-year-old farm (where he and his wife Margo also breed Morgan horses), Gary Koehler builds carriages from scratch using original antique irons. All carriage work leaves Koehler's shop "in the white," with iron and iron-to-wood surfaces primed. The carriages are then assembled (he also carves all the intricate woodwork and moldings required by the antique styles), fitted, and painted.

Although Koehler prefers to make the slat-sided phaetons of the type shown here in his wife's pen-and-ink drawing, he will also do custom work from three-view drawings or good photos.

BRIAR ROSE FARM

Gary Koehler
RR 1, Box 174
Layton Road
Woodstown, NJ 08098
Tel. 609/769–1452

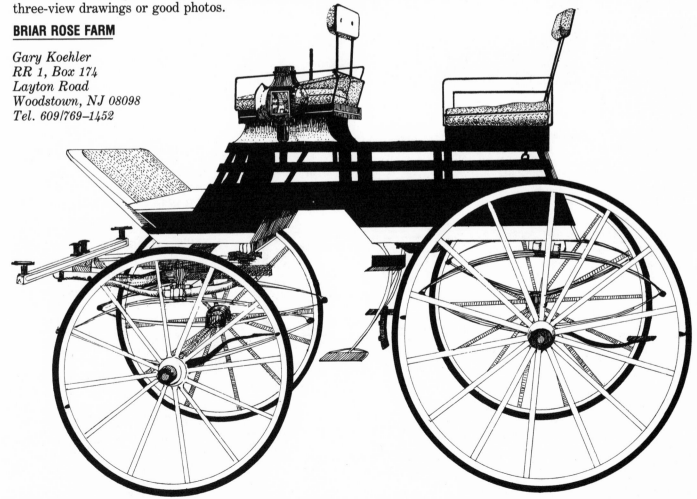

H. McCUE, WHEELWRIGHT

Harry McCue's artistic background tells in the distinctive workmanship and grace of his wagons and buckboards. More than ten years ago, after receiving his Bachelor of Fine Arts from Pratt and his Master of Fine Arts from the University of Colorado, McCue apprenticed himself to Amish wagon builders. It was first his intention to build a business in the repair and restoration of horse-drawn vehicles, but in the past few years he has taken to building the vehicles instead. During this period he has made more than sixty, including many buggies.

For further information contact:

H. McCue, Wheelwright
Skinner Road
Lodi, NY 14860

WESTERN CONCORD STAGECOACHES

In 1858 the Overland Mail Company was established by John Butterfield to haul passengers and mail from St. Louis to San Francisco. Butterfield's stagecoaches called at 160 stations along the 2,800-mile route (it sagged south to El Paso at the behest of southern politicians but was straightened out during the Civil War), making the trip in about twenty-four days.

Butterfield used Concord coaches (what we refer to when we use the term "stagecoach")—leafsprung nine-passenger coaches weighing 2,500 pounds and costing about $1,250. Their name comes from Concord, New Hampshire, where they were first built in 1827. In 1866 Butterfield sold his company to Harry Wells who had formed Wells, Fargo & Company in 1852.

It may be said of the stagecoach that it was the most well-known American vehicle prior to the Model T. Authentic replicas of these raw products of the Yankee's mechanical bent may be ordered custom built by the Frizzell Coach and Wheel Works of Oklahoma City. John D. Frizzell sent the following:

The Frizzell family and the Frizzell Coach and Wheel Works are known throughout the world as the expert source for western American stagecoaches. . . . Our equipment is among the most specialized in the trade, ranging from modern machines to those a century old. Some of these were obtained from among the foremost manufacturers of the past, including the Lemon Wagon Works of Greenville, Tennessee, and the Fulbright Wagon Factory of Fayetteville, Arkansas, which was owned by former Senator Fulbright's father.

Frizzell's stagecoach bodies are framed in the traditional manner using select quality oak, ash, and hickory. Body panels are made of premium Baltic birch and fitted with hand-forged roof rails and body irons. All the latches, hinges, and other metal trim are also hand-forged.

Similarly, all draft components, running gear, wheels, and axles are made with select hardwoods and hand-forged ironware, as per original Concord specifications.

FRIZZELL COACH AND WHEEL WORKS

P.O. Box 82001
Oklahoma City, OK 73148
Tel. 405/943-8038

VEHICLES FROM THE CUMBERLAND CARRIAGE WORKS

The Cumberland General Store's Carriage Works will custom-build these horse-drawn vehicles to your order. The carriages they sell are newly manufactured from original plans and specifications, using the original machinery, and in a few cases, second- and third-generation buggy and wagon craftsmen. "They are absolutely the finest conveyances built," claims Cumberland's catalog, "being continuously manufactured since 1884." The following appears as it does in the Cumberland "Wish and Want Book":

"Wish and Want Book" available, $3.75.

CUMBERLAND GENERAL STORE

Route 3
Crossville, TN 38555
Tel. 615/484–8481

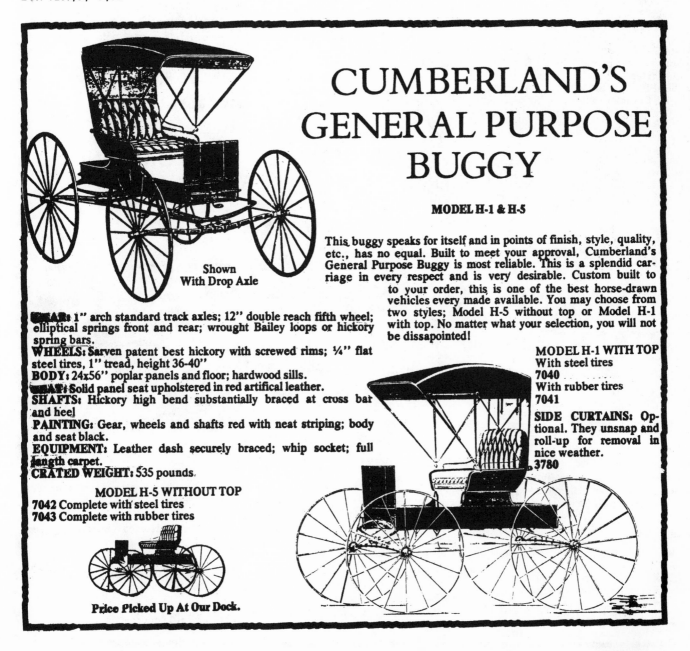

CUMBERLAND'S GENERAL PURPOSE BUGGY

MODEL H-1 & H-5

This buggy speaks for itself and in points of finish, style, quality, etc., has no equal. Built to meet your approval, Cumberland's General Purpose Buggy is most reliable. This is a splendid carriage in every respect and is very desirable. Custom built to to your order, this is one of the best horse-drawn vehicles ever made available. You may choose from two styles; Model H-5 without top or Model H-1 with top. No matter what your selection, you will not be dissapointed!

Shown With Drop Axle

GEAR: 1" arch standard track axles; 12" double reach fifth wheel; elliptical springs front and rear; wrought Bailey loops or hickory spring bars.
WHEELS: Sarven patent best hickory with screwed rims; ¼" flat steel tires, 1" tread, height 36-40"
BODY: 24x56" poplar panels and floor; hardwood sills.
SEAT: Solid panel seat upholstered in red artifical leather.
SHAFTS: Hickory high bend substantially braced at cross bar and heel
PAINTING: Gear, wheels and shafts red with neat striping; body and seat black.
EQUIPMENT: Leather dash securely braced; whip socket; full length carpet.
CRATED WEIGHT: 535 pounds.

MODEL H-1 WITH TOP
With steel tires
7040
With rubber tires
7041

SIDE CURTAINS: Optional. They unsnap and roll-up for removal in nice weather.
3780

MODEL H-5 WITHOUT TOP
7042 Complete with steel tires
7043 Complete with rubber tires

Price Picked Up At Our Dock.

☛ SPRING WAGON ☚

MODEL H-15

A stylish, easy running, comfortable wagon. It is made of the best grade materials. It is very carefully finished and makes a wagon we are as proud to sell as you will be to own.

GEAR: 1⅛'' steel axles, 12'' fifth wheel with double reaches, front spring 1½'' leaves, rear springs half-platform style.

WHEELS: Sarven patent best grade hickory with screwed rims; 1¼'' tread, ¼'' steel tires, height 36-40''.

BODY: 34'' by 90'' with drop end gate.

SEATS: Solid panel style; well ironed throughout, trimmed in red artificial leather. Rear seat is removeable.

SHAFTS: Heavy easy bend surrey shafts well ironed with cross and heel braces.

PAINTING: Gear is painted red with neat striping. Body and seats are black with fine line striping on the body and risers.

SHIPPING WEIGHT: 615 lbs. crated.

7068 Complete with steel tires
7069 Complete with hard rubber tires

MODEL H-16

This wagon is the same as H-15 except without the rear seat. Shipping wt. 575 lbs.

7070 Complete with steel tires
7071 Complete with hard rubber tires

Price Picked Up At Our Dock.

A GOOD, STRONG, WELL-BUILT, WELL-PROPORTIONED COMBINATION BUSINESS AND PLEASURE WAGON!

ONE HORSE FARM WAGON

NO. 350 GENERAL PURPOSE

Farm Wagon is made by expert wagon makers according to standard specifications. These specifications include the best materials to make a strong yet easy running wagon.

SHAFTS: Easy-bent.
TIRES: 1½'' by ⅜''.
WHEELS: Sarvin patent. Wheels measures 36'' in front and 42'' rear.
BOX: 90'' long by 40'' wide by 12'' deep.
SEAT: Spring type.
CRATED WEIGHT: 755 pounds.
Basic Wagon with Easy-bent Shafts
7044

Add for 10'' side boards as pictured
7045
Add for Gear Type Brake with Box Attachment
3745
Add for Drop Tongue for Two Horses (Interchangeable with Shafts).
3746
Add for Lazy Back on Seat
3747

Price Picked Up At Our Dock.

EXTENSION TOP CARRIAGE

A SPLENDID CARRIAGE IN EVERY RESPECT!

GEAR: 1'' arch long distance axles; 12'' fifth wheel; double reaches; wood spring bar; elliptical springs.
WHEELS: 1'' Sarven Patent best hickory with screwed rims; ¼'' flat steel tires with 1'' tread; height 36-40 or 38x42 (please specify).
BODY: 28x70'', with roomy high panel seat; rear seat and top removable.
SEAT: Regular panel upholstered in deep red or black leatherette (please specify color).
SHAFTS: Heavy easy bend surrey shafts, well ironed with cross and heel braces.

TOP: Heavy rubber roof; black curtain and head lining.
PAINTING: Gear, wheels and shafts red with neat striping; body and seat black.
EQUIPMENT: Patent leather dash and rear fenders, securely braced; whip socket.
CRATED WEIGHT: About 600 pounds.
3742 Complete with steel tires.................$4600.00
3743 Complete with rubber tires $4775.00

Price Picked Up At our Dock.

GENERAL ORDERING INFORMATION FOR HORSE DRAWN VEHICLES

> **Prices are based on customer picking up at our dock. It is quite costly to crate in the substantial manner required so that the vehicle will arrive without damage. If it is impossible for you to pick up, add $300.00 for crating.**

Wood wheel pony vehicles except pony wagons, please specify height of pony (measured at withers). Wheels and shafts will be supplied in proper size as follows:

FOUR WHEEL VEHICLES
Pony 42 to 50 inches: wheels 30-34 inches, shafts 60 inches.

THESE EXTRAS AVAILABLE FOR PONY VEHICLES
P-5, P-10, P-11
Pole in addition to shafts........................$386.00
Extra Shafts complete with Singletree $180.00
Top for Pony Buggy $585.00
Pole in place of Shafts..........................$225.00

OPTIONS
WHEEL DIAMETER: On horse size vehicles can be changed from 36-40 to 38-42 inches at no added cost. Please specify.
PAINTING: In any color can be done for small extra charge. Add $53.00
SEATS: Upholstery; black or dark red. Please specify.
POLES: For team can be furnished in place of or in addition to shafts. See special note below:

EXTRAS
For Cumberland's General Purpose Buggy, Surreys, Delivery Wagon, Spring Wagon, Utility Wagon and Extension Top Carriage.
7064 POLE IN PLACE OF SHAFTS .... Add $225.00
7065 POLE IN ADDITION TO SHAFTS .... Add $386.00
7066 EXTRA SHAFTS WITH SINGLETREE.......$180.00

Shipped FOB Crossville, Tn.

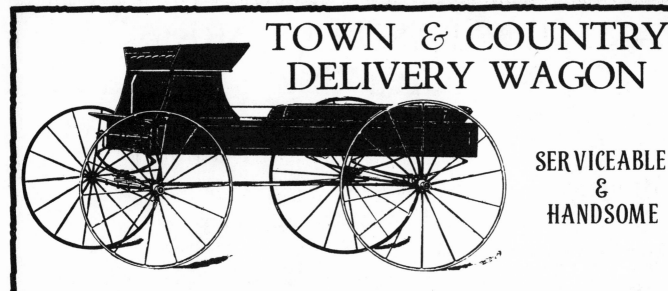

TOWN & COUNTRY DELIVERY WAGON

SERVICEABLE & HANDSOME

High quality Town and Country Delivery Wagon can be put to a variety of uses. Built by experts, this wagon will give many, many years of dependable service.

GEAR: 1⅛" long distance axles, heavy fifth wheel with double reaches, ironed full length and well braced. Heavy leaf front spring and two springs in rear.

WHEELS: Sarven patent best grade hickory with screwed rims; 1¼" tread; ¼" steel tires, height 36-40".

BED: 84" long by 34 inches wide with extension toe board, fitted winged flare boards as shown and drop end gate.

SEAT: Wagon style as illustrated with cushion trimmed in red artificial leather.

SHAFTS: Heavy easy bend surrey shafts well ironed with cross and heel braces.

PAINTING: Gear painted red with neat striping. Body and seat are black with fine line striping on the body and risers.

7050 Complete with steel tires
7051 Complete with hard rubber tires

Price Picked Up At Our Dock.

PONY BUGGY

For ponies, small horses and mules this buggy is hard to beat! It is well crafted and beautifully appointed. Every detail about this buggy has received full attention!

MODEL P-5

GEAR: 1" arched steel axles, 48" track.

WHEELS: Wood wheels, 1" tread. See general specifications for diameter.

BODY: 18x50" body; leather dash.

SEAT: 15x29" seat and lazy back upholstered in red artificial leather.

SHAFTS: Bent hickory shafts with singletree.

PAINTING: Gear, shafts and wheels painted red, neatly striped. Body and seat are black.

CRATED WEIGHT: 370 pounds.

7095 Complete with steel tires
7096 Complete with hard rubber tires

Price Picked Up At Our Dock.

HIGH GRADE PONY BUGGY

CUMBERLAND'S ═UTILITY WAGON═

A Very Attractive & Fine Appearing Wagon

A fine general purpose wagon. Cumberland's Utility Wagon very convenient for carrying parcels and gear. Hinged lids close to protect enclosed items.

GEAR: 1" arch long distance axles; 60" wide track. Double elliptical rear spring. Hickory spring bar.
WHEELS: Sarven Patent best hickory with screwed rims; ¾" flat steel tires, 1" tread, height 38" and 42".
BODY: 28"x60". Poplar panels and floor; hardwood sills.
SEAT: Lazy back type upholstered in red artificial leather.
SHAFTS: Bent hickory shafts with singletree.

PAINTING: Gear, shafts and wheels painted red, neatly striped. Body and seat are black. Utility wagon does not have scroll design as shown.
EQUIPMENT: Leather dash securely braced; whip socket. Full length carpet.
CRATED WEIGHT: About 600 lbs.
3744 Complete with steel tires $3450.00
3776 Complete with rubber tires $3625.00

Price Picked Up At Our Dock.

A GOOD CHOICE FOR THE BEGINNING HORSE AND DRIVER!

CUMBERLAND'S High Grade ═ROAD CART═

This cart is as well known among users of road carts as any staple article in a merchandise store.
SEAT: It has wide seat for two passengers; slat bottom with full seat rail; hung on hickory supports; oil tempered steel spring hung in adjustable loops on heel of shafts.
WHEELS: Sarven patent, 44 inches high, 1 inch best steel tire.
GEAR: Axle is 1 inch, the best refined steel. Width of track, 4 feet, 8 inches.

BODY: Seat, posts, foot rack, shafts, cross bar and single tree are made of the best carefully selected material.
PAINTED: Red.
CRATED WEIGHT: About 150 lbs.
3778 Complete with steel tires.................. $870.00
3779 Complete with rubber tires................ $960.00

Price Picked Up At Our Dock

PIONEER PLACE HORSE-DRAWN ROAD VEHICLES

As Amish farmers, Mark and Elmo Stoll are familiar with the value and efficiency of the horse for small-scale farming. "The struggle between tractor power and horse power is like the race between the tortoise and the hare," they say. "The steady, plodding horse is going strong, while stalled tractors search for fuel."

But as travelers to rural Pennsylvania well know, the Amish use of the horse-drawn vehicle isn't limited to the field, and Pioneer Place's buggy maker stands ready to spread the gospel of "horsepower for the masses" with the following vehicles.

AMISH SURREY

There was a rank of stately hacks and barrouches, and light, wood-colored surreys and phaetons.

—*William Dean Howells*, Day of Their Wedding, *1895*

The surrey, a four-wheeled, two-seated family carriage (often with a fringed, rectangular top) is frequently used by the Amish for excursions to town and church, or for social visits. Pioneer Place's surrey has an optional fringe and offers a choice between steel and hard-rubber tires. With shaft for one horse or a pole for two.

Price: $1,500.

AMISH OPEN BUGGY

"A sensible vehicle of the type built fifty years ago," Mark and Elmo maintain, "but with such modern improvements as Timken bearings and a stronger fifth wheel." All heavy-duty material and quality construction. Available with steel or rubber tires.

Price: $1,500.

Mail-order catalog available.

THE PIONEER PLACE

9938 County Road 39
Belle Center, OH 43310

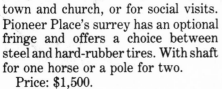

WAGON WHEELS

Established in 1868, the George E. Daniels Wagon Factory has been manufacturing wagon wheels using the same equipment at the same location ever since.

Price list available on request.

GEORGE E. DANIELS WAGON FACTORY

Daniels Road
Rowley, MA 01969
Tel. 617/948-3815

HARNESS The increasing use

of draft animals may again make harness a common article of farm and riding equipment. Big Sky Leatherwork's team harness, horse collars, and hames are made in the old way.

Catalog available, $2.

BIG SKY LEATHERWORKS

Route 3
Billings, MT 59101
Tel. 406/373-5937

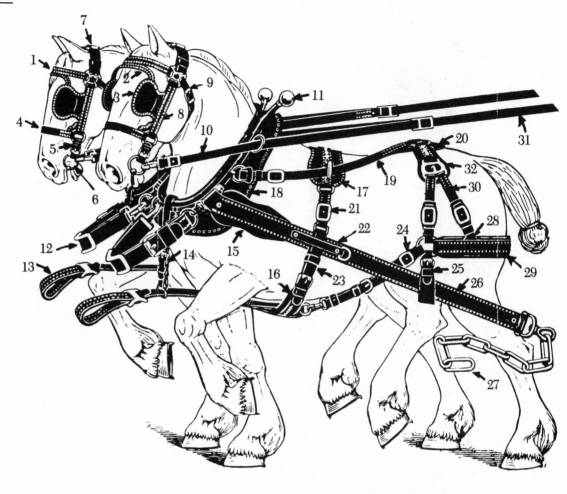

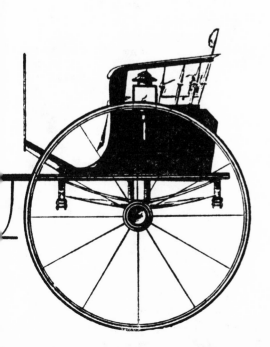

1-BRIDLE FRONT
2-WINKER BRACE
3BLIND OR WINKER
4-NOSE BAND
5-BIT STRAP
6-BIT
7-CROWN PIECE
8-BRIDLE CHEEK
9-THROAT LATCH
10-LINE - FRONT PART
11-HAME
12-BREAST STRAP
13-POLE STRAP
14-COLLAR STRAP
15-SAFE ON TRACE
16-BELLY BAND

17-BACK BAND
18-COLLAR
19-BACK STRAP
20-RUMP SAFE
21-BACK BAND BILLET OR
　　MARKET STRAP
22-LOOP ON TRACE
23-BELLY BAND BILLET
24-QUARTER STRAP OR SIDE STRAP
25-LAZY STRAP OR MUD CARRIER
26-TRACE OR TUG
27-HEEL CHAIN
28-LAYER LOOP
29-BREECHING
30-HIP STRAP
31-LINE - HAND PART
32-TRACE CARRIER

HIGH-WHEELER BICYCLES
Rideable Antique Bicycle Replicas has been building new, old-fashioned, full-size replicas of nineteenth-century bicycles in Oakland, California, for the past decade. Several models are offered: the three-passenger Courting Cycle (with a seat, no doubt, for a chaperone), a copy of the 1882 Rudge Sociable; a 38- and 48-inch Penny Farthing (following their development in 1870, high-wheelers were often referred to as "penny farthings"); and a low-wheel 1840 Hobby Horse.

"To keep the old-fashioned look," Rideable Replica's bicycles are handmade, and are designed to provide maximum strength and reliability. Each bicycle has been fully tested and is warranteed. The firm welcomes custom orders.

Brochure and price list available.

RIDEABLE ANTIQUE BICYCLE REPLICAS, INC.

2447 Telegraph Avenue
Oakland, CA 94612
Tel 415/444–1666 or 451–2838

BRASS SLEIGH BELLS
Crazy Crow's brass sleigh bells are exact replicas of nineteenth-century cast bells. They are available in either round or hexagonal shapes, and have holes to attach them with pop rivets.

Catalog available, $2.

CRAZY CROW TRADING POST

P.O. Box 314
Denison, TX 75020
Tel. 214/463–1366

BUGGY UMBRELLAS
Gohn Brothers is a retail supplier to Amish Mennonite orders throughout the U.S. and Canada. Their large (50-inch-diameter) black buggy umbrellas come with either a wooden or metal shaft.

Prices: No. 8 (metal shaft) costs $12.79, and No. 16 (wood shaft) costs $13.19 (plus $2.10 each for postage and handling).

Catalog of Amish and plain clothing available.

GOHN BROTHERS

Box 111
Middlebury, IN 46540
Tel. 219/825–2400

HIGHEST GRADE GROCERIES
AT LOWEST CHICAGO WHOLESALE PRICES

SAVE ONE-THIRD ON YOUR GROCERY BILLS

by buying all your groceries from us. Write for our Free Grocery Price List today. We have the largest grocery store in the world, the sales amounting to more than the sales of several of the largest wholesale grocery houses in Chicago combined. We guarantee to furnish you absolutely the best and highest grade groceries obtainable, and guarantee our prices to be the lowest ever named. DON'T PAY RETAIL PRICES FOR GROCERIES.

WON'T YOU JUST DO US THIS FAVOR

Write us a postal card or letter and say, "Please send me your big Free Grocery List," and we will mail you at once free and postpaid the latest edition of our big 64-page Grocery List, quoting you THE LOWEST CHICAGO WHOLESALE PRICES ON ABSOLUTELY THE HIGHEST GRADE GROCERIES, enabling you to make a saving of one-third.

SIX GREAT GROCERY LISTS FREE

FOR 1908   FOR 1908

A NEW BOOK EVERY TWO MONTHS

IT IS WONDERFULLY CONVENIENT TO ORDER YOUR GROCERIES BY MAIL

from us. We offer a greater variety than you can get in any local grocery store. Every item is absolutely guaranteed by us to be strictly high grade, thoroughly in accordance with the National Pure Food Law of 1906. You can make up your grocery order very easily, we provide you an order blank which explains itself. You can make up an order at your convenience and enclose our price in the form of a Postoffice or Express Money Order, Bank Draft or currency in a Registered Letter mail it to us and we will ship you the goods very neatly and carefully packed, guaranteeing to furnish you fresh, high grade goods throughout. In a short time your shipment will be at the depot and you can get it just as readily as you would by buying your groceries at a retail grocery store, and then, THINK OF THE SAVING WE MAKE FOR YOU!

WE GUARANTEE TO SATISFY YOU OR REFUND YOUR MONEY

You take no risk. Everything we offer is strictly guaranteed. If goods we send you are not satisfactory in any way with any of the goods we send return it to us at our expense and we will pay you back every cent including transportation charges you paid. You will not be out of one cent. Our Grocery Price List which is issued every two months, and don't fail to observe the wonderful grocery offers we make you in this catalogue which show you some of the values we are able to quote.

FOOD AND DRINK

TWO OFFERINGS FROM OUR GROCERY CATALOGUE

INCLUDE A CANISTER OF TEA OR COFFEE WITH YOUR ORDER AND TEST THE QUALITY OF THESE GOODS AND COMPARE THE PRICES WITH THOSE ORDINARILY PAID FOR SUCH QUALITIES AT RETAIL.

OUR MALDEN COFFEE   19 CENTS PER POUND

Put up in airtight 5-pound canisters. The equal of coffee sold as high as 30 cents by other dealers.

A combination of choice old, well matured Mexican and South American coffees, especially rich in their cup qualities. It really isn't so strange that we can offer you this rich, smooth flavory coffee at the marvelously low price of 19 cents, when you consider the fact that we import our own coffees and do our own roasting, mixing and blending. And it isn't strange that we can offer you so excellent a quality, a quality the equal of which cannot be purchased for less than almost double our price, when you realize that we buy nothing but the very finest grades to be procured in the coffee markets of the world. We employ experts to test the coffees, experts who buy direct from the producer, after having been on the ground and having seen and tested the article.

If you have been buying a 15-cent grade of coffee you will find our 19-cent Malden Blend better and actually cheaper, because you will get more cups of the same strength from the same quantity.

No. 7K500   Per 5-pound canister................ $ 0.95
No. 7K5017   Per case of six 5-pound canisters..... 5.70
No. 7K5027   Per case of twelve 5-pound canisters.. 11.40
No. 7K5037   Per case of twenty 5-pound canisters.. 19.00
We do not sell less than a 5-pound canister of Malden Coffee.

APALDA BRAND TEAS   39 CENTS PER POUND

UNDER OUR APALDA BRAND WE OFFER A SELECTION OF THE FOLLOWING VARIETIES OF TEAS IN AN AIRTIGHT MOISTUREPROOF CAN.

This is a special selection of early crop teas from the best tea growing countries of the world. A line of teas if bought of the wholesaler in the regular way could not possibly be sold at less than 50 cents per pound. This variety is selected with special reference to its cup qualities. We import our own teas, buy direct from the resident agents in the several tea growing countries, thereby saving the profit usually paid the importer and the jobber, which explains why we can furnish this grade of tea at the remarkably low price of 39 cents per pound. We ask you to include in your next order a canister of this tea, making your selection from the list below, and we feel sure that you will agree with us that the quality of the tea we send you is superior to the teas you have been purchasing at from 60 to 70 cents.

Apalda Brand we offer a special selection of the following varieties of teas:

SUN DRIED JAPAN. A green tea draws beautiful light liquor.
No. 7K200   Per 1-pound canister............$0.39
No. 7K201   Per 3-pound canister............ 1.14

REGULAR JAPAN. A green tea, draws fragrant light liquor.
No. 7K202   Per 1-pound canister............$0.39
No. 7K203   Per 3-pound canister............ 1.14

BASKET FIRED JAPAN. A black tea, draws a very pale liquor.
No. 7K204   Per 1-pound canister............$0.39
No. 7K205   Per 3-pound canister............ 1.14

GUNPOWDER. A green tea, draws light aromatic liquor.
No. 7K206   Per 1-pound canister............$0.39
No. 7K206   Per 3-pound canister............ 1.14

IMPERIAL. A green tea, draws fine, pale liquor.
No. 7K209   Per 1-pound canister............$0.39
No. 7K210   Per 3-pound canister............ 1.14

YOUNG HYSON. A green tea, draws medium light liquor.
No. 7K211   Per 1-pound canister............$0.39
No. 7K212   Per 3-pound canister............ 1.14

ENGLISH BREAKFAST. A black tea, draws fine amber liquor.
No. 7K213   Per 1-pound canister.....$0.39
No. 7K214   Per 3-pound canister..... 1.14

OOLONG. A black tea, draws medium amber colored liquor.
No. 7K215   Per 1-pound canister.....$0.39
No. 7K216   Per 3-pound canister..... 1.14

INDIA-CEYLON. A black tea, draws dark amber colored liquor.
No. 7K218   Per 1-pound canister.....$0.39
No. 7K219   Per 3-pound canister..... 1.14

GREEN AND BLACK MIXED. A blended tea, draws medium amber colored liquor.
No. 7K220   Per 1-pound canister.....$0.39
No. 7K221   Per 3-pound canister..... 1.14

SPECIAL BREAKFAST. A blended tea, draws medium dark, very fragrant liquor.
No. 7K222   Per 1-pound canister.....$0.39
No. 7K223   Per 3-pound canister..... 1.14

The early rising cow-boys were off again to their work; and those to whom their night's holiday had left any dollars were spending these for tobacco, or cartridges, or canned provisions for the journey to their distant camps. Sardines were called for, and potted chicken, and devilled ham: a sophisticated nourishment, at first sight, for these sons of the sage-brush. But portable and ready-made food plays of necessity a great part in the opening of a new country. These picnic pots and cans were the first of her trophies that Civilization dropped upon Wyoming's virgin soil. The cow-boy is now gone to worlds invisible; the wind has blown away the white ashes of his campfires, but the empty sardine box lies rusting over the faces of the Western earth.

So through my eyes half closed I watch the sale of these tins, and grew familiar with the ham's inevitable trade-mark—that label with the devil and his horns and hoofs and tail very pronounced, all colored in a sultry prodigious scarlet.

—*Owen Wister,* The Virginian, *1902*

GRANULAR-CURD AMERICAN CHEESE

Although he never seemed to say it when posing for a photograph, the word "cheese" was an important one in Calvin Coolidge's vocabulary. In 1890, the Plymouth Cheese Company of Plymouth, Vermont, was founded by the president's father, and for decades now it's been run by Calvin's son John, whose enthusiasm for the business seems unaffected by semi-retirement. **Yankee flintiness** is a misunderstood thing. The dour facade is used as an effective foil against charlatans, the mask of people whose natural friendliness may need restraint. It's a bluff, a dog barking while his tail wags with abandon. John Coolidge is as delightfully arid as any old Vermonter, but the revelation that I was calling from Springfield, Massachusetts (his boyhood was partly spent in nearby Northampton), released so ready a bonhomie as to make me wonder if his father's fabled frostiness might not be relegated to that part of the Smithsonian reserved for such bogus presidential lore as Washington's wooden teeth.

In his youth John apparently loved the sights and smells of his grandfather's little industry, but six years after he was graduated from Amherst it began to fail. "I couldn't stand to see it go to rack and ruin," he confided, "it was a boyhood thing with me."

The Kraft slices that the term "American cheese" brings to mind have little to do with Plymouth Cheese's product. The term originally arose after the Revolutionary War when Americans, missing the English cheddar they were accustomed to, developed a domestic version with a good republican name. Plymouth's American follows an authentic early Vermont process of agitating cheddar and plat curd in the vat, and has won the certain praise of even the most xenophilic devotees of imported varieties. "We make old-fashioned rat-trap store cheese," says Mr. Coolidge in response to praise, "and we're the only purists in the business, I think."

Visitors welcome.

PLYMOUTH CHEESE COMPANY

P.O. Box 1
Plymouth, VT 05056

Bent's

JOSIAH BENT'S CELEBRATED WATER CRACKERS

In the rural town of Milton, Massachusetts, by the Blue Hills and the Neponset River, along which ran the trails of the few remaining Indians of the Ponkapog tribe, lived a man whose name has become a household word, not only in the United States, but the entire world. This man was Josiah Bent. He made the first Water Cracker bearing that name. At first they were made in small quantities, and he traveled from town to town selling the crackers from saddle bags across the horse's back, employing his own children to make them; he made good and provided for his family.

This was the infancy of the world-famous Water Cracker of the present day. . . .

Sounding for a moment like Longfellow when he was in school, the above "History of the Bent's Water Cracker" is the work of George H. Bent, one of Josiah's descendants. Written in 1914, it evokes the wish that the "powder keg that was Europe" might not have erupted so that the world could lavish its attention on the Bent's Water Cracker a while longer. But the Great War proved uncommonly cruel, and would spare the Water Cracker's fame no more than it would an Alsatiân farmhouse.

Some people might therefore be surprised to learn that the Josiah Bent Water Cracker never left us.

Hearty enough to have found its way onto tea traders and whaling ships, and genteel enough to have been an integral part of the nineteenth-century Boston Brahmin's dinner (served with cheese), the honest good flavor of the Bent's Water Cracker comes from its 183 years of using only pure spring water and stone-ground flour. No salt ever goes into one.

So if the current worldwide celebration of Triscuits is as unfathomable to you as it is to me, and if you think you'd like a cracker you can sink your teeth into ("provided you have good teeth," says the company), then try Josiah Bent's Water Crackers. Here's a recipe for cracker pudding which the Bent company provided:

G. H. Bent's 100-Year-Old Recipe for Common Cracker Pudding

1 pint (2 cups) cracker crumbs	1 tsp. salt
3 pints milk	½ tsp. cinnamon
1 cup sugar	1 Tbsp. butter
	1 cup raisins

Soak cracker crumbs in milk, and mix in sugar, salt, and cinnamon. Butter a deep-dish earthenware container, pour in crumbs and other already-mixed ingredients, and bake. While mixture is baking, puff up the raisins over steam, and after half an hour of baking, stir the raisins into the mixture, adding additional milk around the edges (not in the middle). Bake for another 2½ hours (maybe less).

Prices for Bent's Water Crackers (postage included): two packages, $4.81; four, $7.42; six, $10.05; eight, $13.26; ten, $15.28; twelve, $18.

G. H. BENT COMPANY

7 Pleasant Street
Milton, MA 02186
Tel. 617/698–5945

POLAND WATER

POLAND WATER **At the end of the eighteenth century, one Joseph Ricker of Poland Spring, Maine, lay dying.** To ease his fever, a boy was sent to fetch some water from the old glacial spring that had been discovered on the property in 1793. Near death, Joseph drank the mineral water and lived to tell the story for another fifty-two years.

In fact Joseph told his story so often and so well that before very long the Rickers were bottling Poland Water and distinguished visitors from the world over were finding their way to the Ricker's remote Yankee health spa. Word of the water's reputed curative powers spread and eventually created a broad European market for it. At the Columbian Exposition of 1893, Poland Water won the Medal of Excellence over "all the other waters of the world."

Known today as Poland Spring, the water is distributed only in the northeastern United States. It's bottled at the same icy granite source where it began nearly two centuries ago.

POLAND SPRING

777 West Putnam Avenue
P.O. Box 2313
Greenwich, CT 06836

NEW ENGLAND COB-SMOKED TURKEY AND HAM

Harrington's of Vermont is a century-old business famous for their hams and turkeys that are slowly smoked over maple wood and corncobs ("We don't use hickory, never have") in the nineteenth-century Vermont fashion.

Seasonal catalog of mail-order foods available.

HARRINGTON'S

618 Main Street
Richmond, VT 05477
Tel. 802/434-3411

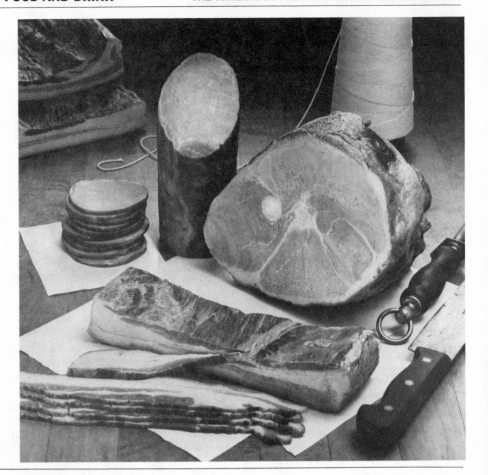

"1852 BRAND" HONEY

Honey was a common sweetener in both England and the American colonies, where honey bees were introduced (to Massachusetts Bay) in 1639. C. F. Diehnelt, a beekeeper in Germany before he came to Wisconsin, began the production of honey there in 1852. Today his descendants, who still own Honey Acres, preserve the memory of this event with their 1852 Brand honey, a "gourmet-quality" line packaged in replica nineteenth-century glass jars.

Price and dealer information available.

HONEY ACRES

Ashippun, WI 53003
Tel. 414/474-4411

PURE SORGHUM

Cumberland General Store's sorghum is grown, processed into syrup, and packed by their Amish neighbors. The new crop "comes ready" in the early fall, and the store may run out of it during the following year. The sorghum is put up in quart jars weighing 40 ounces (shipping weight: 6 lbs.).

Price: $5.95, F.O.B. Crossville, Tennessee.

"Wish and Want Book" available, $3.75.

CUMBERLAND GENERAL STORE

Route 3
Crossville, TN 38555
Tel. 615/484-8481

BOTTLED BEER
Portland's Blitz-Weinhard Brewery makes a regional beer—an important enough matter in this age of undifferentiated amber wash—and although it's the oldest brewery in continuous operation west of the Mississippi, it's not famous.

Blitz-Weinhard was founded in 1856 by Henry Weinhard, an immigrant from Germany, where he was a master brewer. The company was originally located in the Oregon Territory near Fort Vancouver, where the beer was quaffed with the kind of hearty appreciation one might expect from cavalrymen. But lest the Weinhard Brewery's early reputation rely solely on the undiscriminating palates of soldiers, it should also be noted that a contemporary newspaper described it as being "unsurpassed by any other native product of its kind."

As good as this standard brew seems to have been, it wasn't as good as Henry Weinhard's premium, which he prepared in small batches to serve to his friends. Using superior cascade hops, substantial amounts of the Klamath Basin's rare two-row barley, and their founder's nineteenth-century brewing techniques, Blitz-Weinhard has lately succeeded in reproducing Henry's premium. The beer has been christened "Henry Weinhard's Private Reserve," and bears a label design taken from the one on the founder's old beer glass. Because of its "handmade" character (they just about double the time required to brew standard beer) and the fact that it still can be made only in small quantities, Henry Weinhard's is still somewhat private. Patience may be required when ordering it from beyond the pale of the brewery's market area, but the rewards are worth it.

THE BLITZ-WEINHARD BREWERY

1133 West Burnside
Portland, OR 79209
Tel. 503/222-4351

TABASCO PEPPER SAUCE

As if geologically destined for historic importance, Avery Island rises dramatically out of the Louisiana Gulf Coast's marshy flats, some 162 feet of solid salt covered by tidewater forest. After the beginning of the War between the States, John Marsh Avery, scion of the family who owned Avery Island, worked its brine springs for salt to supply the Confederate Army. This made the island a military target, and in April 1863 Union troops under the command of Gen. N. P. Banks advanced from New Orleans (then under Federal control, having been taken a year earlier after a daring maneuver by Admiral David Farragut) to destroy the Avery Island salt mines. Judge D. D. Avery and his family were forced to flee into Texas for safety.

In the summer of 1865, with the war over, the Averys returned to ruins. Although everything on Avery Island had appeared to have been destroyed, in the midst of the old judge's trampled kitchen garden one plant defiantly flourished: the fiery capsicum (chili) pepper—an ancient Central American plant that had taken root there only a decade earlier. Edmund McIlhenny, the judge's son-in-law and a gourmet, was taken with the piquant flavor of the peppers and began to experiment with them—first crushing and straining them into a mash, then adding salt and vinegar, and aging the mixture in wooden barrels. The hot sauce he developed lent some needed zing to the plain fare of Reconstruction, and by 1868 Mr. McIlhenny was selling hundreds of one-ounce bottles of what he called Tabasco Pepper Sauce. Within two years the sauce received its patent, and by 1872 he had to open a London office to handle the European demand. Today the pepper sauce from the plant that was unbowed by Federal occupation is internationally acknowledged as an American classic.

Owing to the scarcity imposed by Reconstruction, pea- and bean-based meals were household staples. Hopping John, a popular Civil War-era dish (traditionally eaten on New Year's Day) benefits greatly from the use of Tabasco Pepper Sauce. This 1868 recipe was supplied by the McIlhenny Company:

Reconstruction Hopping John

1 lb. dried blackeye peas	2 Tbsp bacon fat or lard
3 pints cold water	2 medium onions, chopped
½ lb. sliced salt pork or bacon	1 cup uncooked long-grain rice
1 tsp. Tabasco Sauce	1½ cups boiling water
½ tsp. salt	

Cover the peas with cold water in a large kettle. Soak overnight. [The modern method for cooking dried peas involves bringing them to a boil, simmering them for two minutes, and letting them stand for an hour.] Add salt pork, Tabasco, and salt. Cover and cook over low heat about 30 minutes. Meanwhile, cook onions in bacon fat until yellow and add to peas with rice and boiling water. Cook until rice is tender and water is absorbed, about 20 to 25 minutes, stirring occasionally. Yield: about eight servings.

Recipe booklet available.

McILHENNY TABASCO COMPANY

Avery Island, LA 70513

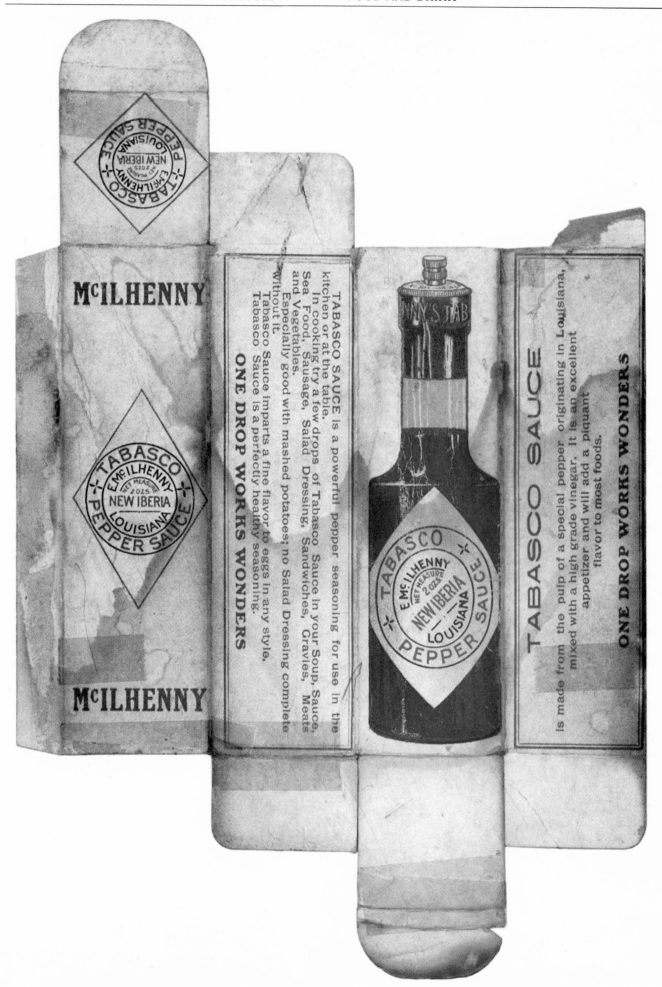

HAROLD'S CABIN CHARLESTON SPECIALTIES

Despite the rustic sound of its name Harold's Cabin doesn't operate in a copse of plantation pine, but out of a Charleston supermarket. Of course, Charleston being the place that it is, this supermarket isn't just any downtown foodliner. What it is, according to Harold's brochure, is "the fabled Meeting Street Piggly Wiggly."

There is perhaps no city on the continent that can offer a history buff more than does Charleston. But a *fabled* Piggly Wiggly? I hope the National Trust has looked into this.

"SLAVE BENNE" Regarding the history of the benne they sell, Harold's Cabin offers the following:

When slaves first came to the coastal areas of Georgia and South Carolina, they brought with them—as their most valued possession—a little handful of benne seed (Sesamum indicum) which they believed held for them the secret of health and good luck.

Planted near the slave quarters of the early plantations, benne became a traditional part of "the Old South." Cooks in the "Big House" kitchens knew just how to use this rich, spicy honey-colored seed to make delicious and exotic concoctions that have since been famous recipes of "dabuckra" [as whites are referred to in the Gullah dialect that was spoken by slaves and can still be heard in the Carolina low country].

Price: Dark or light benne, $1.49 per pound.

"SLAVE RECIPES" Harold's Cabin also sells a variety of candies once prepared by the plantation slaves of the Carolina low country.
Apricot Leather costs $3.50 for a quarter pound, $7 for a half pound.
Peach Leather costs the same.
Onslow's Benne Stick Candy costs $2.50 for half a pound.

PEPPER-COATED COUNTRY HAMS "Cured from a famous old plantation receipt." Average weight is 12 lbs.

Price: about $33.50. All prices F.O.B. Charleston, South Carolina.

Brochure of Charleston and Carolina low country specialties available.

HAROLD'S CABIN

In the Fabled Meeting Street Piggly Wiggly
445 Meeting Street
Charleston, SC 29403
Tel. 803/722-2766

BELL'S SEASONING The army-green herb seasoning for stuffing that for generations has been the very aroma of Thanksgiving was created by William G. Bell, a trained engineer who was a pioneer in the development of refrigeration. Bell founded his company in 1867 and owned it until 1917, when it was purchased by the D. L. Slade Company of Boston, a regional spice concern. Today both companies are owned by Brady Enterprises, Inc.
Throughout its history Bell's Seasoning has never changed its formula—including rosemary, thyme, marjoram, oregano, ginger, pepper, and Dalmatian sage, which contributes the most to its distinctive flavor.

Recipe booklet available.

THE WILLIAM G. BELL COMPANY

P.O. Box 99
East Weymouth, MA 02189
Tel. 617/337-5000

CZARIST VODKA

CZARIST VODKA On a visit to Paris in 1716, Czar Peter the Great was alarmed to find that he had only a single bottle of vodka remaining in his supply. "I don't know what to do," he wrote home to the czarina in despair. But the imposing czar (he stood six feet eight inches) was not undecided for long. Realizing that the situation offered him no choice, Peter immediately left his state duties and returned to the Kremlin. Vodka drinking was then unknown in the West, but today many Americans can sympathize with the czar's dilemma.

In those days the Russians drank their vodka (meaning, roughly, "dear, little water") icy cold from small silver or crystal glasses, throwing the stuff straight to the back of the throat in the belief that it was vodka's fumes that caused intoxication. Russians still prefer their national drink "with a tear," a phrase referring to the condensation that quickly forms on the outside of a chilled glass when the vodka is poured.

When Arsenii Petrovich Smirnoff began his small distillery in 1818, Moscow was still in ruins following Napoleon's invasion. Under the direction of his son Peter (Piotr Arsenievich) Smirnoff, the little distillery's vodka began to win many international medals and awards, and by the middle of the nineteenth century had been appointed purveyor to the czar, as well as to the king of Sweden. Because the vodka was so favored, the Smirnoff family was allowed to continue to make their Smirnoff de Czar even after the Russian government took over vodka production in 1894. But at the time of the Russian Revolution, Peter's son Vladimir was forced to escape to the West with only his family's prized recipes.

Today Smirnoff vodka is made in Hartford, Connecticut, by the Heublein Company. Their newly introduced Smirnoff de Czar vodka is a sweetened spirit, flavored with citrus (as was long traditional, particularly before charcoal distillation was invented), and packaged in a replica czarist-era bottle. The Smirnoff Company recommends that it be drunk in the traditional manner, "with a tear."

THE CZAR'S DISTILLER: PIERRE (PIOTR ARSENIEVICH) SMIRNOFF IN 1882.

WILBUR'S BREAKFAST

COCOA A pound and a half of Wilbur's Breakfast Cocoa, made according to the original 1894 formula, is available through the company in this replica of that era's tin can. Indicate preference for milk chocolate or "dark sweet chocolate buds."

Price: $9.95, delivered.

Chocolate products catalog available.

WILBUR CHOCOLATE COMPANY, INC.

48 North Broad Street
Lititz, PA 17543
Tel. 717/626–1131

123

942　SEARS, ROEBUCK & CO., Cheapest Supply House on Earth, Chicago.　CATALOGUE No. 111.

Fairy Bust Forms.

No. 18R4865 Fairy Bust Form. The lightest, most attractive bust form on the market; thoroughly hygienic, is adjusted to corset, conforms with every movement of the body, gives figure a graceful form. Made of fine quality lawn, edged with Valenciennes lace. Weight, only 2 ounces. Colors, black, white or drab. Price, each............25c

If by mail, postage extra, 4 cents.

No. 18R4867 Fairy Bust Form. Same style as above, made of fine quality Japanese silk, edged with silk Prussian binding. The only bust form that can be worn with evening dress. Weight, 2 ounces. Colors, black, white, pink or blue.

Price, each..............50c
If by mail, postage extra, 4 cents.

The Hygeia Bust Forms.

No. 18R4868 The Hygeia Bust Forms, made of the finest tempered braided wire. Oval in shape. Adjustable. Light as a feather. Comfortable and non-heating. They cannot injure the health nor retard development. Covered with fine lawn, and in such a way that the forms can be removed and the covering washed. A great improvement over any other form on the market. Covered in black if desired. Price..............44c

If by mail, postage extra, 5 cents.

The Parisienne Wire Bustle.

No. 18R4876 The Parisienne Woven Wire Bustle, made of highly tempered, black enameled, woven wire. The best shape, which it will always retain.
Price, each............19c

If by mail, postage extra, 5 cents.

Parisienne Hip Pad and Bustle.

No. 18R4880 The Parisienne Hip Pad and Bustle, made of best tempered, black enameled, woven wire with hip pads of padded cloth. Perfect in shape, and light in weight. Very durable.
Price, each............46c

If by mail, postage extra, each, 10 cents.

The Duchess Hip Pad and Bustle.

No. 18R4884 The Duchess Woven Wire Hip Pad and Bustle, made of best woven white wire, correct shape, very light and durable, and equal to any sold elsewhere for 75 cents or $1.00.
Price, each............39c

If by mail, postage extra, each, 11 cents.

The Lenox Glove Fitting Hip Bustle.

No. 18R4886 It rounds out the figure and produces the effect desired in prevailing fashions, extending over the hips very slightly and gracefully. Made of fine black tempered steel and cannot get out of shape, neither can it be detected. Suitable for rainy day skirts.
Price, each............37c

If by mail, postage extra, 10 cents.

CORSETS.

WE PRESENT TO OUR FRIENDS AND CUSTOMERS A REVISED ASSORTMENT OF CORSET SHAPES. The models and styles illustrated and described were selected to suit every taste, to fit every form, and the prices we name enable you to buy a high grade corset for less than you can get elsewhere.
WE SELL ONLY SUCH CORSETS AS WE CAN GUARANTEE AND RECOMMEND. They have been tested and tried by thousands of our customers, AND THEY BUY THEM AGAIN.
BE SURE AND GIVE YOUR WAIST MEASURE and observe the following rules in taking your measure: if you measure with corset on, deduct 2 to 2½ inches from waist sizes as shown on tape; this allows for spread of lacing in back. For example, if waist measure is 24 inches over corset, order size 21. If you take actual body measure, without corset or underclothing, you should deduct 3 or 4 inches, depending on how tight you lace. For example, if your waist measure is 25 inches without corset or underclothing, your size would be 21 or 22.
Allow 15 cents extra if you want a corset sent by mail.

Our Special Four-Hook Corset, 50 Cents.

50¢

No. 18R4900 Four-Hook Short Corset for medium form. This is a finely made corset of fine jeans, well boned and side steels, boned bust. A perfect fitting corset and meeting with popular favor. We predict an immense sale on this number, and especially at the price we quote. Colors, white, drab or black. Sizes, 18 to 30. Be sure and give waist measure.
Price, each............50c
If by mail, postage extra, each, 15 cents.

The Kabo Fitting Corset for the Average Figure, 88 Cents.

No. 18R4902 Long waist, medium form, five-hook. This is a corset made of fine French coutil strips of French sateen with silk edging. Molded on a perfect French model, stayed with double girdles at the waist lines. The bones and steels are made with a protecting covering for the ends, which prevents cutting through. A perfect fitting garment that will give entire satisfaction. Equal to the $1.50 kind elsewhere. Made in white, drab and black. Be sure to give waist measure.
Sizes, 18 to 30. Price, $0.90
Sizes, 31 to 36. Price, 1.15
If by mail, postage extra, each, 15 cents.

High Class Four-Hook Corset, 73 Cents.

$1.00 VALUE 73¢

No. 18R4904 Our new four-hook, 13-inch Front Steel Corset, for medium figure; the new medium length waist and medium low bust. Made of very fine quality sateen lined with French coutil, handsome lace trimming both top and bottom with baby ribbon drawn through lace. The best quality and most stylish fitting corset to be had, and the equal of any $1.00 corset today on the market. Colors, black, drab or white. Sizes, 18 to 30. Be sure to give waist measure. Price, each............73c
If by mail, postage extra, each, 15 cents.

Bias Gored, Straight Front, Perfect Fitting, Erect Form, 50 Cents.

50¢

No. 18R4906 A new, popular, bias gored, straight front corset, with set in gored busts. The latest low bust effect. Made of good imported coutil with extra heavy 10-inch front steel. This is equal to many of the regular $1.00 straight front corsets sold elsewhere. Colors, white or drab. Sizes, 18 to 30. Always give waist measure.
Price, each............50c
If by mail, postage extra, each, 15 cents.

Medium Figure, Erect Form, Full Gored, Straight Front, French Modeled Corset, 82 Cents.

82¢

No. 18R4996 A full gored, straight front, French modeled corset, adapted to the slight and medium figures, affording freedom to the respiratory organs, possessing exceptional fitting qualities for figures that possess fine outlines of form, embodying perfect workmanship. Materials, drab and white coutil and sateen. Equal to the $1.25 kind. Always give waist measure. Sizes, 18 to 30.
Price, each............82c
If by mail, postage extra, each, 15 cents.

No Brass Eyelets.

88¢

Ladies' Straight Front Corset, made of the best quality of corset jeans and boned with Kabo, with the looped lacer—no brass eyelets. Lace trimmed top and bottom. The straight front corset gives the military figure and the desired fullness at back and over hips. The Kabo straight front has all the good points. We are placing this corset on sale, value equal to the regular $1.50 style as sold elsewhere. Colors, black, white or drab. Sizes, 18 to 30. Be sure and give waist measure. Price, each............88c
If by mail, postage extra, each, 15 cents.

Flexibone, French Model Military Figure, Suitable for the Average Shape, $1.33.

$1.33

No. 18R4912 A Bias Cut Full Gored Corset, in which are combined the qualities of perfect workmanship, durability and graceful shape. This garment is designed to mold the figure into graceful and well proportioned outlines, at the same time allowing the greatest freedom to the muscles. Has low bust, long skirt, with tabs for hose supporters. Made in fine coutil, drab and white, and in black sateen. Trimmed with handsome lace and ribbon. Sizes, 18 to 30. Be sure and give waist measure.
Price, each............$1.33
If by mail, postage extra, each, 15 cents.

Clothes make the man. Naked people have little or no influence upon society.

　　　　　　　　—Mark Twain

"BOILED" COLLARLESS SHIRTS

The sombrero and the flannel shirt he scorned and sported a derby and "biled" goods instead.
　　　　—Outing, February 1892

Taking their name (in part) from the method used to launder them, late-nineteenth-century dress shirts generally had detachable collars. As the above quotation indicated, these fancy shirts were often curiously favored by cowboys for working garments. Red River Outfitters of Tujunga, California, makes boiled collarless shirts that are virtually identical to those made from the 1870s through the turn of the century. These come in pinstriped patterns of red on white and blue on white; they button all the way down the front and feature a small white neckband with collar-button holes.

Available in neck sizes 15, 15½, 16, 16½, and 17 inches.

Price: $24.95 (plus $3 for shipping and handling).

Catalog of frontier clothing, western, and military Americana available, $2.

RED RIVER FRONTIER OUTFITTERS

P.O. Box 241
Tujunga, CA 91042
Tel. 213/352–0177

PIONEER SHIRT A very democratic shirt, this pioneer garment was worn during the early nineteenth century "by most anyone of the period from blacksmiths to men of our government." It is comfortable and roomy, with dropped shoulder seams and wooden buttons. Made of unbleached muslin or lightweight unbleached cotton Osnaburg.

Sizes extra-small to extra-large.
Price: $22.95, ppd.

ALICE'S COUNTRY COTTAGE

Box 3
Rohrersville, MD 21779
Tel. 301/432–5527

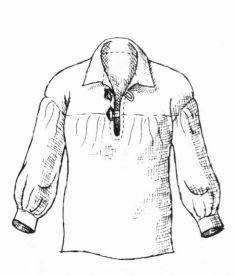

CLOTHING FROM LA PELLETERIE DE FORT DE CHARTRES

Pat Tearney runs La Pelleterie (French for "a fur-trading establishment") de Fort de Chartres along with his wife Karalee. Their business specializes in the accurate replication of historical garments, particularly those of the French and Indian War period (1754–1763) and the era of early westward expansion, defined by Mr. Tearney as occurring between 1820 and 1850. The Tearneys enjoy a solid reputation for historical accuracy that has garnered them assignments consulting with museums in St. Louis and San Diego, where Pat helped put together the Bicentennial display at the Museum of Man. The Tearneys were also costume makers on the set of *The Mountain Men*, a film that starred Charleton Heston and Brian Keith. Examples of the Tearneys' handiwork will be found throughout this book, the more rugged among them in the section on Early Frontier Items.

BROADFALL TROUSERS (circa 1830) Very similar to

trousers worn in the paintings of George Caleb Bingham (1811–1879), La Pelleterie's broadfall trousers are after a pair in the Chester County, Illinois, Historical Society collection.

Prices: linen, $75; fustian, $80; wool, $80; buckskin, $135.

ST. LOUIS TROUSERS Fashionable dur-

ing the period from 1810 to 1830, the St. Louis trouser was an early type of slit-fly pantaloon that eventually replaced drop-front pants.

Prices: linen, $85; fustian, $90; wool, $90; buckskin, $145.

WOMEN'S BODICE A women's waistcoat

available in either linen or wool, fully lined with linen with front lacing.

Price: $85.

MERCHANT'S
SHIRT Full-bodied with a fold-over collar, this shirt was part of the standard apparel for men during the eighteenth and early nineteenth centuries.

Prices: linen, $39.50 (kit, $31.50); Osnaburg (a heavily woven cotton), $29.50 (kit, $19.50).

1815 WAISTCOAT This
vest, following the original design, is cut square at the waist and fits snugly there. The collar is of a high-standing style, and the large lapels stand out when worn.

Price: $85.

GERMAN-STYLE
CAP Similar in style to those worn by German immigrants to rural Pennsylvania during the nineteenth century. Made of fine linen.

Price: $18.95.

The above items each require $3 to cover the cost of UPS shipment when ordered within the continental U.S.

Catalog of historical clothing and accessories available, $3 (refundable with purchase of $30 or more).

**LA PELLETERIE DE
FORT DE CHARTRES**

*P.O. Box 267
Chester, IL 62233
Tel. 618/826–4334*

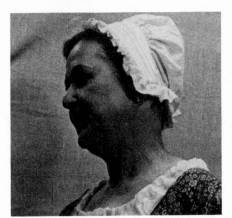

SHAKER CLOTHING

SHAKER CLOAKS

Hancock Shaker Village's cloaks are scrupulously fashioned in the traditional Shaker style but fit in well with contemporary dress. The entire cloak, including shoulder cape and the pleated, lined hood, is made from 100 percent wool melton cloth. The cloaks have been cut very full, so the Hancock Village suggests that they be judged by shoulder width. The standard lengths are 52 and 55 inches, but special orders are accepted.

Specify size (small, medium, or large) and color (navy blue, forest green, or maroon).

Price: $165 (plus $4 for shipping).

SHAKER SHIRT

This pattern was adapted from a nineteenth-century brethren's dress shirt and is made of 100 percent cotton broadcloth.

Women's sizes: small, medium, large, and extra-large. Men's sizes: small, medium, and large. White only.

Price: $42.50 (plus $4 for shipping).

"Products of Industry" catalog available.

HANCOCK SHAKER VILLAGE

U.S. Route 20
Hancock, MA 01237
Tel. 413/443-0188

AMAZON DRYGOODS' LADIES' AND GENTLEMEN'S FURNISHINGS

SUNBONNET

A woman dressed in bright-red calico . . . and shingle sunbonnet, sat there sewing on a muslin of gay colors.
—Sara T. D. Robinson, Kansas: Its Exterior and Interior Life, *1856*

Janet Burgess of Amazon Drygoods relates this bit of sunbonnet lore:

The original from which this pattern is made is 200 years old. The style was adapted from the bonnet that the French brought to America, although theirs were, without exception, starched pure white. We brought color and calico to the sunbonnet, thereby fashioning a distinctly American head covering. When you are inside its deep brim, you'll never wonder what people once did for lack of sunglasses. Fold the brim back on overcast days. The sunbonnet was worn in parts of the U.S. from the late eighteenth century to the Second World War.

Print pattern. Available in baby, child, and women's sizes.

Price: $2.50 (plus $1.50 for shipping).

MAN'S FROCK COAT

The frock coat first appeared on the continent during the 1840s in marked contrast to the ostentatious pinched-waist and padded-shoulder coats of the previous decade. Amazon Drygoods' version, made of black gabardine with black collar and cuffs, is in the long "Abe Lincoln style" of the mid-to-late nineteenth century.

Sizes: 36 to 48. (The coats are easily altered and run large, so Janet Burgess suggests that you order a size smaller than you normally would.)

Price: $55.75 (plus $3 for shipping).

VICTORIAN CORSET

Back lacings, front "busc" closing, and thirty-seven bones. White. Washable, with lace and ribbon trim. To order, send waist measurement.

Price: $59.95 (plus $3 for shipping).

"GAY NINETIES" BATHING COSTUMES

In washable cottons for ladies and gents. The ladies' three-piece outfit consists of a tunic top with a middie collar and tie, ruffled pantalettes, and a matching mobcap. Color availability varies, so state preferences.

Sizes: small (8–10), medium (12–14), and large (17–18).

The men's bathing suit is a striped, two-piece affair. It has a long top, with elbow-length sleeves and pants that extend to below the knees. State color preference.

Sizes: small (36–38), medium (39–41), large (42–44).

Prices: ladies' bathing costume, $38.95 (plus $3 for shipping); men's bathing costume, $32.50 (plus $3 for shipping).

GIBSON GIRL SKIRT AND BLOUSE

"The Gibson Girl," as defined by Stuart Berg Flexner in his book *I Hear America Talking* (Van Nostrand Reinhold, 1978), was the

typical, idealized 1890s girl as portrayed by (and in a large measure created by) illustrator Charles Dana Gibson in his many drawings for such popular magazines as the old Life, Scribner's, *and* Collier's Weekly. *The Gibson girl's soft, wide pompadour, parasol, and clothing influenced styles until the late 1930s. Gibson drew her in what became known as a* Gibson girl blouse, *a starched, tailored* shirtwaist *(an 1879 word) with leg-of-mutton sleeves and a high collar with an ascot tie at the neck.*

Amazon Drygoods' Gibson Girl blouse is available in sizes 32 through 42. An accompanying skirt (appropriately black and floor length) has a "flattering four gore skirt back and self ruffle" in waist sizes 24 through 42.

Prices: Gibson Girl blouse, $26.25; Gibson Girl skirt, $29.95 (plus $3 for shipping either, or both when ordered together).

40-page catalog, Christmas catalog, and seasonal mailings available, $2.

AMAZON VINEGAR & PICKLING WORKS DRYGOODS

Department AH
2218 East 11th Street
Davenport, IA 52803
Tel. 319/322–6800

TOP HAT AND DERBY

Many [English tourists wear] various modifications of the Derby, with long, light veils draped thereon with studied carelessness.
—*Walter G. Marshall,* Through America, *1881*

The top hat was the essential piece of nineteenth-century head covering, first appearing in modified form as a kind of English equestrian crash helmet during the late eighteenth century, and still very proper for formal dress early in the twentieth.

Amazon Drygoods' top hat comes in black or gray wool felt with a black band, in sizes medium, large, and extra-large. (Janet Burgess suggests that you either provide your hat size when ordering or send along a piece of string cut to size.) First color choice may be unavailable. Derby hat in black only.

Price: $13.75 (plus $3 for shipping).

LADIES' SHOES

The expansive crinoline skirts worn during the 1840s were supposedly symbolic of the unapproachability of women. But in their constant state of agitation, there was also something seductive about the enormously expanded skirts, although they never revealed more than a glimpse of the wearer's ankle. This may be why it was during this period that the diminutive slipper-like shoes worn by women began to be replaced by high-topped boots, sensible shoes that would last until the Armistice.

Made of black kid leather, Amazon Drygoods' nineteenth-century-style ladies' shoes have laced tops, leather soles, and 1½-inch heels. They are American made and fully lined for comfort.

Sizes: 6AA to 10AA, 6½A to 10A, 5B to 10B, and 4 to 10 in C, D, E, EE, and EEE widths. (Janet Burgess suggests that you send along a foot tracing as the shoes tend to run large.)

Price: $68, ppd. (60-inch replacement laces, $2).

Sewing Patterns

OLD WORLD SEWING PATTERN COMPANY

The Old World Sewing Pattern Company features a line of full-size men's and women's patterns designed to recreate, with complete historical accuracy, prominent fashions of the nineteenth century. Printed on long-fiber brown paper (the very type used during the 1800s for this purpose), their current line comprises seven female and two male patterns, including an 1805 Empire gown (reflecting the Napoleonic curtailment of extravagance in French fashion), an 1840s men's long frock coat with trousers, an 1860 crinoline dress, and an 1870 bustle dress.

Women's sizes: 8, 10, and 12. Men's sizes: 38 and 40.

Price: $9.95 each.

Catalog available, 75¢.

OLD WORLD SEWING PATTERN COMPANY

Route 2, Box 103
Cold Spring, MN 56320

OLD WORLD
SEWING'S

CALICO DAY DRESS

Thar war Mam, fust on one side, then on t'other, her new caliker swelled up around her like a bear with the dropsy.
—Henry Clay Lewis, Odd Leaves from the Life of a Louisiana Swamp Doctor, *1890*

During the 1880s day dresses were typically high in the neck and finished with a "runching" or large bow of tulle (a thin, fine net of silk).

FOLKWEAR PATTERNS

Founded in 1975, Folkwear was the first company to provide sewers with historical patterns.

Folkwear's pattern makes a dress (or blouse) that is fitted in back and adjustable in front. Optional yoke and shoulder ruffles. Sizes 6–16.

VICTORIAN SHIRT

A pattern for a late-nineteenth-century men's dress shirt described by Folkwear as "also today's full 'tuxedo' shirt for women's 6–22, men's 32–46."

EDWARDIAN UNDERGARMENTS

Everything was somewhat larger than life during the Edwardian period that followed the turn of the century. Edward VII's reported taste for "city men, millionaires . . . American heiresses and pretty women" was in part reflected by the appearance of frilly cotton underthings sometimes called flimsies, or trousseau sets.

Folkwear's Edwardian undergarment patterns are available in women's sizes 6–16.

Literature and price list available.

FOLKWEAR PATTERNS

Box 3798
San Rafael, CA 94912
Tel. 415/457–0252

TRADITIONAL NIGHTCAP

A homemade red flannel nightcap is periodically offered by Putnam Antiques of Middlefield, Massachusetts. Hand-finished with tassel.

PUTNAM ANTIQUES

3 Pond Road
Middlefield, MA 01243

MEN'S LONG UNDERWEAR

The Crazy Crow Trading Post offers authentic 100 percent cotton red long-handled underwear (or long johns) for $20.95.

Catalog available, $2.

CRAZY CROW TRADING POST

P.O. Box 314
Denison, TX 75020
Tel. 214/463–1366

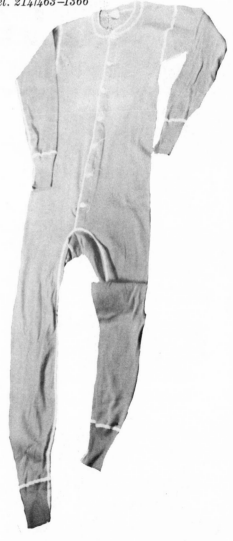

130

SEARS, ROEBUCK & CO., Cheapest Supply House on Earth, Chicago. CATALOGUE No. 111. 327

EARLY FRONTIER ITEMS

A Few Words About Gun Wads.

There is considerable difference of opinion among shooters about the best method of loading shells, with reference to the wadding. We have gone into this matter extensively and our experience is as follows: That if you place one cardboard wad next to the powder, then use one or two of ¼-inch black edge wads (according to the length of the shell), after this put another cardboard wad over the black edge wads, then put in your shot and a thin cardboard wad over the shot, leaving about ¼-inch of the shell to be crimped, you will get as good results as you will from any fancy loading, all other things being equal. **When loading with nitro powder** it is a good plan to put a thin cardboard wad next to the powder, then you may use either one or two of ¼-inch black edge or may use one or two dry felt wads (wads which contain no lubricant), either one of these will produce good results. **The object of putting in a cardboard wad next to the powder,** is that the powder will not tear the felt wad badly as the cardboard wad protects the felt wad. **The object of placing a thin cardboard wad next to nitro powder** is to prevent the nitro powder from absorbing the lubricant of the felt wads which is said to deteriorate the force of the powder. In our opinion the above methods of loading will give you a good average result. Should you not get good results from these two methods, the fault is not with your loading, but with the boring of your gun barrel. **The main scientific principles in shooting is to confine the gas generated by the burning powder behind the shot;** if loading as above mentioned does not give the proper pattern we advise you to try one size larger felt wads. For instance, if you do not get good results with No. 12 black edge wads, try No. 11 wads, for it sometimes happens that the diameter of one gun barrel is a mere trifle larger than another. **If you are doing rapid shooting,** enough so as to cause the barrel of your gun to become heated, bear in mind that this heating process expands the bore of the gun, though not enough to notice it with the naked eye, still enough to impair the shooting qualities. If you have ever so fine a gun and the [illegible] barrel becomes heated, do not blame the gun [illegible] is caused by the [illegible] heat.

Cardboard [illegible]

Made from [illegible]

[illegible] Cardboard Wads, to be used next to the powder, but may be used over the shot also. Weight, about 1½ pounds per 1000.

	Per box of 250	Per 1000
7 or 8-gauge wads	5½c	21c
[illegible]	[illegible]	[illegible]

[illegible] postage extra, box, 5c

No. 6R33[illegible] [illegible] Wads [illegible] the [illegible]ot, w[illegible] per [illegible]00. [illegible] spe[illegible]

	Per box of 250	Per 1000
9 or 10-gauge	5c	18c
11 to 20-gauge	4c	15c

If by mail, po[illegible]ge extra, box, 5c

Black Edg[illegible] [illegible] Inch [illegible]

No. 6R333[illegible] [illegible] black powde[illegible] but may [illegible] over smokele[illegible] powder [illegible] you put a ca[illegible] wad next [illegible] powder. We[illegible] 3¼ pounds, according to size.

	Per box	Per 1000
6-gauge, box of 250, weight, 9 oz.	24c	96c
7-gauge, box of 250, weight, 9 oz.	17c	65c
8-gauge, box of 250, weight, 8 oz.	17c	65c
9 or 10-gauge, box of 250, weight, 8 oz.	14c	56c
11 to 20-gauge, box of 250, weight, 7 oz.	12c	48c

If by mail, postage extra, per box, 5 cents.

Black Edge ¼-Inch Wads.

No. 6R3340 For use over black powder, but may be used over smokeless powder also if you put a card wad next to the powder. Weight, per 1000, 2¼ pounds. Packed 250 in a box.

	Per box	Per 1000
9 or 10-gauge	22c	85c
11 or 12-gauge	18c	72c

If by mail, postage extra, per box, 13 cents.

Black Edge Wads, ⅜ Inch Thick.

No. 6R3350 Black Edge Wads, ⅜ inch thick, for use over black powder, but may be used over smokeless also. One of these is equal to three of the ⅛-inch wads. 125 in a box.

	Per box	Per 1000
9 or 10-gauge	28c	$2.20
11 or 12-gauge	25c	2.00

If by mail, postage extra, per box, 14 cents.

NOTICE—In 12-gauge brass shells, use 10-gauge wads. In paper shells, use wads the same size as shell. Always put the wad down to place flat and evenly, otherwise the shooting quality of your gun will be greatly impaired.

Nitro Felt Wads.

Made of elastic felt, soft and pliable, unlubricated, perfectly dry, and free from all greasy matter, for use over nitro powder. 125 in a box, ⅛, ¼ and ⅜ inch thick.

			Per box	Per 1000
No. 6R3360	⅛-inch	9 or 10-gauge	7c	56c
		11 or 12-gauge	6c	48c
No. 6R3370	¼-inch	9 or 10-gauge	11c	84c
		11 or 12-gauge	9c	72c

If by mail, postage extra, per box, 10 cents.

Pink Edge Felt Wads, ⅛ Inch Thick.

No. 6R3410 For use over black powder, but may be used over smokeless powder if you put a card wad next to the powder. Weight per 1000, 1¾ to 3 pounds, according to size. These wads come 250 in a box.

	Per Box	Per 1000
6-gauge, pink edge, per box of 250	35c	$1.40
7-gauge, pink edge, per box of 250	30c	1.20
8-gauge, pink edge, per box of 250	30c	1.20
9 or 10-gauge, pink edge, per box of 250	25c	1.00
11 to 20-gauge, pink edge, per box of 250	20c	.80

If by mail, postage extra, per box, 10 cents.

Pink Edge Felt Wads, ¼ Inch Thick.

No. 6R3420 For use over black powder, but may be used over smokeless powder if you put a card wad next to the powder. 250 in a box.

	Per box	Per 1000
11 or 12-gauge	25c	$1.00
9 or 10-gauge	30c	1.20

If by mail, postage extra, per box, 13 cents.

White Felt Wads, ⅜ Inch Thick.

No. 6R3430 For use over black powder, but may be used over smokeless powder if you put a card wad next to the powder. One of these is equivalent to three ⅛-inch wads. Weight, per 1000, 5 to 6 pounds. 125 wads in a box.

	Per box	Per 1000
7-gauge, box of 125	40c	$3.20
8-gauge, per box of 125	40c	3.20
9 or 10-gauge, per box of 125	30c	2.40
11, 12, 16, 20-gauge, per box of 125	28c	2.20

If by mail, postage extra, per box, 18 cents.

SMOKELESS POWDERS.

A FEW VALUABLE POINTERS ABOUT NITRO POWDERS.

1—**Don't guess at the quantity; measure it with a good measure and you won't have anything to regret afterwards. It is weighed by apothecary weight.**

2—**Use wads enough to confine the gas produced by the explosion, or there will not be force enough to carry the shot.**

3—**Don't use a too heavy load of nitro powder; it's not good for the gun.**

NOTICE—**Be careful in loading nitro powders. Don't deviate from the directions on the powder [illegible]**

[illegible]OTICE—Smokeless powder is only half as [illegible]vy as black powder; for instance, if you have a [illegible]ound black powder can you will fill it with [illegible]-half pound of smokeless powder.

SCHULTZE Smokeless Powders.

This is one of the very best and safest of nitro powders. Can be loaded with a black powder and shot measure.

Schultze Powders for shotguns, very little smoke.

No. 6R3501 1 pound can (actual weight ½ pound.) 54c

No. 6R3502 10-pound can (actual weight 5 pounds.) $4.86

Follow the directions on can for loading.

E. C. Smokeless Powder.

E. C. Shotgun Powder, little or no smoke. It is becoming more popular every year.

No. 6R3505 1 pound can (actual weight ½ pound). Price, per can 54c

No. 6R3506 10-pound can (actual weight 5 pounds). Price, per can $4.86

Great care must be taken in loading these powders to obtain the best results. Directions on each can.

The great advantage of Du Pont's Smokeless, Schultze and E.C. Powders over common powders is the fact that there is much less recoil and no smoke to prevent seeing game or target for second shot.

NOTICE. Don't load shotgun powder in rifle cartridges. When loading smokeless powder by weight, use an apothecary scale, which weighs 5,750 grains to the pound.

DU PONT Smokeless or Nitro Powder.

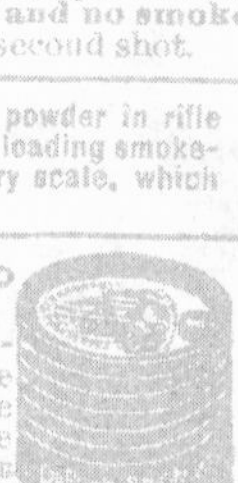

The Du Pont Smokeless Nitro Powder is a fine grain, hard powder, safe and reliable. It may be loaded the same as black powder, except the quantity should be less; use paper shells only. If you use a regular black powder measure, load in 16-gauge 2 to 2¼ drams; in 12-gauge 2½ to 3 drams; in 10-gauge 2¾ to 3½ drams. This is one of the most satisfactory nitro powders.

No. 6R3510 12½-pound can, equal in bulk to 25 pounds of black powder $11.38

No. 6R3511 6¼-pound can, equal in bulk to 12½ pounds of black powder $6.09

No. 6R3512 3⅛-pound can, equal in bulk to 6¼ pounds of black powder $3.10

No. 6R3513 ½-pound can, equal in bulk to 1 pound of black powder 54c

NOTICE—All nitro or smokeless powder can be shipped by express or freight, either alone or with other goods.

Du Pont's Smokeless Rifle Powder.

No. 6R3514 Du Pont's Smokeless Rifle Powder, No. 1, for rifle cartridges from 25-20 to 45-90; see directions for loading with each can. This powder is put up in 1-pound cans only.

Price, per can (actual weight, ½ pound) $1.00

No. 6R3515 Du Pont's Smokeless Rifle Powder, No. 2, for all pistol cartridges and rifle cartridges 38-40 and 44-40; directions with can, 1-pound cans only. Price, per can (actual weight, ⅝ lb.) $1.00

No. 6R3518 Du Pont's Smokeless Special, for 30-caliber rifles, 1-pound can (actual weight, ½ lb). $1.25

BLACK POWDER.

Du Pont Rifle and Shotgun Black Powder.

Our Special Prices for Du Pont's Special Powder ought to induce every buyer of powder to give us his order. **OUR LOW PRICES** are based on actual cost to manufacture with but our one small profit added.

THIS DU PONT'S POWDER IS GUARANTEED, you can get nothing better in black powder for all around use.

Remember we are absolutely headquarters for these powders and they are made specially for us. Cheap powders do not give good penetration and are liable to lead the inside of the gun, but these powders are made from the best ingredients which go into the manufacture of powder.

This powder is made especially for us from the best grades of refined saltpetre, willow or elder charcoal, refined sulphur and nitre.

Don't buy cheap powder which gives poor penetration. Pay a few cents more and get better satisfaction.

Cut showing size of grains of different powders. Hazard Powder same price as Du Pont.

The Messrs. Du Pont & Co. are the oldest powder makers and have the most extensive works in the country. We consider their powder the best. Every pound warranted good and clean. In air tight metallic kegs; **Fg is coarse; FFg is medium and FFFg is fine grain. (See cut.)**

When ordering state which grain you prefer.

PRICES.

No. 6R3530 In F, FF or FFF grain, per 25-lb. keg $4.00

No. 6R3532 In F, FF or FFF grain, per 12½-lb. keg $3.25

No. 6R3534 In F, FF or FFF grain, per 6¼-lb. keg $1.25

No. 6R3536 In F, FF or FFF grain, per 1-lb. can 30c

Powder cannot be sent by express. It must be sent by freight on regular powder trains. Freight charges on powder are double first class.

THERE ARE 256 DRAMS OF BLACK POWDER TO THE POUND IF YOU WISH TO LOAD YOUR OWN SHELLS.

Du Pont Choke Bore Black Powder.

Excellent powder made especially for choke bored guns. See illustration.

No. 6R3540 Kegs, Nos. 5 or 7 grain, 25 lbs. $5.00

No. 6R3542 ½-kegs, Nos. 5 or 7 grain, 12½ lbs. 2.75

No. 6R3544 ¼-kegs, Nos. 5 or 7 grain, 6¼ lbs. 1.50

No. 6R3546 1-lb. cans, Nos. 5 or 7 grain .... .35

NOTE—**We furnish Hazard powder in the same numbers and same size kegs at the same price as Du Pont's when desired. Hazard powder is good.**

Du Pont Eagle Duck.

This is the very finest grade of black powder.

No. 6R3550 Kegs, Nos. 1, 2 or 3 grain, 25 lbs. $8.00

No. 6R3552 ½-kegs, Nos. 1, 2 or 3 grain, 12½ pounds 4.25

No. 6R3554 ¼-kegs, Nos. 1, 2 or 3 grain, 6¼ pounds 2.25

No. 6R3556 1-lb cans, Nos. 1, 2 or 3 grain .... .45

Powder cannot be shipped by express, but must be sent in separate kegs or cases and marked "gunpowder," and sent by freight on regular powder trains. Freight charges are double first class rates on powder.

Du Pont's Special V. G. P. Brand.

No. 6R3560 The New Trap Powder—black, moist, quick, clean and strong (not a nitro). 6¼-pound kegs ....$1.25 12½-pound kegs $2.25

Special Blasting Powder.

No. 6R3565 Du Pont Blasting Powder. In ordering state for what purpose it is wanted. Price, per 25-pound keg ....$1.6[illegible]

DO NOT CUT, TEAR OR MUTILATE THIS CATALOGUE. Order by number and we wil[l] know just what is wanted. Pre[serve] this book carefully. **IT IS YOUR GUIDE TO ECONOMICAL BUYING.**

CRAZY CROW HEADGEAR

COONTAIL CAP

As for . . . plains-men and coon-skin-capped hunters . . . of the "West" . . . you see no more of them.
> —Harper's Magazine, *April 1881*

And will not, it might've been added, until another century passes and the current revival of black-powder hunting begins.

Crazy Crow's cap is not referred to as "coonskin" because, while only genuine animal fur is used to make it, the tail is the raccoon's only contribution. Lined.

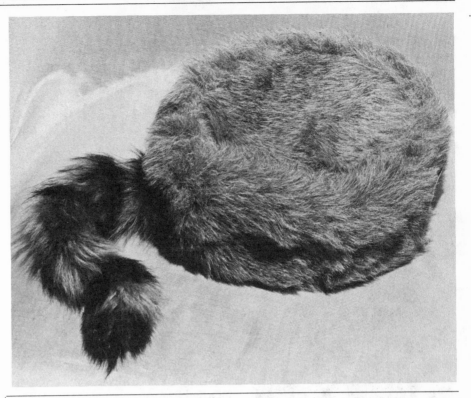

BEAR HAT KIT

When first my father settled here,
T'was then the frontier line:
The panther's scream filled night
*   with fear*
And bears preyed on the swine.
> —Abraham Lincoln, "The Bear Hunt"

While during the nineteenth century bears preyed on swine, many would have it that the reverse is true today. Crazy Crow Trading Post will provide you with enough black bear fur from tanned hides along with instructions to make the type of bear cap worn when young Lincoln was a poet.

Catalog available, $2.

CRAZY CROW TRADING POST

P.O. Box 314
Denison, TX 75020
Tel. 214/463–1366

CAPOTES

Found a small red capot hung upon a tree; this my interpreter informed me was a sacrifice by some Indian to the bon Dieu.
> —Zebulon M. Pike, An Account of Expeditions to the Sources of the Mississippi, *1810*

The capote is a long, loose-fitting blanket coat that was worn by the coureur des bois (the usually unlicensed traders of the eighteenth-century French-Canadian frontier), voyageurs (eighteenth- and nineteenth-century canoe-borne French trappers of the North American West), and long hunters. Along with their kindred but more elaborately tailored "duffle coats," these fringed and hooded (or collared) coats are strikingly colorful garb, well suited to life in the woods.

Several types of capotes are made by Northwest Traders of Dayton, Ohio: Frontier, Coureur des Bois, and Bourgeois ("booshway," or buffalo scout). Prices are available on request.

Brochure of frontier clothing, accouterments, and supplies available.

NORTHWEST TRADERS

4999 Packard Drive
Box 24305 H.H. Br.
Dayton, OH 45424
Tel. 513/236-3930

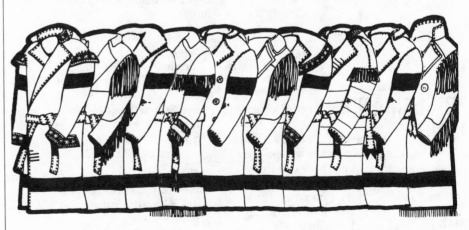

Pat Tearney and his wife Karalee own and operate La Pelleterie, a trading post at the Fort de Chartres Historic Site in Prairie du Rocher, Illinois. They have been offering historical reproductions for over a quarter of a century, and have supplied numerous museums and movie companies. They custom-manufacture all their garments, and authenticate everything they sell.

LA PELLETERIE'S "FUR TRADE ERA" CLOTHING

RIFLEMAN'S COAT

The buckskin rifleman's coat may have been worn as early as the French and Indian War; it was certainly still in use as late as the 1860s. The rifleman's coat was as popular with the mountain men of the 1830s as it was with the long hunters of the East. La Pelleterie's coat is a composite design derived from period drawings and from an original at the Valentine Museum in Richmond, Virginia. **The rifleman's coat** hangs to the lower thigh, and is fringed at the collar, cuffs, bottom, and front and back sleeve seams. The attached cape is also fringed. These were often greased with bear oil for further weatherproofing. There are no buttons, as this style was meant to be closed with a sash.

Price: $225.

TRAPPER'S SHIRT

Pat Tearney derived the design of his trapper's shirts from the portraits of George Caleb Bingham (1811–1879), whose citation in Eleanor S. Greenhill's *Dictionary of Art* (New York: Dell Publishing Company, 1974) reads in part:

> "To the following year [1845] belongs the celebrated canvas, Fur Traders Descending the Missouri . . . in which the turquoise shirts of the two traders in the dugout and the subtle luminosity of the mists rising from the river—at once brilliant and soft—testify to his contact with sophisticated models."

Prices: linen (white, rust, blue), $39.50 (kit, $31.50); Osnaburg, $29.50 (kit, $19.50); calico, $29.50 (kit, $19.50).

RIFLEMAN'S SHIRT

In place of a coat, a slipover buckskin shirt such as one following an original at the Fort Ticonderoga Museum, was sometimes worn. This shirt is typical of those worn by eastern long hunters during the late eighteenth century.

Price: $185.

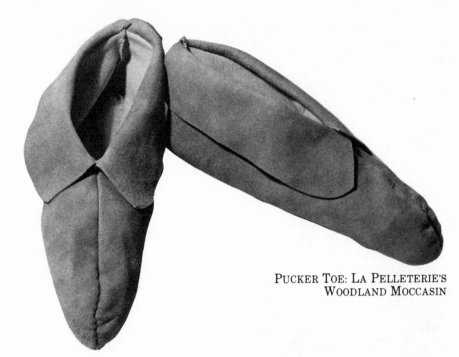

MOCCASINS Moccasins were the universal footwear of the fur trade era.

Customarily insulated with dried leaves or deer hair, they were quite comfortable in cold weather. But like any buckskin clothing, this was not the case when it was wet; after being soaked with water, moccasins were, according to one contemporary description, "just a decent way of going barefooted."

La Pelleterie's moccasins are made of soft tanned cowhide (the soles are of tough chrome tan leather), and come in varieties styled after those worn by "plains and woodlands Indians from New York to the Rocky Mountain beaver country."

Woodland: The eastern style—often called pucker toe—is made of heavy buckskin and has a hand-sewn center seam.
    Price: $32.50.

Rendezvous: An early plains moccasin popular ever since the early nineteenth century. Authentically soft soled.
    Price: $22.50.

WOOLEN TOQUE

Pronounced "tewk," this headgear was worn by the French voyageurs, the coureurs des bois, and early militiamen. Available in white, red, and blue.
    Price: $24.

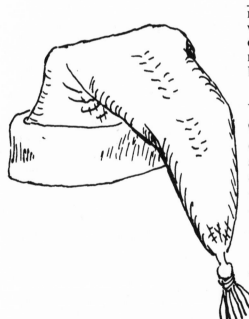

Within the continental U.S., add $3 to cover the cost of UPS shipment.

Catalog of historical clothing and accouterments available, $3 (refundable with purchases of $30 or more).

Visitors are welcome to the La Pelleterie shop at the Fort de Chartres State Historic Site in Prairie du Rocher, Illinois.

LA PELLETERIE DE FORT DE CHARTRES

P.O. Box 627
Chester, IL 62233
Tel. 618/826-4334

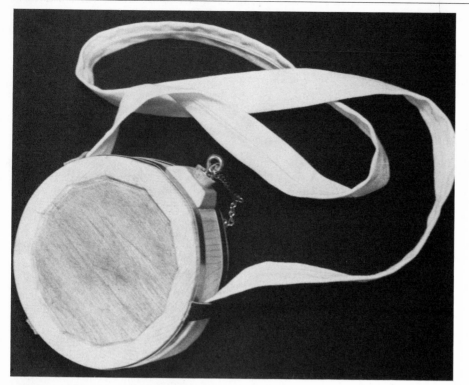

CRAZY CROW CAMP GEAR

WOODEN CANTEENS Crazy Crow's wooden canteen is a hand-made replica of the type used during the American Revolution and up through the Civil War. It's made of white pine, and furnished with a cloth strap and iron bands.

Also available is a single-quart wooden barrel canteen (paraffin-line) replicating one used during the eighteenth century.

HUDSON BAY COMPANY RATION BOX

Constructed of solid pine, this grub box precisely follows the dimensions of an original in the collection of the Museum of the Fur Trade. Complete with handles, hinges, and hasp.

Dimensions: 20 inches long 14 inches wide, and 11 inches deep.

HUDSON BAY CASSETTE

"The really authentic way to transport your plunder to rendezvous," claims Crazy Crow. It follows an original described in the *Museum of the Fur Trade Quarterly*. Complete with handles, hinges, and lock.

Dimensions: 24 inches long, 14 inches wide, and 14 inches deep.

TIN BOX WITH HARD TACK

Hard Tack was the stony bread ("tack" is an eighteenth-century word for food) used by hunters and trappers. Crazy Crow's three-by-five hard tack is the "original type," and its container the old-style tin box.

Catalog available, $2.

CRAZY CROW TRADING POST

P.O. Box 314
Denison, TX 75020
Tel. 214/463–1366

BOUDIN BLANC

Although the origins of this ever-praised dish are hidden from us, the Blackfoot, Crow, and Sioux Indians were all known to have prepared it. Its name—meaning white pudding—was bestowed on it by appreciative French voyageurs who along with other early explorers (Capt. Meriwether Lewis called it "one of the greatest delicacies of the forest") never failed to allude to it in their accounts of food. The following recipe appeared in "Food of the French Explorers and Mountain Men" by H. Jane Nauman in March-April 1983 issue of *American West* magazine:

Cut a section of large intestine from a freshly butchered buffalo (or beef cow). The intestine should be well covered with soft, snowy white fat. Clean and rinse the fatty section of the intestine in water; then turn the casing inside out (so that the fat will be inside during the cooking process) and wash once more. Tightly stuff the casing with finely chopped tenderloin that has been well seasoned with salt and pepper. (Hump meat from the buffalo can also be used.) Tie both ends of the sausage securely with cord, and roast over hot charcoal, turning frequently to prevent burning. After 20 minutes on the coals, drop the sausage into a pot of boiling water for 10 minutes. Serve piping hot.

LOG CABIN CAMP ITEMS

VOYAGEUR'S LEAN-TO

My canoes were three times unladen . . . and carried on the shoulders of voyageurs.
—*Alexander Henry*, Travels and Adventures in Canada and the Indian Territories, 1760–1776

In pursuit of the fur trade, French Canadian voyageurs would paddle all day, portage loads of more than a hundred pounds, cordel upriver, and if they didn't finish off their supply of rum the very first night, carouse drunkenly before the campfire.

When the voyageur finally did retire, it was sometimes to a lean-to like the one replicated by the Log Cabin Shop. Made of 10-ounce canvas duck, this primitive tent has a floor measuring 8 feet by 8 feet at its widest points. It includes all ropes and ties necessary for erection (poles and stakes not included). Weight: 16 lbs. Log Cabin catalog #81010. Price: $95.

COMBINATION TRIPOD AND CROSSBAR COOKING SET

Hand-forged in the traditional manner, this set consists of three interlocking bars of ⅜-inch-square steel. The upper ends of two bars are hammered to form hooks, and the third locks all three securely to form a tripod. To use as a crossbar, stick the two hooked-end bars vertically (and securely) into the ground, and place the third in between as a horizontal cross-member. Strong enough for coffee pots and heavy cooking kettles. Log Cabin catalog #81FTCS (32 inches long). Price: $22.50. Log Cabin catalog #81020 (44 inches long). Price: $24.50.

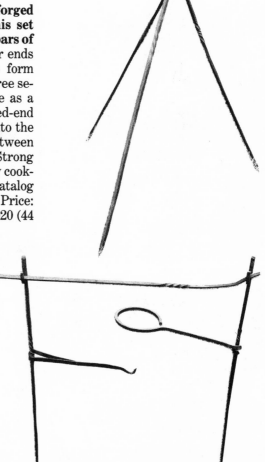

HAND-FORGED COOKING UTENSILS

Forged to meet the demands of primitive camp use, these tools are all approximately 177 inches long, with handles formed from ¼-inch round-bar stock. The bowl of the spoon and the spatula blade are hammered from 16-gauge sheet steel. A 19-inch "ram's horn" wall bracket is optional.

Fork, Log Cabin catalog #81005. Price: $9. Spoon, Log Cabin catalog #81006. Price: $10. Spatula, Log Cabin catalog #81007. Price: $9.50. Bracket, Log Cabin catalog #81009. Price: $9. Postage and handling are additional.

Catalog of black-powder supplies and accessories available, $4. Visitors welcome.

THE LOG CABIN SHOP

P.O. Box 275
Lodi, OH 44254
Tel. 216/948–1082

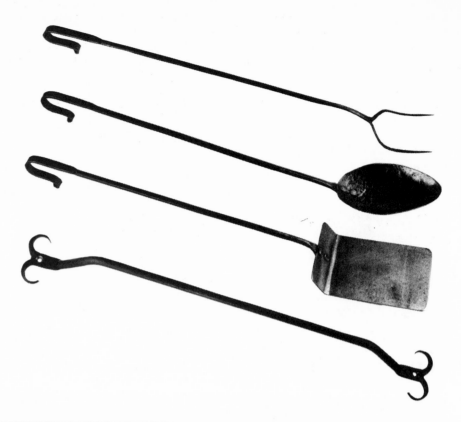

BIRCHBARK CANOES

The product of primeval northeastern woodlands, the bark canoe first emerged from its aboriginal home during the eighteenth century to carry French voyageurs westward in pursuit of the fur trade. So well suited was the bark canoe to wilderness travel that it seemed organically a part of it—the *forest's* expression of man's desire for passage within it. White men recognized the bark canoe's superiority from the moment of their arrival, and in time learned to use it to traverse the vast network of wilderness rivers and lakes that connected New York to the Northwest Territories.

From today's perspective the bark

canoe seems almost as much a natural formation as a man-made object. Yet in a time when space satellites can read the numbers off license plates—for strength, durability, beauty, and versatility, nothing has come along to surpass it.

Possibly because its construction was the master craft of the eastern Indians, by the mid-nineteenth century the bark canoe seemed doomed: "It will ere long, perhaps, be ranked among the lost arts," wrote Henry David Thoreau in his *Journals*. But for the purpose of suddenly depositing the substance of the past on the banks of the present, rivers flow through time as well. Today in New Hampshire—a state where the old ground is broken most often to make way for computer software firms—Henri Vaillancourt wields his crooked knife to make a canoe of tree bark.

Young Vaillancourt has taught himself his craft by following the examples of early-twentieth-century Malecite Indian canoe builders and assiduously studying the work of Edwin Tappan Adney (1868–1950), whose many sketches and models of various Indian bark canoes provided him with an apprenticeship. Of the very few men who can now build these canoes, Vaillancourt is the best; his craft are "Perfect in their symmetry," writes Vaillancourt's biographer, John McPhee. "Their ribs, thwarts, and planking suggest cabinetwork. Their authenticity is lashed in, undeniable."

Vaillancourt, who is descended from French trappers, resists any romantic notions about the upheaval of ancestral memory embodied in his craft. In the modern world his work has simply provided him with a livelihood—while to the modern world it has returned the birchbark canoe.

Most of Henri Vaillancourt's canoes are patterned after the Malecite St. Lawrence River type and are made by hand in the ancient way, using axe, crooked knife, awl, and froe. The woodwork—ribs, planking, stems, thwarts, and gunwales—are made from white cedar and ash or birch. The canoe's skin is white birchbark, sewn with split pine root in the traditional manner.

The flare-sided St. Lawrence River canoe has a beam of 34 inches and is 11–12 inches in depth. The tumble-home type (a tumblehome is the area enclosed by this kind of canoe's large, parenthesis-shaped curves at the bow and stern), with either a high or low end, is available in 16- and 18-foot lengths only. Fur trade canoes may be ordered in any length from 20 to 37 feet.

Prices range from $1,200 for a 10-foot canoe weighing 40 pounds, to $6,000 for a 37-foot fur trade canoe. For another $200, canoes may be ordered with traditional scraped-bark decorations on the sides.

HENRI VAILLANCOURT

P.O. Box 142
Greenville, NH 03048

SNOWSHOES

Henri Vaillancourt writes:

The natives of the northern U.S. and Canada have developed ways of coping with and using the environment that are unique among the world's peoples. They alone have mastered the skills necessary for independence and survival in an environment generally considered uninhabitable by modern man. Perhaps no more efficient harness for practical snowshoeing can be found than that used by the Indians of the north, despite the manufacturer's struggle to create a harnessing system that is more complicated and less efficient than that invented thousands of years before.

Snowshoes are Mr. Vaillancourt's wintertime occupation. Some, such as those he found still being made by the Indians of Québec, are made of birchwood. Several, in Mr. Vaillancourt's own words, are "the fanciest of the traditional Indian kind."

In addition to a plain trail-style snowshoe are three with geometric woven patterns: the square-toe Penobscot, the long pointed-toe Cree, and the Cree beavertail style.

HENRI VAILLANCOURT

P.O. Box 142
Greenville, NH 03048

THE CROOKED
KNIFE
No book entitled *The Maine Woods* can fail to refer to the crooked knife, the aboriginal carving tool from up in the forests of Down East. Henry Thoreau's book, derived from his journals and published in 1864, contains this passage:

When I awoke in the morning the weather was drizzling. One of the Indians was lying outside, rolled in his blanket, on the opposite side of the fire from want of room. Joe had neglected to wake my companion, and he had done no hunting that night. Tahmunt was making a crossbar for his canoe with a singularly shaped knife such as I have since seen other Indians using. The blade was thin, about three-quarters of an inch wide, but curved out of its plane into a hook, which he said made it more convenient to shave with.

Although this tool had been used by the Indians of the Maine woods (primarily to fashion the bark canoe) for thousands of years, a century after the publication of Thoreau's book it was about as extinct as transcendentalism. By the mid-twentieth century the only crooked knives to be found were likely in the weathered hands of New Brunswick's Malecite Indian tribesmen. Certainly the modern world has little use for the crooked knife, and there's small enough reason for Sears to carry it. Still, even for those who have diligently searched for it, the tool can be stubbornly evanescent—as if expressing a will to be part of history.

When Mainer John Gould was a boy, a Malecite whom he called Chief Pugwash made him a crooked knife. In 1947 when the knife was stolen from his toolbox in Freeport, Gould began the search for a replacement that has taken up almost all the intervening years. Along the way Gould became an expert in the lore of the crooked knife, from its Stone Age origin to its probable inclusion among the articles carried west by Lewis and Clark in 1804. But as Gould was to learn, the knife is faithful to its home, and doesn't travel well too far from the misted Maine coast.

In 1975 a twenty-one-year-old bark canoe builder named Henri Vaillancourt (whose canoes are described earlier in this section) was interviewed by John McPhee for *The New Yorker* magazine. Despite his evidently French ancestry, New Hampshireman Vaillancourt's a singularly taciturn Yankee—yet when properly motivated he'll quote Thoreau with the verve that most of his peers reserve for hockey scores. While impressing McPhee with the crooked knife's Maine roots, Vaillancourt inadvertently mixed his tenses to reveal something of its recurrent nature as well: "Where the crooked knife was," he said "the bark canoe was. People from Maine recognized the crooked knife. People from New Hampshire do not. All they knew was the draw knife."

As a builder of the traditional bark canoe, Vaillancourt is something of a historical recurrence himself. *His* crooked knife, he told McPhee, was ordered from the Hudson's Bay Company.

John Gould finished reading the Vaillancourt interview exulting that his search was nearly over. "But of course," he would later write, "since 1760 the Hudson's Bay Company has outfitted the voyageurs, the coureurs des bois, the Indians and the Eskimos who made history not only in Canada but down the Mississippi. . . . Think how many millions of knives that the Bay has sold from the Gaspé to the Aleutians!" Gould wrote off to Hudson's Bay straightaway, but got only a baffled letter in response. From its Toronto headquarters, the 300-year-old multinational was asking him what a crooked knife was and how it was used. "I'd just as soon expect a Full Gospel minister to ask me what the Bible was for," he lamented.

The knife had receded into the mists again.

John Gould's search ended anticlimactically enough in 1980, when a friend who was also a director of the Woodcraft Supply Corporation listened to the tale of his thirty-three-year quest only to allow that, right then, the knives were being sold by Woodcraft. Sure enough, the crooked knife had been appearing (or, one is tempted to say, revealing itself) in Woodcraft's tool catalog since 1977. Today, $5.50 will buy one from them, packed in styrofoam popcorn and sheathed in the history of the Indians of Maine.

Color tool catalog available, $3.

WOODCRAFT SUPPLY CORPORATION

41 Atlantic Avenue
P.O. Box 4000
Woburn, MA 01888
Tel. toll free (orders only)
* 800/225–1153*

LOG CABIN SHOP'S EDGED WEAPONS

SENECA TOMAHAWK

From the days of the earliest white settlers to the end of the fur trade era, the steel tomahawk (in all its variations) was in constant use as a tool and weapon. The Log Cabin Shop's replica (made by the H&B Forge) has been hand-forged and hammer-welded into a sturdy and functional axe. The head has been decorated with the original Seneca "weeping heart" piercing, and the hickory handle embedded with forty-four solid-brass tacks, a favorite Indian decoration. Overall length: 19 inches. Weight: 1½ lbs. Log Cabin catalog #76T17. Price: $40.

HUDSON BAY CAMP KNIFE **This model is "copied directly from a knife so common among early North American fur trappers** that it was dubbed the Hudson Bay knife after the famous fur company," writes Eric Kindig of the Log Cabin Shop. Their replica is fitted with horn slab handles that are secured by brass pins. Solid brass bolster. Overall length: 14 inches; blade length: 8 inches. Weight: 1¼ lbs. Log Cabin catalog #75HB1. Price: $28.50.

FLINT-STRIKER KNIFE **The flint-striker knife served two purposes on the frontier:** it was a small-bladed (3¾-inch) sheath knife and a flint striker, its U-shaped handle providing a shower of incendiary sparks. Weight: 3 ounces. Log Cabin catalog #77FS7. Price: $15 (flint and tinder not included).

MISSOURI WAR HATCHET **In 1805 the Lewis and Clark Expedition found this axe in use by Mandan Indians along the Missouri River.** Describing the axe in his journal, Meriwether Lewis related that the Mandans withheld a supply of corn destined for the expedition's larder until the white blacksmith agreed to duplicate several of the axes that the Indians used. Designs similar to this one were common below the Great Bend of the Missouri and remained so into the 1850s.

Log Cabin's replica hatchet is 8 inches long, 4¾ inches high, and has a round eye 1 inch in diameter. The hickory handle is 20 inches long. This pattern is listed in *American Indian Tomahawks*, by Harold L. Peterson. Log Cabin catalog #76T11. Price: $17.50.

BLACKFOOT DAG **With minor variations this knife was used by Indians and traders from coast to coast throughout the fur trade era.** Supplied by British traders, it served as an effective weapon for both sides in many conflicts. The Log Cabin replica is faithful in detail to the original, and is fitted with hardwood handles secured by brass pins. Overall length: about 11 inches; blade length: 6 inches. Weight: 13 ounces. Log Cabin catalog #75TK1. Price: $24.50.

Add shipping charges and $1 for handling to all prices. Major credit cards accepted.

LOG CABIN SHOP

P.O. Box 275
Lodi, OH 44254
Tel. 216/948–1082

TRADE AWL **An old-style iron awl** of the type used during the eighteenth and early nineteenth centuries for trade with the Indians.

Price: $3.50 (plus $1.20 for shipping and handling).

Catalog of military and camp items available, $1.

PRODUCTS OF THE PAST

P.O. Box 12
West Main Street
Wilmington, VT 05363
Tel. 802/464-5569

KENTUCKY RIFLE (.45 Caliber)

*But Jackson he was wide
awake and wasn't scared at
trifles,
For well he knew what aim we
take with our Kentucky
rifles;
So he led us down to Cypress
Swamp, the ground was low
and mucky,
There stood John Bull in
martial pomp, but here was
old Kentucky.*
*—From the original
"Ballad of New Orleans," 1814*

Rifling—the practice of cutting spiral grooves into the bore of a gun—has been used in the manufacture of firearms in Central Europe since the sixteenth century. It's a small wonder then that the Kentucky rifle (or Pennsylvania rifle, as it was originally known) was first developed by Swiss and German gunsmiths who had settled into Lancaster County, Pennsylvania.

No one can identify the exact year when the Kentucky rifle appeared, but it is recognized that after 1720 these artisans began adapting such old-world hunting rifles as the German jaeger to the requirements of the American frontier. They developed a longer (hence "long rifle," another name for the gun; and "long hunter," the eighteenth- and early nineteenth-century frontiersman who carried it), leaner weapon that carried a smaller charge, a rifle that would become as essential as the axe to life on the frontier.

"If your for a buck, or a little bear's meat, Judge," said James Fenimore Cooper's Natty Bumppo, "you'll have to take the long rifle, or you'll waste more powder than you'll fill stomachs." All frontiersmen, fictional or not, made use of the Kentucky rifle's deadly accuracy both to stock their larders and to protect themselves and their families from Indian raiders. And although the tactics of eighteenth-century warfare ensured the use of French and English smoothbores well past the Revolutionary War, General Washington once noted that even at 400 yards a rifleman using a long rifle could hit an 8- by 10-inch piece of paper three shots out of five. By comparison, a musket could send a ball only 150 yards, and wasn't accurate at all.

It wasn't until the ballad quoted above (celebrating Andrew Jackson and the 2,000 Kentuckians he led in the Battle of New Orleans in 1814) became popular that this rifle became known as a "Kaintuck." But by then the coming of percussion-fired weapons had numbered the days of the old Pennsylvania rifle, although many would be converted. In a short time, however, the era of the solitary gunsmith would be replaced by the early-nineteenth-century firearms factory.

But if such craftsmen gradually disappeared during the nineteenth century, they have gradually reappeared during the twentieth. One such is Larry Mrock, a gunsmith long fascinated by the legend of the Kentucky rifle, who in a way has resurrected it. Mr. Mrock's fidelity to detail in crafting these pieces extends to his replication of a variety of long rifles, each corresponding to the various schools that were developed in the eastern counties of Pennsylvania. As the eighteenth-century originals become increasingly scarce, contemporary long rifles such as those so authentically crafted by Mr. Mrock have come into greater demand from collectors. "It is not only the beauty and history of the Kentucky rifle that inspires me to build them," notes Larry, "but also the satisfaction of creating this piece of art with my own hands."

LAURENCE MROCK, RIFLESMITH

*Box 207
Woodhill-Hooksett Road
Bow, NH 03301*

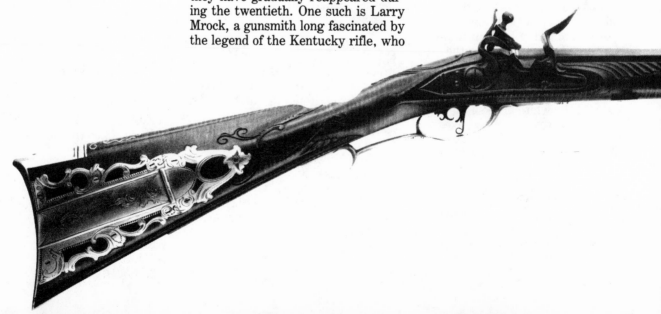

LOG CABIN SHOP FIREARMS

HARPERS FERRY 1806 FLINTLOCK PISTOL (.58 Caliber)

Made at Harpers Ferry between 1806 and 1809, this weapon was one of the first military handguns ever to be manufactured at a national armory. The Log Cabin Shop's replica features a round barrel with brown finish, polished brass hardware, and a color-case-hardened lock.

The walnut stock extends to half the 10-inch barrel length. Overall length: 16½ inches. Weight: 2½ lbs. Log Cabin catalog #10NHF06. Price: $150. Add postage and a $1 handling charge.

HARPERS FERRY 1803 FLINTLOCK RIFLE (.58 Caliber)

It is believed that this rifle was designed by Meriwether Lewis, while he was at the U.S. Arsenal at Harpers Ferry, specifically for his 1804 expedition with William Clark. The Log Cabin replica features a blued, half-round, half-octagonal barrel, color-case-hardened lock, brass hardware, and a push-button release patch box.

Overall length: 50 inches; barrel length: 35 inches. Weight: 8½ lbs. Log Cabin catalog #12NHF03. Price: $300.

Catalog of black-powder supplies and accessories available, $4.

THE LOG CABIN SHOP

P.O. Box 275
Lodi, OH 44254
Tel. 216/948–1082

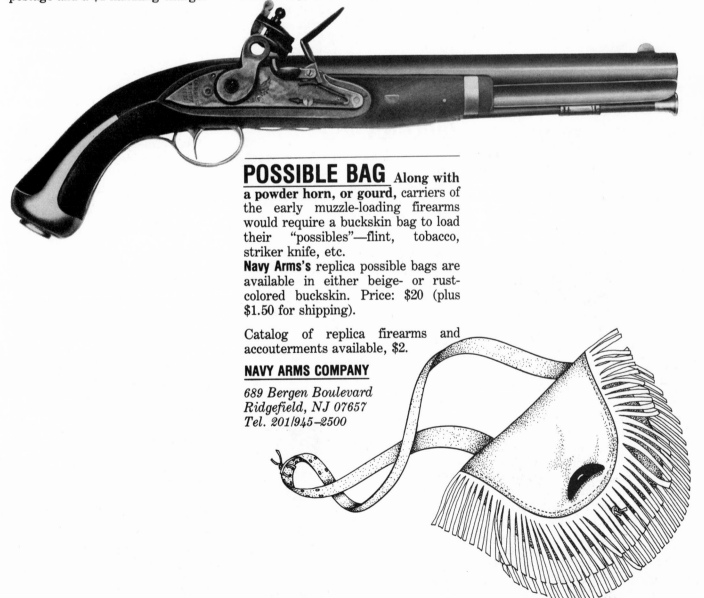

POSSIBLE BAG

Along with **a powder horn, or gourd,** carriers of the early muzzle-loading firearms would require a buckskin bag to load their "possibles"—flint, tobacco, striker knife, etc.

Navy Arms's replica possible bags are available in either beige- or rust-colored buckskin. Price: $20 (plus $1.50 for shipping).

Catalog of replica firearms and accouterments available, $2.

NAVY ARMS COMPANY

689 Bergen Boulevard
Ridgefield, NJ 07657
Tel. 201/945–2500

LA PELLETERIE BLACK-POWDER ACCOUTERMENTS

HUDSON'S BAY BLANKET
GUN COVERS

After a style popular in the East and North from the eighteenth century onward, this gun cover's Hudson's Bay blanketing is trimmed with buckskin fringe. Available in red, green, or candy-stripe wool (specify first and second color choice).

Price: $30 (kit, $25); add $3 each for postage.

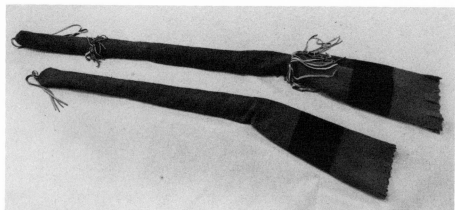

POWDER HORNS

La Pelleterie's powder horn is made of good-quality material, and according to Pat Tearney, "looks right." The small powder horn will contain about 5 ounces of powder, the large horn about 12. Price: either size, $7.50 (plus $2 for postage).

VOYAGEUR BAG

This bag is particularly suited to early rifles and trade guns. It has pockets for small tools and flints, a partition, and a gusseted bottom.

Dimensions: 7 inches by 8 inches. Price: $34.50 (plus $3 for postage).

Catalog of historical clothing and accouterments available, $3 (refundable with purchases of $30 or more).

LA PELLETERIE DE FORT DE CHARTRES

P.O. Box 267
Chester, IL 62233
Tel. 618/826-4334

LOG CABIN BLACK-POWDER SUPPLIES

TINDER BOX

Before matches, one of the fastest fire-starting methods required striking flint against steel. These items were carried in tinderboxes similar to this one available through the Log Cabin Shop. Copied from original fur-trade-era boxes, it measures 3½ by 2¼ by ⅞ inches. Flint, steel, and charred cloth are not included. Available in solid brass or German silver. Weight: 3 ounces.

Brass tinderbox, Log Cabin catalog #77TB2. Price: $14. Silver tinderbox, Log Cabin catalog #77TB3. Price: $16.75.

LEATHER HUNTING BAG

At his side were his tobacco pouch, fire-tongs, pipe, and knife, his hunting-bag and powder-horn.
—David Zeisberger, Diary of David Zeisberger's Journey to the Ohio, *1885*

Like the powder horn, its constant companion the hunting bag was a standard part of every backwoodsman's equipment. It was made of whatever leather was available and was treated hard and repaired often. Few of the original hunting bags of the nineteenth century have survived to the present day.

The Log Cabin Shop's replica leather hunting bag is 7½ inches wide and 9 inches deep. It's made of heavy top-grain cowhide and contains several inside pockets. A ¾-inch-wide carrying strap and patch knife sheath are included. Weight: 10 ounces. Log Cabin catalog #3830. Price: $28.50. Add postage and a $1 handling charge.

Catalog of black-powder supplies and accessories available, $4.

THE LOG CABIN SHOP

P.O. Box 275
Lodi, OH 44254
Tel. 216/948-1082

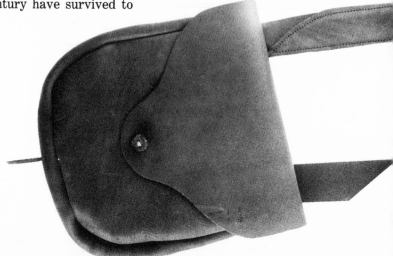

143

SEARS, ROEBUCK & CO., Cheapest Supply House on Earth, Chicago. CATALOGUE No. 111.

Our $3.88 Misses' or Girls' Saddle.

No. 10R1560
This Saddle is made on a 15½-inch English tree.

Skirts, Fancy Pigskin Impression.

Carpet seating pad, full English drill lined, ¾-inch stirrup leather, 3-inch super-cotton girth.

Weight, about 8 pounds.

Price.................$3.88

Our Special. The Princess Side Saddle.

OUR SPECIAL PRICE. $9.47

No. 10R1565 Tree. The tree used in the manufacture of this our special Princess Side Saddle, is a strictly first class Ruwart tree, with bars of saddle padded with sheepskin, so as to be soft and easy on the horse's back. Leather. The leather used in the manufacture of this saddle is of the very finest selection of russet skirting, highly polished well finished edges, leather tanned expressly for saddles and guaranteed to be superior to leather used in a great many other saddles at a great deal higher price than our special price, $9.47, on this saddle. Seating. The seating of this saddle is of the finest quality of buckskin, handsomely ornamentally stitched, making a very soft and easy cushion. This saddle is made with large jockey on back, the skirting is handsomely stamped four pieces, pigskin impression body, extra heavy 1¾-inch leather surcingle with ¾-inch stirrup strap, fine buckskin impression hooded stirrup, leather bottomed, lined with sheepskin, leaping horns seamed and buckskin lined, heavy double under rigging with woven hair cinches with 1½-inch tie straps on each side. We want your order for this saddle, not so much for the small amount of profit there is in it for us, but because we know that you will be well satisfied with this saddle and it will be a great advertisement for us. If you order this saddle and do not find it the greatest bargain you have ever seen for the money, you can return it to us at our expense and we will refund you the money paid for this saddle.

No. 10R1565 Our special price on this saddle $9.47. Weight, about 16 pounds; boxed for shipment, 30 pounds.

Our Special South-West Side Saddle, $14.00.

No. 10R1567
This Saddle is made of oiled California skirting, double rigged seamed leaping horn, made on the western style tree, and heavy rolled cantle, the same as man's heavy stock saddle. The tree used in this saddle is the genuine Ruwart tree; skirts, wool lined, 12½ inches wide and 28 inches long on the near side and 12½ inches wide and 23½ inches long on the off side. The illustrations will show both sides of this saddle. The seat is all leather covered, seat basket stamped pattern, hand stitched solid rolled cantle. Makes a very firm, strong, durable side saddle. Stirrup straps, ¾-inch, with 2½-inch hooded, wool lined stirrup;

cinches, 30-strand white Angora hair, with tongs; 1¾-inch buckle tie strap on the off side and 1½-inch buckle tie straps on the near side. This is one of our special leaders for 1902.

Price of this saddle.................$14.00
Weight, about 21 pounds; boxed, 35 pounds.

Sears, Roebuck & Co.'s Special Iowa Side Saddle.

The Greatest Value Ever Offered for the Money.

OUR SPECIAL $6.95 PRICE.

No. 10R1580
Our Special Iowa Side Saddle, made on 18-inch Ruwart tree, skirts fancy stamped pigskin impression with fancy figured seating. Has heavy padded bars so as not to hurt the horse, 1½-inch tie strap on cinches, ¾-inch stirrup leathers with metal shoe stirrup, 4-inch soft woven hair cinches and seamed buckskin lined leaping horn. An extra good double clinch ladies' side saddle.

Price, each.......$6.95
Weight, about 14 lbs.

Add extra for changes of stirrup on any saddle the difference in price of stirrups on page 419.

Ladies' $4.25 Saddle.

No. 10R1585 This Saddle is made of russet leather, has an 8-inch Ruwart tree, pigskin impression skirts, seating of figured carpet with roll. Pad, bars padded, duck lining, hair stuffed. 1½-inch tie strap, ¾-inch stirrup leather, 4-inch soft woven hair cinch. Stirrup is an XC plated shoe. Horn is carpet lined. Price, $4.25

Weight of saddle, about 11 lbs.

Ladies' $5.42 Saddle.

No. 10R____
Saddle is made ___ ___ leather, ha__ ___ Ruwart tree, ___ with fancy imp___ ing of figured carpet with leather roll. Pad, bars padded, duck lining, hair stuffed, 1½-inch tie straps, ¾-inch stirrup leathers, 2½-inch corded cotton girth, 4-inch woven soft hair cinch, plated shoe stirrup. If ___ leather lined and leath___ faced. Our price.......$____

Our Special Alice Improved Southern Side Saddle.

No. 10R1592 Made on the improved 18-inch Ruwart tree, with roll. Fine plush seating, plush leg fender and plush trimmed skirt. The skirt on

Weight, boxed, about 25 lbs.

this saddle is 18 inches wide and 15 inches deep, which is very large, and protects ladies' dresses. Soft, gray hair cinches. A double rig side saddle, with iron slipper stirrup strap; sheepskin padded bars; soft and easy on the horse's back. This is an entirely new and handsome side saddle. Satchel hook on off side.

Price, without leaping horn.......$7.97
Price, with leaping horn.......$8.55

Our Bessie Texas Side Saddle.

No. 10R1593 Made on improved Ruwart tree, with velvet carpet seating. Roll seat and velvet carpet leg fender. A very rich and tasty side saddle. The skirt is 16½ inches wide and 13½ inches deep. Heavy cotton strand Texas girth, double clinch Texas side saddle; sheepskin padded bars. Satchel to hook on off side. A strictly up to date rich looking side saddle. Made only without leaping horn. Oiled tan California skirting throughout.

Weight, boxed, about 25 lbs.

Price, each.......$6.55

Our Great Western Special Cow Girl Saddle.

$14.25

Weight, boxed for shipment, about 25 pounds.

No. 10R1595 This Side Saddle is made on genuine 18-inch Ruwart tree, strong seating of fine skirting leather, pigskin quilted skirts, extra heavy wide fender, wool lined, stirrup leathers each by 5½ feet long and ___ ___ ___ ___ leather side; Tapidero stir___ on ___ ___ of leaping horn; extra ___ ___ ___ girths, with leather chafe and connecting strap; front girth heavy cotton string and back girth heavy cotton web. Nothing like this saddle ever sold before at this low price.

Our special price.......$14.25

Our Improved Western Side.

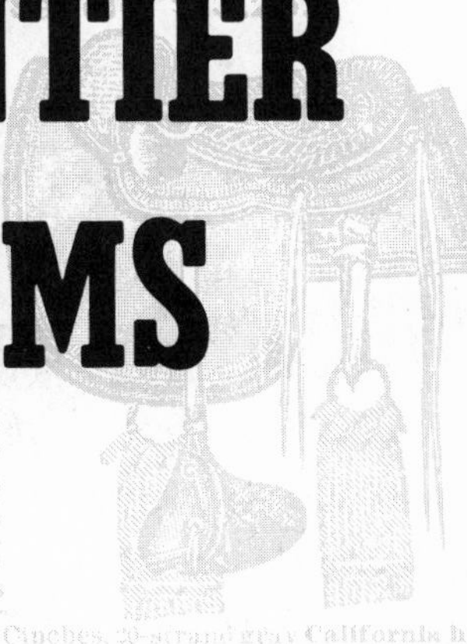

Our Improved Western Style Side Saddle, and one of the best grades of California skirting, plain, under-skirts square wool lined. Seating of genuine buckskin ornamentally stitched, has ¾-inch stirrup leather. Cinches, 29-strand gray California hair, 1½-inch tie straps, leaping horn genuine buckskin seamed. A regular double clinch rigged saddle.

Our price.......(Weight, 19 pounds).......$13.25

Our Special Colorado Stock Side Saddle.

$22.98

No. 10R1605 Sears, Roebuck & Co.'s Special Cow Girl Colorado Stock Side Saddle made on an 18-inch Ruwart rawhide covered tree, heavy ironed and one of the best trees on the market. Seating and jockey of the saddle are in one piece with head to lace and the leaping horn is handsomely

hand stamped in diamond pattern. Skirts extra heavy oil tanned skirting, round cornered, 22 inches long and 16 inches wide with sheepskin lining. The rigging you will notice on the saddle is our sawbuck style with covered rings, the flap of each strap is sewn by hand, making it very firm and strong, short buckle clinch strap on near side and long buckle clinch strap on off side, wood stirrups, leather bottom and large tapideros, wool lined. Cinches, the front cinch is made of soft woven hair with wool lined chafes and buckle ring with connecting strap. This is a strictly high grade Western Saddle, and we guarantee it in every respect in style, quality of leather and workmanship. Our special price.......$22.98

Weight, about 20 pounds; boxed, 40 pounds.

LEVI'S BUTTON-FLY DENIM TROUSERS

The television ad usually appears during the evening news, a jut-jawed cowboy silhouetted against a roseate sky. "In the last known photograph of the Dalton Gang," the voiceover intones as the cowboy wheels his horse and canters down a dry riverbed, "Bob and Brad Dalton were both wearing original Levi's Blue Jeans." The lone rider is joined by one, then another cowboy. Together they ride into the haze of the setting sun.

Well, shown here is what ought to be that last photograph. It was taken at Coffeyville, Kansas, on Wednesday, October 5, 1892, just after the Daltons' final bank raid—one aborted by a spontaneous uprising of townspeople against the robbers.

For the Coffeyville raid, Bob Dalton can be seen wearing his glenplaid-pattern trousers. And as for brother "Brad"—well, despite the Levi's account, of the ten Dalton boys, five were outlaws and five were not, but *none* was Brad. Bob was joined in their last photo by brother Grot (really Grattan—brother Emmett survived Coffeyville but was later killed), a man expunged from the Levi's version of western history for not having a breezy enough name with which to sell blue jeans. Incidentally, Grot's wearing striped trousers. Now we know something of how those folks at Coffeyville must've felt.

Actually, the Levi Strauss Company has been making dungarees for far too long to have to manufacture any history about them. In fact the Levi's 501 button-fly jeans sold today have been virtually unchanged (copper rivets were added in 1870 and beltloops replaced the cinch waist during the 1920s) since the first pair of denims were fashioned by Levi Strauss himself back in 1850. Strauss, a Bavarian-Jewish immigrant, was responding to the advice of an old forty-niner who told him that he "should've brought pants" along to sell on a visit to the California gold country. "Pants don't wear worth a hoot up in the diggins," the prospector is said to have told the merchant, giving him an idea with seemingly endless value.

To make tougher pants—or waist-high overalls as they were then called—Strauss first used canvas and only later switched to denim (a strong cotton fabric loomed in Nîmes, France, and called *serge de Nîmes*). A special indigo dye, which could be depended on for its unvarying color quality, was then developed to color the overalls. From the time of their mid-nineteenth-century beginnings until their popularization east of the Rockies in the 1930s, Levi's jeans were the standard working clothing not just for cowboys, but also for the miners, loggers, and railroad men of the West. Several pairs of these Levi's are today part of the Smithsonian Institution's Americana Collection.

LUCKLESS AND JEANLESS: THE DALTON GANG IN FINAL REPOSE. COFFEYVILLE. KANSAS. OCTOBER 5, 1892. COURTESY KANSAS HISTORICAL SOCIETY.

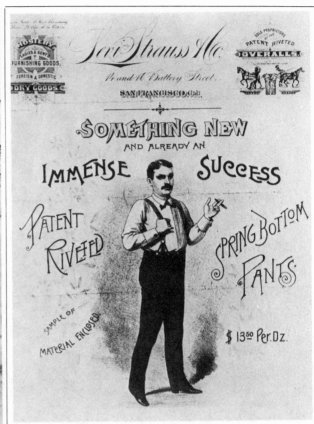

WORKING THE LAST CHANCE MINE IN LEVI'S OVERALLS. PLACER
COUNTY, CALIFORNIA, 1882.

RED RIVER FRONTIER OUTFITTERS

"We don't cater to the shoot-'em-up crowd," confided Phil Spangenberger of Red River Frontier Outfitters. "We are striving to satisfy the purist, and to maintain a high degree of both quality and authenticity."

These winning remarks are borne out by Red River's track record. Since going into business in 1970, the company has been supplying living-history buffs and the National Park Service with an impressive array of authentic frontier clothing and accessories. Red River's list of customers includes the U.S. Army's 1st Cavalry Regiment at Fort Hood, the Fort Laramie National Historic Site, and the Golden Spike National Historic Site, among others.

Also, Red River's stock in Hollywood has risen along the angle traced by the growing sensitivity of filmmakers to the value of straightforward depictions of the nineteenth-century West. In recent years the firm has supplied historical props, clothing, and leather goods to the Disney Studios, Stembridge Gun Rentals (Hollywood's major rental house for firearms), and for the films *The Legend of the Lone Ranger* and *Barbarosa* (here they made star Willie Nelson's personal holsters and belts). Their television credits include "How the West Was Won," "Hearts of the West," "Father Murphy," and "Little House on the Prairie." Naturally, all of Red River's customers can expect to benefit from their serious approach to historical replication: "Don't call our outfits 'costumes,' " Spangenberger unnecessarily insisted. "We make historical frontier clothing." Below and elsewhere in this section are a few examples of these.

GREAT PLAINS

HAT An accurate re-creation of a **popular 4-inch-brim hat** correct for any period from 1820 to 1900. 5X beaver fur felt. Available in sizes 6¾ through 7½. Tan only. Price: $60.

BIB-FRONT

SHIRTS
The 1800s "bib-front" or "shield-front" shirt was worn by every specie of westerner—cowboy, miner, soldier, and farmer—from the Canadian Rockies to the Rio Grande. Red River's 1870s bib-front shirts come in four styles and a range of authentic colors and fabrics. Available in small, medium, large, and extra-large sizes. Prices: cotton bib shirt, $59.95; wool-flannel bib shirt, $87.50.

SPLIT-EAR

HEADSTALL
This was the cowboy's favorite type of bridle. With a single ear hole cut into the crown, this headstall simply slips over the horse's head behind the left ear and over the right. It's an exact replica of an original in the Red River collection, complete with solid-brass oval buckles. Available plain or with border stamp-tooling, and with or without concho. Natural (russet), oil finish only. Reins and bits not included.

Prices: plain headstall, $32.50; concho, $3 (allow several weeks for delivery; include $3 to cover shipping and handling).

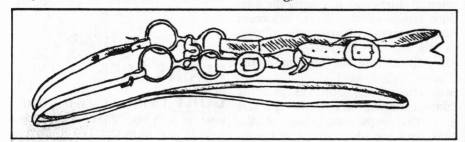

COWBOY BANDANAS
The frontier's face mask (although usually worn as a protection against dust, not detection), arm sling, bandage, water strainer, sweat mop, and tobacco wrapper, cowboy neckerchiefs were available in every color and variety of floral and geometric design. Red River's bandanas come from Mexico and are in the true 1870s–1880s style. State preference for first three colors when ordering. Price: $3 each. Include $3 to cover postage and handling.

Catalog of frontier clothing, western, and military Americana available, $2.

RED RIVER FRONTIER OUTFITTERS

P.O. Box 241
Tujunga, CA 91042
Tel. 213/352–0177

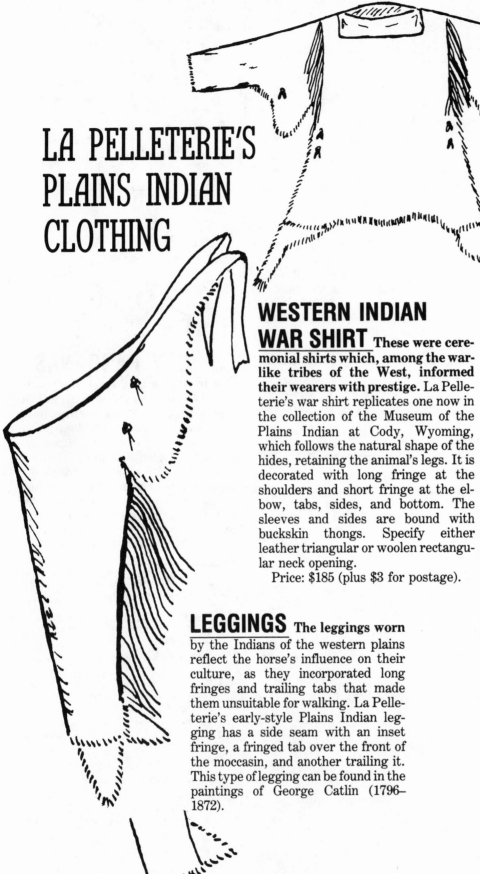

LA PELLETERIE'S PLAINS INDIAN CLOTHING

WESTERN INDIAN WAR SHIRT

These were ceremonial shirts which, among the warlike tribes of the West, informed their wearers with prestige. La Pelleterie's war shirt replicates one now in the collection of the Museum of the Plains Indian at Cody, Wyoming, which follows the natural shape of the hides, retaining the animal's legs. It is decorated with long fringe at the shoulders and short fringe at the elbow, tabs, sides, and bottom. The sleeves and sides are bound with buckskin thongs. Specify either leather triangular or woolen rectangular neck opening.

Price: $185 (plus $3 for postage).

LEGGINGS

The leggings worn by the Indians of the western plains reflect the horse's influence on their culture, as they incorporated long fringes and trailing tabs that made them unsuitable for walking. La Pelleterie's early-style Plains Indian legging has a side seam with an inset fringe, a fringed tab over the front of the moccasin, and another trailing it. This type of legging can be found in the paintings of George Catlin (1796–1872).

PLAINS CREE COAT

La Pelleterie refers to this coat as a "Cree" coat because it's a copy of one from that tribe now in a private collection. Pat Tearney notes that this coat is nearly identical to those worn by other tribesmen, including two as geographically and chronologically distant as an eighteenth-century Iroquois and an 1860s Crow.

The Plains Cree coat has fringed shoulder seams, and fringed collar, cuffs, and bottom. The front opening is buttonless, as if meant to be belted.

Price: $225; northern plains tack belt, $55 (plus $3 each for postage).

THE CHEYENNE DRESS

After one in the Museum of the Plains Indian, this early-style northern plains dress was very popular among Cheyenne women. It's a full-length buckskin dress, fringed at the waist and hem and doubly fringed at the sleeves. The skirt is decorated with a thong-fringed back and front.

Price: $215 (plus $3 for postage).

Catalog of historical clothing and accouterments available, $3 (refundable with purchases of $30 or more).

LA PELLETERIE DE FORT DE CHARTRES

P.O. Box 627
Chester, IL 62233
Tel. 618/826-4334

PRAIRIE EDGE STUDIOS

Just over a hundred years ago lived a proud people whose horsemanship, bravery, and colorful regalia captured the imagination of the world. They were the Cheyenne, Crow, Sioux, and Blackfoot of the northern plains. Their mystical lifestyle has inspired writers and artists for generations.

It was with deep respect for those proud people and their artistic traditions that Prairie Edge was created. We are located in the heart of the plains, at the very edge of the Paha Sapa, the sacred Black Hills.

In everything we offer, Prairie Edge strives to be faithful to the original spirit and design sensibilities of the finest artisans of these northern plains tribes. We use the same techniques and materials they did, except where impossible to do so.

Every single item in these entries is unique and made by hand. Because the detail work is so painstaking, and because of our vigorous insistence on authentic materials, quantities are limited.

—Ray Hillenbrand, Prairie Edge

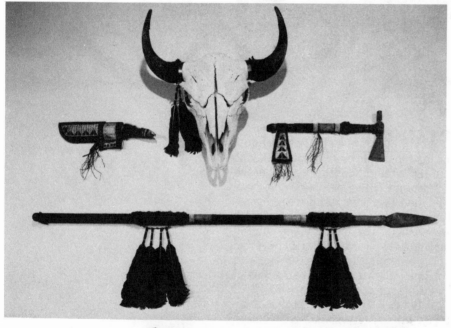

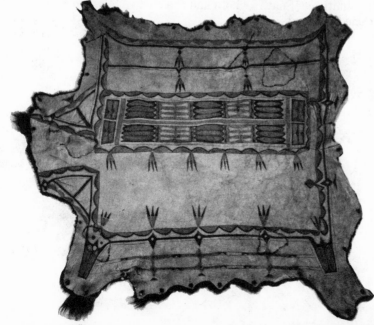

BUFFALO-HONORING

COLLECTION To the Indian of the northern plains the buffalo was the center of life itself, providing food, medicine, clothing, and shelter to the entire tribe. The western Sioux and other northern plains tribes believed that the buffalo was related directly to the Great Spirit and stood as a natural symbol for the universe. Many parts of the animal were used in religious and spiritual ceremonies.

The Buffalo-Honoring Collection is Prairie Edge's assemblage of those items with which the tribes of the northern plains would ceremoniously honor the buffalo. Included are the buffalo ceremonial lance, the buffalo jaw knife and sheath, the buffalo ceremonial pipe tomahawk, and the buffalo-honoring skull, which honors the spiritual power of the beast.

PAINTED

BUFFALO ROBE The Plains Indians recorded their history by painting their buffalo robes with depictions of true accounts. In this way a document was created that could be passed on to future generations.

Prairie Edge's painted buffalo robe portrays in an early geometric design the various parts of the sacred animal: heart, stomach, hump, legs, and horns, emulating the work of a primitive Indian artist. The earthen paint colors (basically red and yellow with a blue-gray outline) have been applied with bone brushes in the traditional manner.

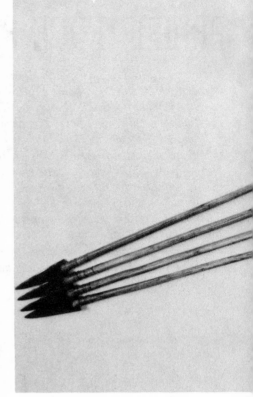

STAR QUILT The first schools
organized in the Sioux territory during the 1860s taught quilting as part of the curriculum. The Sioux star quilt marries the white man's craft with characteristically dynamic Indian use of color and design. The quilt's eight-pointed morning star is the traditional symbol of hope, accounting for its function as a wrapping for infants and a ceremonial covering for adopted relatives.

Prairie Edge's star quilts are made by Sioux women from the reservation communities of South Dakota and are stitched by hand.

HORSE
DANCE STICK A horse killed
in battle was the Lakota Sioux warrior's fallen comrade, a brother to be honored by the creation of a piece of art in his memory. By making and then carrying the horse dance stick in warrior society dances, the Sioux brave would publicly demonstrate his grief for the loss of his horse.

The horse dance stick was uniquely Sioux. The honoring warrior would carve his horse's head and hoof onto it, embellishing the image with beads showing his family's colors. The brave would then use his horse's hair to fashion a mane on the stick, over which a bridle would be placed. The horse stick would be finished off with decorative brass tacks, brain-tanned hide, earth paints, wild turkey feathers, and trade cloth.

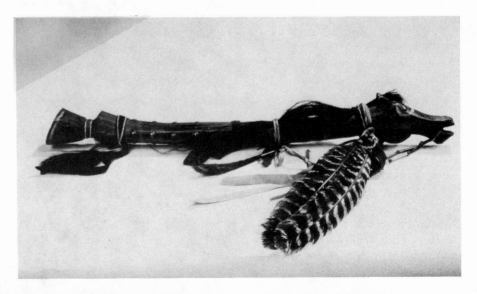

WAR ARROWS

WAR ARROWS Steel-pointed arrows with short, sturdy shafts and long feather fletchings were used by the Teton Lakota or western Sioux throughout the last century. The Indians abandoned the use of stone points as soon as metal became available from traders, often filing them from barrel hoops, as does Prairie Edge.

The arrow's shafts are short because the small and powerful bow that propelled the arrow was plucked rather than pulled. The arrow would be shot by the brave at hip level and at close range as he rode his horse at a gallop.

Earth paint and dye markings on an arrow identified its owner and established the credit for fallen enemies and game. Wild turkey feathers were used for fletching, and like the metal points, were attached to the shafts with sinew.

As it was considered the mark of a truly brave warrior to get close enough in battle to use a bow and arrow, they were carried long after firearms became prevalent on the plains.

WAR WEAPONS COLLECTION

WAR WEAPONS COLLECTION This collection, consisting of shield, tomahawk, and lance, is Prairie Edge's tribute to both the bravery and success in battle of Plains Indian warriors.

The Bear Society shield, originally created by the Kiowa nation more than a century ago, imparted to its owner the spirit and fighting strength of the bear. It includes a medicine bundle for the owner's personal medicine—in this case scraps of buffalo wool, sweet grass, and a buffalo tooth. The colors are earth pigments, authentically applied by bone brush. Following tradition, the shield is arrayed with trailers of trade cloth onto which a warrior could attach charms and the coup feathers and scalp locks he earned in battle. The long length of the collection's tomahawk and lance reflect the requirements of mounted warfare.

The central design theme (in both beadwork and blade cutouts) is the forward-pointing triangle, symbolic of advancement in battle. The lance's dominant red coloration represents its power to shed the blood of an enemy; the yellow beadwork, symbolic of the sun, courts its power; dew claws of a deer are intended to impart that animal's speed and agility; and spent cartridges count the enemies dispatched by the lance. Each eagle feather that hangs from the lance marks a coup, or the brazen and nonharmful touching of an enemy in battle, executed by its owner.

HORSEHEAD MIRROR BOARD

In the warrior society of the Sioux, vanity was the prerogative of the male. The tribe's ceremonial dances were in one respect an exhibition of this vanity, emphasizing the warrior's ability to maintain a fierce image.

A dancing warrior would carry a mirror board to aid him in adjusting his regalia and to admire his fearsome visage. The brave would also use the mirror board to flirt while he danced—reflecting sunlight off it onto the maiden he fancied.

Prairie Edge's mirror board also reflects the Lakota Sioux's concern with the decoration of everyday objects. The horsehead style shown is one of the more prestigious (and elaborate) versions. Made of lead-inlaid walnut, it has a trade mirror and decorative brass tacks.

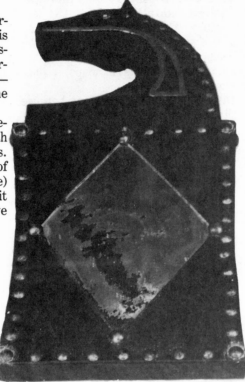

GUN STOCK WAR CLUB

After the musket was introduced to the Sioux by eighteenth-century fur traders, the shape of the Indian's war clubs began to emulate those of guns in order to capture some of the latter's impressive power, or "medicine." That these efforts were unsuccessful may be seen in the musket's ability to eliminate much hand-

PEACE PIPE

Among the Lakota tribes, male artisans have created porcupine-quill pipe stems for more than 150 years. Today this craft is practiced by only a handful of men.

In this traditional masculine art form, ash is cut green and then stored to allow it to dry and straighten. It is then bored out and sculpted into the forms of antiquity. Elements of the pipe represent all creation: the red, catlinite bowl is Mother Earth, a sacred altar upon which the tobacco is smoked; the stem represents a man's life, ideally straight and true; the sweet grass is symbolic of purity and growing things; and the quilled wheel stands for the four cardinal directions central to Indian creation myths.

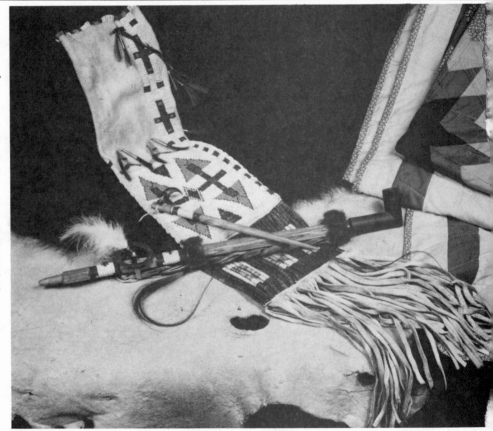

to-hand combat, which made the war club obsolete.

Still, late-nineteenth-century Sioux warriors retained the gun stock war club as a part of their traditional regalia, and many are to be seen proudly displayed in period photographs.

Prairie Edge's replica war club has a heavy, hand-forged iron spear point and is decorated with brass tacks, red earth paint, and feathers.

PIPE BAGS The modern Sioux

artisans who create these bags for Prairie Edge also make them for the tribe's ceremonial use, including the fasting, praying, and healing ceremonies. No artisan will make any two bags exactly alike.

Pipe bags are considered to be religious objects and have undergone little change in the past 130 years. The classic beaded pipe bag was developed by the 1850s, when the basic elements of fringe, quilled tabs, and beaded design were accepted conventions. One of the Sioux holy man's most valued possessions, the fully beaded pipe bag was considered a tribute to the sacred qualities of the pipe and tobacco it contained.

Brochure and price list available.

PRAIRIE EDGE

P.O. Box 8303
Rapid City, SD 57709
Tel. 605/341-4525

PLAINS INDIAN SHOOTING BAG Closely patterned after

an early original, this bag and strap are made from Hudson's Bay blanketing. The 7- by 8-inch bag is attached to the strap with buckskin thongs and wooden toggles. A matching powder-horn strap (with or without the horn) is also available.

Prices: shooting bag, $19.50 (plus $3 for postage); horn and strap, $10 (plus $2 for postage); strap only, $3.50 (plus $1.25 for postage).

Catalog of historical clothing and accouterments, available, $3 (refundable with purchases of $30.00 or more).

LA PELLETERIE DE FORT DE CHARTRES

P.O. Box 627
Chester, IL 62233
Tel. 618/826-4334

PLAINS INDIAN BOTANICALS In their beliefs and talismans,

all Indian religions are rooted in the immediate natural environment. To almost every Indian, all men, plants, and animals have souls permeated by a supernatural overforce. Indian priests and medicine men used grasses and herbs not only for the ritual communication with this spirit world, but also in conjunction with it as curatives. Although many whites considered Indian medicine men to be charlatans, their use of these botanicals was routinely effective, and their belief in the supernatural deeply held.

The Crazy Crow Trading Post offers several varieties of botanicals used by the Indians of the plains. Among these are sage, a fragrant plant used as incense and burned at religious ceremonies; sweet flag root, a Sioux medicine chewed for sore throats and toothaches; cedar, used by peyoteists and straight dancers as a perfume; and sweet grass.

Catalog available, $2.

CRAZY CROW TRADING POST

P.O. Box 314
Denison, TX 75020
Tel. 214/463-1366

PLAINS INDIAN

TIPIS

The Sioux word *tipi* (meaning a place in which to dwell) succinctly captures a sense of the conical tent's serenity and comfort. Throughout all the seasons of their long use, in fact, tipis have provided room and agreeable shelter at every latitude of the Great Plains—a matter of some consequence to its nomadic buffalo hunters. Moreover, the tipi was easily broken down for transport into a travois, which could then be dragged by either dog or horse to a new site where the tipi could be resurrected by a single man, if need be. Even the most modern tents must strive unevenly against a tendency to be cramped, poorly lit and ventilated, or ugly looking—but the tipi simply has none of these failings; it is rather a stately dwelling that combines its naturalistic beauty with human cunning to reflect the dignity and grace so important to the everyday life of the Plains Indian.

The tipi can be distinguished from the smoky dens that were the skin tents of other (usually circumpolar) peoples by its use of smoke flaps—the external wings that flank the tipi's smoke hole and are infinitely adjustable by means of outside poles. These flaps ensure amenity by regulating the draft of the tipi, ventilating it and carrying its smoke out and away from its occupants. The unique smoke flaps were alluded to in the explorer Don Juan de Oñate's 1599 account of an encounter with Apaches. Here he described an assembly of ". . . 50 tents made of tanned hides, very bright red and white in color and bell-shaped, with flaps and openings, and built as skillfully as those of Italy . . ." [Herbert Eugene Bolton (ed.), *Spanish Exploration in the Southwest, 1542 to 1706* (New York: Charles Scribner's Sons, 1916), p. 223.]

The tipi's refined adaptation to both its purpose and environment has left it virtually unchanged (save for the regular substitution of canvas for hide during the late 1800s) for centuries. During their early winter campaigns on the frontier, shivering U.S. cavalry-men so envied the Indians their warm tipis that elements of the design were later (unsuccessfully) incorporated into the Silbey tent that was used during the Civil War. Tipis served as the portal for many historic councils, and the homes, at times, for such frontier scouts, soldiers, and writers as Kit Carson, Buffalo Bill Cody, Jim Bridger, Joe Meek, William Bent, and Gen. John Charles Frémont.

The Blue Star company of Missoula, Montana, offers both three- and four-pole tipis, the former based on the designs of the Blackfeet and Crow, the latter upon those of the Sioux and Cheyenne. These range in size from 12 to 24 feet and are available in authentic Grade-A #12 cotton duck as well as in polyester and flame-retardant blends. Interior liners, *ozans* (Sioux for cover, a flat interior ceiling to retain heat), and lodgepoles are also available.

Detailed price list and brochure obtainable.

BLUE STAR TIPIS

P.O. Box 2562
Missoula, MT 59806
Tel. 406/728-1738

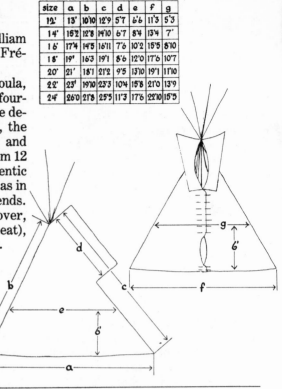

size	a	b	c	d	e	f	g
12'	13'	10'10	12'9	5'7	6'6	11'3	5'3
14'	15'2	12'8	14'10	6'7	8'4	13'4	7'
16'	17'4	14'5	16'11	7'6	10'2	15'6	8'10
18'	19'	16'3	19'1	8'6	12'0	17'6	10'7
20'	21'	18'1	21'2	9'5	13'10	19'1	11'10
22'	23'	19'10	23'3	10'4	15'8	21'0	13'9
24'	26'0	21'8	25'5	11'3	17'6	22'10	15'5

TACK SHEATH

Tack-decorated sheaths were favorites of both the Plains Indians and the whites who adopted their ways. La Pelleterie makes four types of these, each copied from nineteenth-century originals. Fashioned from top-grain cowhide, the sheaths are studded with solid-brass-headed tacks. Send a tracing of your knife and specify the style you desire. Available in natural, black, and dark brown.

Prices: complete sheath, $27.50 (plus $3 for postage); kit (undyed only), $13.50 (plus $2.50 for postage).

Catalog of historical clothing and accouterments available, $3 (refundable with orders of $30.00 or more).

LA PELLETERIE DE FORT DE CHARTRES

P.O. Box 627
Chester, IL 62233
Tel. 618/826-4334

COFFIN BOWIE KNIFE

Scarcely were these words uttered when another of the party reached over and struck Joaquin a severe blow to the face. The latter sprang for his Bowie knife . . . when Rosita, instinct with the danger such rashness threatened, threw herself before him and . . . frantically held him. For the intruders to thrust aside the woman and strike the unarmed man senseless was the work of the moment. When Joaquin awoke to consciousness, it was to find Rosita prostrate, her face buried in her clothes, sobbing hysterically. Then he knew the worst.
—Hubert Howe Bancroft, "Joaquin Murieta: The Terror of the Stanislaus,"
  California Pastoral: 1769–1848, *1888*

*His blade was tempered and so was
  he;*
indestructible steel *was he.*
Jim Bowie, Jim Bowie,
*he was a fightin' and fearless, and
  mighty adventurin' man.*
—Theme from the 1950s television
  series "Jim Bowie"

The Bowie knife, long associated with Jim Bowie, the valorous Mexican hero of the Alamo, was actually named for its original maker, Bowie's brother Rezin. The early Bowie knife was a large 9- to 15-inch sheath knife, often fashioned by frontier blacksmiths from old files and horse rasps. The Bowie knives therefore varied widely in pattern and use. **Navy Arms's coffin Bowie knife** is so named because of its use of "coffin" handles of American walnut. It has a high-carbon-steel blade, and has been hammer-forged, then tempered and fully sharpened.

Dimensions: 7-inch blade, 12 inches overall. Weight: 1 lb. Available fully finished or as a kit.

Prices: finished Bowie knife, $37.50; kit, $27 (plus $1.50 for shipping).

Color catalog of replica arms and accessories available, $2.

NAVY ARMS COMPANY

689 Bergen Boulevard
Ridgefield, NJ 07657
Tel. 201/945–2500

HAWKEN RIFLES (.50, .52, .54, .58 Caliber) It was

1822 when brothers Jacob and Samuel Hawken began to make Hawken rifles in their St. Louis shop. As Sam's account of an event that took place the following year shows, acceptance of the gun was nearly immediate:

Paul Anderson's expedition was the first I fitted out. He and Chambers went to Santa Fe and gave such good reports about my guns that every man going west wanted one. [Gen.] William Ashley's men were the next to go out. . . . The boys . . . ran out of provisions and had to kill a mule. Ashley told me that he was riding on a white horse looking for game one day and sighted a buffalo. He could hardly believe the shot was effective at so great a distance, and rode up to take another shot at short range, but found the buffalo dead, shot through. . . . Ashley was offered $150.00 [for the gun] out west, but he would not take it.

—"Testimony re Hawken's Rifles," Jefferson National Expansion Memorial, St. Louis

The fame of the Hawken half-stock rifle grew steadily throughout the era of westward expansion, and it became a favored weapon among such adventurers, explorers, and scouts as Kit Carson, Jeremiah Johnson, Jim Bridger, and Francis Parkman.

A precise replica of the slant-breech rifle built by the Hawken brothers, Primitive Arms's half-stock Hawken has been cited by the authoritative *Guns & Ammo* magazine as a "truly authentic version of the St. Louis originals . . . deserving of the Hawken name." The company offers both percussion and flintlock models. Overall length: 50¼ inches. Weight: approximately 9½ lbs.

Literature available, $1.

PRIMITIVE ARMS

Route 1
Box 42–A
Ashdown, AR 71822
Tel. 501/898–2345

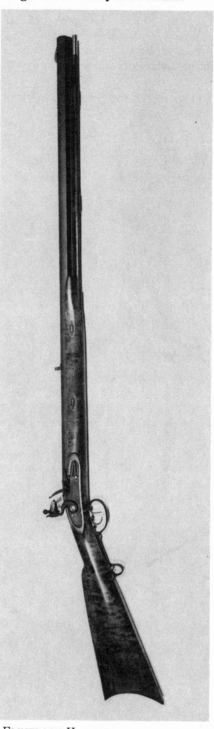

FLINTLOCK HAWKEN

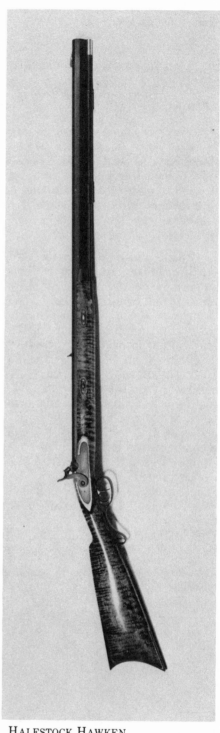

HALFSTOCK HAWKEN

Western Handguns

HANDGUNS FROM NAVY ARMS

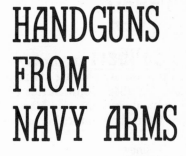

The following account by John Reno, the "inventor" of train robbery, describes the train ride to the Jefferson City, Missouri, prison after his capture by Pinkertons in 1868. Because it was planned that during this journey Reno's brother Frank and their comrades would raid the train and rescue him, John anxiously sizes up his guards:

I was a little uneasy on the morning we left Gallatin to see the guard so strong—there were six or eight armed soldiers, well weaponed, but I knew they were not all going on the train and hoped they would leave us before my brother might make his attack. As I did not know where the attack was to be made, however, I was very restless, watching for them at every station. . . . I dreaded to see the time come, for I feared there would be some hard fighting. The guards were all provided with long "navies" and had a reputation of being men with steel nerves.

Because gang members had "missed train connections at Quincy," Frank never mounted his attack. If John Reno was disappointed when he entered the Missouri Penitentiary, he hid it manfully:

When we arrived at the prison gate I looked up and read in large letters over the entrance: "THE WAY OF THE TRANSGRESSOR IS HARD. Admission, twenty-five cents," but I was on the dead-head list and went in free.

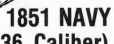

1851 NAVY (.36 Caliber)
This was the revolver that John Reno eyed so nervously on his way to prison. Originally manufactured by Colt from 1850 through 1876, it was the company's prime medium-caliber handgun during the percussion period. Lighter and handier than the Dragoon pistol, it was also a popular Union Army weapon. Navy Arms notes that the original Colt was also a favorite dueling weapon during the California Gold Rush.

The Navy Arms replica features a steel frame, octagonal barrel, and a six-shot cylinder engraved with a period naval battle scene. The backstrap and trigger guard are both of polished brass.

Dimensions: overall length, 14 inches; barrel length, 7½ inches. Weight: 2 lbs.

Price: finished model, $118.95

NEW ORLEANS ACE (.44 Caliber)
The original "gambler's companion," the Ace was designed in France and popularized by New Orleans gunsmiths during the 1840s. It is claimed that the easily concealed Ace was used fatally by John Beauregard to settle a cardplayer's dispute with Beau Jackson in one of Bourbon Street's plush casinos.

Available either rifled or as a smoothbore, the Navy Arms replica Ace is a percussion pistol with a 3½-inch barrel and an overall length of 9 inches. Weight: 1 lb.

Prices: smoothbore finish, $58.50; rifled finish, $64.25. Include $4 per handgun to cover the cost of shipping and handling.

Color catalog of replica arms and accessories available, $2.

NAVY ARMS COMPANY

*689 Bergen Boulevard
Ridgefield, NJ 07657
Tel. 201/945–2500*

THUMB-HAMMER PEPPERBOX REVOLVER

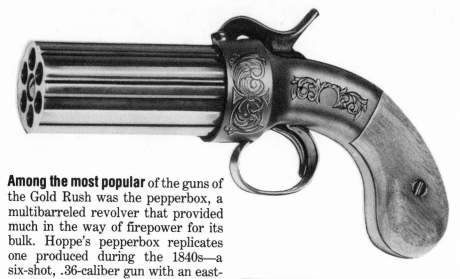

(.36 Caliber)

At Sutters Mill, California, on the evening of Friday, January 28, 1848, John Sutter confided to his diary that "Mr Marshall arrived from the mountains on very important business." As Mr. Marshall's business concerned the discovery of gold in the American River, Sutter's entry contends as the supreme understatement of the nineteenth-century American West.

Within a year of this event, Alta, California's pastoral landscape, fragrant with juniper, would become a frantic duchy of ramshackle towns, thick with drifters and scoundrels in search of fast wealth. For many men of the California Gold Rush, stealing the stuff was as good as panning for it; and so for each man, good and bad, there was a gun.

Among the most popular of the guns of the Gold Rush was the pepperbox, a multibarreled revolver that provided much in the way of firepower for its bulk. Hoppe's pepperbox replicates one produced during the 1840s—a six-shot, .36-caliber gun with an eastern American walnut grip.

Price: $75.48.

HOPPE'S

c/o Penguin Industries, Inc.
Airport Industrial Mall
Coatesville, PA 19320
Tel. 215/384-6000

RED RIVER OUTFITTERS' WESTERN ACCOUTERMENTS

FRONTIER CARTRIDGE BELTS

A re-creation of an early-style belt, handmade of the same weight leather as were the originals. "These authentic cartridge belts bring to mind the old towns of Tucson, Denver, Abilene, and El Paso, as well as the men who tamed them," says the Red River catalog.

Each belt is made with 30–36 cartridge loops to accommodate either .38, .44, or .45 caliber bullets. Heavy, old-style buckles are used, and each belt is available either plain or border-stamped. Natural oil-finish only.

Prices: plain belt, $45; border-stamped, $50. Include $3 per item to cover postage and handling.

Catalog of frontier clothing, western, and military Americana available, $2.

RED RIVER FRONTIER OUTFITTERS

P.O. Box 241
Tujunga, CA 91042
Tel. 213/352-0177

THE BUNTLINE SPECIAL (.44 Caliber)

Ned Buntline (1823—1886), actor, soldier of fortune, and western romance writer, gave versions of the long-barreled Colt revolver that had been made especially for him (and exhibited at the 1875 Philadelphia Industrial Show) to such celebrities of the sage as Bat Masterson and Wyatt Earp. By one account, to William F. Cody he gave the sobriquet "Buffalo Bill."

Allen Fire Arms's Buckhorn S. A. Buntline revolver has a fully adjustable blade rear sight and ramp front sight.

Dimensions: overall length, 23 inches; barrel length, 18 inches. Weight: 3.59 lbs.

Catalog of firearms and accessories available.

ALLEN FIREARMS COMPANY

1107 Pen Road
Santa Fe, NM 87501
Tel. 505/983-1961 or 982-3399

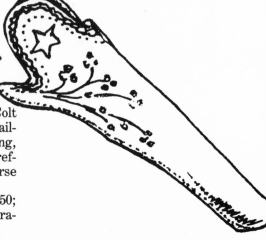

1850s–1870s FORM-FIT HOLSTER

This holster is handmade and duplicates what was likely the most popular style of the entire percussion era. It is suitable for the Colt-Paterson or Dragoon (any model), the 1851 and 1861 Colt Navies, the 1861 Remington Army or Navy, the 1860 Colt Army, and the 1873 Colt single-action Army revolvers. Available plain or with border stamping, natural oil-finish only. Indicate preference for butt-forward or reverse style, right or left side.

Prices: plain form-fit, $27.50; border-stamp tooled, $32.50; extra-fancy tooled, $37.50.

Family Compartment Tents.

Oblong, with square ends. Weights without poles, 50 to 100 pounds.

Tents made of 8 oz. double filling, brown and white or blue and white stripe, same as 10 ounce double filling white.

These tents are especially designed for families or parties who must have separate rooms. It is accomplished as perfectly as at home. It is divided into four bed rooms on sides and dining room in center. The awning as shown in this tent is not extra to the tent, but part of the wall lifted up, thus forming an awning affording free circulation of air through the tent, as well as complete shade. The prices include everything complete, ready for putting up.

No.	Size	Wall	Pole	White 10 ounce double filling or ounce army duck.	White 12 ounce double ounce army duck.
49199	8 x16½	4 ft	10 ft	$20.96	$23.70
	9 x19	6 ft	10 ft	22.75	26.00
	12 x19	6 ft	11 ft	26.90	30.60
	12 x21½	6 ft	11 ft	29.60	33.35
	14 x21½	6 ft	11 ft	32.20	36.60
	14 x23½	6 ft	12 ft	34.25	38.90
	16½x23½	6 ft	12 ft	38.85	44.40

Dimensions of bed rooms and dining room.

2 bedrooms	5½x9	Dining room	5 x9
2 bedrooms	6 x9	Dining room	6½x9
4 bedrooms	6 x7	Dining room	7½x12
4 bedrooms	6 x7	Dining room	7½x12
4 bedrooms	7 x7	Dining room	7½x14
4 bedrooms	7 x7	Dining room	7½x14
4 bedrooms	8½x8½	Dining room	7½x10½

The above prices include everything complete ready for putting up.

NOTE—When 8 oz. stripe blue or brown is wanted the price will be the same as 10 oz., double filling.

The Protean Tent.

49200

It is the best all 'round tent for camping purposes in the world. It is compact, roomy, easy to put up, and suitable for both hot and cold weather; only one pole required. The tent has a sod cloth 9 inches wide all around to keep out wind and mosquitoes. The tent has also a "fly" that can be used in many ways, as a fly protecting the roof and part of sides or as an awning in front of tent, or as a store house. It has other advantages too numerous to mention here, and circulars showing the different shapes it can be made into with illustrations free.

Prices of Protean tents, including fly, sod cloth, ash pole and pins complete ready to set up.

Order No. 49200.

Size on Ground.	Height, Rear Wall.	Height of Pole.	8 oz. Duck, Single Filling.	10 oz. Duck, Single Filling.	Additional for 3 Joint Pole.	Additional for Com- stock's Carry Bag With Shoulder Straps.
6½x6½	2 ft	6ft 9 in.	$6.60	$7.80	$1.25	$1.00
7 x7	3 ft	7ft 3 in.	8.00	9.40	1.70	1.40
8 x8	2½ ft	8ft 9 in.	10.00	11.50	1.70	1.40
9 x9	3 ft	9ft 9 in.	13.25	15.10	2.10	1.90

Comstock's Carry Bag.

49201 It is a very simple and inexpensive bag for carrying tent, jointed pole, pegs and blankets or extra clothing. It is light and convenient, and carries the load in comfortable position on the back. The bag can be instantly opened without removing the straps. The straps and cords can be instantly detached and stowed in top of bag for shipment. When ordering these bags for Protean tents, column in tent list above marked "additional for patent carry bags with shoulder straps" will give price of bag for any sized tent. Tent, jointed pole, etc., when packed in this bag can be checked as baggage. Each $1.30

Comstock's Malleable Iron Tent Peg.

49202 One set of these pegs will last a lifetime, as they cannot be broken. They are fully as light as wooden pegs of the same holding power, and will pack in one quarter the space. They save time and labor in putting up any tent.

	Doz
Short pegs, 8½ inches, weigh 4½ to 5 ozs.	$0.75
Long pegs, 13½ inches, weigh 7 to 7½ ozs.	1.00

Each set of one dozen or more put up in 12 oz. canvas bag. If you own a tent send for a set of these pegs.

Wall Tents.

We can furnish tents in large or small quantities on short notice generally. Our tents are the best grade, they are all full size, and all have a good "pitch" or roof, to turn rain, and all made in a durable substantial manner. Prices in lots of 5 or more furnished on application. Tents will not be sent C. O. D., they have to be made to order.

We warrant them to be exactly as represented. In ordering give catalogue number, length and breadth and price.

We can make to order all kinds of tents, canopies, etc.

Wall Tent No. 49215

Wall Tents.

Weights without poles, 7x7, 30 lbs.; 9½x12, 40 to 50 lbs.; 14x18, 96 to 76 lbs.; 16x24, 120 to 130 lbs.; 18x32, 147 to 160 lbs. Ridge poles weigh 23 ounces to the foot. Upright poles, 14 oz. to the foot. Pins weigh ¼ to ½ pounds each. All of our 12 ounce duck tents are double filling, best quality.

No.	Length and Breadth. Feet	Height Wall. Feet	Height Pole. Feet	Price with Poles, Pins, Guys, etc. Complete ready to set up		
				8 oz. Duck.	10 oz. Duck.	12 oz. Duck.
Order 49215	7 x 7	3	7	$3.70	$4.30	$5.80
	7 x 9	3	7	4.35	5.10	6.70
	9 x 9	3	7½	5.05	5.90	7.50
	9½ x 12	3	7½	5.95	6.95	9.20
	9½ x 14	4	7½	6.75	7.85	10.40
	12 x 12	3½	8	7.05	8.25	10.90
	12 x 14	3½	8	7.95	9.30	12.35
	12 x 16	3½	8	8.85	10.30	13.75
	14 x 18	3½	8	9.80	11.45	15.05
	14 x 14	4	9	9.45	11.10	14.75
	14 x 16	4	9	10.45	12.25	16.30
	14 x 18	4	9	11.65	13.70	18.15
	14 x 20	4	9	12.95	15.05	19.70
	14 x 24	4	9	14.60	17.00	22.10
	16 x 16	5	11	12.95	15.25	20.25
	16 x 18	5	11	14.25	16.65	22.00
	16 x 20	5	11	15.70	18.30	23.95
	16 x 24	5	11	17.85	20.80	27.15
	16 x 30	5	11	21.02	26.00	32.90
	16 x 35	5	11	24.20	28.25	36.90
	18 x 18	5	11	17.05	19.45	25.40
	18 x 20	5	11	17.95	20.95	27.45
	18 x 24	5	11	20.05	23.40	30.55
	18 x 30	5	11	24.60	28.90	39.75
	18 x 35	5	11	26.95	31.20	41.55

Photographers' Tent.

49220 Weight, without poles, 60 to 176 pounds. Ridge poles, 22 to 25 oz. per foot in length.

Size	Pole.	Wall	Price, complete, without dark room.		
			8 oz. single filling duck	10 oz. single filling duck	10 oz. double filling duck
12x16 ft	11 ft	6 ft	$13.55	$15.20	$18.20
12x21 ft	11 ft	6 ft	16.55	19.10	22.54
12x24 ft	11 ft	6 ft	18.40	21.15	24.85
14x16 ft	12 ft	6 ft	15.20	17.95	21.60
14x21 ft	12 ft	6 ft	18.40	21.15	25.55
14x24 ft	12 ft	6 ft	20.00	23.25	27.60
14x28 ft	12 ft	6 ft	22.75	26.45	31.20
16x18 ft	13 ft	6 ft	17.95	20.95	25.05
16x24 ft	13 ft	6 ft	21.10	25.75	30.60
16x28 ft	13 ft	6 ft	25.10	29.20	34.75
16x30 ft	13 ft	6 ft	26.90	31.30	37.25

Prices on tents include poles, pins, guys, etc. Tent complete ready to set up.

Dark rooms extra, 6x6 feet, $7.80; 4½x4½ feet $6.50. Our dark rooms are made of same material, same weight and color as the tent—all white. We make the room only, the artist can darken it to suit his own taste. We use black sheeting, some yellow, etc.

MILITARY GOODS

Palmetto, or Lawn Tents.

These are positively the best tent made for lawn, croquet or picnic parties. They are made of 8 ounce awning duck, color, blue and white, or brown and white, alternate shades. They have but one pole, and that in center. Top is supported by wood frame umbrella shape. It can be set up in three to five minutes and taken down as speedily as the closing of an umbrella. The cut shows this tent with awning extension.

Size of Base.	Size of Top.	Height in Center.	Height at Side.	Price, without Awning.	Price with Awning.
7 x 7	2 ft. 4 in.	7 ft. 6 in.	6 ft.	$4.30	$5.95
8 x 8	3 ft. 4 in.	8 ft.	6 ft.	4.95	6.50
9 x 9	3 ft. 6 in.	8 ft. 6 in.	7 ft.	6.25	7.95
10 x 10	3 ft. 6 in.	9 ft.	7 ft. 6 in.	7.00	9.00

Black Oiled Wagon Cover.

These covers are made from 8 oz. duck and although black and called tarpaulins, have no tar in their composition. Our water proof dressing is an oil preparation, and is entirely free from anything calculated to rot or burn the canvas, but adds to the durability of the cover, being impervious to water, and very soft and pliable. It will neither rot nor mildew from damp, nor break from being too hard. They are invaluable to all persons who are shipping and receiving goods which are liable to damage from wet weather. In ordering, give catalogue number, size and price.

Weight to 28 pounds. 8x12, 12 lbs; 6x6, 9 lbs; 7x12, 10 lbs; 7x14, 14 lbs.

No.	Size.	Price.	Size.	Price.	Size.	Price
49227	6x 8 ft	$2.50	7x 9 ft	$3.30	8x10 ft	$4.00
	6x 9 ft	2.85	7x10 ft	3.65	8x12 ft	5.15
	6x10 ft	3.10	7x12 ft	4.40	8x14 ft	5.85
	6x12 ft	3.75	7x14 ft	5.10	8x16 ft	6.65
	6x14 ft	4.35	7x16 ft	5.80	9x14 ft	6.60

TRY AND GET INTO THE HABIT OF THINKING about the goods that you will need two or three weeks hence. This plan will double the advantages of buying away from home.

CIVIL WAR FLAGS

At first when the Union,
was loyal to a trust.
Like friends and like brethren,
kind we were, and just.
But now when Northern treachery
attempts our right to march,
we hoist on high the Bonnie Blue
*   Flag*
that bears the single star.
        —"The Bonnie Blue Flag"
        by H. MacCarthy. (A popular
        secessionist rallying song)

The single star on the Bonnie Blue Flag represented South Carolina, first state of the Confederacy. Despite the rebellion it helped to foment, the pale-blue secessionist standard was never adopted by the C.S.A.—but it remained unchallenged as a symbol for "The Cause" until after the first Battle of Bull Run (July 1861) when the Confederate Battle Flag was adopted.

This flag, with its starry blue St. Andrew's Cross shielding a red field, is today the country's second most popular. Revived throughout the U.S. during the Civil War centennial of the early 1960s—a period also characterized by (relatively subdued) national upheaval—the "Stars and Bars" was a salient emblem of "Surrender, Hell!" obduracy. Since then, the old Confederate Battle Flag has stayed on to symbolize something of a more benign national independence of mind. That may be the reason why, although thousands of their ancestors died fighting against it, it's a facsimile of the Stars and Bars that's the preferred front-bumper license plate of as many modern New Englanders.

In addition to those flags shown, Authentic Reproductions of Ashland, Ohio, manufactures a replica of the thirty-three-star Union flag, the one fired upon at Fort Sumter the day the war began.

Bonnie Blue Flag: 3 feet by 5 feet. Price: $63.25.

First Confederate National (the true "Stars and Bars"): 3 feet by 5 feet. Price: $41.25.

Confederate Battle Flag: 3 feet by 5 feet. Price: $59. Cavalry: 32 inches by 32 inches. Price: $59. Artillery: 38 inches by 38 inches. Price: $81. Infantry: 51 inches by 51 inches. Price: $145.

Second Confederate National: 3 feet by 5 feet. Price: $49.50.

Third Confederate National: 3 feet by 5 feet. Price: $49.50.

Add $2.50 for shipping and handling.

AUTHENTIC REPRODUCTIONS

1031 Old Nankin Road, R-3
Ashland, OH 44805
Tel. 419/289-6642

BONNIE BLUE
In 1860, the BONNIE BLUE flag was unofficially used throughout the south. This flag was never adopted by the Confederate States of America. Solid light blue field with white star in center. White star represents SOUTH CAROLINA, first state to secede from the Union.
SIZE: 3' x 5'

FIRST CONFEDERATE NATIONAL
Adopted March 4, 1861, this was the first flag of the Confederacy. Also called the "STARS AND BARS." Red and white bars with blue field and white stars.
SIZE: 3' x 5'

BATTLE FLAG
The second flag of the Confederacy, this flag was red with a blue St. Andrews Cross containing 13 white stars.
SIZE: 3' x 5'
REGULATION SIZE:
Cavalry: 32" x 32"
Artillery: 38" x 38"
Infantry: 51" x 51"

SECOND CONFEDERATE NATIONAL
Also called the "JACKSON FLAG," this was the third flag of the Confederacy and was adopted May 1, 1863 to replace the "stars and bars."
SIZE: 3' x 5'

THIRD CONFEDERATE NATIONAL
This was the fourth flag of the Confederacy, adopted March 4, 1865. A broad vertical red bar was added to the right hand edge of the "Second Confederate National" flag so that it could not be mistaken for a flag of truce.
SIZE: 3' x 5'

Civil War Uniforms

THE C & D Jarnagin Company of Corinth, Mississippi, manufactures replica nineteenth-century military (primarily Civil War) uniforms, equipment, and accoutrements. Regarding the authenticity of these, a single fact culled from a sidebar in their catalog can make the point standing alone: For its Confederate uniforms, Jarnagin identifies and replicates *five* shades of gray (including the brownish Tuscaloosa gray that was earmarked for the Eastern Theater; and the dark Richmond gray, so called because it was worn by soldiers who defended the Confederate capital) and *four* shades of butternut. This attention to detail extends to each cut, stitch, and drape of every item produced. "We're not a merchandise mart," said John Jarnagin while leveling a gaze at me over the telephone, "we're a military reproduction service."

"Service" is very much the operative word here. Prospective customers are invited to fill out "Service Cards" as long as passport applications. These address special fitting problems, inquire after favored activities involving use of the item, and assign a "seniority number" to the customer. All this fidelity to both authenticity and customer care on the part of the Jarnagin Company evokes a strong bond with the customer, and a sense of family pervades the place. John Jarnagin will not suffer fools (or the "frivolous"—nonhistorical—use of uniforms) gladly, but he works long hours in aid of the serious educator, historian, and military-history buff. "Here at least," he advised me, "nice guys come in first."

Although I spent a good deal of time both in correspondence and on the telephone with Mr. Jarnagin, when his company's catalog finally arrived the range of items it contained was still startling. Below (and elsewhere in this section) is a sampling of these:

UNITED STATES ARMY

FORAGE CAP in 1858 a board of officers designed the forage cap—closely following the French "kepi"—for general use by the army. The design was adopted in part because it allowed for machine manufacture and thereby reduced expenses. During the war, literally all enlisted men were issued a regulation forage cap of dark-blue wool stiffened with buckram, and having a pasteboard crown reinforcement, a polished cotton lining, a crescent-shaped leather visor, and two General Service brass buttons. The only acceptable substitute for the regulation forage caps were those brought into the service through private means. Sometimes scorned as "shapeless feedbags," these forage caps stood high on the head and were relatively unattractive.

Nowadays the junk cap market makes forage-style caps that have become popular among inner-city street gang

MODEL 1852

SHIRT **Prior to the issuance of this shirt, the army acquired shirts on the open market, contracting for them to no specific pattern.** The 1852 shirt is a four-button pullover with a yoke in the back, single-button cuffs, and a square-bottom plaquet in front. Before the war a gray wool shirt was specified, but during it a white muslin shirt of the same pattern was very much in evidence. Civilian production provided colored and print shirts of a similar cut.

members and bikers. I asked one of the latter just what they called these blue caps and was told "rebel hats." Damned close enough.

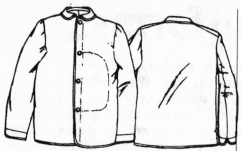

MODEL 1851 JEFFERSON BROGAN

Although quality varied, the "bootees" or shoes that were issued to the troops were better made than their civilian counterparts. Also called "mudscows" or "gunboats," these M1851 brogans were rights and lefts, unlike the straight-last types that preceded them. Other changes included a shortening of the upper so that it came to just above the ankle, and a reduction of the lace holes from five or six down to four.

The Jarnagin Company's Jefferson brogans are made of moderately heavy oak-tanned leather, with black "rough out" exteriors. The soles of heavy leather are fastened with wooden pegs.

FATIGUE JACKET

This is the four-button "sack" coat that was the mainstay of all service branches during the war. The fatigue jacket is fashioned of 12-ounce dark-blue wool, unlined, with an inside left-hand breast pocket (lined coats were supposedly issued to recruits). The comfort and usefulness of the sack coat made it a popular garment during the war.

MOUNTED SERVICES OVERCOAT

Made of a heavy, sky-blue wool, the mounted troops' overcoat is double-breasted, and has a wrist-length cape and a stand-and-fall collar. Should they wish, mounted officers could substitute dark-blue woolen material.

ARMY-PATTERN UNDERWEAR

The soldier of the 1850s and 1860s was issued underwear of a heavy cotton "canton" flannel. John Jarnagin noted that the undershirt was mainly used (except during cold weather) as a regular shirt worn around camp. The drawers, he continued, were worn long as issued during the winter, and then cut off above the knee in spring. C & D Jarnagin uses the same material as the originals, and have sized them so that they will fit after one washing in hot water, and then shrink no further.

CONFEDERATE ARMY

Confederate Army Regulations prescribed uniforms for all branches of the service, but particularly in the last years of the war few Confederates were well supplied with them. Many 1861 volunteers wore militia uniforms and homespun clothing, and in some instances stripped the uniforms from the bodies of the enemy dead. Shorn of their insignia and (in some commands) dyed gray, they then served the Confederate cause. Especially prized were "Yankee overcoats," also known as the foot overcoat.

C & D Jarnagin's Confederate uniforms follow the regulations of the Confederate War Department and, worn all together, would not represent a realistic "mustering out." The typical uniform of the rebel guerrilla would be a hodgepodge of homespun and official garb.

COMMON SHELL JACKET

The common shell or roundabout jacket was the basic style used throughout the war in all theaters and by all service branches. It's a reasonably close-fitting, waist-length jacket, with a stand-up collar. Each jacket is lined with either muslin or polished cotton and has an inside breast pocket. Fronts have five to ten buttons, seven or nine being most common in the Eastern Theater (and

in the early war everywhere), six or eight in the Western, or Trans-Mississippi, Theater. These jackets may have service-branch-trimmed collars or cuffs, and either solid-color or piped edges.

KEPI, CHASSEUR-STYLE FORAGE CAP

Somewhat more stylish than the Federal-based forage cap, the rakish chasseur-style hat was very popular among Confederate forces. C & D Jarnagin's replicas have been patterned after originals, featuring a heavy leather brim and a lining of polished cotton with drawstring adjustment. These caps are distinctly more substantial than the U.S. model 1872 forage caps with which they are often confused. As with the regulation C.S. forage caps, the Jarnagin Company's chasseur-style kepis may be ordered either in a solid color or with a dark-blue bottom band and tops distinguished by arms-of-service colors—red (for artillery), light blue (infantry), or yellow (cavalry).

CONFEDERATE FROCK COAT

"The uniform shall be a double-breasted tunic of gray cloth, known as cadet gray, with the skirt extending halfway between the hip and the knee." So stated the Confederate War Department regulations promulgated in 1861, but as C & D Jarnagin notes, seemingly never enacted. While very few of these double-breasted coats were ever noted in the field, a large number of single-breasted coats were worn, and these are what the Jarnagin Company replicates.

The single-breasted Confederate frock coats are fully lined in heavy muslin and have two tail pockets. They also have either seven- or nine-button fronts, and may be dressed plain or with trimmed collar and cuffs.

Catalog and price list of nineteenth-century military uniforms and equipment available, $2.

C & D JARNAGIN COMPANY

Route 3, Box 217
Corinth, MS 38834
Tel. 601/287-4977 for customer service, or toll free 800/647-7084 for new orders only.

MILITARY HEADGEAR

Militaria, Inc., of Kearny, New Jersey offers several Civil War (and other nineteenth-century) military hats and caps not in the Jarnagin catalog. These are of "museum quality," and made of wool or fur felt. All of Militaria's headgear comes with appropriate leather chin straps, sweat bands, and visors. Included are U.S. and C.S. fur felt hats, and U.S. Indian War fur felt hats. Civil War uniforms, insignia, and trim are also offered.

Catalog and price list available, $1.50.

MILITARIA, INC.

138 Kearny Avenue
Kearny, NJ 07032
Tel. 201/998-7471

UNITED STATES ARMY CAMPAIGN HATS

MODEL 1885–1898

A precise replica of the hat worn by Teddy Roosevelt's Rough Riders at San Juan Hill, the Model 1885 campaign hat differs slightly from the actual type worn earlier by Indian fighters. In 1885 these hats used small brass-screen ventilators; Red River has been unable to locate these, so the replicas lack them. The 1889 model had a star pattern punched into the crown, which Red River will reproduce on request.

This hat is made of 5X-quality beaver fur felt, with the proper pattern grosgrain ribbon band and the two-line stitched border at the brim as per the originals. Tan only. Sizes: 6¾ to 7½.

Price: $50 (plus $3 for shipping and handling).

MODEL 1875

One of the earliest campaign hats issued by the army, the Model 1875 was worn by troopers during the many western campaigns of the 1870s and 1880s (including Custer's defeat at the Little Big Horn on June 25, 1876; and Geronimo's surrender on September 4, 1886, ending the Apache Campaign). Because of the poor quality of the black wool felt originally used, few specimens of these hats now exist.

Red River Outfitters' replica Model 1875 campaign hat is faithful to the originals in all but material. They have substituted a 5X-quality beaver fur felt that would outlast the original material even if it had been worn at Pleiku rather than on the Upper Platte. The Red River Model 1875 Campaign Hat has the authentic grosgrain ribbon band and regulation folded brim. Sizes: 6¾ to 7½.

Price: $50 (plus $3 for shipping and handling).

Catalog of frontier clothing, western and military Americana available, $2.

RED RIVER FRONTIER OUTFITTERS

P.O. Box 241
Tujunga, CA 91042
Tel. 213/352–0177

1883 ARMY CAMPAIGN SHIRT

Designated the "Model 1883 Army Overshirt," this blue wool garment was adopted as an alternative to the heavier five-button blouse that had seen earlier service on the frontier. A simple, practical, and comfortable shirt, the Model 1883 found ready favor from among the officers and enlisted men of all branches of the army.

The 1883 campaign shirt clad the backs of the cavalry and infantrymen who for many months guarded the waterholes and mountain passes in the Arizona and New Mexico Territories during the Geronimo Campaign of 1885–1886; it was standard issue to troops on the northern plains, and saw service during the last, cold campaign that devastated the already defeated Sioux near the Pine Ridge Agency at the end of 1890. Later, this shirt was used as the standard uniform blouse in Cuba during the Spanish-American War, and was worn by the Rough Riders. Before the Model 1883 was retired it also saw duty in the Philippines and at the Chinese Boxer Rebellion.

Red River's replica has been copied from existing original shirts and conforms to period army regulations. Its accuracy in style, detailing, buttons, and material extends to its use of cotton ivory-glaze cloth and an inner yoke as per the originals. Made to your measurements.

Price: $90 (plus $3 for shipping and handling).

Catalog of frontier clothing, western and military Americana available, $2.

RED RIVER FRONTIER OUTFITTERS

P.O. Box 241
Tujunga, CA 91042
Tel. 213/352–0177

C & D JARNAGIN CIVIL WAR ACCOUTERMENTS

During the Civil War the term was the more Gallic "accou*tre*ments," meaning equipment other than weapons and clothing that was carried by a soldier. Here they are mentioned in Ambrose Bierce's late-nineteenth-century short story "An Affair of Outposts":

> *The Governor went forward alone and on foot. In a half-hour he had pushed through a tangled undergrowth covering a boggy soil and entered upon more firm and open ground. Here he found a half-company of infantry lounging behind a line of stacked rifles. The men wore their accoutrements—their belts, cartridge boxes, haversacks, and canteens. Some lying full length on the dry leaves were fast asleep; others in small groups gossiped idly of this and that; a few played at cards; none were far from the line of stacked arms. To the civilian's eye the scene was one of carelessness, confusion, indifference; a soldier would have observed expectancy and readiness.*

CARTRIDGE BOXES These replica cartridge boxes, all made of oak-tanned leather and stitched with natural linen thread, extend back to the Revolutionary War. Each box uses interior tin liners and wooden cartridge blocks as per the original upon which they're based. Included are the militia-type cartridge box for flintlock musket (the "Lafayette"); the improved U.S. Model 1808; the U.S. Model 1841, designed for use with the Mississippi rifle; the British Enfield Infantry, circa 1853, which was imported for use during the Civil War; the U.S. Model 1855 .58-caliber box; and several purely Confederate cartridge boxes, including three types for muskets.

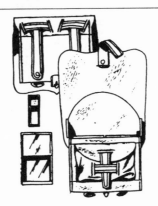

BELTS Naturally, the Jarnagin Company manufactures a full complement of replica nineteenth-century military belts. These include the Model 1840 U.S. regulation sword belt with "puppyfoot" oval belt buckle; the Type of 1839 waistbelt, most commonly used by Confederate troops; the Model 1851 regulation waistbelt for noncommissioned officers; and the Model 1854 regulation waistbelt, most common of the Civil War.

OVAL CONFEDERATE BELT PLATE The Civil War waistbelt was fastened by a lead-filled belt plate of stamped brass, generally oval in shape and with its block lettering indicating either a "C.S." or "U.S." issue. This was the type most often found in all fields of conflict during the war.

The Jarnagin Company also has available an oval U.S. belt plate, an arrow-back wartime type; and several box plates representing both sides.

U.S. MODEL 1858 "SMOOTHSIDE" CANTEEN

The following appears as written in the C & D Jarnagin catalog:

> *This is the first general-issue "modern-style" canteen of the U.S. Army. The first lot delivered—over 20,000—was covered with sky-blue wool. During the war years, covers were also issued in dark blue, various grays, and several shades of brown or tan.*
>
> *The canteen consists of two dish-shaped sides, so formed that they seal together with a solder joint. On the top, a shaped shield mounts a pewter spout. Three strap carriers are soldered to the body. The whole is then covered by wool and a strap attached . . . of natural white military drill. This is three-quarters-of-an-inch wide, double-folded and sewn up on each side. . . .*
>
> *We offer the M1858 canteen in sky blue, dark blue, brown, and gray covers; each having an inspector's cartouche on the strap, as per the originals. This canteen was one of the most essential items of a Federal soldier's gear, and was also preferred by many Confederates when they could get them.*

The Jarnagin Company also offers the general-issue round-drum C.S. canteen, the U.S. M1858 style, and the U.S. "Bullseye" canteen.

FEDERAL REGULATION HAVERSACK,

EARLY WAR When in the field, each soldier would carry his rations in a haversack made of either canvas or leather. In theory these were waterproof affairs, but a downpour would usually render them as unprotective as any cloth bag. The effects that this would have both on the haversack's contents and on the bag itself (most were issued white) were often barely tolerable, even by a foot-soldier's standards. As one wrote: "By the time one of these haversacks had been in use for a few weeks as a receptacle for chunks of fat bacon and fresh meat, damp sugar tied up in a rag—perhaps a piece of an old shirt—potatoes and other vegetables that might be picked up along the route, it took on the color of a printing office towel."

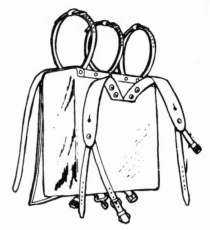

The early-war haversack was first issued to U.S. soldiers during the 1850s and carried into the Civil War by the First Massachusetts Volunteer Infantry, among other regular troops. It is similar to, but smaller than, the wartime version (also offered by the Jarnagin Company) and is made with special military drillcloth treated with black weatherproofing. The early-war haversack contains an inner bag fastened by three bone buttons; the outside strap closure is effected by means of a leather strap and buckle, which bear inspector's marks.

The Jarnagin Company also manufactures an early 1800s haversack known as the Mexican War Type, and both types of C.S. haversacks.

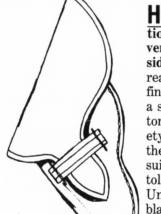

CONFEDERATE

HOLSTER "Be aware," cautions the Jarnagin catalog, "that very many Confederates wore their sidearms on the right side, butt to the rear." The firm's replica C.S. holster is finished in black or russet leather, has a strap-and-tab fastener, and no bottom plug. It is but one of a great variety of holsters that were employed by the Confederacy. Jarnagin's replica is suitable for the Colt Army/Navy pistols, the Remington Army, and other Union and Confederate handguns. A black leather U.S. holster with a brass tab latch (after an original in the Jarnagin collection) is also available.

NONREGULATION SINGLE-BAG

KNAPSACK Civil War knapsacks were notoriously punishing to carry, but this was one of the more comfortable ones. Modeled after an original in the Jarnagin collection, it was one of three types most used by Confederate forces. The original is made of black weatherproofed drill, has leather strappage that has been sewn by hand with linen thread, and includes separate blanket straps. The large bag is divided by a wall of ticking. The Jarnagin Company replica is also available in untreated white drill "to illustrate the Southern lack of resources."

C & D Jarnagin also has available the U.S. regulation 1851 (hardpack, or Mexican War) knapsack; and the U.S. double-bag knapsacks, Types I, II, and III. The Type III double-bag made up more than 90 percent of all the knapsacks used by Federal forces during the war.

OTHER MILITARY

ACCOUTERMENTS In addition to all the above, the C & D Jarnagin Company offers a similar range of replica nineteenth-century scabbards, frogs, cap pouches, and slings.

Catalog and price list of nineteenth-century military uniforms and equipment available, $2.

C & D JARNAGIN COMPANY

Route 3, Box 217
Corinth, MS 38834
Tel. 601/287-4977 for customer
* service, or toll free 800/647-7084 for*
* new orders only*

U.S. 1860 CAVALRY

SABER In 1860 a lighter military saber was introduced to replace the 1840 "Old Wristbreaker" model that had previously been used by the cavalry. The narrower bladed Light Model 1860 saw extensive service during the war.

Characterized as a "good representative modern copy," Dixie Gun Works's replica 1860 cavalry saber features a 35½-inch plated blade, with both hilt and guard made of polished brass. The wooden handle is covered with brown leather and wire-wrapped in the original fashion. The scabbard features an authentic trail drag and rings for attaching to a sword belt.

Catalog of gun supplies available, $3.

DIXIE GUN WORKS, INC.

Gunpowder Lane
Union City, TN 38261

CIVIL WAR CAMP ITEMS

FEDERAL-ISSUE SHELTER TENT
Also known as the *tente d'abri,* **pup, or dog tent,** the shelter tent became available in early 1862 when 300,000 of them were issued to Federal forces. The shelter tent was the most common type of the war.

Troops gave them the "dog tent" name in derision, but in time their versatility—as sunshades, lean-to's, and ground cloths—made them favored gear.

The shelter tent was comprised of two pieces, usually of cotton drill, each carried by a single soldier. The first of these was 5 feet 2 inches by 4 feet 8 inches. The men would combine in threes and use the extra half to block up one end of the structure; or two men would use an overcoat or ground cloth for the same effect. In 1864 a larger tent was issued, complete with a triangular endpiece.

The Jarnagin Company offers replicas of both the 1862 and 1864 model shelter tents. Each half is fully buttonholed on three sides and comes with stamped metal buttons, comparable to the originals, sewn in place. Each half has upper corner reinforcements on which brass grommets have been fixed.

C & D Jarnagin also replicates the U.S. and C.S. Old Army Type wedge tent, the tipi-like U.S. Silbey tent, and a small hospital tent.

TIN ARMY CUP
This is the large-style mug that accompanied the coffee boilers of both armies. "You can stick this one in the fire and boil us a cup of 'java' or 'muck' . . . at any short-half during the march," says the Jarnagin catalog.

COFFEE POT
After an original **dug up by the Jarnagin Company** at the camp occupied by (U.S.) Gen. William S. Rosencrans's Army of the Cumberland before the Battle of Iuka, Mississippi. The tapered pot is about 8½ inches in diameter at the base and 9 inches high. Also available are a small coffee pot, a lidded camp pot, and a washbasin.

FEDERAL DOUBLE BLANKET
Blankets were normally issued to men before they left their home state, but by 1862 the influx of volunteers and militia exhausted supplies. The double blanket, devised as a way to make up for this shortage, was issued "off the roll," giving each soldier a double length of about 11 feet.

The Jarnagin Company offers a replica of this blanket in either single or double length. Brown, with dark-brown end stripes. A Federal regulation saddle blanket is also available.

PLAYING CARDS

Bristol threw down a flyspecked ten,
"Theah," he said in the soft, sweet drawl
That could turn as hard as a Minie-ball,
"This heah day is my lucky day,
And Shepley nevah could play piquet,"
He stretched his arms in a giant yawn,
"Gentlemen, when are we movin' on?
I have no desire for a soldier's end,
While I still have winnin's that I can spend.
And they's certain appointments with certain ladies
Which I'd miss right smart if I went to Hades,
Especially one little black-eyed charmer
Whose virtue, one hopes, is her only armor,
So if Sargent Wingate's mended his saddle
I suggest that we all of us now skedaddle
To employ a term that the Yankees favor—"
—Stephen Vincent Benét,
John Brown's Body, 1927

Poker was the game in most regiments. Francis Lord's *Civil War Collector's Encyclopedia* notes that in the 150th Pennsylvania it was described after the war as the "absorbing occupation" of private soldiers and officers alike—the former "risking his scanty allowance as heedlessly as the latter their liberal stipend." Both sides also enjoyed playing cribbage and euchre.

The Jarnagin Company's Civil War playing cards have been "painstakingly reproduced" from an original deck. Their patriotic military motif is reminiscent of those made by the American Card Company, "the first and only genuine American cards ever produced," according to one contemporary advertisement. The replica cards employ the highest quality color-separation techniques, and have been shellacked by hand in the old way. Each deck has been boxed.

Catalog and price list of nineteenth-century military uniforms and equipment available, $2.

C & D JARNAGIN COMPANY
Route 3, Box 217
Corinth, MS 38834
Tel. 601/287–4977 for customer service, or 800/647–7084 for new orders only

CAMP ITEMS FROM DIXIE GUN WORKS

CIVIL WAR

WALLET Although styles varied greatly, most wallets used during the Civil War were made of pliable brown leather and simply designed. Francis A. Lord's *Civil War Collector's Encyclopedia* notes that most were 4 to 4½ inches long and 2½ to 3 inches wide. Dixie Gun Works offers what it believes to be a highly representational replica of the Civil War wallet, measuring 3 by 5¼ inches and including four inside pockets. Shipping weight: 1 lb.

DEERSKIN

GAUNTLETS Part of the Civil War officer's dress uniform included gauntlets, many of which were elaborately embroidered. Due in part to their utilitarian value, the gauntlet's popularity continued on after the war, well into the late 1800s.

Dixie Gun Works of Union City, Tennessee, offers deerskin gauntlets very similar to those worn during the Civil War. These are large cuffed and tight fitting, but are extremely soft and flexible. Machine stitched.

CONFEDERATE MONEY

"In the North a carpenter got three dollars," said Twain's Connecticut Yankee, "in the South he got fifty—payable in Confederate shinplasters worth a dollar a bushel." Dixie Gun Works's Confederate bills are "reasonable facsimiles" costing somewhat more and capable of buying even less. $1, $5, $10, $50, and $100 notes all included.

Catalog of gun supplies available, $3.

DIXIE GUN WORKS

Gunpowder Lane
Union City, TN 38261

CONFEDERATE ARMY SOUP AS MADE AT GENERAL PICKETT'S HEADQUARTERS

One ham bone, one pod red pepper, black-eyed peas. Boil in a mess pot. Splendid on a wet day.
—*Mrs. Frances E. Owens,*
Mrs. Owen's Cook Book, 1882

MILITARY PISTOLS AND REVOLVERS

Val Forgett founded the Navy Arms Company back in 1958 after his experience with the North-South Skirmish Association (a Civil War reenactment group) triggered in him an awareness of the need for authentically replicated historic firearms. All of Navy Arms's guns are shooting pieces, far safer than their "guess and by God" antecedents.

The word "navy" had been used to identify U.S. military firearms for nearly two centuries before the Navy Company got started. The earliest citation appears in a 1777 description of battle by an officer in the Continental Navy, and later the word most often referred to the .36-caliber 1861 Colt revolver described in the section on "Late Frontier Items."

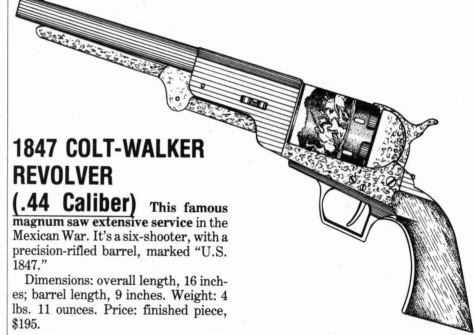

1847 COLT-WALKER REVOLVER
(.44 Caliber) This famous magnum saw extensive service in the Mexican War. It's a six-shooter, with a precision-rifled barrel, marked "U.S. 1847."

Dimensions: overall length, 16 inches; barrel length, 9 inches. Weight: 4 lbs. 11 ounces. Price: finished piece, $195.

"REB" MODEL 1860 REVOLVER
(.36 or .44 Caliber) At the beginning of the Civil War, the largely agricultural South faced difficulties in procuring arms for the fight. Other than the old flintlock and percussion rifle muskets that volunteers could bring into battle from home, before the Confederacy developed sufficient importation of arms (mainly from England) it had to rely on captured weapons and the product of its smattering of arms manufacturers. The most consequential of these was the firm of Griswold and Gunnison, of Griswold, Georgia. Under contract to the C.S.A. from 1862 to 1864, the company produced the Model 1860 percussion revolver.

Navy Arms's replica features a brass frame and backstrap with a steel barrel and cylinder.

Dimensions: overall length, 13 inches; barrel length, 7½ inches. Weight: 2 lbs. 12 ounces.

Prices: finished .36-caliber piece, $93; finished .44-caliber piece, $93.

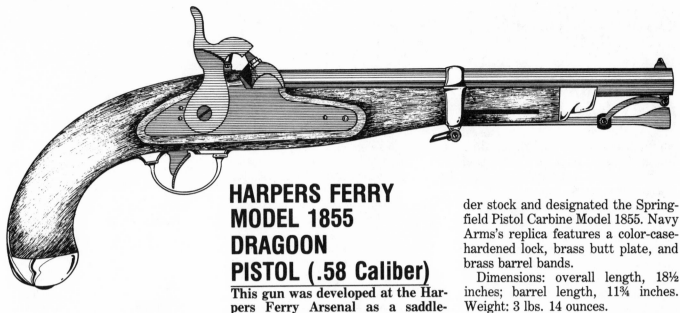

HARPERS FERRY MODEL 1855 DRAGOON PISTOL (.58 Caliber)

This gun was developed at the Harpers Ferry Arsenal as a saddle-holster pistol for the U.S. Mounted Rifles. It was later fitted with a shoulder stock and designated the Springfield Pistol Carbine Model 1855. Navy Arms's replica features a color-case-hardened lock, brass butt plate, and brass barrel bands.

Dimensions: overall length, 18½ inches; barrel length, 11¾ inches. Weight: 3 lbs. 14 ounces.

Prices: finished piece, $218.50; shoulder stock, $45.

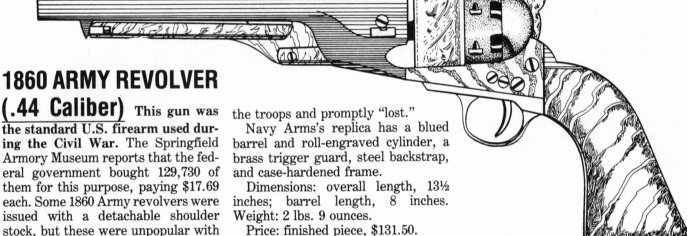

1860 ARMY REVOLVER (.44 Caliber)

This gun was the standard U.S. firearm used during the Civil War. The Springfield Armory Museum reports that the federal government bought 129,730 of them for this purpose, paying $17.69 each. Some 1860 Army revolvers were issued with a detachable shoulder stock, but these were unpopular with the troops and promptly "lost."

Navy Arms's replica has a blued barrel and roll-engraved cylinder, a brass trigger guard, steel backstrap, and case-hardened frame.

Dimensions: overall length, 13½ inches; barrel length, 8 inches. Weight: 2 lbs. 9 ounces.

Price: finished piece, $131.50.

SPILLER & BURR REVOLVER (.36 Caliber)

This percussion revolver was originally produced for the Confederacy by Spiller & Burr of Atlanta between 1862 and 1864. After the company proved unable to comply with an order for 15,000 pieces, the Confederate government purchased it and moved it to the Macon Armory.

Navy Arms's replica comes with a brass frame, trigger guard, backstrap, and top strap. It has an octagonal blued barrel and cylinder.

Dimensions: overall length, 12½ inches; barrel length, 7 inches. Weight: 2 lbs. 8 ounces.

Price: finished piece, $109.

When ordering any of the above, include $4 to cover shipping, handling, and insurance.

Catalog of replica firearms and accessories available, $2.

NAVY ARMS COMPANY

689 Bergen Boulevard
Ridgefield, NJ 07657
Tel. 201/945-2500

ALLEN FIREARMS'S REVOLVERS

1858 REMINGTON ARMY (.44 Caliber)

This is the gun that Colt's closest competitor, the firm of E. Remington & Sons, placed on the market after Sam Colt's patent on muzzle-loading revolvers expired. Despite its single drawback—difficulty of cleaning—the 1858 Army's sturdy construction and precision aim made it a favorite among Civil War troopers. In fact, at the end of the war when the U.S. government offered to sell each of its soldiers the weapon they had been issued, the Remingtons were most often selected.

Allen Firearms's replica 1858 Remington is a six-shot muzzle-loader with a blued-steel frame and brass trigger guard. It has a two-piece walnut grip and a tapered octagonal barrel.

Dimensions: overall length, 13¾ inches; barrel length, 7½ inches. Weight: 2.65 lbs.

Price: $198, ppd.

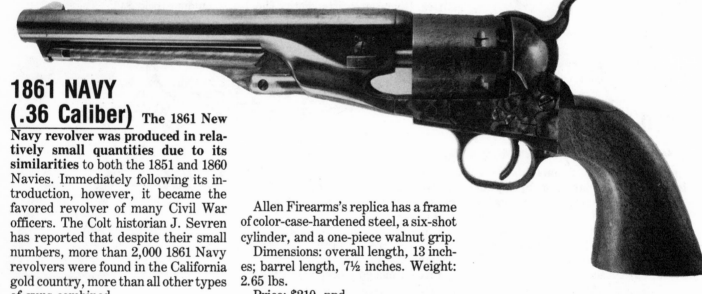

1861 NAVY (.36 Caliber)

The 1861 New Navy revolver was produced in relatively small quantities due to its similarities to both the 1851 and 1860 Navies. Immediately following its introduction, however, it became the favored revolver of many Civil War officers. The Colt historian J. Sevren has reported that despite their small numbers, more than 2,000 1861 Navy revolvers were found in the California gold country, more than all other types of guns combined.

Allen Firearms's replica has a frame of color-case-hardened steel, a six-shot cylinder, and a one-piece walnut grip.

Dimensions: overall length, 13 inches; barrel length, 7½ inches. Weight: 2.65 lbs.

Price: $210, ppd.

TEXAS CONFEDERATE DRAGOON (.44 Caliber)

In 1862 the Confederate State of Texas commissioned Tucker, Sherrard & Company of Lancaster, Texas, to make 3,000 revolvers in lots of a .44 caliber (dragoon) and a .36 caliber (navy). Allen Firearms's Texas Dragoon model replicates the characteristics of the originals faithfully, right down to their cylinder engravings.

Dimensions: overall length, 13½ inches; barrel length, 7½ inches. Weight: 3.97 lbs.

Price $239, ppd.

Catalog of firearms and accessories available.

ALLEN FIREARMS COMPANY

1107 Pen Road
Santa Fe, NM 87501
Tel. 505/983–1961

NAVY ARMS'S MILITARY RIFLES

1841 MISSISSIPPI RIFLE

The old Mississippi Rifle, carrying a half-ounce ball, is a favorite with them.
—Rodney Glisan, Journal of Army Life, *1874*

This .58-caliber percussion lock weapon gained its name during the 1846 Mexican War after Jefferson Davis's Mississippi Regiment used it to turn back Santa Anna at the decisive battle of Buena Vista. Although the rifle was obsolete by 1855, its reputation caused the Colt Company to rebuild it to accommodate the Union Army's .58-caliber mini-ball in 1861.
Navy Arms's replica Mississippi rifle features a browned barrel, polished brass fittings, and a patchbox for tools and spare parts. It has a color-case-hardened lock, a walnut stock, and brass buttplate, trigger guard, and patchbox.

Dimensions: overall length, 48 inches; barrel length, 33 inches. Weight: 9½ lbs.

Price: finished model, $263 (plus $6 for shipping, handling, and insurance).

THREE-BAND ENFIELD, MODEL 1853

The .58-caliber Enfield Model 1853 was made chiefly at the London Armoury Company in Enfield, England, and was considered to be one of the best of the foreign arms to see service during the Civil War.

Similar to the Springfield Rifle (the machine tools at the Enfield armory were actually direct copies of the U.S. armory at Springfield, Massachusetts), the Enfield was admired in one contemporary account as "a beautiful arm [that] presented a natty appearance." Enfields were purchased in large amounts by both the Union and Confederate governments.

Navy Arms's replica Three-Band Enfield percussion long gun features the traditional Enfield folding-ladder rear sight and inverted-"V" front sight.

Dimensions: overall length, 54 inches; barrel length, 39 inches. Weight: 9½ lbs.

Prices: finished model, $315; Enfield bayonet and scabbard, $30 (plus $6 or $3, respectively, for shipping, handling, and insurance).

1863 SPRINGFIELD RIFLE

America's "most historical firearm" was the .58-caliber muzzle-loading Springfield percussion rifle, brought into the Civil War for its ability to stabilize the dreaded mini-ball. As described in the *Civil War Collector's Encyclopedia*, the 1863 Springfield was a variation of the 1861 model (a.k.a. the U.S. Rifle-Musket) that was so advanced for its time as to cause one of the 52nd Massachusetts Volunteers to write home in a torrent of admiration:

Our guns were issued to us the other day, beautiful pieces; of the most improved pattern—the Springfield rifled musket. . . . Mine is behind me now, dark black—walnut stock, well oiled, so that the beauty of the wood is brought out, hollowed at the base, and smoothly fitted with steel, to correspond exactly to the curve of the shoulder, against which I shall have to press it many a time. The spring of the lock, just stiff and just limber enough; the eagle and stamp of the government pressed into the steel plate; barrel, long and glistening—bound into its bed by gleaming rings—long and straight and so bright that when I present arms, and bring it before my face, I can see the nose and spectacles and the heavy beard on lip and chin. . . .

Navy Arms claims to have carefully replicated the 1863 Springfield rifle down to its most minute detail. Their piece is a full-size three-band musket with a precision rifled barrel that is identical to the original.

Dimensions: overall length, 56 inches; barrel length, 40 inches. Weight: 9½ lbs.

Price: finished model, $380 (plus $6 for shipping, handling, and insurance).

Color catalog of replica arms and accessories available, $2.

NAVY ARMS COMPANY

689 Bergen Boulevard
Ridgefield, NJ 07657
Tel. 201/945–2500

1860–1874 ISSUE FULL-FLAP CAVALRY HOLSTER

This handmade replica of the holster used by Federal cavalry troopers throughout the War between the States has been patterned after an original in the collection of Red River Outfitters.

The holster is made of oak-tanned leather and will hold all Civil War-era Colts and Remingtons, as well as certain other large cavalry pistols of the period. Black only.

Price: $30 (plus $3 for shipping and handling).

Catalog of frontier clothing, western and military Americana available, $2.

RED RIVER FRONTIER OUTFITTERS

P.O. Box 241
Tujunga, CA 91042
Tel. 213/352–0177

CIVIL WAR WOODEN ARTILLERY BUCKETS

During the Civil War, according to Francis Lord's *Civil War Collector's Encyclopedia,* buckets were used to carry cartridges from the magazines to the gun batteries. The cartridges were then transferred to haversacks or "pass-boxes" for distribution to the individual artillery pieces.

Catalog of military and camp items available, $1.

PRODUCTS OF THE PAST

P.O. Box 12
West Main Street
Wilmington, VT 05363
Tel. 802/464–5569

WALKER-DRAGOON FLASK

During the 1830s and 1840s the powder flask gradually replaced the horn, although there are accounts of some rural Confederates' using the latter in the early days of the Civil War. The Log Cabin Shop's powder flask is a replica of one originally used to charge such large muzzle-loading revolvers as the famous Colt-Walker or the Dragoon. This flask features an adjustable charger head that automatically throws a correctly measured charge.

Dimensions: 8½ inches high. Weight: 9 ounces. Log Cabin catalog #35F3. Price: $16.50.

Catalog of black-powder supplies and accessories available, $4.

THE LOG CABIN SHOP

P.O. Box 275
Lodi, OH 44254
Tel. 216/948–1082

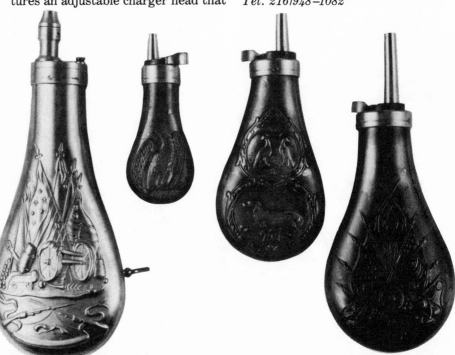

ORDNANCE RIFLE

BARREL

A three-quarter-scale replica of the Federal 3-inch rifled gun that revolutionized siege warfare in 1862, when ten such guns (and twenty-six smoothbores) enabled Gen. Quincy Adams Gillmore to breach the Confederate line's 7½-foot-thick brick walls at Fort Pulaski. The siege lasted only twenty-four hours, and Gen. Gillmore's batteries fired from a point one mile from their target! The 3-inch rifled guns were manufactured in large quantities and were considered among the most important weapons of the war.

Dixie Gun Works's ordnance rifle barrel has an overall length of 55⅛ inches and a smooth bore of 2⁵/₁₆ inches. Weight: 340 lbs.

A 2⁵/₁₆-inch smoothbore carriage-mounted replica Civil War field cannon and a replica 1836 mountain howitzer barrel are also available.

Catalog of gun supplies available, $3.

DIXIE GUN WORKS

Gunpowder Lane
Union City, TN 38261

MINI-BALLS AND

MOLD

The mini-ball was the 1848 invention of Capt. Claude Minié of the army of France. It was a bullet that revolutionized nineteenth-century warfare.

Cast as a projectile, the true mini-ball was hollowed at the base for about one-third of its length. When the gun was fired, this configuration allowed the explosive gases to force the lead into the barrel's riflings with increased velocity, giving the bullet greater smashing power. The U.S. Army adopted the mini-ball in 1855, and it was used extensively in the .58-caliber rifle muskets.

Prices: .58-caliber mini-balls, twenty for $4; mini-ball mold, $28.75 (plus $1.50 each for shipping and handling).

Catalog of replica firearms and accessories available, $2.

NAVY ARMS COMPANY

689 Bergen Boulevard
Ridgefield, NJ 07657
Tel. 201/945-2500

GATLING GUN

Improving on the technology previously provided by the Ager "Coffee Mill" (1852) and the Barnes Machine Cannon (1856), Richard Jordan Gatling patented his "revolving gun battery" in November 1862. His invention has been widely acknowledged as the forerunner of the modern machine gun.

Believing that use of his rapid-fire gun would hasten a Federal victory, Gatling's efforts to sell the U.S. Army on his gun met with bureaucratic stonewalling, an ancient institution even then. The inventor persisted, however, and was eventually able to induce Gen. B. F. Butler to observe a demonstration of the weapon. Butler was so impressed that he paid a thousand dollars apiece for twelve Gatlings and personally directed their use during Grant's nine-month siege of Petersburg, Virginia. The U.S. Army's untimely adoption of the weapon took place in 1866, a year following Lee's surrender; but for forty years thereafter, the Gatling gun was used by virtually every major power in every major conflict (including the Franco-Prussian and Spanish-American Wars) throughout the world.

George Shimek, a "forge and anvil" blacksmith out of Waterloo, Iowa, became interested in the Gatling gun after he saw a replica of one at a 1982 Civil War battle reenactment in East Davenport. Using copies of the original drawings submitted by Gatling for his patent, Shimek began building his replica in January 1983, taking about 250 hours to complete the piece. Mr. Shimek's Gatling is a replica of the 1862 model, a .50-caliber, black-powder percussion instrument. It will fire 200 rounds per minute and, according to Shimek, is highly accurate.

Dimensions: overall length, 38 inches; barrel length, 22 inches. Weight (without carriage): 135 lbs.

Price: $10,000; complete mechanical blueprints, $25.

CUSTOM BLACKSMITHING AND MANUFACTURING

827 Commercial
Waterloo, IA 50702
Tel. 319/291-2095

BOOTH'S
DERRINGER

During the April 14, 1865, performance, of *Our American Cousin* at Ford's Theatre, young Julia Shephard sat in the audience excitedly writing a note to her father back home:

The President is in yonder upper right hand private box so handsomely decked with silken flags festooned over a picture of George Washington. The young and lovely daughter of Senator Harris is the only one of the party we can see, as flags hide the rest. But we know "Father Abraham" is there, like a father watching what interests his children. . . . How sociable it seems, like one family sitting around their parlor fire. . . . The American Cousin has just been making love to a young lady who says she will never marry but for love, yet when her mother and herself find he has lost his property they retreat in disgust at the left of the stage, while the American Cousin goes out at the right. We are waiting for the next scene.

The next scene would be the final one in a chapter of American history: the crack of the assassin's pistol and his leap onto the stage. Many recognized the actor John Wilkes Booth, and until they learned of the president's mortal wound, believed his dramatics to be a new part of the play. Lincoln was carried across the street to the Petersen House, where he died the next morning. Twelve days later Booth, while hiding in a tobacco barn near Port Royal, Virginia, was surrounded by soldiers. He was shot in the neck and died shortly thereafter, meeting the same fate as his victim.

Dixie Gun Works offers a replica of the .41-caliber pistol wielded by Booth at Ford's Theatre that they call the "Lincoln Derringer." As described in their catalog, the gun has a "two-inch browned barrel . . . and will shoot a .400 patched ball. Top barrel flat and lock is marked 'Deringer Philadela.' . . . German silver furniture includes triggerguard with pineapple finial, wedge plates, nose inlay, wrist inlay, side inlay, and tear-drop inlay on the birdhead grip. Walnut-stained wood with a checkered grip. Brass front sight with rear sight positioned on the tang of the breechplug. Case hardened lock, hammer, and trigger. . . . An excellent high-quality reproduction. . . . Made in Italy." Shipping weight: 3 lbs.

Catalog of gun supplies available, $3.

DIXIE GUN WORKS

Gunpowder Lane
Union City, TN 38261

WASHINGTON IRVING FACSIMILE LIBRARY

Hailed by William Makepeace Thackeray as "the first ambassador whom the New World of Letters sent to the Old," Washington Irving (1783–1859) was indeed the first American writer to attain recognition abroad for his literary works. The Sleepy Hollow Press, an educational service of Sleepy Hollow Restorations (which owns and maintains several historic sites in the lower Hudson Valley, including Sunnyside, Irving's Tarrytown, New York, home) has reprinted a series of Irving's nineteenth-century editions, first published by G. P. Putnam. "Faithful to the original editions as contemporary book manufacturing and materials will allow," Sleepy Hollow Press has made a great effort to match the original volumes in both quality and authenticity.

"HE WAS A SMALL, BRISK-LOOKING OLD GENTLEMAN, DRESSED IN RUSTY BLACK COAT, A PAIR OF OLIVE VELVET BREECHES, AND A SMALL COCKED HAT." SO IRVING INTRODUCES "DIEDRICH KNICKERBOCKER," THE HISTORIAN HE INVENTS TO WRITE *A HISTORY OF NEW YORK* (1809), A SATIRICAL AND STILL FUNNY ACCOUNT OF THE EARLY DUTCH SETTLERS OF "MY BELOVED ISLAND OF MANNA-HATA!" THE SKETCH OF FATHER KNICKERBOCKER IS BY IRVING'S FAVORITE BOOK ILLUSTRATOR, F.O.C. DARLEY.

DIEDRICH KNICKERBOCKER'S
A HISTORY OF NEW YORK

Diedrich Knickerbocker *I have worn to death in my pocket.*
—*Charles Dickens*

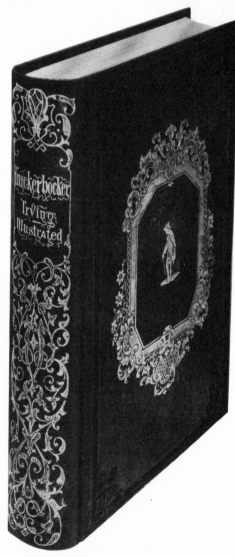

Although Washington Irving had a close friend named Herman Knickerbocker, he stoutly maintained that he fashioned the name of his book's hero from the Dutch words *knicker*, to nod, and *boeken*, a book. The doughty Knickerbocker, then, was one who dozes over books.

This satirical depiction of the period when the Dutch ruled New York was America's first humorous book and signaled a coming of age for American letters. That the English loved the book is hardly surprising, and Sir Walter Scott's report that ". . . our sides were absolutely sore with laughing [at the story]" was not echoed by anyone in Holland's aristocracy. This book is a facsimile of G. P. Putnam's 1854 illustrated edition, 496 pages, with sixteen illustrations by F. O. C. Darley. Introduction by the noted Irving scholar Andrew B. Myers.

Price: clothbound, $23.95.

THE ALHAMBRA Irving
served as a U.S. diplomat in Spain between 1826 and 1829, and remains a popular and often-read figure there. This is in some measure due to the warmth and brilliance of his portrayal of Moorish Spain in *The Alhambra* (1832), which according to a contemporary review in the Richmond (Virginia) *News Leader* "retells the legends of the area with all the grace of the tales of Scheherezade." Sleepy Hollow's facsimile edition replicates G. P. Putnam's 1851 book, with text from the Author's Revised Edition of 1848. 464 pages with fifteen illustrations by F. O. C. Darley. Introduction by Andrew B. Myers.

Price: clothbound, $23.95.

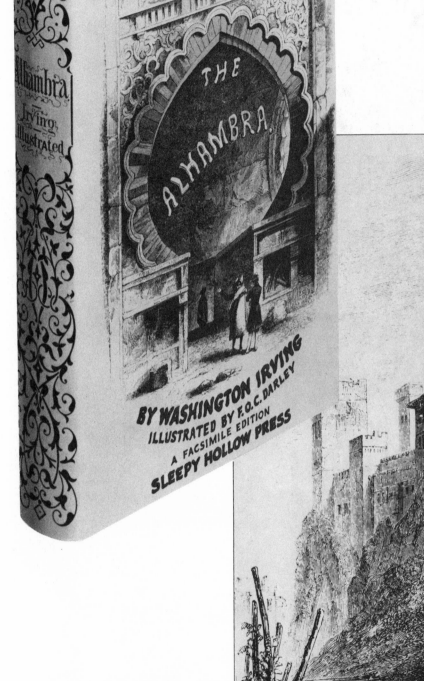

AN ORIGINAL DARLEY ILLUSTRATION FROM *THE ALHAMBRA*, REPUBLISHED BY SLEEPY HOLLOW PRESS IN HONOR OF THE 1983 BICENTENNIAL OF WASHINGTON IRVING'S BIRTH.

THE SKETCH BOOK

Every reader has his first book: I mean to say, one book among all others which in early youth first fascinates his imagination, and at once excites and satisfies the desires of his mind. To me, this first book was The Sketch Book *of Washington Irving.*

—Henry Wadsworth Longfellow

The Sketch Book was originally published in seven parts during 1819 and 1820. Containing such universally beloved stories as "Rip Van Winkle" and "The Legend of Sleepy Hollow," the book is pervaded by Irving's clear, colorful, and humorous American style. Sleepy Hollow's facsimile of the 1852 G. P. Putnam edition takes its text from the 520-page Author's Revised Edition of 1848 and includes twenty-two original illustrations by F. O. C. Darley.

Price: clothbound, $23.95; leatherbound, $47.50.

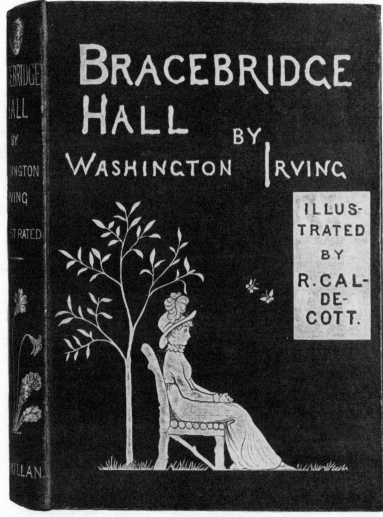

BRACEBRIDGE

HALL   Like *The Sketch Book,* **which it followed,** *Bracebridge Hall* also emphasized English settings, but was Irving's least successful book. This is a facsimile of a first edition published by the MacMillan Company in 1876. 320 pages with 118 illustrations by Randolph Caldecott. Introduction by Andrew B. Myers.

Price: clothbound, $12.

Books in the Washington Irving Facsimile Library may be ordered directly from the publisher if accompanied by a check or money order (no credit-card orders accepted). Postage and handling require $1.25 for the first book in each order, plus 25¢ for each additional copy. Retail discount schedule available.

Catalog obtainable.

SLEEPY HOLLOW PRESS

c/o Sleepy Hollow Restorations
150 White Plains Road
Tarrytown, NY 10591
Tel. 914/631–8200

BOOKS ON LIGHTING AND ARCHITECTURE

THE AMERICAN BUILDER'S COMPANION,
by Asher Benjamin. First published in 1827, this book was widely used as an architectural style book covering the Colonial through the Greek Revival periods. Seventy plates show construction details, floor plans, and elevations. 114 pages.

Price: $6 (plus $2 for shipping).

THE OCTAGON HOUSE,
by O. S. Fowler. This reprint of an 1853 edition focuses on the curious octagon house, many examples of which can still be found in Connecticut and other areas. Construction plans include such innovations for the time as central heating and an indoor water closet. 192 pages.

Price: $4 (plus $2 for shipping).

VICTORIAN LIGHTING: THE DIETZ CATALOGUE OF 1860
The complete 1840–1860 catalog of the R. E. Dietz Company of Syracuse, New York, America's leading manufacturer of Victorian kerosene lamps. Ulysses G. Dietz, a descendant of the company's founder and now curator of decorative arts at the Newark Museum, discovered the sole remaining original from which this facsimile has been taken. 128 pages, forty-one plates (of which six are in color), with a new history of "Dietz and Victorian Lighting" by Ulysses G. Dietz. Published in 1982.

Price: $30 (plus $2 for shipping).

AMAZON PICKLING & VINEGAR WORKS DRYGOODS

Department AH
2218 East 11th Street
Davenport, IA 52803
Tel. 319/322-6800

McGUFFEY'S READERS

The Author has long been of the opinion that a mischievous error pervades the public mind, on the subject of juvenile understanding. Nothing is so difficult as "nonsense." Nothing so clear and easy to comprehend as the simplicity of wisdom.

So wrote William Holmes McGuffey in the preface to one of his early *Eclectic Readers,* **the schoolbooks first published in 1836** that would dominate classroom education for the following three-quarters of a century. Widely regarded as a monument in American education, more than 122 million copies of the *Readers* were to be published prior to their decline in the 1920s. South of the Mason-Dixon line, their popularity was exceeded only by that of the Bible.

In terms of marketing the books, all of the simple wisdom involved was comprehended by McGuffey's nineteenth-century publishers, who paid the author no more than $1,000 for his work and craftily billed him on the title pages as a "late professor at the University of Oxford." If the reader surmised that the Oxford referred to was England's great gothic academy and not *Ohio's,* so much the better.

Except for his leather bullwhip, McGuffey himself was every inch the didactitian. The whip—a red one—was used by McGuffey to keep at bay the mudslinging schoolboys (in winter snow was used) that he somehow attracted wherever he lived. It was as if the boys could calculate the number of hours of study that 122 million textbooks would in time bring upon their class. But the *Readers* were extremely well suited to the requirements of nineteenth-century study. Beginning with a primer and going on through six volumes of increasing difficulty, schoolhouse students not segregated by grade could advance each at his own speed.

The *McGuffey's Readers* never shrank from lessons in morality, except where certain contemporary nineteenth-century controversies were involved. The books stoutly advocated temperance, but carefully sidestepped such other political issues of their time as slavery, secession, and trade unionism. Similarly, although the *Readers* included selections from the works of the highest order of poets and writers (Shakespeare, Dickens,

Hawthorne, and Wordsworth are all represented), they also much preferred the hale verse of Longfellow and Holmes to Poe's fevered images or Emerson's abolitionism.

Yet these criticisms are made negligible by the *McGuffey's Readers'* effective value. They may not be *Catcher in the Rye,* as a Van Nostrand Reinhold spokesman said, but a leisurely perusal of the books soon has one marveling at their richness and gently graduated complexity. What's more, their moral and religious philosophy seems more quaint than overbearing, and the values taught—honesty, industry, courage, charity, and polite-

ness—are all old American ones sorely in need of restoration.

And this brings me to a modern matter known in some circles as the "McGuffey's Phenomenon." Although the *Readers* have not been out of print since they were first introduced, recent sales of the books have climbed from 10,000 in 1975 to a 1982 figure ten times that! Several school districts have returned to using the books as a part of their recommended curriculum, winning the approval of parents, teachers, and students in each case.

The Van Nostrand Reinhold Company of New York began publishing their

current series of *McGuffey's Readers* after one of their authors discovered the original copper plates of the 1879 editions while doing some research in the (now-defunct.) American Book Company's printing plant in Cincinnati. These were then used to prepare the facsimile editions that Van Nostrand Reinhold has been selling since 1969, seven to the set, all handsomely (and authentically) printed and bound.

Price: complete set, $29.95, ppd.

VAN NOSTRAND REINHOLD CO., INC.

135 West 50th Street
New York, NY 10020
Tel. 212/265–8700; request customer service

(7)

THE McGUFFEY'S
ECLECTIC PRIMER'S FIRST LESSON.

CIVIL WAR BOOKS

THE COLLECTORS LIBRARY OF THE CIVIL WAR

As the general was not awakened by the noise we made in entering the room, I walked up to his bed and pulled off the covering. But even this did not arouse him. . . . So I pulled up his shirt and gave him a spank. Its effect was electric. The brigadier rose from his pillow and in an authoritative tone inquired the meaning of this rude intrusion. . . . I leaned over and said to him, "General, did you ever hear of Mosby?" "Yes," he quickly answered, "have you caught him?" "No," I said. "I am Mosby—he has caught you."

Col. John S. Mosby—the Gray Ghost—was so nicknamed because his troop of cavalry was the Confederacy's most elusive guerrilla force. *Mosby's Rangers*, written by James J. Williamson (one of his men) and originally published in 1896, is a volume in the Collector's Library of the Civil War, one of two series of rare nineteenth-century narratives that have been republished by Time-Life Books. **These hand-rubbed leather editions** are remarkably detailed and gratifyingly authentic. Assembled with the assistance of two noted authorities on the Civil War (one, Thomas Broadfoot, is a noted dealer in rare Civil War editions), the series includes: *Campaigning with Grant*, an account by Gen. Horace Porter, aide to U. S. Grant, vividly recalling some of the war's bloodiest episodes; *Daring and Suffering*, William Pittenger's recounting of the capture of the Confederate locomotive *The General* by Union raiders, originally published in 1864; *Hardtack and Coffee*, John D.

Billing's anecdotal memoir of a foot soldier's life in the Army of the Potomac, originally published in 1887; and *One of Jackson's Foot Cavalry*, John H. Worsham's portrait of life among Stonewall Jackson's rebel troopers, published in 1912.

These and other editions of the Collector's Library of the Civil War are available in bookstores or by subscription through Time-Life Books.

Brochure available.

TIME-LIFE BOOKS

Time-Life Building
Chicago, IL 60611
Tel. 312/329–6349

PHOTOGRAPHIC VIEWS OF SHERMAN'S CAMPAIGN

A reprinting of a landmark 1866 volume containing sixty-one plates of his campaign made by his official photographer. 80 pages.

Price: $5 (plus $2 for shipping).

AMAZON VINEGAR & PICKLING WORKS DRYGOODS

Department AH
2218 East 11th Street
Davenport, IA 52803

CLASSICS OF THE OLD WEST

Like its elegant companion series, the Collector's Library of the Civil War, Time-Life's selection of these historical accounts of life in the nineteenth-century West was based on their vivid literary quality as well as their rarity. The following passage is from *Life Among the Apaches*, a book by Indian War cavalryman John C. Cremony:

> . . . the dust rose in blinding clouds, hurried up by the trampling feet of the contending men. . . . I was just reloading a six-shooter, when a robust and athletic Apache stood before me. He was naked with the single exception of his breech cloth, and his person was oiled from head to foot. . . . The instant we met he advanced upon me with a long and keen knife with which he made a plunge at my breast.

The Classics series carries on the Civil War Library's exquisite detailing through the use of hand-tooled leather covers highlighted by gilt stamping. These enclose pages that are gilded on all three edges, and retain the typography, title pages, and illustrations (including many by such famous western artists as Frederick Remington) of the originals.

Some other titles in this series are: Charles A. Siringo's *A Texas Cowboy*, an accurate and colorful account of cowboy life that was remembered by Will Rogers as "the cowboy's bible when I was growing up" (originals of this book have brought $4,000 at auction); *The Life of Honorable William F. Cody*, Buffalo Bill's audacious autobiography first published in 1879; *The Authentic Billy, The Kid* by one he helped make famous, Sheriff Pat

FROM TIME-LIFE BOOKS'S *A TEXAS COWBOY* BY CHARLES A. SIRINGO.

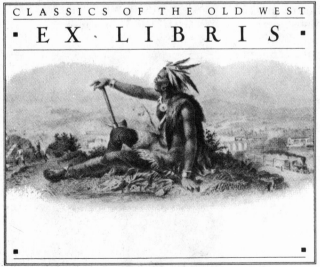

Garrett, originally published in 1882; and *The Captivity of the Oatman Girls*, an account relating an 1857 capture by Apache Indians.

These and other editions of the Classics of the Old West are available in bookstores or through Time-Life Books.

Brochure available.

TIME-LIFE BOOKS

Time-Life Building
Chicago, IL 60611
Tel. 312/329-6349

CHILDREN'S BOOKS

BOOKS FROM VICTORIAN ACCENTS

In the mid-1830s George Cruikshank, an illustrator of popular English children's literature, was among the first to have his works printed in color. The advent of color printing spelled the end of laborious and expensive hand-tinting, and brought colored books into the hands of children at all levels of English society.

Cruikshank's *Comic Alphabet* and his *Toothache* foldout books are unique among children's literature of the period in that rather than preach, they are intended solely to amuse.

Victorian Accents' spectacular facsimile edition of *A Day at the Zoo*, a late-nineteenth-century foldout book, opens to more than 6 feet in length and 12 inches high, revealing eight panels depicting a day's visit to the zoo.

Prices: Cruikshank's *Comic Alphabet* and *Toothache*, $4 each (plus $1.95 for postage and handling); *A Day at the Zoo*, $11.95 (plus $3.50 for postage and handling).

Catalog of Victoriana available, $1.

WATTLE & DAUB'S VICTORIAN ACCENTS

661 West 7th Street
Plainfield, NJ 07060
Tel. 201/757–8507

FROM VICTORIAN ACCENT'S *COMIC ALPHABE*

MERRIMACK PUBLISHING COMPANY

Merrimack Publishing is the imprint of the B. Shackman Company, a firm that has been in business on Manhattan's lower Fifth Avenue since 1898. Merrimack specializes in the replication of nineteenth-century printed paper products including postcards, valentines, and children's books. They are primarily wholesalers but have consented to provide the readers of *The American Historical Supply Catalogue* with retail prices for mail orders over $10 on the following full-color paperback reprints of original nineteenth-century editions:

Prices: *Kate Greenaway's Mother Goose*, $2 each; *A Peep at Buffalo Bill's Wild West*, $2.50 each; *Rip Van Winkle*, $2.50 each.

MERRIMACK PUBLISHING COMPANY

85 Fifth Avenue at 16th Street
New York, NY 10003
Tel. 212/989–5162

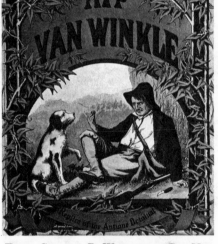

FROM GEORGE P. WEBSTER'S *RIP VAN WINKLE* BY THE MERRIMACK PUBLISHING COMPANY.

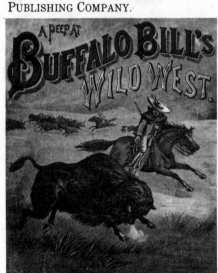

FROM *A PEEP AT BUFFALO BILL'S WILD WEST* BY THE MERRIMACK PUBLISHING COMPANY.

"POP-UP" AND "DISSOLVING-VIEW" BOOKS

Toward the end of the nineteenth century, "pop-up" and "dissolving-view" books achieved enormous popularity on both sides of the Atlantic. The dissolving-view, or revolving-picture, books incorporated scenes that a child could "magically" change by rotating a ribboned tab. The moveable books manufactured between 1891 and 1900 by Ernest Nister are considered the finest of the genre.

Philomel Books has replicated a series of four of these books: *Animal Tales* (1894), *Magic Windows* (originally

C
Chimpanzee

D
Dining out

E
Equality

Y GEORGE CRUIKSHANK.

published as *In Wonderland*, 1895), *Land of Sweet Surprises*, and *Merry Magic Go-Round* (both 1897). In addition Philomel has republished the pop-up book *The Little Actor's Theater*, originally published in Germany in 1883.

Prices: *Animal Tales, Magic Windows, Land of Sweet Surprises*, and *Merry Magic Go-Round*, $8.95 each; *The Little Actor's Theater*, $10.95.

PHILOMEL BOOKS

*The Putnam Publishing Group
200 Madison Avenue
New York, NY 10016
Tel. 212/576–8900*

N. C. WYETH ILLUS-TRATED EDITIONS OF *KIDNAPPED* AND *TREASURE ISLAND*

Fac-simile editions of Robert Louis Stevenson's *Kidnapped* **and** *Treasure Island* **have been reissued by** Charles Scribner's Sons in commemoration of the first books' 1982 centennial. Both books are reproductions of editions that were published into the early twentieth century and which were illustrated by N. C. Wyeth. The original paintings from which the illustrations were copied now hang in the Brandywine River Museum in Chadds Ford, Pennsylvania.

"This reprint is a model of restoration," enthused *Time* magazine's reviewer over the 1982 *Kidnapped*. "The very typeface bespeaks adventure, and the artworks are reproduced with even greater fidelity than the plates in the rare first edition."

Price: $17.95 each.

CHARLES SCRIBNER'S SONS

*597 Fifth Avenue
New York, NY 10017
Tel. 212/486–2888*

TREASURE ISLAND
BY
ROBERT LOUIS STEVENSON

Illustrated By N. C. WYETH

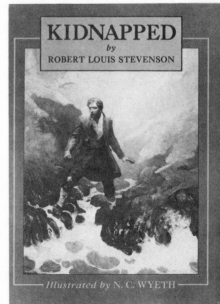

KIDNAPPED
by
ROBERT LOUIS STEVENSON

Illustrated by N. C. WYETH

186

SEARS, ROEBUCK & CO., Cheapest Supply House on Earth, Chicago. CATALOGUE No. III.

THE SEARS SPECIAL FILM CAMERAS
AT $3.60 AND $5.70.

WE HAVE THIS SEASON closed a contract with the leading manufacturer of Film Cameras, which enables us to furnish the highest grade film cameras at prices heretofore unknown in the camera business.

OUR FILM CAMERAS are manufactured exclusively for us; they are made under contract that calls for the very best materials, the very best of

ACHROMATIC LENSES

and the most perfect workmanship throughout.

THEY ARE EQUIPPED with all the latest improvements and we can guarantee them in every way, both as to materials, workmanship and picture making qualities.

...OUR...
FILM CAMERAS
use the
CARTRIDGE SYSTEM OF DAYLIGHT LOADING FILMS
and they may be loaded and unloaded in broad daylight.

FILM CARTRIDGES are unbreakable; their weight and bulk as compared with glass plates is practically nothing; the results obtained are in every way equal to pictures made upon glass plates, and one-half dozen film cartridges, each sufficient for twelve pictures, may be carried in the pocket without inconvenience.

THE No. 1 SEARS SPECIAL FILM CAMERA, for 3½x3½ pictures. Measurements, 4¼x4½x5½ inches. Capacity, six exposures. Weight, 20 ounces.
No. 20R2116 Price...$3.60
THESE PRICES DO NOT INCLUDE FILMS.

THE SEARS SPECIAL FILM CAMERAS represent a type of camera that is complete in itself, with no removable parts. They are fitted with the finest high grade fixed focus achromatic lenses, and are provided with a set of three diaphragms.

THE SHUTTER is suitable for both time and instantaneous exposures, and the speed may be regulated in accordance with the brightness of the light.

EACH ...

THE ... sockets. The covering is the best quality of black morocco leather, and all metal parts are finely nickel plated.

THE No. 2 SEARS SPECIAL FILM CAMERA, for 4x5 pictures. Measurements, 5x5½x6½ inches. Capacity, twelve exposures. Weight, 28 ounces.
No. 20R2118 Price...$5.70
THESE PRICES DO NOT INCLUDE FILMS.

FILMS FOR THE SEARS SPECIAL FILM CAMERAS. This Film is put up in light-tight rolls, or cartridges, all ready to go into the camera, and may be put in at any time or place in broad daylight.
No. 20R2125 Daylight Loading Film Cartridge, for six exposures, 3½x3½ Price...26c
　　　If by mail, postage extra, 3 cents.
No. 20R2126 Daylight Loading Film Cartridge, for twelve exposures, 4x3½ Price...52c
　　　If by mail, postage extra, 4 cents.
No. 20R2127 Daylight Loading Film Cartridge, for six exposures, Price...39c
　　　If by mail, postage extra, 4 cents.
No. 20R2128 Daylight Loading Film Cartridge, for twelve exposures, 4x5 Price...78c
　　　If by mail, postage extra, 5 cents.

PHOTOGRAPHIC GOODS

$11.98 BUYS ... PERFECTION VIEWING OUTFIT
5 x 7 PICTURES.

NO. 20R2135
ORDER BY NUMBER.

THE PERFECTION VIEW CAMERA is a thoroughly up to date, well made, substantial camera. It is made from the best seasoned mahogany, finely finished and highly polished, and all metal parts are nickel plated.

THE PERFECTION VIEW CAMERA
FOLDS UP COMPACTLY, has rising and falling front for adjusting relative amount of sky or foreground, and is provided with a first class swing back, a very valuable feature, especially when photographing buildings.

THE LENS is our Monarch Single Achromatic, a strictly high grade lens, manufactured especially for us by the Bausch & Lomb Optical Co., and guaranteed to be

The Best Single Achromatic Lens that can be made.
The Monarch Single Achromatic Lens is suitable for general all around photography including landscapes, groups, portraits, etc.

THE PERFECTION VIEW CAMERA
is made with **REVERSIBLE BACK,** thus permitting the camera to be used for either vertical or horizontal pictures without changing its position on the tripod.
THE BELLOWS is made from the very best quality of black gossamer cloth of double thickness and is cone shaped. Both the cone shaped bellows and the reversible back are features which have never before been offered except in high priced cameras.

THE PERFECTION VIEWING CAMERA makes pictures 5x7 inches; the most popular size both for professional and amateur purposes.
THE TRIPOD is our best quality sliding tripod, thoroughly substantial and rigid.
REMEMBER $11.98 includes the entire outfit just as listed and described.

THE COMPLETE OUTFIT CONTAINS:
1 5x7 Perfection Viewing Camera, with Monarch Achromatic Lens, Sliding Tripod, Canvas Carrying Case, and one Double Plate Holder.
1 Metal Ruby Lamp.
3 Compressed Fiber Trays for developing, fixing and toning.
1 8-ounce Measuring Glass.
1 5x7 Printing Frame.
1 4-inch Ruler.
1 2-inch Paste Brush.
2 Dozen Sensitized Paper.
1 Dozen Dry Plates.
25 Card Mounts.
1 Package Concentrated Developer.
1 Package Concentrated Toning and Fixing Solution.
1 Package Hypo.
1 Tube of Paste.
1 Fine Gossamer Focus Cloth.
1 Copy of "Complete Instructions in Photography."
No. 20R2135 The Complete Perfection Viewing Outfit. Price, $11.98
No. 20R2136 Extra Plate Holders for Perfection View Camera. Price, each..55

THERE are no extras to buy before you can commence work. The outfit contains absolutely everything necessary for starting into a pleasant and good paying business.

SUCCESS IS CERTAIN, even though you have never had the slightest experience in photographic work. You will be able to turn out good pictures right from the start, as our new 112-page Instruction Book, which we include absolutely free with every one of these outfits, makes everything so plain and easy that failure is practically impossible.

IF YOU WISH TO SEE THE STYLE and quality of work that can be done with the Perfection Viewing Camera we will be pleased to mail you a sample picture made with this Camera, upon receipt of 10 cents.

VIEW CAMERA

VIEW CAMERA During the nineteenth century the paper used in the photographic printing process was so insensitive to light that the only way to expose it properly was to make a "contact print" from a full-size negative onto the paper using sunlight. The size of the print, therefore, was determined by the size of the negative. If you wanted a big print, you needed a camera that would produce an equally big negative.

Such a camera was the 5- by 7-inch Premo View developed by Laban F. Deardorff during the 1880s. The Premo View helped establish the Deardorff Company's reputation for the manufacture of superlative cameras—a reputation carried on by its successor, the 5- by 7-inch View Camera. The mahogany-bodied View Camera is completely collapsible for field use.

Price: 5- by 7-inch View Camera, $1,930.

L. F. DEARDORFF & SONS
315 South Peoria Street
Chicago, IL 60607
Tel. 312/829–5655

PHOTOGRAPHIC PRINTS

Taking its name partly from the prevailing nineteenth-century photographic printing process, Chicago Albumen employs this and other original methods to authentically reproduce the photographs of such nineteenth- and early-twentieth-century masters as Mathew Brady, Eadweard Muybridge, and William Henry Jackson.

In each case, photographic prints are made from the photographer's original negative using the same process—albumen, salted paper, gelatin POP, platinum paper, or gum bichromate—that the photographer himself employed. Chicago Albumen's historically accurate process has brought them to the attention of several major photographic collections, and both the Atget Collection at the Museum of Modern Art and the Meserve Collec-

tion at the National Portrait Gallery have employed their services to reproduce prints from museum negatives.

Finished prints are available and range in price from $100 to $400.

Brochure available.

CHICAGO ALBUMEN WORKS

P.O. Box 379
Front Street
Housatonic, MA 01236
Tel. 413/274-6901

STEREOSCOPES AND VIEWCARDS

Victorian Accents' "Museum-quality Stereoviewer" is a direct reproduction of the 1859 viewer patented by Oliver Wendell Holmes. It features a carefully detailed walnut finish, with brass fittings and a velvet-lined hood. The New Jersey firm also offers a "Popular-quality Stereoviewer" in oak, with a plain, unlined hood. Both viewers use the same precision optic lenses and come with bases and a sample set of ten views. Naturally, both will also accept antique viewcards.

A selection of sixty replica viewcards is also available. The originals are from the famous Keystone and Underwood Studios and include views of scenic natural wonders, city scenes, and "melodramas." In addition, Victorian Accents offers eight supplementary sets (eighteen to the set) depicting either Victorian Christmas, the Old West, the San Francisco Earthquake, Industry, Suffragettes, the Alaska Gold Rush, New York City, or the Civil War.

NEW YORK CITY

Keystone View Company COPYRIGHTED MADE IN U.S.A. *Publishers*
Manufacturers

Meadville, Pa., New York, N.Y., Chicago, Ill., London, England.

26511 T   The Leviathan, Originally the Vaterland — a Palatial Ocean Liner with a Notable War and Peace Record.

Prices: Museum-quality Stereoviewer with base, $64.95 (plus $8 for postage); Popular-quality Stereoviewer with base, $52.95 (plus $6.50 for postage); 60 views, $17.95 (plus $3.50 for postage); supplementary sets, $6.95 each (plus $1.95 postage).

Catalog of Victoriana available, $1.

WATTLE & DAUB'S VICTORIAN ACCENTS

661 West 7th Street
Plainfield, NJ 07060
Tel. 201/757-8507

DAGUERROTYPE
BOXES Invented in 1839 by the

Frenchman Louis J. Daguerre, the daguerrotype process recorded an image on a silver plate made light sensitive with iodine. The first American daguerrotypes were made with the aid of Samuel F. B. Morse, inventor (in 1837) of the "American electromagnetic telegraph."

Daguerrotypes were all the more treasured for their fragility, and were kept in leather or gutta percha boxes for their protection.

Some of the lids of the very few of these boxes that have survived the ravages of time have been hand-cast in ivory-finished composition material to form the covers of Victorian Accents' replicas:

Children with Lambs: 3½ inches high, 3⅞ inches wide, and 1¾ inches deep. Price: $17.

Mother and Child: 3⅜ inches high, 3¾ inches wide, and 1¾ inches deep. Price: $17.

Baby Moses (oval): 2¼ inches high, 2¾ inches wide, and 1¼ inches deep. Price: $11.95.

Children with Butterfly: 2⅝ inches high, 3 inches wide, and 1¾ inches deep. Price: $13.95.

Add $3.50 postage for each item ordered.

Catalog of Victoriana available, $1.

WATTLE & DAUB'S VICTORIAN ACCENTS

661 West 7th Street
Plainfield, NJ 07060
Tel. 201/757–8507

OUR CELEBRATED MARCEAU BAND INSTRUMENTS.
GREATEST BARGAINS IN BAND INSTRUMENTS EVER OFFERED TO THE BANDMEN OF AMERICA.

THIS IS ONE OF THE FINE LINES of band instruments which we have been handling for years and which have given such immense satisfaction.

MUSIC RACKS and INSTRUCTION BOOKS are sent with all of these Instruments.

WE GUARANTEE EVERY INSTRUMENT in this line and sell them on the same terms that we sell all of our other band instruments. Each horn is fitted with celebrated French piston light action valves and is splendid in model and finish. Beware of the cheap lines of instruments handled by dealers throughout the country. They only sell a very limited quantity of goods, and no manufacturer of any reputation whatsoever can entrust his agency to them.

Marceau E Flat Cornet.

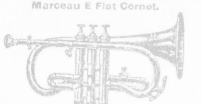

A clear toned, splendid instrument for the use of leaders. Guaranteed in every way. Beautiful in model, perfect in tune and tone. The E flat cornet is never used except for playing in a band. If you wish a cornet for general playing, you should order a B flat cornet.

No. 12K7980 Brass, highly polished.... **$6.65**
No. 12K7981 Nickel plated, highly polished.. 7.55

Marceau B Flat Cornet.
SINGLE WATER KEY.

MUSICAL INSTRUMENTS

is a fine B Flat Cornet in every way and is

We can also furnish this cornet in the key of C at the following prices:
No. 12K7988 Brass. Price............ **$6.95**
No. 12K7989 Nickel plated. Price........... 7.85

Marceau B Flat Cornet.
DOUBLE WATER KEY.

This Double Water Key Cornet has been a favorite with bandmen for a long time on account of its beautiful model and splendid tone. It is furnished with an A shank for use in orchestra and is a fine instrument in every way.
No. 12K7993 Brass, polished. Price.... **$7.95**
No. 12K7994 Nickel plated, highly polished. Price............ 8.95

Marceau Solo Altos.

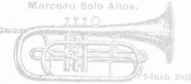

7-inch Bell.

These instruments are manufactured for solo alto purposes and have been great favorites ever since their appearance. They are easy blowing, have a splendid tone and a handsome appearance.
No. 12K8011 Brass, highly polished.... **$10.45**
No. 12K8012 Nickel plated, highly polished.... 11.95

Marceau Valve Trombones.
SPECIAL HILLYARD LONG MODEL.

No. 12K8023 6½-inch Bell.   No. 12K8029 7-inch Bell.

These Trombones are all fine in every respect and have that deep, rich tone so peculiar to trombones. Each band should be fitted with at least two of these, as they give a coloring harmony which could be obtained in no other way.

No. 12K8023 E Flat Alto Trombone, brass. Price.... **$11.65**
No. 12K8024 E Flat Alto Trombone, nickel plated. Price...... 13.15
No. 12K8029 B Flat Tenor Trombone, brass. Price.... 13.55
No. 12K8030 B Flat Tenor Trombone, nickel plated. Price..... 15.45

Marceau E Flat Altos and B Flat Tenors.

Altos 8-inch Bell.

Tenors 8½-inch Bell.

These instruments are splendid for harmony work in a band, and we recommend them highly for those who desire fine altos and tenors at extremely low prices. They have a splendid tone, a beautiful model and a handsome appearance. They are perfect in tune and tone and so well constructed that they will last a lifetime. The action of the valves is extremely light and either one of these instruments can be used very nicely for solo purposes. We guarantee them to be satisfactory, and we believe that alto and tenor players will find in these instruments just what they desire at a very small cost. We desire to place them in the hands of all who are looking for something in this line at a moderate cost, and we do not ask the customer to take any chances as we assume all the risk of shipping.

No. 12K8013 Alto, brass, polished..... **$10.75**
No. 12K8014 Alto, nickel plated, polished 13.25
No. 12K8015 Tenor, brass, polished.... 12.60
No. 12K8016 Tenor, nick'l plat'd, polish'd 14.70

For Band Instrument Supplies of all kinds refer to Our Special Band Catalogue

Marceau B Flat Baritone.

9½-inch Bell.

These instruments have been used with great success in all sorts of solo playing and general band work. A large number of bandmen have pronounced them the finest baritones on the market for less than double the price given below. Their tone is full and sonorous without being dull, and is light and clear without being too snappy. The model is handsome and the general workmanship on the instruments is all that can be desired. We recommend these baritones highly to baritone players throughout the country and we are always willing to have them compared with instruments offered by other dealers for twice the price.

No. 12K8017 Brass, highly polished. Price............ **$14.15**
No. 12K8018 Nickel plated, highly polished. Price............ **$16.65**

Marceau F Circular Alto. 10-inch Bell.

This style of alto horn has become very popular with all kinds of military and concert bands in the last few years on account of its beautiful mellow tone. It is used almost exclusively by all of the larger bands and we recommend its use to all bandmen. Its circular model makes it a very easy blowing and sensitive instrument and not only does it add to the appearance of the band, but it gives the music a coloring which can be obtained in no other way. It is made by the same celebrated makers who manufacture the balance of this line, and is a valuable addition to the well known Marceau Co. band instruments which we have handled so successfully for years. If your band does not possess altos of this model you should by all means procure them without delay, and you will find that the beautiful effect which you will obtain will much more than compensate for the small expense incurred. It is furnished with three additional crooks, Eb, D and C, thus enabling the performer to play in four different keys. All crooks are fitted with water key, enabling the performer to quickly remove the accumulation of saliva, a feature to be found only on our instruments.

No. 12K8033 Brass, highly polished. Price.... **$19.95**
No. 12K8034 Nickel plated. Price.... 22.45

Marceau B Flat Bass.

10½-inch Bell.

These instruments can be used with excellent effect to fill in between the E Flat Bass and the B Flat Baritone. They are very effective when used in the bass solos which frequently occur in band selections, and they serve to balance up the instrumentation in excellent shape. Their tone is everything that could be asked for in an instrument of this nature and in model and finish they are splendid in every way.

No. 12K8019 Brass, highly polished. Price.... **$15.40**
No. 12K8020 Nickel plated, highly polished. Price.... $17.95

Marceau E Flat Bass.

11½-inch Bell.

We wish to call your attention particularly to this instrument and will say without fear of contradiction, that it has never been equaled, price considered. It has a deep, rich tone and furnishes an excellent fundamental bass for any brass band. It has enough volume to answer for a large instrumentation and the tone is full and sweet enough for use, if desired, in orchestras. The model is fine and the tubing is so thoroughly braced and reinforced that it will not break down under severe use. The valves are all quick and responsive and we guarantee the instrument to be satisfactory in every particular.

No. 12K8021 Brass, highly polished. Price.... **$21.25**
No. 12K8022 Nickel plated, highly polished. Price.... $25.15

Marceau E Flat Contrabass. 15-inch Bell.

This instrument is of exactly the same splendid model and construction as our No. 12K8021, only it is of extra large proportions, and is very deep and rich in tone. We recommend it very highly to all band organizations. The bell is of a flaring model.

No. 12K8021½ Brass, highly polished. **$24.60**
No. 12K8022½ Nickel plated, highly polished. 28.60

Marceau Slide Trombones.

7-inch Bell.

We know that these instruments will appeal to all trombone players who desire good, serviceable trombones at an extremely low price. For band and orchestra use they will be found equal to all requirements. For solo playing they have given general satisfaction. The slide works with ease and rapidity and the tone is mellow and powerful.
No. 12K8031 Brass, highly polished. Price.... **$6.95**
No. 12K8032 Nickel plated, highly polished. Price.... 8.55

TRADITIONAL DULCIMERS

APPALACHIAN
DULCIMER
Among the many ancient things carried into this century by our mountain culture is a biblical instrument—the dulcimer. The sound of the dulcimer, a haunting fusion of the wild and lyrical, somehow reflects the character of Appalachia itself—both in culture and in terrain.

Jeremy Seeger has been handcrafting traditional Appalachian (or mountain) dulcimers for fifteen years. Each instrument is individually built of selected woods and is crafted to produce consistently excellent sound. A variety of wood combinations and designs are available.

    Prices range from $250 to $600.

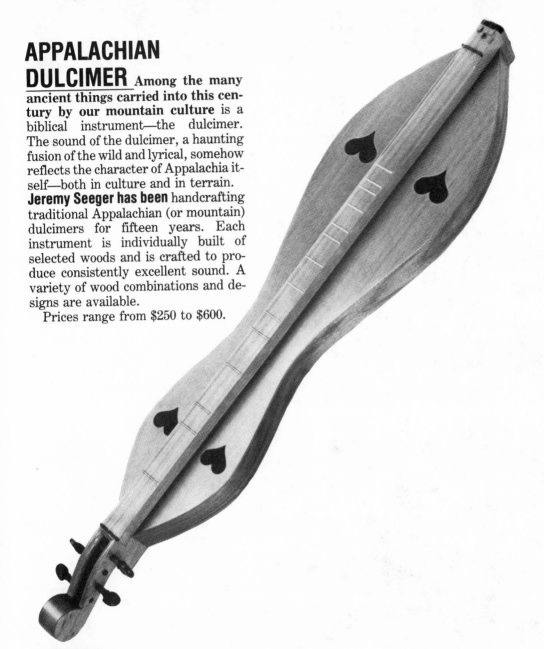

HAMMER
DULCIMERS
Hammer dulcimers have a rich, full sound and good volume. Mr. Seeger's instruments, with twelve courses of treble strings and eleven courses of bass strings, are constructed of maple and spruce. Hammer dulcimers must either be hand-delivered or picked up at Mr. Seeger's Vermont studio.

    Prices range from $250 to $600.

Brochure available.

MOUNTAIN DULCIMERS

P.O. Box 117, Fassett Hill
Hancock, VT 05748

HOHNER HARMONICAS

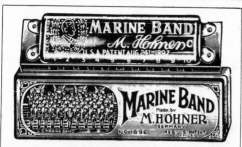

No. 1896. "MARINE BAND." Hohner Harmonica. Length 4 inches. The instrument with an international reputation. Its accuracy of tone and simplicity have made it the choice of music teachers and professional players everywhere. 10 single holes, 20 reeds, brass plates, heavy convex covers, finely nickel-plated. In hinged box bearing photograph of The United States Marine Band. Available in all keys.

A Danbury boy of ten winters . . . stole a harmonica Friday evening to serenade his girl with.
—James M. Bailey, Life in Danbury, 1893

Scorned by the great masters of music, the Harmonica still produces more music for its size than any other instrument known to the musical world, and at the least cost.
—From the 1907 Hohner catalogue

No. 607. "ECHO." Hohner Harmonica. Length 6⅛ inches. Large double sided tremolo instrument in two different keys, having 40 double holes and 80 perfectly tuned reeds, brass plates, finely nickel-plated covers with turned in ends. Packed in a very attractive hinged box with pictorial design in many colors. Available in key combinations "A-D," "B♭-F," "C-G."

HOHNER, INCORPORATED

Lakeridge Industrial Park
Sycamore Drive, P.O. Box 15035
Richmond, VA 23227

Since Will Hohner turned out his first 650 harmonicas in 1857, his name has been virtually interchangeable with the word "harmonica."

As the accompanying old catalog entries show, many Hohner harmonicas produced today are the same as they were at the turn of the century and before.

Catalog of harmonicas, melodicas, and accordions available.

No. 34B. "OLD STANDBY." Hohner Harmonica. Length 4 inches. An ideal instrument, and popular everywhere. 10 single holes, 20 reeds, brass plates, finely nickel-plated covers. Furnished in a neat hinged box. Available in all keys.

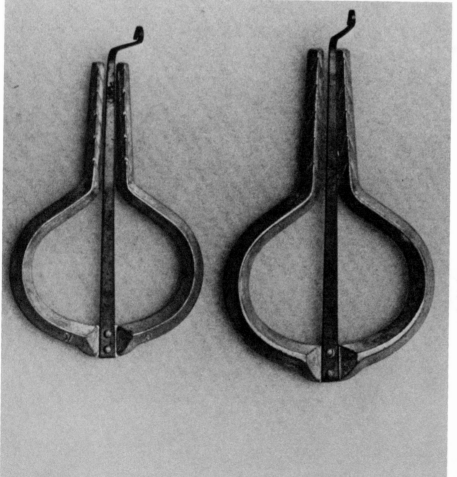

JAW HARPS **Once commonly called "Jew's harps,"** they are available from La Pelleterie in two sizes: 3 inches and 3½ inches.

Prices: $1 and $1.25, repectively (plus $1.25 for postage).

LA PELLETERIE DE FORT DE CHARTRES

P.O. Box 627
Chester, IL 62233
Tel. 618/826-4334

CONFEDERATE BUGLE

Dixie Gun Works's Confederate infantry bugle is a copy of one dug up at the site of the Battle of Stone's River, near Murfreesboro, Tennessee. It is a genuine musical instrument that replicates the original down to its use of a double-thickness brass bell, made entirely of polished brass. Overall length: 10½ inches.

Catalog of gun supplies available, $3.

DIXIE GUN WORKS

Gunpowder Lane
Union City, TN 38261

CHILD'S FURNITURE.

Order No. 25238.

A description and the illustration of crib does not do justice to this line of goods. The pieces are imitation enamel, corrugated, finished in white and gold, and are large enough to be of practical value.

Beds.

18 inch. Price, each	$1.00
21 inch. Price, each	1.25
24 inch. Price, each	1.50

Cribs.

18 inch. Price, each	1.25
21 inch. Price, each	1.50
24 inch. Price, each	1.88
Child's Rocker. Price, each	1.50
Child's Chair. Price, each	1.35
Child's Settee. Price, each	2.50
Dolls' Chair. Price, each	.38
Child's Chair. Price, each	.75
Child's Table. Price, each	1.13
Child's Table. Price, each	.75

Black Boards.

25240 One of the finest and most complete blackboards made. A well arranged combination of easel and desk, having a movable sawed extension, with designs for drawing on either side. The board is made of new material of best quality, smooth and warranted not to check. The desk is provided with an extra large drawer with ornamented front. The board drops forward to form the desk, showing additional designs for drawing. It is made in a substantial manner and folds very closely for shipping. Height, 48 in. Size of board, 16x19 in.
Price....$1.00

25241 A perfect Blackboard and Easel; no cut. Has fluted standards. Complete alphabet on the frame of the board. A movable extension having designs for drawing on both sides. The back support can be easily removed so as to make a very thin package; height, 41 inches. Size of board, 18½x12¼ inches.
Price....$0.45

DOLLS.

Jointed Dolls, Bisque Heads, with Chemise.

25249 Jointed Dolls, bisque heads, flowing hair, teeth, and long plaited chemise. Length, 16½ inches.
Price....$0.50

25250 Jointed Dolls, with bisque heads, flowing hair, teeth and long chemise. Length, 19 inches.
Price....90

25251 Jointed Dolls, extra large and fine, with flowing hair, teeth and long chemise, bisque heads. Length, 25 inches.
Price....1.00

Kid Body Dolls, Not Dressed, Jointed.

25252 Kid Body Dolls with bisque heads, flowing hair, teeth and solid eyes. Length, 12 inches.
Price....$0.25

25253 Kid Body Dolls with bisque heads, woven wig, flowing hair, teeth and solid eyes. Length 15 in.
Price....50

25254 Kid Body Dolls, bisque heads, woven wig, flowing hair, and teeth. Length, 17 inches.
Price....75

25255 Kid Body Dolls, with bisque heads, flowing hair, woven wig, teeth and solid eyes. Length, 21 inches.
Price....1.25

25257 Kid Body Doll, patent hip joint, jointed arms, fine bisque head, flowing hair on full woven wig, teeth, closing eyes, open work stockings, and shoes.
Length, 23 inches.
Price....$2.45

Dressed Dolls, Patent Indestructible Heads.

25268 Indestructible head Dressed Doll. Same as above, 30 inches long. Price.... $0.60

25269 Indestructible Head Dressed Doll

Dressed Dolls, Cloth Bodies, with Kid Joints.

25275 Dressed Dolls, with kid joints, bisque heads and arms, teeth and flowing hair, dressed in handsome costume, length; 13 inches.
Price....$0.50

25276 Dressed Dolls, cloth body, kid joints, bisque heads and arms, flowing hair, teeth, shoes, stockings. Dressed in costume of handsome design and good material; length, 14½ inches.
Price....$0.65

25277 Dressed Dolls, cloth body, kid joints, bisque head and arms, flowing hair, teeth, solid eyes, shoes and stockings; dress is of the best *materials*, in fashionable colors and well made; length, 17 inches. Price....$1.00

25278 Dressed Dolls, cloth body, kid joints, bisque heads, flowing hair, teeth, *solid eyes*, shoes and stockings, dressed in an elaborate costume of satin, with large turned-up hat; length 20 inches.
Price....2.00

Dressed Baby Dolls, Jointed.

25280 Full Jointed Dolls, finest bisque head, flowing hair, solid eyes; long baby dress of woolen stuff and silk, neatly trimmed. See cut. Price....$1.00

25281 Same description but larger size, and more elaborate dress. Price....$1.45

25282 Superior quality, superfine dolls, jointed, with bisque heads, flowing hair, teeth, shoes and stockings. Dressed in "Baby" costume of nun's veiling, with cap to match. Length, 12 inches.
Each....$0.65

25283 Same description as above, but larger. Each....$0.90

25284 Large size "Baby" doll. Length, 16 inches. Price....$1.50

Jointed Dolls, Dressed.

bisque heads, solid eyes, flowing hair, shoes and stockings. Superior quality dolls. Dress made of cotton stuff, trimmed, silk bonnet. Price....$0.50

25287 Same description; dress of muslin and lace, bonnet trimmed with ribbon. Price....1.00

25288 Same description, dress and bonnet of double silk trimmed with ribbons. Price....1.15

25289 Same description; dress, finest muslin, run through with ribbons. Full silk bonnet with strings and balls. Price....1.25

25290 Same description; dress of fine woolen goods, trimmed with silk ribbons or embroidered. Some hair lace hats, some bonnets.
Price....2.00

25291 Same description; dress, fine cashmere, trimmed with silk and lace. Full silk bonnet, lace trimmed. Price....2.25

25292 Same description; dress, full winter costume of fine woolen goods, trimmed with plush and ribbons. Bonnet to match. Price....3.50

Columbus Dressed Dolls.

The costumes are works of art, made of the finest silk velvets and satin, in contrasting colors. Each Cavalier wears at his side a tiny sword. The broad cap is surmounted with an ostrich plume, while the inscription, "1493 C. Columbus, 1893" is emblazoned upon its front.

25293 Columbus Doll, jointed, bisque head, flowing hair, teeth, solid eyes. Length, 15 inches.
Price....$1.80

25294 Columbus Doll, same description as above. Length, 18 inches. Price....$2.50

25295 Columbus Doll, large size. Length, 21 inches. Price....$3.25

Dolls and Dollhouses

TOYS FROM THE ENCHANTED DOLL HOUSE

From where it's "nestled" in the Green Mountains of Vermont, the Enchanted Doll House does business on two-tone pink stationery, calls its staff "resident elves," and posts catalogs that gush as if written by hand puppets. Now, as one who can slip into pie-eyed semi-consciousness at the memory of meeting the *actual* Santa Claus at Santa's Workshop, New Hampshire, in 1950 (well, he had a real beard!) I don't want to be a killjoy. I don't expect the folks at EDH to come across like Sergeant Fury and his platoon mopping up at some Chi-Com machine gun nest or anything. I just figure that any treacle that would sicken Mr. Rogers would also turn the stomachs of kids and has to be intended for sentimental adults.

Not that the Enchanted Doll House's claim to having "the most endearing, stimulating, and worthwhile quality playthings available" is out of line. Nossir. The miniatures in particular are mesmerizing in their quality and detail. For pages, photos of tiny replica items from all periods—a dwarf 1810 Pennsylvania cupboard with lilliputian stonewear, a minikin 1927 tubular-metal Breuer chair, a jar of Hellmann's mayonnaise that would nicely fit a five-inch supermarket shelf, a 1 foot = 1 inch scale Vermont barn with perfect little tools—invite prolonged gazing and summon up profound yearnings, even in the tough, take-all-comers breasts of the grizzled veterans of Santa's Workshop.

From among their antique replica dolls and doll things, the Enchanted Doll House has supplied the following examples:

REPLICA DOLLS The Enchanted Doll House offers several replicas of nineteenth-century dolls including Nancy Girl, a 6-inch cherub based on a turn-of-the-century original; and Nichole, the elegant Victorian illustrated, a 13-inch cloth doll from the "Heirloom Collection of Louis XVII by Louis Nichole." "Reminiscent

of days gone by, a touch of the Renaissance, a soup-con [*sic*] of Victorian and an enormous amount of talent," says the EDH catalog about either Mr. Nichole or his doll.

Prices: Nancy Girl, $65, ppd.; Nichole, $225, ppd.

VICTORIAN DOLL CARRIAGE

This woven-wicker carriage has a metal frame and wheels, and its hood and lace-trimmed lining are removable.

Dimensions: 39 inches high, 31 inches long.

Price: $287, ppd.

Catalog of reproduction dolls, doll accessories, and handcrafted miniatures available, $2.

ENCHANTED DOLL HOUSE

Manchester Center, VT 05255

DOLLHOUSE KITS

These are not reproductions of antique dollhouses but modern kits depicting period buildings. The Victorian mansion shown is a 1-inch-scale model of the 1870 Ellwanger house in Rochester, New York. Its kit comes with gingerbread trim, a latticework porch, steeply pitched gables, and a box-bay window, all precut from ⅜-inch plywood. All window trim, stairs, chimneys, front steps, Plexiglas windows, hinges, and instructions for assembly are included.

Dimensions: 40 inches wide, 36 inches high, and 22 inches deep.

Price: $445, ppd.

ADDITIONAL DOLL-HOUSE KITS

Doll House Factory Outlet of Boonton, New Jersey, offers a well-detailed line of kit doll-houses patterned after actual nineteenth-century buildings. The "Americana Farmhouse" illustrated is 1 : 12 scale model measuring 21 inches deep, 36 inches wide, and 29 inches high. As with their other dollhouse kits, including a Victorian mansion and a southern Colonial, solid-pine clapboard walls, individual wood shakes, and windows are standard. A full line of miniature furnishings for each model is available separately.

Color catalog available, $2.

DOLL HOUSE FACTORY OUTLET

325 Division Street
Boonton, NJ 07005
Tel. 201/335–5501

PORCELAIN DOLLS

"My dolls are priced from $15 to $550," writes **Marilyn Ainsworth of MJA Porcelain Dolls.** "We have more than 150 faces that we make and my husband and I do all the work by hand following a 100-year-old process. We use only human hair, imported hand-blown glass eyes, and handmade leather shoes. The dolls are all signed and dated." Mrs. Ainsworth fashions all of the doll's clothing herself, following diligent research into period fabrics and styles.

MJA PORCELAIN DOLLS

Sunset Drive
Hope Valley, RI 02832
Tel. 401/539–2209

VICTORIAN ACCENTS' WOODEN TOYS

PULL TOYS "In the days of America's advancing frontier," relates Victorian Accents' Dan Damon, "children of homesteaders and farmchildren generally labored hard, helping with the field work and chores. In addition, boys worked with the men in building houses and barns, making furniture, and a few wooden toys for the younger children. The most popular items were rocking horses and pull toys consisting of animals mounted on wooden-wheeled platforms."

Victorian Accents' pull toys are hand-carved and painted, closely following nineteenth-century originals. Their heights vary from 4½ inches for the cow to 7½ inches for the horse.

Price: $18 each (plus $3.50 for postage and handling).

NOAH'S ARK TOY The Noah's Ark is a Lord's Day, or Sabbath Day, toy considered permissible for play on Sunday because it imparted biblical knowledge. Victorian Accents' handmade replica has twenty-nine figures (including Noah and his wife), plus a removable roof and gangplank, and comes with a calico sack for storage.

Dimensions: 17 inches long, 7 inches wide, and 10½ inches high.

Price: $165 (plus $9.50 for postage and handling).

Catalog of Victoriana available, $1.

WATTLE & DAUB'S VICTORIAN ACCENTS

661 West 7th Street
Plainfield, NJ 07060
Tel. 201/757–8507

CAST-IRON BANKS Shortly after the Civil War, brightly painted
cast-iron mechanical banks made their appearance. Although parents bought
them as devices to encourage thrift among children, the youngsters became so
enthralled by their ingenious mechanisms that many buttons were stolen out of
sewing boxes to be saved when pennies were scarce. The complex movements of
the banks often depicted actions and characters reflecting the cultural and
political atmosphere of the time: from a circus dog jumping through a hoop to
deposit a coin in a barrel, to a smiling Uncle Sam salting his coins away in a
valise.

By the 1880s mechanical banks had become so popular that the *Book of Knowledge*,
a highly respected source of information, published a compilation of the
most popular ones. Hand-painted, cast, and assembled according to nineteenth-century methods, Elizabeth Edge Studios' replicas each carry a certificate of authenticity from the Book of Knowledge Collection.

The Organ Grinder bank depicted was first crafted in 1892. As you turn the
handle, the boy and girl begin to dance, bells chime, and the monkey deposits the
coin from his tray while politely tipping his hat. Other penny banks available are
Jonah and the Whale (1890), American Eagle (1883), Hometown Battery, and
William Tell (1896).

Brochure available.

ELIZABETH EDGE STUDIOS

Department AH
5060 West Lake Road
Canandaigua, NY 14424
Tel. 716/394-0656

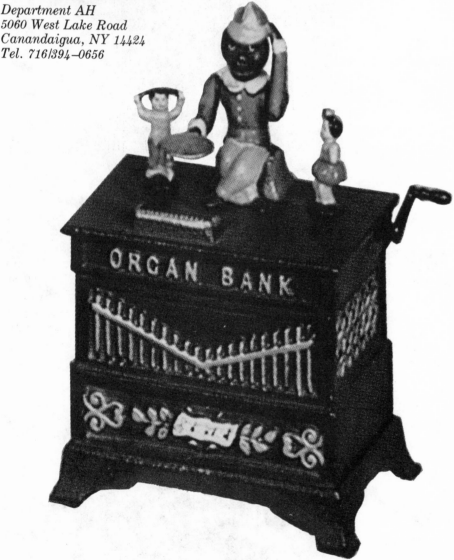

CHECKERBOARDS Cabi-
netmaker Michael L. Lester fashions checkerboards typical of many
made during the nineteenth century.
Made of hand-planed poplar and
painted in traditional colors, the
boards have spoke-shave moldings
that are applied with cut nails. Available in red oxide on dark green or yellow ochre on red oxide.

Prices: 12-inch square, $33; 14 by 23
inches, $47 (plus $3.50 each for shipping).

FOLK ART STUDIOS

611 West 12th Street
Bloomington, IN 47401
Tel. 812/336-5575

HOBBY HORSE Copied from
a nineteenth-century original in
the Charleston Museum, Historic
Charleston Reproduction's hobby
horse has the profile of a galloping
steed over each rocker supporting a
baby's seat in between. The hand-
painted toy is of solid pine.

Dimensions: 25½ inches high, 16
inches wide, and 43 inches long.

Price: $225 (freight collect).

Color catalog of antique reproduction
home furnishings and price list available.

HISTORIC CHARLESTON REPRODUC-
TIONS SHOP

105 Broad Street, Box 622
Charleston, SC 29402

FRENCH PLAYING CARDS

La Pelleterie replicates a deck of cards designed in France and printed in 1805.

Price: $5 (plus $1.25 for postage and handling).

Catalog of historical clothing and accouterments available, $3.

LA PELLETERIE DE FORT DE CHARTRES

P.O. Box 627
Chester, IL 62233
Tel. 618/826-4334

1890 FIELD DRUM

In the winter of 1854 Silas Noble and James P. Cooley began the manufacture of drums in the kitchen of Noble's farmhouse. So great was their initial success that by 1856 they were able to build their first factory. In 1860 Noble and Cooley made a drum from a rail split by Abe Lincoln—this was used by the Great Emancipator in political rallies in Connecticut and Massachusetts, and may even have had something to do with the firm's landing several contracts for drums for Northern regiments.

By 1873 Noble and Cooley were manufacturing 100,000 drums a year, including toy drums. These required special machinery to aid in the difficult process of steam bending, decorating, and fabricating the drum parts. The 1890 Field Drum is still made by this nineteenth-century equipment.

The 1890 "cord and ear" Field Drum is an authentic vintage toy. It features a brightly lithographed and embossed shell 9 inches in diameter, strung with white cord through leather ears. Drumsticks and carrying sling included.

Price: $9.95.

NOBLE & COOLEY COMPANY

Water Street
Granville, MA 01034
Tel. 413/562-9694

WOODEN TOP AND CLAY MARBLES

La Pelleterie offers an old-fashioned top of hand-turned hardwood and handmade clay marbles.

Prices: top, 95¢; marbles (ten in a leather bag), $2.75 (plus $1.25 for postage and handling).

Catalog of historical clothing and accouterments available, $3.

LA PELLETERIE DE FORT DE CHARTRES

P.O. Box 627
Chester, IL 62233
Tel. 618/826-4334

POOL TABLES

Pre-1900 Brunswick and English Thurston pool tables are replicated by the Adler company of Los Angeles. The Adlers offer a range of types, each handcrafted from 1 1/16-inch Pennsylvania slate and kiln-dried hardwoods. Weighing more than 1,600 pounds apiece, the pool tables may be ordered with any one of several finishes, cloths, frieze, and pocket treatments. Each is built to meet the commercial specifications of the Billiard Congress of America.

Prices range from $1,250 to $7,995.

Brochure available.

POOL TABLES BY ADLER

820 S. Hoover Street
Los Angeles, CA 90005
Tel. 213/382-6334

JANESVILLE BALL BEARING COASTER WAGON

Beginning in the year 1900 and for three decades thereafter, the Janesville Ball Bearing Coaster Wagon was the standard, as the copy line goes, by which all other such toys were judged. The solid-oak Janesville wagon was the model of versatility—it was a racer, a covered wagon (when properly fitted out), a farm wagon, and a bus. When necessary, the durable plaything could also be pressed into service aiding adults with shopping and laundry—serious tasks that it performed with happy aplomb. The Janesvilles got passed on from one generation to the next, and today they are valuable collector's items.

The Wisconsin Wagon Company began producing the "Series II" Janesville Ball Bearing Wagon in 1979, intent on sacrificing none of the quality of the originals to contemporary standards of workmanship and design. As a result, the Series II precisely replicates their design details, retaining the solid-oak body, the ball-bearing wheels, the unique bracing, the front axle pivot system, as well as all other features.

Dimensions: 16- by 33-inch box with 4-inch sides.

Price: $160 (plus $10.50 UPS charge).

Brochure available.

WISCONSIN WAGON COMPANY

10 South Locust Street
Janesville, WI 53545
Tel. 608/754–0026

201

SEARS, ROEBUCK & CO., Cheapest Supply House on Earth, Chicago. CATALOGUE No. III.

REMEDIES AND TOILET ARTICLES

Dr. Worden's Female Pills for All Female Diseases.

Retail price 50c
Our price, per box $0.35
Our price, per dozen boxes 3.00

'his is acknowledged as one of the GREATEST REMEDIES of the age.

A GREAT BLOOD purifier and nerve tonic. Cures all diseases arising from a poor and wasted condition of the blood, such as pale and sallow complexion, general weakness of the muscles, loss of appetite, depression of spirits, lack of ambition, anæmia, chlorosis or green sickness, palpitation of the heart, shortness of breath on slight exertion, coldness of hands and feet, swelling of the feet and limbs, pain in the back, nervous headache, dizziness, ss of memory, feebleness of will, ringing in the ears, early decay. ALL ORMS OF FEMALE WEAKNESS—leucorrhœa, tardy or irregular periods, uppression of the menses, hysteria, locomotor ataxia, partial paralysis, iatica, rheumatism, neuralgia. Cures all diseases depending on vitiated umors in the blood, causing scrofula, swelled glands, fever sores, rickets, ip joint diseases, hunchback, acquired deformities, decayed bones, chronic rysipelas, consumption of the bowels and lungs. In invigorating the blood ystem when broken down by overwork, worry, iseases, excesses and indiscretions of living, his is a most wonderful medicine.

One of our best sellers. Women who have used these pills will gladly recommend them to others. They will increase your sales and profits immensely. . . . . . .

HESE FEMALE PILLS are not a purgative medicine: they are not a cure-ll. They contain nothing that could injure the ost delicate system but act upon the diseases ependent upon poor and watery blood or a achectic state of that fluid.

'OMEN CAN BE BEAUTIFUL, their complexion perfect, nervous stem normal, circulation perfect. All weakess and disease removed by taking these pure vegetable pills. Thousands f women have been cured by using Dr. Worden's Pills, after all other emedies and physicians had failed.

'E GUARANTEE A CURE. One single box will furnish great relief. Six boxes are usually sufficient to cure cases that are not of oo long standing, while ten to twelve boxes will cure any case for the treatent of which these pills are prepared. We positively guarantee to cure ny case of female weakness if the treatment is proceeded with in a sysmatic manner, and for a reasonable length of time.

No. 8R39 Our special price, per dozen boxes, $3.00; per box 35c
If by mail, postage extra, per box, 2 cents.

Cathartic Pills, Only 10 Cents per Box.

Retail price 25c
Our price, per box $0.10
Our price, per dozen boxes .... .90

HIS IS THE OLD FASHIONED UGAR COATED CATHARTIC PILL the U. S. Pharmacopœia, the me as Ayer's, Brandreth's, aynes' and other much adverised pills. They act principally the liver, and move the bowels ntly without griping. These lls are carefully prepared from esh vegetable extracts, and can be thoroughly relied upon. For this reason ey are much superior to many others sold at double their price.

No. 8R42 Price, per dozen boxes, 90c; per box containing 25 pills 10c
If by mail, postage extra, per box, 2 cents.

Wonderful Little Liver Pills.

Retail price 25c
Our price, each $0.13
Our price, per dozen 1.00

ntirely vegetable in their composition. These wonderful little pills operate without disturbance to the system, diet or occupation.

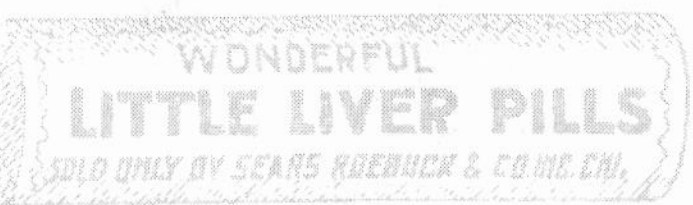

CONSTIPATION, that most hideous and deathly demon of sickness, is an easy enough thing to cure if you will only persist in taking proper treatment. It is one of the commonest troubles and often thought to be a very little thing. Yet we say that nine-tenths of human sickness is due to this one thing. When the bowels do not move gularly the natural drainage tract in the human system is dammed up, composition ensues and poisonous gases and liquids are carried all rough the system. The result is jaundice, torpid liver, biliousness, llow skin, indigestion, foul breath, coated tongue, loss of appetite, mples, belching foul gases, blotches, boils, dizziness, headache, cramps, lle, etc. You can easily avoid all these troubles and keep your system re and healthy by taking from time to time one or two of our WONDER- L LITTLE LIVER PILLS. Some of our customers call them "LITTLE ANTS," they are so small in size and so easy to swallow, yet so effective l mild in their operation. Whenever your stomach, liver and bowels get t of order take one or two of our LITTLE WONDERS and notice the ick effect and great relief you will experience. Keep a box always beside u. Use them occasionally and you will always feel well and look the ture of health.

No. 8R45 Price, per dozen boxes, $1.00; each 13c
If by mail, postage extra, per box, 2 cents.

Do You Sneeze? Camphor Pills.

Retail price .... 25c and $1.00
Our price, 25c size, each $0.18
Our price, 25c size, per dozen 1.50
Our price, $1.00 size, each .... .50
Our price, $1.00 size, per dozen 4.80

VE BEEN LONG USED BY THE OLD SCHOOL PHYSICIANS, a remedy for cold in the head, cramps, colic, diarrhœa and olera morbus and other annoying troubles resulting from catchcold. Also for menstrual colic. A bottle of these pills ought be carried in the pocket continually by those who are travel-, or outside most of the day exposed to all weathers. Though ry effective in performing cures, they are small and can be conniently kept in the vest pocket.

No. 8R48 Price, regular size, per dozen $1.50; each 18c
If by mail, postage, extra, small, 2 cents.

Large size (containing four times as much as small ones). Price, per dozen, .80; each .... (If by mail, postage extra, large, 16 cents.) 50c

Dr. Hammond's Nerve and Brain Pills.

GUARANTEED THE HIGHEST GRADE ON THE MARKET.

A BOON FOR WEAK MEN.

Retail price $1.00
Our price, each $0.60
Our price, per dozen 6.00

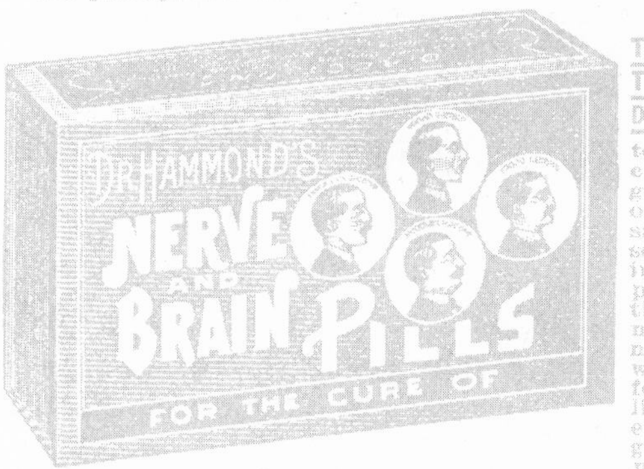

SIX BOXES POSITIVELY GUARANTEED TO CURE ANY DISEASE for which they are intended. This will cure you if you feel generally miserable or suffer with a thousand and one indescribable bad feelings, both mental and physical, among them low spirits, nervousness, weariness, lifelessness, weakness, dizziness, feeling of fullness like bloating after eating, or sense of goneness or emptiness of stomach in morning; flesh soft and lacking firmness, headache, blurring of eyesight, specks floating before the eyes, nervous irritability, poor memory, chilliness, alternating with hot flushes; lassitude, throbbing, gurgling or rumbling sensations in bowels, with heat and nipping pains occasionally; palpitation of heart, sho[illegible]h on exertion, slow circulation of blood, cold feet, pain and oppression [illegible] weariness of the lower [illegible]ness at night, languor in [illegible]mething awful was going [illegible]

IF YOU HA[illegible]D BRAIN [illegible]u. No matter what the cause may be or how severe your trouble is, DR. HAMMOND'S NERVE AND BRAIN PILLS will cure you. These pills have a remarkable effect on both old and young. They cannot be equaled by any other medicine as a cure for impotency, spermatorrhœa, night sweats, emissio[illegible], weakness of both brain and body arising [illegible] the whole nervous [illegible]r depressed you ma[illegible] bold again; they wi[illegible]

BEWAR[illegible] paying money [illegible] Our Nerve and Brain Pills are compounded from a prescription of one of the most noted German scientists, and are the same as have been used in German hospitals for years with marvelous success. HOW TO CURE YOURSELF and full and explicit direct[illegible] enclosed with every box. All orders and inquiries concerning the[illegible] will be treated confidentially, and all shipments made in plain sealed [illegible]

ONLY $3.0[illegible] case, no matter [illegible] long standing, whether ol[illegible] $3.00 and we will send [illegible] package, with full instru[illegible]

If you need these pills don't delay. This is the first time the American people have had an opportunity of getting the genuine Dr. Hammond's Pills, and the first time they have been sold anywhere at anything like our price.

No. 8R51 Price, per dozen boxes, $6.00; each 60c
If by mail, postage extra, per box, 2 cents.

Our Famous Blood Pills.

A WONDERFUL PURIFIER.

Retail price 50c
Our price, each $0.22
Our price, per dozen 1.80

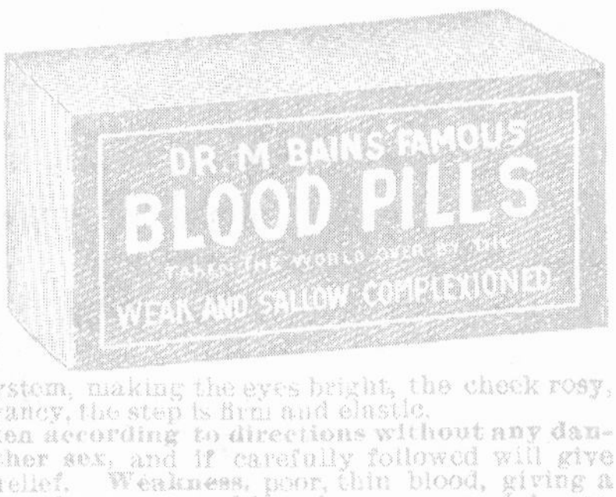

For men and women that require a nerve tonic, blood purifier or builder.

Over one hundred thousand sold last year, which shows what is thought of these pills when known. Others sell them at 50 cents per box.

FOR FEMALE TROUBLE they are an unfailing remedy, and guaranteed far superior to any other pills on the market at any price. They give tone to the whole system, making the eyes bright, the cheek rosy, and, through strength and buoyancy, the step is firm and elastic.

OUR BLOOD PILLS can be taken according to directions without any danger, by either sex, and if carefully followed will give quick results and permanent relief. Weakness, poor, thin blood, giving a sallow or pale complexion, loss of appetite, chlorosis or green sickness, pain in the back, palpitation of the heart, nervous headaches, suppression of menses, leucorrhœa, tardy or irregular periods, hysteria, paralysis, and all diseases resulting from humors in the blood, which cause erysipelas, sores, swellings, and even consumption, also in cases where the system is broken down by overwork of mind or body, or from excesses and indiscretions of living.

THE EFFECT IS WONDERFUL. These pills are not of a cathartic nature; they do not, nor are they intended to purge. They are intended to act on the blood, and supply what is needed in restoring the tone and lacking constituents, stimulating to activity the sluggish system.

FOR WOMEN in case of suppression of menses, leucorrhœa or whites, chlorosis, anæmia, locomotor ataxia, a quick and permanent cure can be effected; in fact, it is the greatest remedy known.

FOR MEN these pills stand without a rival, and should be used in all cases where the patient is suffering from a tainted condition of the blood. They have proved especially valuable in the treatment of blood and skin diseases, and as a rule are prescribed by the most successful physicians in cases of eczema and blood poison. A similar class of pills retails everywhere from 50 cents to $1.00, but they cannot be compared with our famous Blood Pills, which are the grandest prescription in existence for restoring the blood to a natural, healthy and normal condition.

No. 8R54 Price, per dozen boxes, $1.80; each 22c
If by mail, postage extra, per box, 2 cents.

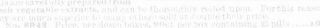

COLOGNE AND AFTER-SHAVE

NUMBER SIX

COLOGNE The Caswell-Massey Company's claim to being "the oldest chemists and perfumers in America" is certainly no idle boast. In fact, if by America we mean the United States, then the New York chemists are *older* than America.

The apothecary was founded in 1752 by Dr. William Hunter, a patron of the arts who helped support Gilbert Stuart when he was a young portraitist. Dr. Hunter was also the first person in America to lecture on anatomy, and displayed an interest in affairs both cultural and scientific reminiscent of those of the Founding Fathers who were his peers. The difference was that Dr. Hunter was a Tory, and one who died with his cause during the Revolutionary War.

Hunter's apothecary was then located in Newport, Rhode Island. Following the Revolution his widow sold this store to a clerk, thereby beginning a tradition that has held on ever since, with one assistant after another succeeding the previous owner.

The Newport store was closed in 1906, leaving only the one in New York City (which since the time of its opening has been located at Lexington Avenue and 48th Street), a sedate, mahogany-paneled place that's, well, somewhat *Tory* in its ambience. It's from New York that Caswell-Massey's products are widely distributed.

And these products, coming from all over the world, themselves embrace centuries. Until a few years ago Caswell-Massey still sold leeches; other items of theirs featured throughout this section, were also used by historic Americans. Dr. Hunter's Number Six Cologne was used, ironically enough, by none other than the Father of our Country.

Still made from the formula that Dr. Hunter brought over from England, Number Six Cologne contains twenty-seven natural ingredients—including bergamot, musk, orange blossom, and lemon—and was so favored by George Washington that as president he sent two bottles over to France for his old ally, Lafayette, to enjoy. Although this formulation is somewhat stronger than the original (in those days "cologne-water" was used for sponge bathing), Dr. Hunter's stipulation that the aging casks be rolled from one end of the laboratory to the other once monthly is still followed faithfully. Available in the traditional "Caswell Round" bottles in 3-, 8-, and 16-ounce sizes.

Prices: 3 ounces, $10; 8 ounces, $20; 16 ounces, $36 (plus 10 percent for shipping). Minimum order $2.

Seasonal catalog available.

CASWELL-MASSEY CO., LTD.

Mail-Order Division
111 Eighth Avenue
New York, NY 10011
Tel. 212/620–0900

LILAC VEGETAL According to the Nestle-LeMur Company, makers of Lilac Vegetal, the lilac-scented after-shave tonic was developed during the 1850s by Édouard Pinaud, *parfumeur* to the court of Napoleon III. M Pinaud was charged with the task of creating a distinctive scent for the contingent of Hungarian cavalry then attached to the monarch's court; the lime-green lotion still to be found in most drugstores was then produced by Pinaud after several months' work.

LIMIMENTS

SLOAN'S

As the early records regarding Dr. Earl Sloan and the liniment he developed in 1885 have been lost, little is known about the beginnings of the product that bears his name. Warner-Lambert, the company that now manufactures Sloan's Liniment according to its original formula, does tell us that at the time he first produced his capsicum-based compound, Dr. Sloan was a veterinarian for the St. Louis Street Car Company. Thus it may be assumed that Sloan's Liniment was preceded by a stronger potion used to relieve the muscular distress of horses.

The packaging of Dr. Sloan's liniment appears unchanged, and features the benign veterinarian, contemplative behind his massive (and from the looks of it, rotating) handlebar moustache.

Available in drugstores everywhere.

PRAIRIE CHIEF

For internal and external use. Contains methyl salicylate, thymol, oil of eucalyptus, oil of camphor, refined oil petrolatum, D&C color. 8 fluid ounces. Shipping weight: 2 lbs.

Price: $2.73, F.O.B. Crossville, Tennessee.

"Wish and Want Book" available $3.75.

CUMBERLAND GENERAL STORE

Route 3
Crossville, TN 38555
Tel. 615/484–8481

SLOAN'S LINIMENT

WITH SAFETY CAP

DrEarlSSloan ®

ACTIVE INGREDIENTS: Capsicum Oleoresin 0.62%, Methyl Salicylate 2.66%, Oil of Camphor 3.35%, Turpentine Oil 46.76%, Oil of Pine 6.74%.

2 FL. OZ.

AIDS IN THE TEMPORARY RELIEF OF MINOR RHEUMATIC AND ARTHRITIC PAINS

REMEDIES

MONROE'S GLYCERATED ASAFOETIDA

Asafoetida is the hardened juice from the root of a Persian plant, once used to cure a wide variety of nervous ailments. The Cumberland General Store notes that when worn about the neck in an "asafoetida poke," the remedy's foul odor is sure to keep all communicable diseases away. Shipping weight: 6 ounces.

Price: 95¢, F.O.B. Crossville, Tennessee.

"Wish and Want Book" available, $3.75.

CUMBERLAND GENERAL STORE

Route 3
Crossville, TN 38555
Tel. 615/484–8481

THAYERS SLIPPERY ELM THROAT LOZENGES

Thayers Lozenges have recently been reformulated to substitute dextrose for sugar, but are otherwise the same product in the same package that has been marketed since 1847.

Thayers' effective ingredient is the bark of the slippery elm, a natural demulcent that has long been a part of the American folk pharmacopoeia.

A regional New England product until about ten years ago, Thayers is now to be found in drug and health food stores throughout North America.

CASWELL-MASSEY SPECIALTIES

PROCTOR'S PINELYPTUS PASTILLES

When singer John Denver sends to the Caswell-Massey Company for his caseload of these throat comforters, he may or may not be aware that Jenny Lind, the "Swedish Nightingale" of the 1850s, also was once the beneficiary of its soothing combination of pine, menthol, and eucalyptus. Miss Lind's order was placed with the apothecary by an admiring P. T. Barnum, who asked that she be sent "a little something—not too expensive—every week, wherever she is."

Price: $4 (plus $2 for shipping).

TONSORIAL SUPPLIES

Relative to the Europeans, Americans have never much gone in for mechanized electronic approaches to shaving. For those among us who will even regard a Trac-Two as too nontraditional, Caswell-Massey offers a sure-fire way to feel like a cowboy first thing in the morning.

Available are three varieties of hollow-ground straight razors imported from France. These arrive with assurances from the ancient American apothecary that straight razors still provide the most effective method of shaving, and are therefore *not* anachronisms. A barber's guidance (and an industrial-size styptic pencil) is advised for beginners.

Several accessories are also offered, including a razor strop made of sturdy leather, a wooden shaving bowl with soap (choice of almond, sandalwood, and verbena fragrances), and imported English badger brushes.

Prices: Sparticus razor, $40; razor strop, $39; shaving bowl and soap, $9.75; gray badger brushes, $45 to $130, depending on brush length (plus 10 percent for shipping each item. Minimum $2).

ALLCOCK'S POROUS PLASTER

An oldtime poultice that "draws out" temporary muscle pain by "counter-irritant action." Contains: burgundy pitch, frankincense, orris root, capsicum, beeswax, camphor, gum of elemi, and gum of myrrh on a natural-rubber base.

Price: $2.50 (plus $2 for shipping).

Seasonal catalog available.

CASWELL-MASSEY CO., LTD.

Mail-Order Division
111 Eighth Avenue
New York, NY 10011
Tel. 212/620-0900

How an ALLCOCK PLASTER draws the pain out

PAINS OF LUMBAGO!   WARMED

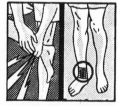

SPRAINS & STRAINS.   SUPPORTED STRENGTHENED!!

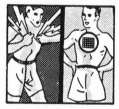

CHEST COLDS.   QUICK RELIEF!!

RHEUMATIC PAIN!   RELIEVED!

PAIN OF SCIATICA!   QUICKLY RELIEVED!!

NEURITIS!   RELIEVED WITH WARMTH!!

CUCUMBER NIGHT CREAM

In 1885 Sarah Bernhardt, then playing the title part in *Hamlet* in her own theater in Paris, cabled Caswell-Massey for thirty jars of their Cucumber Night Cream.

Prices: 4 ounces, $5; 14 ounces, $13.50 (plus $2 each for shipping).

TILBURY TOOTHBRUSH

Identical to the Caswell-Massey toothbrush found in Gen. George Armstrong Custer's personal kit following the Battle of the Little Big Horn. Handmade in England of bone and the finest natural bristle.

Price: $12 (plus $2 for shipping and handling).

Seasonal catalog available.

CASWELL-MASSEY CO., LTD.

*Mail-Order Division
111 Eighth Avenue
New York, NY 10011
Tel. 212/620–0900*

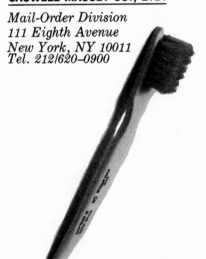

IRON KOLA AND CELERY COMPOUND TONIC

A "System Tonic and Body Builder—Recommended for Men, Women, and Children in weakened or run down condition. Containing: Rhubarb, Sienna, Gensian, Golden Seal, Boneset Herb, Sodium Salicilate, Licorice, Magnesium Sulfate, Extract of Celery, Extract of Kola, Iron Citrate in Sherry Wine. . . . Combines the curative and strengthening powers of celebrated vegetable elements from the finest medicinal herbs."

Price: $3.12, F.O.B. Crossville, Tennessee.

"Wish and Want Book" available, $3.75.

CUMBERLAND GENERAL STORE

*Route 3
Crossville, TN 38555
Tel. 615/484–8481*

ACE HARD-RUBBER COMBS

Made from the material accidentally discovered by Nelson Goodyear in 1851, Ace hard-rubber combs were reputedly found among the remains of Civil War soldiers during archeological excavations of battlefield sites. Found today at drug counters everywhere.

GOLD BOND MEDICATED POWDER

Gold Bond's turn-of-the-century can bristles with fleur-de-lys and contains an original-formula powder "for the relief of bed sores, chafing, sunburn, prickly heat, non-poisonous insect bites, chapped hands, and minor skin irritations."

GOLD BOND STERILIZING POWDER COMPANY

*745 Washington Street
Fairhaven, MA 02719*

206

SEARS, ROEBUCK & CO., Cheapest Supply House on Earth, Chicago. CATALOGUE No. 111.

27 Cents Buys a 50-Cent Pipe.

No. 18R5534 This splendid smoker is a French brier, bulldog shape bowl, with amberoid mouthpiece; the stem between bowl and mouthpiece is genuine Weichsel wood, and will not burn your tongue; worth 75 cents in the regular pipe stores.
Price, each........27c
If by mail, postage extra, 5 cents.

French Brier Pipe for 39 Cents.

No. 18R5538 Handsome French Brier Pipe, straight bulldog shape, with clear Chinese amber stem and decorated band and bowl, latest design. We highly recommend this pipe.
Price, each........39c

The Distiller Pipe, 44 Cents.

No. 18R5542 The Distiller Pipe. Greatest success of the century. Brier bowl with hard rubber stem. Between bowl and stem is a glass tube which takes up the nicotine and saliva. Draw out the mouthpiece and let out the nicotine; stem is easily replaced.
Price, each............44c

German Porcelain Pipes.

No. 18R5546 German Porcelain Pipe, handsome, large size, with long bent stem in five different shades of amber and gold, with fancy porcelain bowl handsomely decorated. The bowl can readily be taken apart for cleaning, thus insuring a clean, cool smoke.
each..........79c

PIPES AND TOBACCO

egg shaped bowl and handsome cherry stem with silk cord and tassel and Chinese amber mouthpiece. An exceptionally handsome article.

No. 18R5550 Price, each........69c
If by mail, postage extra, 6 cents.

Turkish Water Pipe.

No. 18R5554 A genuine Turkish Water pipe; the bowl is made of fine colored glass, prettily decorated, and has a long flexible stem, with small amber mouthpiece connected to pipe. In the center of head is a thin glass tube through which the smoke passes. The cup which holds the tobacco is made of Vienna Meerschaum, which can be replaced, if desired, by the Vienna Meerschaum cigar holder, which comes with the set. Entire height of same is about 16 inches.
Price, each............$1.94
Shipping weight, 1 pound.

No. 18R5558 Turkish Water Pipe, same as above, but having two flexible stems from which two persons can smoke at the same time. The bowl is more elaborately decorated than the above, and a little larger. Entire height about 16½ inches.
Price, each. (Shipping weight, 1 pound)... $2.75

Pipes in Leather Covered Cases.

No. 18R5562 Genuine French Brier Pipe, English bulldog shape. Length, 5 inches. Handsome Vienna amber mouthpiece. Each one of these pipes is put up in a handsome leather covered case, with silk and velvet lining.
Price, each............73c
If by mail, postage extra, each, 5 cents.

79 Cents for a Rosewood Pipe.

No. 18R5566 This is certainly one of the very handsomest pipes made. It is made from highly polished rosewood with removable set in bowl of genuine meerschaum, which can be unscrewed and easily cleaned. Genuine Chinese amber mouthpiece; length, 5½ inches. Put up in handsome leather covered, satin lined case.
Price, each..........79c
If by mail, postage extra, 4 cents.

Most Stores get $1.50 for this Grade.

No. 18R5567 Flat Stem French Brier Pipe, with 1½-inch genuine amber mouthpiece. Has a medium small size bowl and is a very desirable shape. Pipe is very highly polished. Total length of pipe, 5½ inches. Inlaid in fine leather velvet lined case. A very desirable style.
Price, each..........92c
If by mail, postage extra, 4 cents.

A Handsome Shape, $1.75.

No. 18R5569 Highly Polished French Brier Pipe, representing an acorn, bowl carved on top. The under bowl is round, while at end it is flat, with 1½-inch amber mouthpiece. Entire length of pipe is 7 inches. A cool smoke, and a particularly desirable style.
each..........$1.75
If by mail, postage extra, 5 cents.

Bull Dog Style, $1.47.

No. 18R5571 French Brier Pipe, bulldog shape, with 2¼-inch genuine amber mouthpiece and trimmed with a sterling silver band between stem and pipe. Entire length of pipe, 5¼ inches. Large size, highly polished bowl. Inlaid in fine leather plush lined case.
Price, each..........$1.47
If by mail, postage extra, 5 cents.

A Beauty for a Present.

No. 18R5573 Fine French Brier Pipe, bulldog shape, with genuine amber mouthpiece, 5 inches long, highly polished bowl, with band of chased gold, also on stem, in elegant plush lined leather case. $3.75 value. Our price..........$2.29
If by mail, postage extra, 6 cents.

This $5.00 Pipe for $3.25.

No. 18R5575 Finest Quality French Brier Pipe, with heavy, wide, 3½-inch genuine amber mouthpiece. The bowl is ornamented with a heavy 14-karat gold band, and a heavy 14-karat gold band also connects the amber mouthpiece with the brier bowl. Total length of pipe, 6½ inches. Inlaid in an elegant plush lined chamois covered case. There are no finer goods made; red $5.00 value.
Price, each..........$3.25
If by mail, postage extra, 6 cents.

Fancy Egg Shape.

No. 18R5579 This is a fancy, egg shape, French Brier Pipe, with a round stem and ½-inch gold band and 4-inch amber mouthpiece. Entire length of pipe is 11 inches, making a delightful, cool smoke; inlaid in fine chamois, plush lined case. Price, each..........$2.85
If by mail, postage extra, 6 cents.

Finest Quality French Brier Pipe.

No. 18R5581 Finest Quality French Brier Pipe, Bull bitch shape. This handsome pipe has a thick curved genuine amber stem, heavily mounted in real gold, such a pipe as you never expect to pay less than $7.50 for elsewhere.
Price, each..........$3.73
If by mail, postage extra, each, 6 cents.

A Novelty Ball Shape Pipe, $1.85.

No. 18R5583 Fine French Brier Pipe, ball shape. Highly polished bowl, with curved, square, genuine amber stem and trimmed with small gold band. Inlaid in leather lined case. A very desirable small pipe.
Price, each..........$1.85
If by mail, postage extra, 5 cents.

Special Value at $2.75.

No. 18R5585 Highly Polished, Fine French Brier Pipe, bulldog shape, with curved 2½-inch genuine amber square stem; trimmed with gold band at top of the stem between the stem and bowl. A very handsome pipe. Inlaid in leather plush lined case. Price, each..........$2.75
If by mail, postage extra, 5 cents.

Handy Set Pipe, 87 Cents.

No. 18R5586 Well Shaped Brier Pipe, with clear bent Chinese amber stem, inlaid in plush lined pocket case. A real bargain. Price, each..........87c
If by mail, postage extra, 4 cents.

No. 18R5587 Fine French Brier Pipe, with a well shaped, large size, egg bowl; trimmed with curved sterling silver band and 2½-inch genuine amber curved shove bit. Pipe inlaid in chamois, plush lined pocket case.
Price, each..........$1.89
If by mail, postage extra, 4 cents.

No. 18R5589 A well shaped genuine French Brier Pipe. Highly polished, with handsome chased gold bands on stem and top of bowl; genuine amber curved shove bit, 2¾ inches in length. Pipe is inlaid in handsome chamois, plush lined pocket case.
Price, each..........$2.95
If by mail, postage extra, 5 cents.

No. 18R5591 Square Stem, French Brier Bowl, very highly polished, heavy sterling silver band between stem and pipe; 2½-inch genuine amber shove bit; medium large bowl for a good long smoke. Inlaid in chamois plush lined pocket case.
Price, each..........$1.97
If by mail, postage extra, 4 cents.

Smoker's Companion.

No. 18R5594 Smoker's Companion, consisting of two pipes, one straight French brier, bulldog shape, with 2-inch genuine amber mouthpiece, solid gold band, and one bent egg shape, highly polished French brier pipe, with curved 2-inch genuine amber mouthpiece, solid gold band around stem, both pipes inlaid in a beautiful chamois covered and silk plush lined case.
Price, per set..........$2.98
If by mail, postage extra, 6 cents.

FINE MEERSCHAUM PIPES.

No. 18R5597 Chip Meerschaum Pipe, bulldog shape bowl, best English amber mouthpiece. We warrant this pipe to color; with satin lined leather covered case. Do not unscrew stem from bowl.
Price, each....97c
If by mail, postage extra, 5 cents.

Pipes

FROM CRAZY CROW TRADING POST

CLAY PIPES **Replicated to faithfully follow eighteenth- and early-nineteenth-century originals,** clay pipes like those offered by the Crazy Crow Trading Post were likely to have been found in every Hudson Bay and Northwest Company trader's pack. With cherrywood stems.

TRAPPER'S PIPES **For making the bowls of their calumets, the Indians of the upper Missouri River region used a red pipestone found only in one Minnesota quarry.** This quarry and the territory around it were considered neutral land, accessible to those of any tribe who came for the sacred pipestone. In time this Minnesota catlinate was used to fashion the compact, stowable pipes that were smoked (and often worn as pendants) by eighteenth- and early-nineteenth-century trappers. Today this material is still used by Crazy Crow to make their unique replica trapper's pipes.

Catalog available, $2.

CRAZY CROW TRADING POST

P.O. Box 314
Denison, TX 75020
Tel. 214/463–1366

TURK'S HEAD
CLAY PIPE
As the Ohio Valley was settled in the early part of the nineteenth century, pottery factories were soon established to fulfill the pioneers' requirements for crocks, jugs, and tableware. These places also made clay pipe bowls in great quantities, each usually to be fitted onto a reed stem. The Log Cabin Shop has replicated an unusual version of one

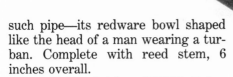

such pipe—its redware bowl shaped like the head of a man wearing a turban. Complete with reed stem, 6 inches overall.

Log Cabin Catalog #83003. Price: $3.50 (plus postage and handling).

Catalog of black-powder supplies and accessories available, $4.

THE LOG CABIN SHOP

P.O. Box 275
Lodi, OH 44254
Tel. 216/948–1082

MARK TWAIN'S 1896 PETERSON

Samuel Clemens's well-known love of tobacco was not without its limits: "I have made it a rule," the Bard of Hannibal, Missouri, was once quoted as saying "never to smoke more than one cigar at a time." As the accompanying photograph shows, this rule applied to pipes as well. But while it may be assumed that Twain smoked a single stogie at a time out of his sense of proper restraint, he kept to one pipe because, from 1896 until his death in 1911, he favored one above the others.

For years it rested almost unnoticed in the Mark Twain Museum, mercilessly misshapen as a result of the author's frequent cleanings. Then one day in 1980 Henry Sweets, curator of the Hannibal museum, received a telephone call from Bill Sweeney, president of Peterson Pipes of Dublin, Ireland. Sweeney had come across the picture of Twain we see here and believed that the pipe cradled in his hand was one once made by the Peterson Company and discontinued early in this century. One look by the curator at the original pipe in the museum's collection instantly confirmed Mr. Sweeney's suspicion.

Sweeney immediately dispatched a company expert from Dublin to Hannibal to record the precise dimensions of Mark Twain's 1896 Peterson pipe. Then, after carefully selecting proper blocks of aged briar with which to reproduce it, in 1981 the Peterson company manufactured a limited run of 400 "Mark Twain System Pipes," and 2,500 "Mark Twain Deluxe Quality System Pipes," dedicated to the great American writer's memory and works.

Prices: Deluxe Mark Twain pipe, $75; Limited-Edition Mark Twain Pipe, $300.

PETERSON OF DUBLIN

P.O. Box 608
Southport, CT 06490

TOBACCO

KINNIKINNICK
In its various forms, the word "kinnikinnick" comes from the Cree or Chippewa dialects of the Algonquin language and means "what is mixed." What *was* mixed by the Indians was originally dried sumac leaves together with other ingredients. As a name for the smoking mixtures used by both red men and white, "kinnikinnick" was widely employed throughout the nineteenth century—Kinnikinnic brand tobacco was sold to Federal troops by Civil War sutlers for a dollar a pound.

The Crazy Crow Trading Post offers several blends of Indian kinnikinnick, loosely replicating what may have been smoked early in the nineteenth century: *Northern Plains*, ". . . a mild blend of . . . tobacco, leaves, and herbs common to the Indians of the upper Missouri River Country"; *Eastern Woodlands*, ". . . a . . . blend of tobacco, roots, and bark preferred by the Indian forest dwellers of the Eastern United States"; *Comanche Straight*, ". . . a nontobacco blend of herbs, bark, and leaves from the Southern Plains"; and *Great Lakes Straight*, "An *all*-herbal blend based upon an old 'good medicine' recipe. The herbs that are used were common to the Indian people of the midwestern woodlands, the Appalachians, and the Ozarks."

TWIST

At eight o'clock, the Posscossohe, Black Cat, grand chief of the Mandans, came to see us. After showing these chiefs many things which were curiosities to them, and giving a few presents of curious handkerchiefs, arm bands, and paint, with a twist of tobacco, they departed at 1 o'clock much pleased.
—The Journal of William Clark, Captain, The Corps of Discovery, November 28, 1804

From the eighteenth century when it was used in trade with the Indians, through the Civil War when it was bought from sutlers, the convenient tobacco twist was a familiar sight. These would be chewed or smoked, and the Indians would make use of them in medicine bundles.

The Crazy Crow Trading Post offers the following varieties of tobacco twist: *American Fur Company Brand*, a sweet chew or smoke; *Rocky Mountain Pride*, described as "natural" by the store; and *Astorian Twist*, a burley tobacco.

Catalog available, $2.

CRAZY CROW TRADING POST

P.O. Box 314
Denison, TX 75020
Tel. 214/463-1366

Containers

TOBACCO CANTEEN
Crazy Crow's handcrafted replica tobacco canteens are rawhide flasks, each with a willow endplug and braided leather thong.

Catalog available, $2.

CRAZY CROW TRADING POST

P.O. Box 314
Denison, TX 75020
Tel. 214/463-1366

FROM THE LOG CABIN SHOP

TOBACCO BOX
A faithful replica of an early-nineteenth-century tobacco box that might have been found on a trade blanket in an Indian camp or in a Boston gentleman's coat. Available in solid brass or German silver, it measures 4 inches by 2 inches by ⅝ inch. Weight: 4 ounces.

Log Cabin catalog #7703 (brass). Price: $16.40. Log Cabin catalog #7701 (German silver). Price: $18.25.

GAGE D'AMOUR
La Pelleterie's heart-shaped tobacco bag (its name means "token of love") has been copied from early drawings of the Plains Indians. Made of finely fringed buckskin, it holds tobacco and carries a clay pipe.

Price: $15 (plus postage and handling).

Catalog of historical clothing and accouterments available, $3.

LA PELLETERIE DE FORT DE CHARTRES

P.O. Box 627
Chester, IL 62233
Tel. 618/826-4334

SNUFF BOX
Made of brass, 2½ inches in diameter and 1 inch high. Press-on lid. Weight: 3 ounces.

Log Cabin catalog #77SB1. Price: $6.95. Add postage and a $1 handling charge.

Catalog of black-powder accessories and supplies available, $4.

THE LOG CABIN SHOP, INC.

P.O. Box 275
Lodi, OH 44254
Tel. 216/948-1082

CIGAR STORE

INDIANS **Unseen in the forest surrounding Claremont, New Hampshire, numberless Indians yet lurk.** These are not wild men, but wooden; and once liberated from the tree trunks that conceal them, are more likely to brandish a fistful of cheroots than a tomahawk. They exist today because of the craftsmanship of Edward Boggis, a former logger, wrestler, and woodcarving instructor who is presently the country's only full-time maker of cigar store Indians. **Since he began** to carve them full size back in 1972, the sixty-year-old Mr. Boggis has turned out well over a thousand wooden chiefs, squaws, and scouts, each crowned with either feathers or (as was often the case historically) tobacco leaves. Mr. Boggis's wooden Indians cleave closely to the traditional and are made by means of a painstakingly authentic process that takes up to nine months to complete. Until the store closed in the mid-1970s the wooden Indians were sold by New York's Abercrombie & Fitch on Fifth Avenue.

When and where the first cigar store figures appeared is not known for certain, but several sources point to an early-eighteenth-century London tobacconist as their originator. This cigar store "Indian" was more likely a Negro, or "black boy" as they came to be called, wooden facsimiles of the West Indian slaves that (along with imported African ones) did the work of the American tobacco industry. Perhaps because Europeans had become aware of both simultaneously, the wild Indian was also associated with tobacco, and in time fanciful red men and women came to replace the wooden slaves at their cigar store stations. Toward the end of the nine-

teenth century the use of wooden figures had spread to other establishments as Chinese mandarins bowed before tea shops, German kings greeted tavern-goers with foaming steins, and legions of carved Punches, Columbines, Turks, and others populated city sidewalks. Early in the 1900s all these fell victim to the traffic ordinances of meddlesome local governments whose ferocious action against them was such that today few survive. Few, that is, except those in the museums, those in our memories, and those still unseen in the forests a short haul from Ed Boggis's shop.

Brochure available.

ED BOGGIS

Old Church Road
Claremont, NH 03743

Our New Hinge Cap Telescope, $3.95.

No. 20K3515 We recommend this glass particularly to those who are willing to pay a little more money for the sake of quality. This instrument comes from a Paris maker, who is noted for the quality of his telescopes, particularly the lenses, which are of higher grade and better quality than the lenses used by other makers. The object glass in this telescope is a very fine achromatic lens, insuring high magnifying power and fine definition. This instrument is strongly and substantially made throughout, finely finished, fitted with the special patented hinge cap, sliding cover in the eyepiece, draw tubes of highly burnished brass, and trimmings of bronzed brass, lacquered. Length, closed, 6⅝ inches; extended, 16¾ inches; magnifying power, twenty times, diameter of object glass, 14 ligues. Price................(If by mail, postage extra, 15 cents)...............$3.95

This Big Marine Telescope, $5.55.

No. 20K3520 This telescope, although designed especially for use on shipboard, is a fine instrument for general purposes. It is a one draw telescope, the draw tube made of highly burnished brass, and all exterior metal work of lacquered brass. Both the object lens and the eyepiece are protected by sliding covers, and the body is covered with a special corded material made from pure linen, ornamental in appearance, and even stronger and more durable than leather. The diameter of this telescope is 2½ inches. The length, closed, is 14½ inches; extended, 24 inches; the magnifying power, twenty-two times. Price...............$5.55
If by mail, postage extra, 37 cents.

No. 20K3520 partly extended.

Special Gun Metal Hinge Cap Telescope, $8.40.

No. 20K3525 This special hinge cap telescope is an exceptionally good telescope in every way, material and workmanship the very best, extra quality achromatic lenses, carefully and accurately adjusted, giving high power and fine definition. The metal parts, including the outside trimmings and the draw tubes, are made with the finest gunmetal finish, a finish that never tarnishes and which insures smooth and perfect working of the draw tubes so long as the instrument may be used. The patented hinged cap affords perfect protection to the object glass and the eyepiece is perfectly protected by a sliding cover. This telescope is made with extension sun shade, by means of which the object glass is perfectly protected from the direct rays of the sun when viewing objects where it is necessary to look toward the west in the evening, and toward the east in the morning. This telescope measures 8 inches long when closed, and 23⅞ inches long when fully extended. The diameter of the object glass is 16 ligues, and the magnifying power is 24 diameters. Price...............$8.40
If by mail, postage extra, 22 cents.

No. 20K3525 partly extended.

Our Special Strap Telescope, $11.95.

No. 20K3530 This high grade, first quality telescope, made with leather caps and shoulder strap, is an ideal instrument for rough work, carrying on horseback, etc., the leather caps and the strong leather covering affording perfect protection to the instrument, no matter how roughly it may be handled. The body of this telescope is covered with high quality, pebbled morocco leather. The caps are of the same durable material, made extra heavy and strong. The metal parts are all made with dead black oxidized finish and the workmanship throughout is the best. This telescope is provided with specially ground achromatic lenses of the highest degree of excellence, carefully and accurately adjusted, and we particularly recommend this telescope to anyone desiring a serviceable, strongly made instrument, of the highest degree of optical perfection. The diameter of the object glass is twenty-two lignes; the length, closed and with the caps on, is 10¾ inches; the length when fully extended is 35¾ inches, and the magnifying power is thirty diameters.
Price...............(If by mail, postage extra, 47 cents.)...............$11.95

This illustration shows the telescope partly extended.

Large Field Extra Luminous Telescope, $17.25.

No. 20K3540 partly extended.

No. 20K3540 This telescope is the highest grade telescope that can be manufactured, representing the very highest degree of excellence in instruments of this kind.

IT IS FITTED WITH GENUINE ANASTIGMAT LENSES, lenses that are free from spherical and chromatic aberration, but also for astigmatism. The greatest possible definition, combined with high magnifying power.

THIS TELESCOPE embraces a wider angle of view than any other telescope made, lenses, both the objective lens and the lenses in the eyepiece, is su...... construction of the instruments are known as "Extra Luminous." This desirable quality is particularly advantageous on dark, cloudy days or when using the instrument along toward evening.

UNDERSTAND, that so far as magnifying power and definition are concerned this is the best telescope that can be manufactured, fully equal in its optical and mechanical perfection to the very finest astronomical telescopes.

THE WORKMANSHIP, FINISH AND MATERIALS used in this telescope are made to co...... optical qualities, all metal parts, both the draw tubes and the extern...... best gunmetal finish and the covering is a very fine quality of blue levant leather. Made with patented hinge cap for protection ...... for the eyepiece, two draws; length, closed, 10¾ inches; extended, 24 inches; diameter of object glass, 19 lignes; magnifying power $17.25
If by mail, postage extra, 33 cents.

NAUTICAL ITEMS

25-Ligne Hinge Cap Telescope, $19.70.

No. 20K3545 This is the most powerful telescope that we handle, a much higher grade telescope than is to be found in the best optical stores in the United States. It is the lenses which make this instrument so much superior to ordinary telescopes, these lenses being especially ground from the finest optical glass, very carefully centered and accurately adjusted. They are made to combine to the greatest possible extent the finest definition and highest magnifying power. For astronomical work this telescope forms an ideal instrument, showing clearly and distinctly the interesting changes and mysterious spots on the surface of the sun, the wonderful mountain ranges and apparently extinct craters of the moon, the satellites and the surface markings of the planet Jupiter, the wonderful rings of Saturn, the canals on the planet Mars, nebulae, double stars, etc. For the observation of the sun a dark glass is mounted in the slide cover of the eyepiece. The magnifying power is 50 diameters.

The draw tubes, trimmings, and all exposed metal parts are made with fine gunmetal finish, the very best and most expensive finish known for optical instruments. This fine steel blue gunmetal finish will never tarnish nor rust and the draw tubes always work smoothly and easily. The body of the instrument is covered with a fine grade of pebbled morocco leather. This telescope is made with sunshade, and instead of the ordinary cap it is provided with a hinged metal cover which affords perfect protection to the object glass. The length, when closed, is 41½ inches; when closed, 12¼ inches. Weight, 50 ounces. The diameter of the object glass is 25 lignes (2¼ inches) and the magnifying power 50 diameters. Price, complete...............$19.70

Astronomical Eyepiece, $5.20.

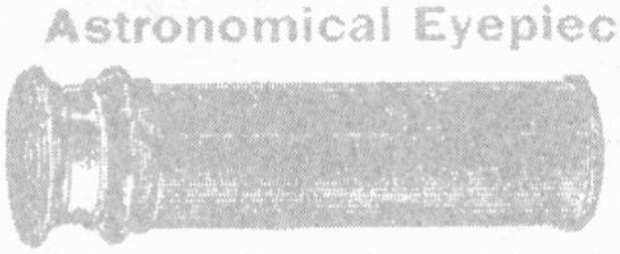

No. 20K3546 This Eyepiece is made for use with our No. 20K3545 telescope, for astronomical observations only and increases the power to 75 diameters. Price. (Postage extra, 10 cents.)...............$5.20

Genuine Stanhope Lens Floroscope, 30 Cents.

No. 20K3600 This Microscope is fitted with an exceedingly powerful Stanhope lens, by means of which the animalculae in stagnant water, entirely invisible to the naked eye, can be distinctly seen. A drop of vinegar seen by this instrument is found to be swarming with living creatures, and yeast water is alive with wriggling germs. Besides the high power Stanhope lens, this Floroscope is also fitted with an ordinary long focus magnifying glass for the examination of insects, flowers, etc. An intensely interesting instrument. Finished in lacquered brass.
Price...............(If by mail, postage extra, 3 cents).30c

Tripod Microscope.

No. 20K3605 Tripod Microscope, adapted to a variety of uses where a short focus and high magnifying power is desirable. Adjustable focus, extra high grade lens, strong, heavy brass mountings, with fine lacquered finish. The best tripod microscope made.
Price...............29c
If by mail, postage extra, 5 cents.

Exultation is the going
Of an inland soul to sea,
Past the houses—past the head-
     lands—
Into deep Eternity—

Bred as we, among the mountains,
Can the sailor understand
The divine intoxication
Of the first league out from land?
                    —Emily Dickinson

HANDMADE
SHIP MODELS

Handcrafted miniatures of eighteenth- and nineteenth-century sailing ships are the work of Piel Craftsmen. From their shop in Newburyport, Massachusetts (where many of the original vessels were built), Piel craftsmen have been carving their ship models from selected, well-seasoned wood for more than thirty-five years.

The completed models measure from 13½ to 28½ inches in length, and from 11 to 17¼ inches in height. Included are the cargo carrier *Benjamin Hale* (Newburyport, 1882); the small merchant brig *Topaz* (Newburyport, 1807), with her characteristic "cod's head, mackerel tail" lines; the clipper *Sea Witch* (New York, 1846), the first ship to sail from New York to San Francisco; the extreme clipper *Red Jacket* (Rockland, Maine, 1853), "one of the seven fastest sailing ships in all history"; the lordly *Sovereign of the Seas* (East Boston, 1852); the *Charles W. Morgan* (Newburyport, 1841); the famous clipper *Flying Cloud* (East Boston, 1851); and the U.S.S. *Constitution*, illustrated.

Prices: $40 to $300 (plus $5 for postage).

Brochure available.

PIEL CRAFTSMEN

307 High Street
Newburyport, MA 01950
Tel. 617/462-7012

SCRIMSHAW CARVINGS

Although Europeans hunted whales at least as long ago as the ninth century, among white settlers of North America whaling began during the seventeenth century, after the Indians of Nantucket Island taught it to them. Within a hundred years of this modest beginning Nantucket whalers were voyaging to the Pacific Ocean, plying the sperm whale's sea lanes in pursuit of its valuable oil. So dependent was nineteenth-century America on the products of whaling that from its industrial centers (New Bedford, Massachusetts, and San Francisco, California) several species of leviathan were hunted to extinction, or nearly so.

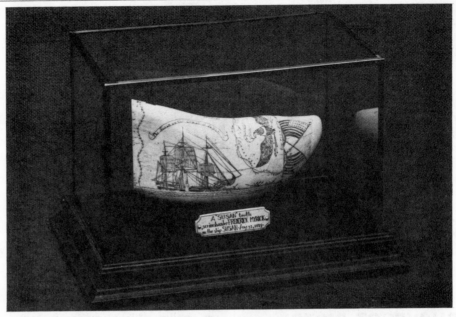

In those days a whale hunt might last from three to five years, and it was during the seaman's long periods of idleness that scrimshaw—the art of carving and decoratively engraving whalebone—emerged. Some of the finest artifacts of nineteenth-century scrimshanders are in the collection of the Nantucket Whaling Museum, which has granted Artek, Inc., the exclusive rights to their replication and sale. Using a non-whale-derived polymer "ivory" to replicate the weight, the color, and even the flawed texture of the originals, Artek's copies can barely be distinguished from them. Shown here is *A "Susan" Tooth*, depicting the whaler *Susan* as it was carved by the reknowned nineteenth-century scrimshander Frederick Myrick. The original of this polymer replica is in the Nantucket Museum.

Catalog available, $2.

ARTEK, INC.

P.O. Box 154
Antrim, NH 03440
Tel. 603/588-6825

NEW BEDFORD WHALING MUSEUM PRINTS

The Old Dartmouth Historical Society's Whaling Museum sits on a hill overlooking the harbor where many nineteenth-century Yankee whalers were berthed. The society sells full-color offset and lithographic reproductions of 1800s prints depicting New Bedford whalingmen, their vessels, and their historic port. Illustrated here is a print entitled "New Bedford, Fifty Years Ago," first published by Charles Taber & Company in 1858. This print is available for $10.

"Catalog of Publications" (including posters and books) available.

OLD DARTMOUTH HISTORICAL SOCIETY

Whaling Museum
18 Johnny Cake Hill
New Bedford, MA 02740

MYSTIC SEAPORT NAUTICAL ITEMS

The Mystic Seaport Museum store offers the following replicas of nineteenth-century nautical items:

BULKHEAD LANTERN

Following the type of lantern used during the late nineteenth and early twentieth centuries on ocean-going vessels, Mystic Seaport's bulkhead lantern is made in the traditional manner. Pure, unlacquered brass with beveled glass. 12 inches high.

Price: $145 (plus $4.50 for packing and delivery).

DUCKFOOT PISTOL (.36 Caliber)

" 'Early Mutiny and Riot Arm,' " the Navy Arms catalog relates. ". . . many sea Captains relied on a brace of these pistols to control a scurvy crew and put down a mutinous rebellion on the high seas. A common sight on the old sailing ships was the first mate standing by with his Duckfoot during ship's punishment at the Captain's Mast. The crack of the whip and the blood drawn by the lash could excite a crew into mutiny. Six simultaneous shots kept the fear of the Lord in a sailor's heart. . . ."

Dimensions: overall length, 10½ inches; barrel length, 2⅞ inches. Weight: 2 lbs.

Price: finished model, $69.95 (plus $4 for shipping and handling).

Color catalog of replica arms and accessories available, $2.

NAVY ARMS COMPANY

689 Bergen Boulevard
Ridgefield, NJ 07657
Tel. 201/945-2500

SHIP SURGEON'S CANDLEHOLDER

Hand-cast in a foundry more than 150 years ago, the original candlestick that Mystic Seaport has replicated was salvaged from a sunken British warship. The ship surgeon's candleholder has unusual heft and a low center of gravity to keep it stable below decks in rough weather. Hand-cast of solid bronze. 4 inches wide.

Price: $50 (plus $3.50 for packing and delivery).

CHESAPEAKE CAPTAIN'S BAROMETER

A replica of a late-nineteenth-century captain's barometer, mounted on solid mahogany. With mercury thermometer, 11½ inches long.

Price: $92 (plus $3.75 for packing and delivery; allow four weeks for delivery).

WHALE CRIBBAGE BOARD

Using polymer-simulated ivory, Mystic Seaport has had replicated this whale-shaped cribbage board, a nineteenth-century museum piece. 13 inch long.

Price: $45 (plus $3.50 for packing and delivery).

Color catalog available.

MYSTIC SEAPORT MUSEUM STORE

Mystic, CT 06355
Tel. 203/536-9957

TOURING AND SOLO-CRUISING CANOES

Wisconsin's Freedom Boat Works is one of several shops responding to the revival of interest in traditional wooden craft. All the models made by the firm on a regular basis are planked with ¼-inch white cedar or select northern pine and fastened onto white oak frames with bronze and copper or brass. Freedom Boat's late-nineteenth-century-style canoes are not precise replicas, but capture the singular grace and sophistication of this "Golden Age" of American canoeing.

MIRAGE LAP-STRAKE TOURING CANOE

Freedom Boat's Mirage is touted as a descendant of the celebrated Ruston Vesper, a cruising canoe of the 1880s. With the capacity for a crew of two (including their stores and gear), she is a traveler's canoe; and although her dimensions have been increased somewhat over those of the Vesper (to better accommodate tandem paddlers), she retains the elegantly long bow and full stern of the original. The Mirage may be fitted with a foot-control rudder and can be rigged for sail.

Dimensions: length overall, 17 feet 7 inches; maximum beam (outside plank), 34⅝ inches; bow height, 20½ inches; height amidships, 13½ inches; stern height, 18½ inches; depth (top keel amidships), 12½ inches. Approximate weight: 70 lbs.

Price: standard model, $2,850.

Catalog of boats and canoes available, $3.

FREEDOM BOAT WORKS

Route 1, Box 12
North Freedom, WI 53951
Tel. 608/356–5861

SOLITAIRE LAPSTRAKE SOLO-CRUISING CANOE

A lengthened version of reknowned builder **J. Henry Rushton's Nessmuk-type canoes,** the *Wee Lassie*, which was built in 1893 and is now on exhibit at the Adirondack Museum at Blue Mountain Lake, New York. Of the Nessmuk, the nineteenth-century author and canoeist George Washington Sears once wrote: "She waltzes on the waves . . . and, propelled by a light double paddle, with a one-fool power in the middle, she gets over the water like a scared loon."

Dimensions: length overall, 12 feet 8 inches; maximum beam (outside plank), 27¾ inches; bow height, 17 inches; height amidships, 12 inches; stern height, 17 inches; depth (top keel amidships), 11¼ inches. Approximate weight: 40 lbs.

Price: standard model, $1,600.

Wagon Covers.

49228 Wagon Covers, white duck (see cut). Always give size when ordering. Weight, 7 to 50 lbs. 10x10, 8 oz., 7 lbs.; 10x13, 10oz., 16 lbs.; 12x22, 30 to 50 lbs.

Size—Feet	8 oz. Duck	10 oz. Duck	12 oz. Duck
10x10	$1.20	$1.50	$2.33
10x12	1.45	1.85	2.75
10x14	1.70	2.15	3.25
10x15	1.80	2.35	3.50
10x16	1.90	2.45	3.70
11x13	1.75	2.20	3.40
11x15	2.05	2.55	3.90
11x18	2.45	3.10	4.75
12x15	2.30	2.85	4.35
12x16	2.50	3.05	4.65
12x20	3.10	3.80	5.85

Stack, Machine and Merchandise Covers, Called Paulins.

Weight from 15 to 100 lbs. 10x14, 10 to 20 lbs; 14x20, 25 to 30 lbs. 20x20, 38 to 45 lbs.

49229 White Duck. Always state size wanted, when ordering. Prices quoted on application, on sizes not mentioned here. Our 12 ounce duck is best double filling. These goods are not tents, but "stack covers" or paulins.

Size.—Feet	8 oz. Duck	10 oz. Duck	12 oz. Duck
10x16	$1.95		
10x18	2.20		
12x14	2.10		
12x16	2.50		
12x18	2.75		
12x20	3.05	3.90	6.60
14x16	3.50		
14x18	3.65	4.45	6.30
14x20	4.05	4.95	7.00
14x24	4.85	5.90	8.40
16x16	3.70	5.55	
16x18	4.20	5.15	
16x20	4.65	5.65	
16x24	5.55		
18x20	5.20		
18x24	6.25		
18x28	7.30		
18x30	7.80	9.60	13.50
20x24	6.90	8.50	12.00
20x36	10.45	12.75	18.00
24x30	10.40	12.70	17.95
24x36	12.50	15.35	21.60
24x40	13.90	17.05	24.00
24x50	17.40	21.30	30.00

Stack covers have short ropes, but no poles, machine and merchandise covers have eyelets around side. Any other size furnished on short notice. Prices on application.

Binder Covers.

49260 Weight, 6½ to 7½ lbs. Fitted to cover the binder and not the whole machine. Will fit any binder. Made of white duck.

	8 oz.	10 oz.
Price, each	$1.85	$2.15

Stockman's Bed Sheets.

Weights, 10 to 22 lbs. Fitted with snap rings or eyelets as may be ordered. Made of very best heavy white duck.

Order No.	Feet	13 oz.	15 oz.	18 oz.
49231	6x12	$2.35	$2.85	$3.05
	6x14	2.70	3.30	3.50
	6x15	2.90	3.50	3.80
	6x18	3.45	4.20	4.45
	7x12	2.75	3.25	3.60
	7x14	3.10	3.75	4.15
	7x15	3.35	4.05	4.45
	7x18	3.95	4.75	5.25
	8x12	3.40	4.10	4.40
	8x14	3.90	4.70	5.15
	8x18	5.00	6.05	6.60

Arctic Sleeping Bags.

49240 The Improved. Made of heavy waterproof tan-colored duck, lined with sheepskin, with the wool left on, inside of sheepskin lining, is a heavy drill lining that can be taken out and cleaned at any time; large enough to cover any man entirely, can cover up "head and ears" and still have plenty of air. Loops on sides so that it can be hung up with ropes, if desired. With these bags all bed and bedding can be dispensed with; it rolls up into small package, so that it can be fastened to a saddle, or "packed on back." The best bed ever invented for outdoor sleeping or tent camping. Weight, about 20 lbs. Each........$15.50

Camper's Clothes Bag.

49241 These bags are made of heavy white duck, round bottom, drawing string top fastening. Handy for extra clothing, shells, boots and other "truck." Regular sailor's bag. Don't cost much, always useful. Every family needs them. Each......$0.50

Campers' "Carry-All" Bag.

(Try one on your next outing trip.)

49243 This bag is made of heavy waterproof tan colored duck, with leather lap over mouth, leather lock strap fastening, mail bag style. Durable and strong, large size. The BEST and most USEFUL bag a "cowboy," hunter or camper could suggest. No campers' outfit complete without one; about 20x30 inches. Each......3.00

Kit Bag.

49245 Made of 10 oz. brown canvas, fastened with straps and buckles, neat, handy and durable. Length, 27 inches; width, 20 inches. Each......$0.75

Folding Canvas Boats.

Send for our Illust'd Catalogue of Folding Boats and Canoes.

The Acme Folding Canvas Boat.

49252 (2) The Acme Folding Canvas Boat. Painted. 12 feet, beam, 45 inches, depth at ends, 18 inches, depth amidships, 14 inches. Weight complete 35 pounds, weight complete. Capacity, one to three passengers. Complete with one pair ash oars, pair adjustable oar locks, adjustable back and shipping box.....$35.00

This is our most popular boat. It is a good general purpose boat. It can be made up in a light form weighing but 35 pounds by leaving out some of the parts which are necessary only when the boat is loaded heavy, and can be made up into two handles and carried with ease in one hand. For from one to three passengers, we recommend it above any of the other boats.

Eureka Canvas Folding Boat.

49255 No. 1.—Length, 10 feet; beam, 30 inches; depth at ends, 20 inches; depth at center, 12 inches; weight, 35 pounds; capacity, one to three passengers. Price, with one pair 4-foot ash oars, malleable rowlocks and two folding seats, Grade A.....$24.00

The No. 1 has a full model, the full beam being carried well up to the ends. It has great carrying capacity for a boat of its length and weight, and is very steady on the water. It is a boat capable of carrying safely two or three persons, yet light enough and compact enough to be easily carried long distances by hand. The Eureka does not fold as compactly as the Acme, and of course is not as well made, but yet is strong and durable.

The Koshkonong Hunting Skiff.

"Sets on the water like a duck."

49260 The Celebrated Koshkonong Hunting Boat is without doubt the best in the world, all things considered. Fifteen feet long, three feet beam, cockpit five feet long, two feet wide, pointed at both ends, deck boarded and canvas covered—can walk all over deck. Folding canvas wing around cockpit. Oarlocks not fitted, can put on any kind of locks desired. Water and air tight chamber in each end, good in open rough, as well as shallow water. Cannot be tipped over, easy rowing, foot rest in bottom made especially for running easily over grass and weeds, sets low on the water. Capacity 1,200 to 1,500 lbs. Just what every hunter and fisherman has been looking for; "easy as a rocking chair." Weight, about 90 lbs. Boat and 1 pair 6 feet ash oars.....$25.00

Buzzacott's "Patent" Complete Camp Cooking Outfit.

SPORTING SIZE, EXTREMELY PORTABLE. Order No. 49270.

49270 Same style as adopted by the United States Army, every part solid and substantial; description, etc. Top engraving shows the entire outfit, 15 pieces nested and packed forming a package for carrying not a foot square. Below are found the various utensils (15) arranged so as to form an idea of one of the many forms of use contents, etc.

THE OUTFIT INCLUDES:

1 Skeleton Stove, 11x14x6 inches (steel); 1 Large Stew Pot, steel, 8 quart; 1 Medium Stew Pot, steel, 6 quart. These combined for an excellent oven, 14xx10x10 inches. Capacity for 12 pound roast, 1 Coffee Pot, solid lip, mincers, 3 quart; 1 Frying Pan, used also for baking and roasting when desired, 12x8x2½, with cover to fit, 1 Boiler, 12x8; used also for pan rest, 1 Ladle Dipper; 1 Ladle Strainer; 1 Spoon; 1 Pancake Turner; 1 Fork, handle 12 inches long; 1 Adjustable handle, a feature so arranged as to fit any utensil for handling in any way when in use; 1 Combination Pan and Pot Cover, 2 Dredges 15 pieces. Price, complete.....$5.50

The "Kankakee."

A Portable Sectional Boat.

49271. CONSTRUCTION.

The frame of the boat is constructed of second growth white oak as to ribs, side slats, top rail, and bow and stern post. Cypress is used for floor, seats, and bow and stern deck. For fastening frame together, brass screws, copper rivets and copper nails are used throughout, which allows no parts to rust or corrode, and makes a very stiff, rigid frame. The outside covering is the best No. 1 galvanized steel, fastened throughout with copper rivets (which adds greatly to the strength) and then soldered over rivets and at all joints. This makes boats water-tight and prevents any action on the different metals when used in salt water.

JOINTS.

The joints are made each with one tongued and one grooved brass casting reaching from rail to rail clear across mid section of boat. The grooved casting being milled out to receive a soft rubber gasket ½ by ½ inch. The milled slot holds gasket in place and the pressure of the tongued casting on the rubber makes a perfect and absolutely water-tight joint. The joints are held together each by four brass clamps, two at bottom of boat and one on each rail at top of joint, as shown in foregoing cut. These four fastenings at each joint are very strong and rigid and so far from being a weak point the joints are the strongest part of boat, and we guarantee more than ample strength to carry all the boat will float, not only in smooth water, but in rough water, over shallow parts, sunken logs, rocks or any other obstructions.

This construction makes boat impervious to the weather as there can be no swelling or shrinkage to cause leakage; prevents being snagged, admits of use in heavy ice without damage, makes the use of paint to preserve unnecessary, does away with all bulkheads thus giving free use of entire boat without obstruction.

As parts are made interchangeable, we have two sizes of boats in one by simply leaving out middle section and joining two end sections. This is a very light, handy boat useful for one man in a great many places where a large boat would be inconvenient. See page 504 for prices.

TOURS AND LODGING

THE DEARBORN INN

As improbable as it seems on the face of it, Detroit's Dearborn Inn ("Colonial Homes and Motor House") offers its guests lodging in any one of five homes replicating the original dwellings of historic American figures. This means that midway between downtown Motor City and the airport you can pass the night in a house an awful lot like the Frederick, Maryland, one from which Barbara Fritchie (1766–1862) waved the flag as the Confederate troop rode through town; or like the Long Island farmhouse where Walt Whitman was born in 1819.

Located near Greenfield Village and the Henry Ford Museums, the Dearborn Inn's replica homes were built in 1937 as a way of accommodating more guests. For a "private area" behind the hotel, Charles M. Hart ("the father of the historic village idea") designed the homes, and landscape architect Marshall Johnson surrounded each with flora appropriate to its original site.

EDGAR ALLAN POE

The exteriors of the replica homes are the same size and made from the same materials as the originals. Although the interiors have been modified both in terms of structural space and to allow for modern conveniences, the entrance halls, stairs, and sitting rooms are "exact copies or close adaptations" of those in the original structures, their sconces and candelabra copied and electrified. Many of the furnishings are reproductions of pieces used in the original homes.

The original of the Dearborn Inn's Poe Cottage still stands near where it was first built in the Bronx (euphemistically, if authentically, called "Fordham, New York" in the hotel brochure) in a tiny park where it is marinated in the rock music from ghetto-blaster radios half the year. Even in the far more civilized Bronx of the 1950s (from which time I can fondly recall it) the simple frame house invited protective worry, walled in as it was by phalanxes of the Grand Concourse's art deco apartment buildings which were then just starting to go to seed. The poverty of Poe's life is reflected by the primitive workmanship of the white cottage, with its cut nails, crude laths, and mud plaster. A colonial influence can be seen in the paneled doors, broad mantels, and small-paned windows. Here is where Poe wrote "The Bells," "Annabel Lee," "Ulalume," and "Eureka."

In addition to the Poe Cottage, the Barbara Fritchie House, and the Whitman farm, there are replicas of the Red Hill, Virginia, home that Patrick Henry bought in 1794; and of the Litchfield, Connecticut, home that was built by Gov. Oliver Wolcott (1726–1797) in 1754, and where Alexander Hamilton, the Marquis de Lafayette, and Gen. George Washington all stayed.

THE DEARBORN INN

20301 Oakwood Boulevard
Dearborn, MI 48124
Tel. 313/271-2700

REPLICA WHITMAN FARMHOUSE

POE'S BRONX COTTAGE
REPLICATED IN MICHIGAN.

HANCOCK SHAKER VILLAGE

Following a visit to the Hancock Shaker community in 1827, James Fenimore Cooper declared, "I have never seen, in any country, villages so neat, and so perfectly beautiful . . . without, however, being picturesque or ornamented, as those of the Shakers." This atmosphere, born of Shaker design and reflecting the sect's spirit of "consecration, peace, order, simplicity, and quiet industry," can still be found at Hancock Shaker Village. Shaker functionalism is said to anticipate that of the twentieth century, while in the other ways mentioned, it provides a refreshing contrast to it.

At the time of Cooper's visit the Hancock Shaker community was just about reaching its peak in members and productivity. During the middle of the nineteenth century its population began (as Shaker celibacy makes almost inevitable) to dwindle, and the last eldress, Sister Frances Hall, died and was buried there in 1959.

Today the Hancock Shaker Village is operated as a public museum presenting the sect's unique culture as it unfolded there during parts of three centuries. Of the nineteen structures at the museum, most are originals that have been restored, although one (the Meeting House) was actually moved to Hancock in 1962 from a closed Shaker community in Shirley, Massachusetts, and another (the Schoolhouse) is a complete reproduction. The Brick Dwelling that was built during the 1830s to house 100 Shakers, the Trustee's Office with its 1895 Victorian facade, and the 1826 Round Barn are each of special interest. During the summer season demonstrations of Shaker crafts and domestic life can be seen at the village, and a special calendar of events is scheduled.

Open June 1 through October 15, 9:30 A.M. to 5 P.M. Guided tours available. Admission: adults, $3.50; children 12 and under, $1.

Brochure available.

HANCOCK SHAKER VILLAGE

U.S. Route 20
Hancock, MA 01237
Tel. 413/443-0188

BLACK CREEK PIONEER VILLAGE

At Black Creek Pioneer Village in Downsview, Ontario, thirty buildings have been restored and furnished in the manner of a typical crossroads Ontario community of the 1830s. Included are a working pioneer farm, harness shop, general store, blacksmith shop, printing office, firehouse, shoemaker's shop, school, church, and flour mill. The Dalziel Barn Museum, housed in a cantilever barn constructed in 1809, contains Canada's largest collection of nineteenth-century toys.

Open Monday through Friday: April, May, June, September, and October, 9:30 A.M. to 5 P.M.; in July and August, 10 A.M. to 6 P.M.; in November and December, 9:30 A.M. to 4:30 P.M.

BLACK CREEK PIONEER VILLAGE

c/o The Metropolitan Toronto
Conservation Authority
Five Shoreham Drive
Downsview, ON
Canada M3N 1S4
Tel. 416/661-6610

MASTED-SHIP CRUISES

The *Mystic Whaler,* a replica of the sharp-shooter schooners that cruised the world's whaling grounds at the end of the nineteenth-century, was launched in 1967. She's "baldheaded" (no topmasts) and has a steel deck and hull that are covered by wooden planking. The *Whaler's* masts are also made of steel—a 68-foot mainmast and a 61-foot foremast—and carry about 3,200 square feet of Dacron sail in the jib, staysail, foresail, and mainsail. The 100-foot vessel has a diesel auxiliary engine.

Leaving from the Whaler's Wharf in Mystic, Connecticut, and the Annapolis City Dock in Annapolis, Maryland, the *Whaler* and her companion ship the *Mystic Clipper* offer two- to five-day cruises along the Connecticut coastline and the Chesapeake Bay. A replica "centerboard Yankee Privateer," the *Clipper* was launched in 1982 and possesses the raked lines and natural speed of the historic Baltimore clipper ships of the early 1800s. As such, she's "the first of her kind to have been built along the northeast coast in 150 years," notes the fleet's brochure.

Color brochure available.

THE GREAT OUT O' MYSTIC SCHOONER FLEET

7 Holmes Street
Mystic, CT 06355
Tel. 203/536-4218

CONNER PRAIRIE PIONEER SETTLEMENT

"A microcosm of Indiana as it was in the 1830s, an exciting period of expansion for the state and region," the Conner Prairie Settlement is located only a few miles from downtown Indianapolis.

The museum began in 1934 when Eli Lilly, grandson of the well-known pharmaceutical pioneer, purchased the estate of William Conner, an Indian trader who was one of the area's first settlers. Conner was the husband of a Delaware Indian woman named Mekinges, and fathered six children by her. In 1820, when the Delawares were forced to withdraw to the western side of the Mississippi River by the Treaties of St. Mary's, Ohio, Mekinges and her children accompanied her tribe on their overland journey. Conner stayed behind, took a new wife, and became a merchant. In 1823 his brick Federal-style house (now included in the National Historic Register), today a part of the Conner Prairie Pioneer Settlement, was built.

After buying the 200-acre estate, Lilly and his wife immediately set about restoring it into a village that would reflect southern Indiana as it existed in the year 1836. At the Conner Prairie Pioneer Settlement costumed blacksmiths, weavers, and farmers conduct themselves as if past were present; and much of the fruit of their labor—including saltglaze and spatterware pottery, ironware, and wooden objects—is available in the Museum Shop.

Open April 1 to December 19, with special programs scheduled regularly.

CONNER PRAIRIE PIONEER SETTLEMENT

13400 Allisonville Road
Noblesville, IN 46060
Tel. 317/773-3633

LIVING HISTORY

FARMS **The lamentable fading of the traditional family farm over recent decades has created** outdoor farm museums to record and preserve their way of life. One of these museums, Living History Farms, is situated on 600 acres some eight miles northwest of Des Moines, Iowa.

Using diligently researched historical lore, the museum's 85 staff members and 200 voluneteers demonstrate midwestern life as it existed from the 1840s to the turn of the century. Included at the Living History Farms are reconstructions of a pioneer trading post, an 1840s homestead, an Iowa town of the 1870s, and a 1900 farm. The museum's newest addition reflects its oldest period: an Ioway Indian village of about 1700.

The Living History Farms are true working farms, where all the spinning, canning, soapmaking, cheese making, cabinetmaking, threshing, and harvesting are done to produce actual goods, as well as to instruct.

Open July 17 through October 30, Monday through Saturday, from 9 A.M. to 5 P.M. (on Sunday from noon to 6 P.M.). Admission: $5 for adults, $4 for those over 65, and $3 for children.

Courtesy Living History Farms

Group rates available.

Brochure obtainable.

LIVING HISTORY FARMS

2600 N.W. 111th Street
Des Moines, IA 50322
Tel. 515/278–5286

WHITE HOUSE

RANCH **The White House Ranch Historic Site is located in the Garden of the Gods Park in Colorado Springs, Colorado.** The museum's exhibits progress through forty years of Colorado history, beginning with a working reconstruction of an 1868 homestead and including an 1895 ranch and the Orchard House, the 1907 mansion of Gen. William Palmer, founder of the Denver & Rio Grande Railroad. The Living History Program and other historically related affairs held at this site are administered by the Colorado Springs Park and Recreation Department.

Open daily from 9 A.M. to 5 P.M. June 11 through September 5. Admission: $1.50 for adults and 75¢ for children aged 6 through 17.

Brochure available.

WHITE HOUSE RANCH

Living History Program
3202 Chambers Way
Colorado Springs, CO 80904
Tel. 303/578–6777

MOHONK MOUNTAIN HOUSE

Perched dramatically on a jagged rock cliff that frames a glacial lake in New York state's Catskill Mountains, the Mohonk Mountain House began in 1869 after two Quaker schoolteachers, Albert and Alfred Smiley, purchased the ten-room tavern that was standing at the site. The sale of the tavern must've come as a disappointment to the revelers of the nearby old Dutch village of New Paltz, for not only were the Smileys strictly religious, but they intended to convert the tavern into their home.

Still, the size of both the Smileys' debt and their newly acquired building was such that in quick order it made sense for them to take in boarders. They somewhat moderated their religious reservations against drinking and smoking (although at Mohonk there is *still* no bar, and smoking is not permitted in the hotel's dining room) and soon Victorian New Yorkers were finding the inn to be an ideal retreat from city life. Greatly in aid of this was the Smileys' interest in conservation and their Victorian notions of landscape design, which today has lent the stately air of an English garden setting to the grounds. Furthermore, the hotel's magnificent 5,000 acres of woodlands (through which several trails and bridle paths wind) have been spared development by the device of a preservation trust.

The hotel's massive lakefront main building was added to incrementally until it reached its present form at about the turn of the century. Its piecemeal architecture was described thus by Elizabeth Cromley in an essay entitled "A Room with a View" (*Resorts of the Catskills*, [New York: St. Martin's Press, 1979]):

Buildings, additions, and replacements for outmoded parts join together in a long, irregular line along the edge of the rock-bordered lake to form the hotel. Wood meets stone, shingle shifts to tile, browns and grays give way to greens and reds—creating a disturbing eclecticism or an enchantingly varied romantic fantasy, depending upon the eye of the beholder.

The list of the Mohonk Mountain House's beholders includes naturalist William Burroughs, industrialist Andrew Carnegie, and four presidents: Theodore Roosevelt, William Howard Taft, Rutherford B. Hayes, and Chester A. Arthur.

Open all year.

MOHONK MOUNTAIN HOUSE

Lake Mohonk
New Paltz, NY 12561
Tel. 914/255-1000

NORLANDS

I hear the talk goin' round about you but I want you ta know I don't believe t'word of it.
—*Mystifying announcement made by "Emeline Hilton" to "Brooksey Waters" at the time of the latter's 1982 arrival at Norlands.*

For those contemplating a trip to Maine there are plenty of nice places to visit, but anyone traveling back into 1870 must book a bedchamber at Norlands.
Norlands, named for the loud whirlwinds that blow through Alfred Lord Tennyson's *Ballad of Oriana*, is a working nineteenth-century farm located on 430 acres in Livermore, Maine. Originally conceived as a down-east Old Sturbridge Village, Norlands (under the direction of Mrs. Billie Gammon) has created so keen an experience of the last century as to make visits to other "living history" museums seem like watching daytime television. The Norlands program even awes the professionals: "A Norlands live-in is the most in-depth experience in America of life as it was lived one-hundred years ago," said Terry Sharer, secretary-treasurer of the Smithsonian-based Association of Living Historical Farms and Agriculture Museums. "I can't think of anything quite like it."

The Norlands' live-in program is a four-day, three-night visit for adults (shorter sessions are available for families with children at least eight years old) conducted from February through November—and it generally begins by making participants a bit uneasy. Clothed "appropriately" in late-nineteenth-century agricultural garb, newly arrived visitors will find themselves addressed as a member of one of two local farm families (the Waters and the Prays) of the period. Moreover, conversation is conducted in the infectious Maine dialect of the time and concerns matters that have long since receded into the pages of the *Farmer's Almanac*. Initially this ritual may impart the giggly feeling of play, but it serves the real purpose of an initiation, a baptism into the past.
A stay at Norlands is as little like a visit to a New England inn as it is to Madame Toussaud's. There is no plumbing or electrical wiring at the farm; and wristwatches, cigarettes, and flashlights must be left at home. Mornings begin at dawn, with the crowing of the cock and the clanging of pots (a warning that breakfast—which

might include either fried liver or ham, scrambled eggs, oatmeal, toast, and plenty of strong, dark coffee—follows early chores at 8:30). Then a day of more work around the farm commences—perhaps including the mucking of the oxen stalls or, in winter, cutting ice—and in evening there's a quiet gathering around the kitchen cookstove where "Shouting Proverbs" may be played over cocoa, and soapstones warmed to be wrapped in flannel and carried off into the cornhusk beds. Any notion of "quaintness" here is certain to die with the rooster that is slaughtered for dinner, or the necessity of using a frigid chamberpot on a midwinter night (Norlands's three-hole privy is a good twenty yards from the cottage), but every visitor seems to take home the experience of a unique moment that these deprivations may have helped to bring about.

It usually comes at a quiet time that has been spent perhaps watching Nathan Bartlett, the farm blacksmith, tending the oxen; or noting with pleasure how vast the stardome is, and how luminous its planets. It is inevitably triggered by a small thing, like the flutter of a flame as a draft passes over a lantern's chimney, but as with Emerson's "crossing of a bare common, in snow puddles, at twilight, under a clouded sky" it is the most mundane circumstance that is also the most transcendent. Suddenly (and quite naturally) it's the world of new-car-model changeovers, chemical dumps, and chicken salad on croissants that seems fantastic, and even dreadful. If anything beyond the farm seems real at all, it's the course of Reconstruction, and the possibility of continued drought until harvest.

In addition to the live-in program Norlands holds a variety of 1½- to 4-hour programs for school groups, and three public festivals a year: Autumn harvest (in October), Christmas at Norlands, and Heritage Days (in late June). The adult live-in program carries three teacher recertification credits through the Maine Department of Education and Cultural Services. Casual visits are discouraged.

Prices for live-in program: $150 for adults, $75 for children.

NORLANDS
Mrs. Alfred Q. Gammon
R.D. 2
Livermore Falls, ME 04254

RIDING THE CARS The

story of a town's being created or becoming successful because of the arrival of the railroad is a familiar one. Particularly during the late nineteenth century, when the railroad companies had power comparable to today's multinationals, many towns were also *founded* by them. Such was the case with Durango, Colorado, which came into being by dint of the Denver & Rio Grande Railway's need for it in 1879. In July 1882 a link to Silverton was completed for the purpose of hauling gold and silver down from the San Juan Mountains, and over the years to follow more than $300 million in precious metals were carried on its narrow-gauge rails.

Ninety-nine years later, with the ore long gone, the (renamed) Denver & Rio Grande Western Railroad sold the Silverton Branch to the Durango & Silverton Narrow Gauge Railroad Company (D&SNG), which put into operation what is now the country's only regulated, 100 percent coal-fired, narrow-gauge railroad.

Faithful to the pledge of the company's president, Charles E. Bradshaw, Jr., that "there will never be a diesel run on D&SNG tracks," the Silverton train employs two early-1920s-vintage steam locomotives to pull their 1880 coaches and open-air gondolas. Many of these cars, such as the parlor car *Alamosa*, were rolling back when the James-Younger gang was riding; and now they make the run between Durango and Silverton in every season but winter, when there's an abbreviated excursion.

The Silverton train travels through a wilderness area, part of the two-million-acre San Juan National Forest, following the Animas River into Silverton. Any other access into this area may only be made on horseback or on foot, making the train a favorite among backpackers and fishermen, for whom it calls at Needleton and Elk Park en route. The Silverton train also serves the Ah! Wilderness Guest Ranch and the Tall Timber Resort, as well as continuing to haul freight.

Round-trip fares are $25 per adult and $12.50 per child.

DURANGO & SILVERTON NARROW GAUGE RAILROAD

479 Main Avenue
Durango, CO 81301
Tel. 303/247-2733

THE HUBBELL TRADING POST CIRCA 1910

HUBBELL TRADING POST

Inside its long, low stone walls is a rectangular iron stove, the center of the "bull pen." During winter it was always stocked with piñon and juniper wood, and the Navajos, talking and laughing, lingered in the warmth. Behind the massive counters are shelves filled with coffee, flour, sugar, candy, Pendleton blankets, tobacco, calico, pocketknives and canned goods. Hardware and harness hang from the ceiling.
—*The Hubbell Trading Post's memory of itself early in this century.*

The Hubbell Trading Post is part of a historic Arizona site operated today by the National Park Service. The trading post itself has been in continuous operation since it was started by John Lorenzo Hubbell in 1878. The son of a Connecticut Yankee, Hubbell's varied career as merchant, sheriff, and member of the Arizona Territorial Council was touchingly enhanced by his unflagging devotion to the Navajo people as a translator, advisor, and friend. His turn-of-the-century home and the trading post have been restored to their original appearance and offer craft demonstrations of Indian weaving, spinning, and silversmithing.

Free admission. Open Easter Sunday through October 30, Monday through Friday from 8 A.M. to 6 P.M.; October 31 through Easter Sunday, Monday through Friday from 8 A.M. to 5 P.M. Closed Thanksgiving, Christmas, and New Year's Days.

HUBBELL TRADING POST

P.O. Box 150
Ganado, AZ 86505
Tel. 602/755-3475

GOLDEN NORTH HOTEL

Built in the "Days of '98" during the era of the Klondike Gold Rush, the Golden North is the oldest operating hotel in Alaska, and was once considered the territory's finest accommodation. The hotel's furnishings include many original pieces brought around Cape Horn at the turn of the century—tintypes, four-poster beds, porcelain water pitchers, oil lamps, and a days-of-'98-vintage piano.

Open all year.

GOLDEN NORTH HOTEL

P.O. Box 343
Skagway, AK 99840
Tel. 907/983–2451

HOTEL DEL CORONADO

The Hotel Del Coronado, a seaside Victorian castle dominating San Diego's Coronado peninsula, is generally considered to be the last of that era's extravagantly conceived ocean resorts. The hotel was the brainchild of Elisha Babcock, a wealthy Hoosier who acquired the 4,100-acre peninsula in 1885 as the future site of a resort hotel that would be the "talk of the Western world."

As a pipeline under the bay from San Diego had to be constructed to supply fresh water to the peninsula, and since both lumber and carpenters needed to be imported from San Francisco, the Hotel Del Coronado took three years to complete. On opening day in February 1888, thousands of people from all over the country passed beneath its great lighthouse turrets and gingerbread arches.

Although minor structural changes have taken place over the past century, many of the original facilities are intact. Notable among these are the Crown Room (where the Prince of Wales was introduced to Wallace Simpson in 1920), with its vast arched ceiling of pegged sugarpine, and the Grand Ballroom.

HOTEL DEL CORONADO

1500 Orange Avenue
Coronado, CA 92118
Tel. 619/435–6611

FORD'S THEATRE John T.

Ford had expected to reopen his E Street theater 2½ months after President Lincoln's April 14, 1865, assassination with the play *Octaroon*. Undeterred by an outpouring of letters threatening both to burn the theater and to murder him, Ford sold 200 tickets for the play's July 7 opening; but that night the War Department ordered Ford's Theatre closed, stationed guards in front of it, and demanded that the proprietor refund the ticket-holders' money. It would be more than a century before the boards of Ford's Theatre would again groan under the performance of a stage play.

In August 1865 the War Department purchased Ford's Theatre for $100,000 and began to dismantle the interior. Over the following century the building would variously be used as a War Department office building, as the home of the Army Medical Museum, and for the storage of government documents. In 1931 it passed into the hands of the Department of the Interior.

On July 7, 1964—ninety-nine years to the day after the army stopped the curtain from rising on *Octaroon*—the 88th Congress appropriated more than $2 million for the full restoration of Ford's Theatre, a painstaking process that involved tracking down elements of the original interior; it took almost three years to complete. On February 13, 1968, Ford's Theatre was again open to the public.

In cooperation with the Ford's Theatre Society, performances are scheduled throughout the year. Also available are free fifteen-minute programs recounting the story of President Lincoln's assassination, an exhibition of the Oldroyd collection of Lincolniana, and visits to the 1849 William Petersen house, directly across the street, where the president finally expired.

Open all year, 9 A.M. to 5 P.M. Closed for matinees on Thursday, Saturday, and Sunday, October through June. Closed December 25.

**FORD'S THEATRE
NATIONAL HISTORIC SITE**

*10th Street NW
Washington, DC 20001
Tel. 202/426-6924*

FORD'S THEATRE IN 1865.

Tenth Street between E and F as it was in 1865. The large building in the center is Ford's Theatre where Lincoln was assassinated.

No. 18K13367 Our finest quality Imported Foliage Effect in combination with half blown buds. Good buyers will appreciate this offer. Comes in natural foliage shades with pink, tea or American beauty red buds. State color wanted. **48c**
If by mail, postage extra, 7 cents.

A Novelty Wreath.

No. 18K13369 Foliage Wreath. Full trimming for one hat. Made up of handsome June rose foliage, liberally mixed with tiny buds. Natural shaded foliage with pink, tea or American beauty red buds as wanted. State color wanted. Price, per wreath. **42c**
If by mail, postage extra, 7 cents.

No. 18K1337. Natural shaded, finest quality Geranium Foliage with tiny buds, containing twenty-one leaves. We show only one quality—the best. Price, per bunch. **18c**
If by mail,

Pretty Styles in Fruits with Foliage.

No. 18K13373 Very showy spray of fine quality imported Cherries branched with natural foliage. Finest quality unbreakable cherries. Very showy trimming. Price, per bunch. **21c**
If by mail, postage extra, 6 cents.

38c

No. 18K13376 Beautiful bunch of imported Cherries branched in three sprays with natural foliage and rubber stems. Very attractive number. Comes in natural shades only. Price, per bunch. (Postage extra, 5c) **38c**

A SPLENDID STYLE. GREAT VALUE.

No. 18K13378 Handsome Cherry Wreath, branched very long. Made up of unbreakable cherries and natural shaded foliage. Exceptional value at our price. Price, per wreath. **38c**
If by mail, postage extra, 8 cents.

48c

No. 18K13380 Our very finest Cherry Wreath Effect, beautifully sprayed with imported foliage and quantities of natural sea moss. A very attractive trimming in a pretty soft effect. Price, per wreath. If by mail, postage extra, 8c. **48c**

44c

Grapes Are Very Popular.

No. 18K13382 A very pretty cluster of natural shaded Grapes, sprayed with natural grape foliage in rosette effect. Regular 75-cent value. Price, per bunch. **44c**
If by mail, postage extra, 5 cents.

67c

No. 18K13384 This beautiful wreath is made up of finest quality Grapes, sprayed with natural foliage and buds. Enough to trim the entire brim of a hat. Nothing better at any price. Price, per wreath. **67c**
If by mail, postage extra, 9 cents.

Handsome June Rose Clusters

No. 18K13387 Showy cluster of twelve good quality muslin June Roses, branched with foliage and long stems. Colors, pink, white, light blue or American beauty red. 25-cent value. State color wanted. Price, per bunch. **15c**
If by mail, postage extra, 5 cents.

38c

No. 18K13389 Beautiful spray of extra quality muslin June Roses, branched in two clusters with leaves and buds. Tremendous value. A great bargain at our price. Colors, white, pink, light blue or American beauty red. State color wanted. Price, per bunch. **38c**
If by mail, postage extra, 6 cents.

No. 18K13392 Our finest June Rose Effect of best quality silk and muslin flowers in combination with buds and beautiful sea moss. Very handsome front trimming with the present style hats, soft and fluffy. Colors, pink, tea or American beauty red. State color wanted. Price. **59c**
If by mail, postage extra, 8 cents.

No. 18K13394 All silk and muslin June Rose Wreath, branched very long with natural moss and imported foliage. Colors, white, pink, tea or American beauty red. State color wanted. Price, per wreath. **45c**
If by mail, postage extra, 8c.

Best Muslin Roses.

No. 18K13396 Good quality three in a bunch muslin Crush Roses, with full centers. Colors, pink, white, tea, light blue or American beauty red. State color wanted. Price, per bunch. **14c**
If by mail, postage extra, 5 cents.

No. 18K13398 Our best quality all muslin six in a bunch Cup Roses, with rubber stems. Colors, white, pink, light blue or American beauty red. State color wanted. Price, per bunch. **23c**
If by mail, postage extra, 5 cents.

Silk and Velvet Crush Roses.

No. 18K13403 All silk and velvet, three in a bunch Crush Roses. First class materials. Colors, white, pink, light blue, tea or American beauty red. State color wanted. Price, per bunch. **13c**
Postage extra, 5c.

No. 18K13413 These beautiful three in a bunch Crush Roses are made of good quality silk, velvet and muslin. Our illustration does not show its real beauty. Colors, pink, white, or American beauty red, brown, shaded with light blue, green shaded with brown. 50-cent value. State color. Price, per bunch. **29c**
Postage extra, 5c.

No. 18K13417 Our very finest quality all silk and velvet Crush Roses, three in a bunch. No better flower at any price than this. Colors, pink, old rose, brown, gray or American beauty red. State color wanted. Price per bunch. **49c**
If by mail, postage extra, 6 cents.

No. 18K13424 Great value in silk and velvet Crush Roses with rubber stems, six in a bunch. Made of good quality materials. Colors, pink, white, light blue, tea, or American beauty red. 50-cent value. Price, per bunch. **29c**
If by mail, postage extra, 7 cents.

No. 18K13430 Our finest quality six in a bunch all silk and velvet Cup Roses with rubber stems. Colors, white, pink, light blue, tea, gray, brown or American beauty red. State color wanted. Price, per bunch. **46c**
If by mail, postage extra, 7 cents.

American Beauty Roses.

No. 18K13432 Three medium size American Beauty Roses of good quality lawn, sprayed with soft natural sea moss and rose foliage. Colors, white, pink, tea or American beauty red. State color wanted. Price, per bunch. **18c**
If by mail, postage extra, 6 cents.

No. 18K13434 Natural American Beauty Roses are always popular. This number contains two beautiful full blown roses with a bud and natural imported rose foliage. A rich trimming. Colors, white, pink, tea or American beauty red. Price, per bunch. **27c**
If by mail, postage extra, 6 cents.

No. 18K13436 Our very finest two in a bunch, Half Blown Rose Effect. Made of silk, velvet and muslin in handsome combination with natural rose foliage and moss. Our illustration does not begin to show the real beauty of these flowers. Comes in white, pink, tea or American beauty red. Price, per bunch. (Postage extra, 7c.) **46c**

No. 18K13438 Handsome spray of six medium size Cup Roses of fine quality lawn, sprayed with soft sea moss, giving it a very dainty effect. Colors, white, pink, tea or American beauty red. State color wanted. Price, per bunch. **33c**

Rose Wreaths Trim Easily.

No. 18K13440 Our leading value in velvet and muslin Rose Wreath, six velvet and muslin roses, wreath effect, sprayed with foliage on chenille stems. One of the biggest bargains ever offered. Colors, white, pink, light blue, tea or American beauty red. Price, per wreath. (Postage 5c.) **27c**

No. 18K13442 A very showy wreath effect of good quality muslin American Beauty Roses, branched with natural foliage and long stems. Colors, white, tea, pink or American beauty red. State color wanted. Price, per wreath. (Postage extra, 7c.) **35c**

No. 18K13444 This handsome cluster contains four half blown muslin Roses of good quality, branched with quantities of fluted imported foliage and tiny buds. Colors, pink, white, tea or American beauty red. State Color Wanted. Price, per bunch. **48c**
If by mail, postage extra, 9 cents.

No. 18K13446 Beautiful wreath of half blown muslin Roses, branched with June rose foliage, natural soft moss and tiny buds. Others ask $1.25 for no better value. Colors, pink, white, tea or American beauty red. State color wanted. Our price, per wreath. **67c**
If by mail, postage extra, 8 cents.

88c

No. 18K13448 Our most beautiful Crush Rose Wreath. The daintiest effect in our complete line. Something entirely new and very attractive. Our illustration does not show the exquisite beauty of these roses. Come in white, pink, tea or American beauty red. State color wanted. Price, per wreath. **88c**
If by mail, postage extra, 8 cents.

Black Foliage.

No. 18K13450 Good quality black Mercerized Satin Foliage for use with black crush roses. Regular 35-cent value. Price, per bunch. **19c**
If by mail, postage extra, 7 cents.

No. 18K13452 Our very finest All Satin Foliage in black only. No better black foliage than this can be bought at any price. Contains twenty-four beautiful leaves handsomely sprayed. Price, per bunch. **33c**
If by mail, postage extra, 8c.

Best Black Flowers.

No. 18K13454 Good quality black Crush Roses with all silk centers, three in a bunch. Great value at our price. Price, per bunch. **14c**
If by mail, postage extra, 5 cents.

No. 18K13456 Fine quality, six in a bunch, black Cup Roses, made of a combination of silk, satin and muslin. Regular 50-cent value. Price, per bunch. **33c**
If by mail, postage extra, 5 cents.

No. 18K13457 Extra fine quality all silk and satin black Crush Roses with very full centers. Three in a bunch. Price, bunch. **46c**
If by mail, postage extra, 5 cents.

No. 18K13459 Very handsome black Crush Rose and Foliage Spray, branched in double sunburst effect. Best silk flowers and all satin foliage. This is a very beautiful number in splendid style. Price, per bunch. **33c**
Postage extra, 7c.

For a full line of Children's and Misses' Wreaths see page 1037.

DECORATIVE CHRISTMAS TREE CANDLEHOLDERS

Prior to the mid-nineteenth century the wax of dripping Christmas tree candleholders was caught in small plates that were set below the branches. The first improvement on this arrangement came in the form of crimped-edge tin dishes onto which the Christmas candles could be skewered. This integrated dish-and-candle design offered only meager benefit, however, as the weight of the melting candle would often tilt the branch, spilling the molten wax anyway, and sometimes starting a fire.

The problem was eventually solved in 1867 by one Charles Kirchof of Newark, New Jersey, who on December 24th of that year (he must've gotten the idea while decorating his tree!) patented the counterweighted candleholder. These devices simply were hooked over the branch of the tree to hold the candle perfectly upright; the counterweights, which were made of unfired clay about the same size and shape as a cherry, were usually painted in bright colors.

The McLeach Company of Fitchburg, Massachusetts, makes handcrafted replicas of Kirchof's candleholders, warning that they are intended strictly as historical ornamentation and are not to be used with lighted candles. They come in boxes of six, with two candleholders in each of red, mustard, and blue colors. Gold, silver, and white candleholders are also available upon request.

Price: $3.50 per candleholder (plus $2.50 for postage and handling).

McLEACH

Box 575
Fitchburg, MA 01420
Tel. 617/386-5323

DECORATIONS AND STOCKING STUFFERS

B. Shackman & Company has been doing business at the same Fifth Avenue location since 1897, and sells many novelty items reminiscent of that time. Their Christmas catalog contains a wonderful array of paper and tinsel Victorian Santas, angels, tree decorations, and cards. A minimum $10 order is required.

B. SHACKMAN & COMPANY

85 Fifth Avenue at 16th Street
New York, NY 10003
Tel. 212/989-5162

OLD
CHRISTMAS As a part of their

Washington Irving Facsimile Library, the Sleepy Hollow Press has also re-published *Old Christmas*, a series of Irving's Christmas tales which pre-date Dickens's *A Christmas Carol* by a quarter century.

Price: clothbound, $10. 208 pages with 106 illustrations. *Old Christmas* may be ordered directly from Sleepy Hollow Press when accompanied by a money order (no credit-card orders are accepted). Postage and handling require $1.25 for the first book, plus 25¢ for each additional copy. A retail discount schedule is available.

SLEEPY HOLLOW PRESS

c/o Sleepy Hollow Restorations
150 White Plains Road
Tarrytown, NY 10591
Tel. 914/631–8200

RANDOLPH CALDECOTT'S ILLUSTRATION OF CHRISTMAS DINNER FROM *OLD CHRISTMAS* BY WASHINGTON IRVING.

CHRISTMAS
POSTCARDS Replicas of Victorian Christmas postcards (and reprints of period cards on a variety of other subjects) are available from both Evergreen Press and the R. J. Fish Publishing Company.

Brochures and order forms available.

R. J. FISH PUBLISHING COMPANY

P.O. Box 1771
Reseda, CA 91335

THE EVERGREEN PRESS

P.O. Box 4971
Walnut Creek, CA 94596
Tel. 415/825–7850

THE NIGHT
BEFORE
CHRISTMAS Originally calling it "A Visit from St. Nicholas," this poem was written by the Hebrew scholar Clement Clark Moore as a Christmas gift for his six children in 1822. A family friend gave the poem to the Troy (New York) *Sentinel* where it was published anonymously on December 23, 1823.

For years newspapers everywhere copied the poem without attribution until finally Mrs. Sarah Joseph Hale, editor of Godey's *Lady's Book* discovered the identity of the author. An edition of Moore's verse published in 1844 included the poem as his own for the first time.

Evergreen Press of Walnut Creek, California, has published a facsimile of the 1870 "Charles Graham" edition of *The Night Before Christmas.* The book's artwork recalls the first time that holly was associated with Christmas and the first representation of Santa Claus dressed in a red cloth coat trimmed with white fur.

Other Victorian Christmas books published by Evergreen are: *Christmas Delights* (turn of the century), and *Santa Claus and His Works* (first published around 1870) with illustrations by Thomas Nast.

THE EVERGREEN PRESS

P.O. Box 4971
Walnut Creek, CA 94596
Tel. 415/825–7850

If you are interested in receiving periodically updated mail-order information on these and other
nineteenth-century-style items, address your request to American Historical Supply, P.O. Box
15428, Springfield, MA 01115.

INDEX

A

accessories, brass, 71
accouterments, Civil War, 165–166, 168, 172
Adney, Edwin Tappan, 137
after-shave tonic, 202
Alhambra, The, 177
aluminum, 20
American Builder's Companion, The, 179
American cheese, 114
American colonial revival design, 55, 179
American Graniteware Assn., 37
Anderson, Paul, 156
Animal Tales, 184–185
apothecary chest, 14
apple parers, 42
apricot leather, 120
arms, Confederate, difficulty of procurement, 168
Army of the Cumberland, 167
arrows, Sioux war, 151
art nouveau, 86
asafoetida, glycerated, 203
Ashley, Gen. William, 156
Athenaeum, the Philadelphia, 55
Authentic Billy, The Kid, The, 183
Avery, John Marsh, 118
awl, 139
axes: broad, 8, 93; Hudson Bay, 92

B

B. Shackman Co., 227
Babcock, Elisha, 224
Bag Balm, 100
Baker, Jim, 29
Baker, John Morgan, 73
bandanas, cowboy, 147
bandboxes, 31–32
Banks, Gen. N.P., 118
banks, toy, 198
Barnes Machine Cannon, 173
Barnum, P. T., 25
barometer, captain's, 214
baskets: lightship, 33; traditional, 33
bathing costumes, 127
bathroom fixtures, 10–11
bathtubs: clawfoot, 10; hip, 40
beams, hand-hewn, 8
beanpot, 46
Beauregard, John, 157
"Belle Époch," 86
Bell's Seasoning, 120

belts: frontier cartridge, 158; military, 165: plates (buckles) for, 165
benches: "Nasturtium," 18; Victorian park, 19
benne seeds ("slave benne"), 120; stick candy, 120
Bent, Josiah, 115
Bent, William, 115, 154
Bernhardt, Sarah, 205
bicycles, 112
Billings, John D., 182
Bingham, George Caleb, 124, 132
bit brace, 93
Black Creek Pioneer Village, 218
blankets: Federal double, 167; Hudson's Bay, 63; New Hampshire, 64
Blitz-Weinhard Brewery, 117
blouse, Gibson Girl, 127
bodice, women's, 124
Boggis, Edward, 210
"Bonnie Blue Flag," 160
Booth, John Wilkes, 174
Borden, Nancy, 65
Boston Tea Party, 35
botanicals, Plains Indian, 153
boudin blanc, recipe for, 135
Bowie, Jim, 155
Bowie, Rezin, 155
bowl, shaving, 204
Boxer Rebellion, 164
Bracebridge Hall, 178
Brady, Mathew, 188
brass beds, 20–21
Bridger, Jim, 154, 156
British East India Company, 35
Broadfoot, Thomas, 182
brooms, 35
Bronx, The, 217
brushes, shaving, 204
buckets, Civil War artillery, 172
bucksaw, 96
Buena Vista, Battle of, 171
buffalo, importance to Plains Indians of, 149
buffalo honoring collection, Plains Indian, 149
Buffalo, New York, 39
buffalo robe, painted, 149
buggy. *See* horse-drawn carriages
buggy umbrellas, 112
bugle, Confederate, 192
Bumppo, Natty, 140
Buntline, Ned, 158
Butler, Gen. B. F., 173
butter churns, 100
Butterfield, John, 104

C

cabins: log, 2; Thoreau's Walden Pond, 2–3
camera, view, 187

camp items: Civil War, 167; fur trader's, 134–136
Campaigning with Grant, 182
candleholders: Christmas tree, 227; ship's surgeon's, 214
candlestand, 24
candlesticks, 29
canoes: birchbark, 136–137; solo-cruising, 215; touring, 215
canteens: Civil War, 165; wooden, 134
cap pouches, 166
capotes, 131
caps. *See* hats
capsicum pepper, 118, 203
Captivity of the Oatman Girls, The, 183
"carpetbaggers," 67
carpetbags, 67
Carson, Kit, 154, 156
cartridge belts, frontier, 158
cartridge boxes, 165
cassette box, Hudson Bay, 134
Caswell-Massey Company, 202
catlinate, use of in peace pipes, 152, 207
ceiling fans, 8
ceilings, metal, 9
ceremonial lance, Plains Indian, 149
chain pump, 95
chairs: Adirondack lawn, 16; bent hickory rocking, 16; Brumby rocking, 17; Hitchcock, 15; low back, 24; Shaker elder's, 22; Shaker rocking, 25; Shaker weaver's, 24
checkerboards, 198
cheese, American, 114
cherry stoner, 43
chest, apothecary, 14
Christmas Delights, 229
churns, butter, 100
cider mill, 98
Clark, William, 141
cloaks, Shaker, 126
clock kits: Aaron Willard, 77; No. 2 regulator, 78; railroad regulator, 78; Shaker tall, 79 Vienna regulator, 79
clocks: English carriage, 79; sharp steeple, 77; Victorian street, 78; 1870 mantle, 79
clothes wringer, 40
coaster wagon, 200
coats: frock, Confederate, 163; frock, men's, 126, 128; Plains Cree, 148; rifleman's, 132; "sack," 162; U.S. Mounted Services, 162
cocoa, 122
Cody, Col. William F. "Buffalo Bill," 154, 158, 183, 184
coffee grinders, 35–36
"Coffee Mill," Ager, 173

coffee pot, Civil War, **167**
Coffeyville, Kansas, **144**
colognes, **202**
Confederate Battle Flag, **160**
combs, **205**
commode, pull chain, **11**; seats for, **11**
Conner, William, **219**
Conner Prairie Settlement, **219**
cooking pot, **37**
cooking utensils, hand-forged, **136**
Cooley, James P., **199**
Coolidge, Calvin, **114**
Coolidge, John, **114**
Cooper, James Fenimore, **140, 218**
Cornelius & Company, **55**
corset, **127**
costumer, brass, **27**
Country Iron Foundry, **28**
coup, Plains Indian battle, **151**
courieur des bois, **131, 133, 138**
cream cans, **99**
Cremony, John C., **183**
cribbage board, whale, **214**
Crossville, Tennessee, **40**
Cruikshank, George, **184**
Cruikshank's *Comic Alphabet*, **184**
Cruikshank's *Toothache*, **184**
cruises, masted ship, **218**
crystal: decanter, **49**; goblet, **49**; plate, **50**; tumbler, **49**
Cumberland, Army of the, **167**
cup, tin army, **167**
Custer, Gen. George Armstrong, **164, 205**

D

Daguerre, Louis J., **189**
daguerrotype boxes, **189**
Dalton, Bob, **144**
Dalton, "Brad," **144**
Dalton, Emmett, **144**
Dalton, Grot, **144**
Dalton gang, **144**
Dalziel Barn Museum, **218**
dance stick, Sioux horse, **150**
Darby, Abraham, **71, 87**
Darby, Francis, **71**
Daring and Suffering, **182**
Davis, Jefferson, **82, 171**
Day at the Zoo, A, **184**
de Oñate, Juan, **154**
Dearborn Inn, the, **217**
Deardorff, Laban F., **187**
decorations, Christmas, **227**
decoys, **74**
Dedham Pottery Company, **45**
deed box, **39**
Denver & Rio Grande Railroad, **220, 223**
Diedrich Knickerbocker's A History of New York, **176**
Diehnelt, C. F., **116**
Dietz, Robert E., **54**
Dietz, Ulysses G., **179**
dinner pail, **40**

"dissolving view" books, **184**
doll house kits, **195, 196**
dolls, **194**; Victorian carriage for, **195**
doorstops, **29**
dough maker, **42**
dresses: calico day, **128**; Cheyenne Indian, **148**; 1805 Empire gown, **128**; 1860 crinoline, **128**
drum, toy 1890 field, **199**
dulcimers, **191**
Durango, Colorado, **223**
Durango & Silverton Narrow Gauge Railroad Company, **223**

E

Edison, Thomas Alva, **61**
Edwardian era, **129**
Emerson, Ralph Waldo, **6, 70, 180, 222**
Enchanted Doll House, the, **194-195**
examplars, **70**

F

farm bell, **95**
Farragut, Adm. David, **118**
ferkin, **45**
Findlay Brothers Foundry, **88**
finials, curtain pole, **73**
firebacks, **28**
fireboards, **29**
flags, Civil War, **160**
floor cloth, **64**
flour mill, **97**
Ford, John T., **225**
Ford's Theatre, **174, 199, 225**
Fort Pulaski, Battle of, **173**
frames, **73**
Frémont, Gen. John Charles, **154**
Fritchie, Barbara, **217**
Frizzel Coach and Wheel Works, **104**
froe, **93**
frontier, North American, **2, 6, 140**
frogs, leather, **166**
fruit press, **43**
"Fur Traders Descending the Missouri," **132**

G

G. P. Putnam Company, **176**
Gandhi, Mahatma, **46**
Garrett, Sheriff Pat, **183**
Gatling, Richard Jordan, **173**
Gatling gun, **173**; plans for a, **173**
gauntlets, deerskin, **168**
gazebo, **3**
General, The, **182**
Geronimo, **164**
Gibson, Charles, Dana, **127**
"Gibson girl, the," **127**
Gillmore, Gen. Quincy Adams, **173**

glassmaking, **49**
gloves, **168**
Godin Foundry, **19, 86**
Gold Rush: Alaskan, **224**; California, **158**
Golden North Hotel, **224**
Gothic revival architecture, **77**
Gould, Jay, **19**
Gould, John, **138**
graniteware, **37**
"Gray Ghost," the, **182**
Great Britain, the, **87**
Great Exhibition, the, **18**
Greek classical design, **55, 179**
grinders, coffee, **35-36**
Griswold & Gunnison Arms Company, **168**
gun covers, **142**

H

Hale, Sarah Joseph, **229**
ham: cob-smoked, **116**; pepper-coated, **120**
Hancock Shaker Village, **218**
handguns: Booth's derringer, **174**; Buntline Special, **158**; duckfoot pistol, **214**; Harpers Ferry Model 1855 Dragoon pistol, **169**; New Orleans Ace, **157**; Pepper-box revolver, **158**; "Reb" Model 1860, **168**; Spiller & Burr revolver, **169**; Texas Confederate Dragoon revolver, **170**; 1806 flintlock pistol, **141**; 1847 Colt Walker revolver, **168**; 1851 Navy revolver, **157**; 1858 Remington Army revolver, **170**; 1860 Army revolver, **169**; 1861 Navy revolver, **170**
hard tack, **134**
Hardtack & Coffee, **182**
hardware, Victorian, **27**
harmonicas, **192**
harness, **111**
Hart, Charles M., **217**
hatchet, **139**
hats: bear, kit for, **131**; C.S. kepis, **163**; coontail cap, **131**; derby, **127**; German-style cap, **125**; Great Plains, **146**; miscellaneous military, **163**; nightcap, **129**; sunbonnet, **126**; top, **127**; toque, woolen, **133**; U.S. forage cap, **161**; U.S. Model 1875, **164**; U.S. Model 1885-1898, **164**
haversacks, military, **166**
Hawken, Jacob, **156**
Hawken, Samuel, **156**
headstall, **147**
hearth accessories, **29**
Hendrick, Tom, **88**
Henry, Patrick, **217**
Hicks, Edward, **29**
Hitchcock Chair Company, **15**
hobby horse, **198**
hoes, **95**

Hohner, Will, 192
Holmes, Oliver Wendell, 188
holsters: C.S., 166; U.S. Civil War, 166; cavalry, 172; 1850–1870 form-fit, 158
Homesteads Project, 40
honey, 116
honeypot, 48
Hopping John, recipe for, 118
horse-drawn carriages: buggy, general-purpose, 105; buggy, open, 110; buggy, pony; 108; extension-top, 107; phaeton, 103; stagecoaches, 104; surrey, 110; wagon, farm, 106; wagon, spring, 106; wagon, town & country delivery, 108; wagon, utility, 109
Hotel Del Coronado, 224
house plans, 4
Hubbell, John Lorenzo, 223
Hubbell Trading Post, 223
Hudson's Bay Company, 63, 138
Hunter, Dr. William, 202
hunting bags: leather, 142; Plains Indian, 153; possible, 141; voyageur's, 142

I

ice box plans, 38
ice cream freezer, 41
In the Maine Woods, 138
In Wonderland, 185
Indians, cigar store, 210
Indians, Malecite, 138
Indians, Mandan, 139
Indians, North American: adaptation to environment by, 137; preparation of tobacco among, 209
Indians, Plains, 148–154
Indians, Sioux: adoption of metal arrow points by, 151; emulation of muskets in design of war clubs by, 152; meaning of a horse killed in battle to, 150; method of discharging arrows practiced by, 151; quilting by, 150; sacredness of buffalo to, 149; vanity among warriors, 152; work for "dwelling," 154
inkwell, 39
interiors, period, 9
Iron Bridge, the, 87
ironware, 36
Irving, Washington, 176–178, 228
Italianate design, 55

J

jackets: C.S. common shell, 162; U.S. fatigue, 162
Jackson, Andrew, 140
Jackson, Beau, 157
Jackson, Mississippi, 82
Jackson, William Henry, 188

Janesville wagon, the, 200
jardinieres, 101
Jarvis, Deming, 49
jaw harps, 192
Jefferson, Thomas, 6
Johnson, Edward, 6
Johnson, Jeremiah, 156
Johnson, Nancy, 41
"Journals," 137

K

Kate Greenaway's Mother Goose, 184
kepis, 163
Kidnapped, 185
King Edward VII, 129
King George III, 35
"kinnikinnick," 209
Kirchof, Charles, 227
Kistler, Steve, 101
kitchen pump, 40
knapsacks, military, 166
knives: Blackfoot dag, 139; Bowie, 155; Buffalo jaw, 149; crooked, 138; flint striker, 139; Hudson Bay camp, 139; Plains Indian, sheath for, 154
Know Nothing Party, 10

L

Lafayette, Marquis de, 202, 217
lamp post, 52
lamps: bracket, Victorian, 60; bracket, wall, 53; desk, 60; kerosene, 53; leaded glass, 53; sewing, 53; whale oil, 52
lance, Plains Indian, 151
Land of Sweet Surprises, 185
lanterns: bulkhead, 214; hall, 53; hurricane, 54; post, 54; tubular, 54; whale oil, 53
lard press, 43
lean-to. *See* tents
Lee, Ann, 22
Lee, Robert E., 82
"Legend of Sleepy Hollow, The," 178
leggings, Plains Indian, 148
Levi Strauss Company, 144
Lewis Meriwether, 135, 139, 141
Lewis and Clark expedition, 138, 139
Life Among the Apaches, 183
Life of the Honorable William F. Cody, The, 183
light bulbs, 61
lighting, Victorian, 55–61
Lilly, Eli, 219
limner artists, 69
Lincoln, Abraham, 174, 199, 225
Lind, Jenny, 204
liniments, 203
Little Actor's Theater, The, 185
Little Big Horn, the, 164

Living History Farms, 220
London Armoury Company, 171
long hunter, 131, 140
long johns. *See* undergarments
longleaf pine, 6
long rifle, 140
lozenges, slippery-elm throat, 203
lumber, 6

M

McCue, Harry, 104
McGuffey, William Holmes, 180
McGuffey's Eclectic Readers, 180
"McGuffey's phenomenon," 180
McIlhenny, Edmund, 118
McPhee, John, 137, 138
Magic Windows, 185
marbles, clay, 199
Massachusetts Bay Colony, 6
meat chopper, 43
medicine bundle, Plains Indian, 151
Meek, Joe, 154
Mekinges, 219
Merrimack Publishing Company, 184
Merry Magic Go-Round, 185
Metro, Paris, 86
Mexican War, 171
milk bottles, 38
milk cans, 95
milk paint, 8
millwork, Victorian, 7
mini balls, 172, 173; mold for, 173
Minié, Capt. Claude, 173
mint julep cups, 48
mirror, 25
mirror board, Sioux, 152
moccasins, 133
Mohonk Mountain House, 221
money, Confederate, 168
Moore, Clement Clark, 229
Morse, Samuel F. B., 189
Mosby, Col. John S., 182
Mosby's Rangers, 182
Mrock, Laurence, 140
Muir, John, 6
Muybridge, Eadweard, 188
Myers, Andrew B., 176, 177, 178
Myrick, Frederick, 213
Mystic Clipper, the, 218
Mystic Whaler, the, 218

N

nails, cut, 94
Napoleon III, 202
National Trust for Historic Preservation, 75
Navy Arms Company, 168
New Orleans: 1814 Battle of, 140; 1863 capture by Federal troops, 118
"Night Before Christmas, The," 229
night cream, 205

Nister, Ernest, 184
Noah's ark, 197
Noble, Silas, 199
Noble & Cooley Company, 199
Norlands, 222

O

Octagon, House, The, 179
"Octaroon," 225
Old Christmas, 228
One of Jackson's Foot Cavalry, 182
Oriental design, 55
"Our American Cousin," 174
Overland Mail Company, 104
ozans, 154

P

padlocks, 39
pails, dairy, 99
paint, milk, 8
Palmer, Gen. William, 220
pants. See trousers
parers, apple, 42
Parkman, Francis, 6, 156
"pass-boxes," 172
pastilles, pinelyptus, 204
"Peaceable Kingdom, The," 29
peace pipe, Sioux, 152
peach leather, 120
Pearson, Adelaide, 46
Peep at Buffalo Bill's Wild West, A, 184
Pennsylvania rifle. See rifles
pepper, capsicum, 118, 203
Peter the Great, 121
Petersburg, Virginia, Siege of, 173
phaeton, 103
photographic printing, 187, 188
photographic prints, 187, 188
Photographic Views of Sherman's Campaign, 183
pie safe, 14
Pinaud, Edouard, 202
Pine Ridge Agency, 164
pipe bags, Sioux, 153
pipes, tobacco: clay, 207; Mark Twain Deluxe, 208; Mark Twain Limited-Edition, 208; trapper's, 207; Turk's head, 207; 1896 Peterson, 208
pistols. See handguns
pitch fork, 95
Pittenger, William, 182
planter, hill-type, 96
plaques, iron, 71
plaster, medicinal, 204
playing cards: Civil War, 167; 1805 French, 199
plow, 96
Poe, Edgar Allen, 180, 217
Poe, cottage, 217
pool tables, 199
popcorn popper, 42
"pop-up" books, 184
Porter, Gen. Horace, 182

portraits, folk, 69
post & beam construction, 6
postcards, Christmas, 229
pottery: Dedham, 45; early Ohio Valley manufacture of, 207; redware, 45; slipware, 45; stoneware, 45
powder, medicated, 205
powder flask, 172
powder horns, 142, 153; strap for, 153
Prairie Edge Studios, 149
prints: advertising, 73; New Bedford Whaling Museum, 213; Shaker, 72
Puritans, 6

Q

Queen Victoria, 55, 101
quilting bees, 65
quilts: Amish, 65; Sioux, 150

R

rag rugs, 66
ranges: Elmira Oval, 88; Findlay Oval, 88; Julia, 88; Princess Atlantic, 85; Queen Atlantic, 85; restored antique, 82; Sweetheart, 88. See also stoves
ration box, 134
razor, straight, 204
Reconstruction era, 67; plain fare of, 118
Red River Frontier Outfitters, 146
redware, 45
registers, hot-air, 11
Remington, Frederick, 183
Reno, Frank, 157
Reno, John, 157
revolvers. See handguns
Ricker, Joseph, 115
rifles: Hawken, 156; Kentucky, 140; long, 140; ordnance barrel, 173; Pennsylvania, 140; 3-Band Enfield, 171; 1803 flintlock, 141; 1841 Mississippi, 171; 1863 Springfield, 172
rifling, 140
Rip Van Winkle, 178, 184
Robbins, Roland Wells, 3
robe, painted buffalo, 149
Robertson, Hugh, 45
Robinson, John, 25
rococo design, 55
Roman classical design, 55
Roosevelt, Eleanor, 40
Roosevelt, Theodore, 164, 221
root beer, 73
Rosencrans, Gen. William S., 167
Rough Riders, 164

S

saber, U.S. 1860 cavalry, 166
St. Louis Stamping Co., 37

St. Mary's, Ohio, Treaties of, 219
sampler kits, 70
samplers, 70
San Juan Hill, 164
Santa Anna, 171
Santa Claus and His Works, 229
sausage stuffer, 43
saws: buck, 96; cross-cut, 93
scabbards, 166
schooners, 218
scrimshaw carvings, 213
Seaman, Eliza, 70
Sears, George Washington, 215
Sears-Roebuck & Co., catalogue, 37, 40
seats, 18
Second Empire period, French, 19
seed box, 101
serving trowel, 48
settee, 23
sewing patterns, 128-129
Shakers, 22, 101, 218
sheath, tack, 154
shelves, 23
Shephard, Julia, 174
shield, Kiowa bear society, 151
Shimek, George, 173
ship models, 212
shirts: bib-front, 147; "boiled" collarless, 124; merchant's, 125; pioneer, 124; rifleman's, 132; Shaker, 126; trapper's, 132; U.S. Model 1852, 161; U.S. Model 1883, 164; Victorian, 128; Western Indian war, 148
shoes: ladies, 127: laces for, 127; U.S. Model 1851 Jefferson brogan, 162
"silent companion," 75
sinks: copper kitchen, 11; pedestal bathroom, 10
Siringo, Charles A., 183
Sketch Book, The, 178
skirts: crinoline, 127; Gibson girl, 127
skull, buffalo honoring, 149
sleigh bells, 112
slings, leather, 166
slipware, 45
Sloan, Dr. Earl, 203
Smiley, Albert, 221
Smiley, Alfred, 221
Smith & Wellstood Ltd., 82
Smith, James, 82
Smith, Robert, 82
snowshoes, 137
snuff box, 209
soap, shaving, 204
soapsaver, 40
sorghum, 116
soup, recipe for Confederate army, 168
Spanish-American War, 164
Springfield (Mass.) Armory, 171
stagecoaches, 104
staircases, 9
"Stars and Bars," 160

stereoscopes, **188**
stereoscopic viewcards, **188**
Stevens, Alfred, **18**
Stevenson, Robert Louis, **185**
stocking stuffers, **227**
Stone's River, Battle of, **192**
stoneware, **45**
Stoughton, Donald, **28**
stoves: Air-Tite parlor, **84**; B&M Station Agent (potbelly), **85**; Belle Époch, **86**; Coalbrookdale Darby, **87**; Esse Queen, **82**; Handy, **84**; Large Round Godin, **86**; Oval Godin, **86**; restored antique, **82**; St. Nicholas parlor, **85**; Sheepherder, **84**; Small Round (Petit) Godin, **86**; soapstone; **83**. *See also* ranges
stow chest, **30**
Strauss, Levi, **144**
strop, razor, **204**
Stuart, Gilbert, **202**
surrey, **110**
Sutter, John, **158**
"Swedish Nightingale," the, **204**
sword, **166**

T

Tabasco pepper sauce, **118**
tables: Alfred Stevens, **18**; bistro, **19**
tankard, **48**
Tea Act of 1773, **35**
telegraph, **189**
tents: Civil War, **154**, **167**; lean-to, **135**; tipis, **154**
Terry, Thomas & Hoadley, **78**
Texas Cowboy, A, **183**
textile furnishings, **65**
Thomas, Seth, **78**
Thoreau, Henry David, **2**, **137**, **138**
tin box, **134**
tinder box, **142**
tinware, **36**
tipis, Plains Indian, **154**
tobacco: bag for, **209**; box for, **209**; canteen for, **209**; kinnikinnick, **209**; twist, **209**
Tocqueville, Alexis de, **2**
toilet, **11**
tomahawks: as part of Plains Indian war weapons collection, **151**; buffalo ceremonial pipe, **149**; Seneca Indian, **139**
tonic, after-shave, **202**
tonic, health, **205**
tonsorial supplies, **204**
toothbrush, **205**
top, **199**
towel rack, **23**
Townshend Acts, **35**
toys wooden: hobby horse, **198**; Noah's ark, **197**; pull, **197**; top, **199**
train rack, **28**
Treasure Island, **185**

trousers: broadfall, **124**; button-fly denim, **144**; St. Louis, **124**
Tucker, Sherrard & Company, **170**
turkey, **116**
Turner, Frederick Jackson, **6**
Twain, Mark, **208**

U

undergarments: corset, Victorian lady's, **127**; Edwardian lady's, **129**; men's longhandles, **129**; U.S. army pattern, **162**
uniforms, Civil War, **161–163**
Union flag, the, **160**

V

Vaillancourt, Henri, **137**, **138**
Van Nostrand Reinhold Company, **180**
Victorian era, **55**
Victorian Lighting, **179**
Visit from St. Nicholas, A, **229**
vodka, **121**
voyageurs, **131**, **133**, **138**

W

waffle iron, **38**
wagons. *See* horse-drawn carriages
wagon wheels, **110**
waistcoat, **125**
Walden, **3**
Walden Pond, **2**
wallet, Civil War, **168**
war club, Sioux, **152–153**
Ward, Artemus, **101**
Wareham, Massachusetts, **94**
war weapons collection, Plains Indians, **151**
washboard, **41**
wash boiler, **41**
Washington, George, **41**, **140**, **202**, **217**
washtubs, **40**
watches: Hamilton reproduction, **80**; railroad pocket, **79**
water, bottled, **115**
water crackers, **115**; pudding recipe for, **115**
watering can, **101**
weather vanes, **12**
Weinhard, Henry, **117**
Wellington monument, **18**
Wells, Harry, **104**
Wells Fargo & Company, **104**
whaling, **213**
wheelbarrow, **92**
White House Ranch, **220**
Whitman, Walt, **217**
wilderness, North American, **2**, **6**, **136**
Willard, Aaron, **77**
Willard, Simon, **77**
William Petersen House, **225**

Williamson, James J., **182**
windmills, **90–91**; towers for, **91**
Wistar, Caspar, **49**
Wolcott, Gov. Oliver, **217**
Wonder-Working Providence, **6**
Worsham, John H., **182**
wringer, clothes, **40**
Wyeth, N. C., **185**

Y

"Young Boy Seated with Dog," **75**

INDEX OF SUPPLIERS & MANUFACTURERS

A A Abbingdon Ceilings   9
2149 Utica Avenue
Brooklyn, NY 11234
Tel. 212/477-6505

Adirondack Store and Gallery   16
109 Saranac Avenue
Lake Placid, NY 12946
Tel. 518/523-2646

Alice's Country Cottage   124
Box 3
Rohrersville, MD 21779
Tel. 301/432-5527

Allen Firearms Company   158, 170
1107 Pen Road
Santa Fe, NM 87501
Tel. 505/986-1961 or 505/982-3399

**Amazon Vinegar & Pickling Works
   Drygoods   39, 127, 179, 183**
Department AH
2218 East 11th Street
Davenport, IA 52803
Tel. 319/322-6800

Antiquity Reprints   4
P.O. Box 370
Rockville Centre, NY 11571
Tel. 516/766-5585

**Architectural Antiques
   Exchange   9**
715 North Second Street
Philadelphia, PA 19123
Tel. 215/922-3669

Artek, Inc.   213
P.O. Box 154
Antrim, NH 03440
Tel. 603/588-6825

Authentic Reproductions   160
1031 Old Nankin Road, R-3
Ashland, OH 44805
Tel. 419/289-6642

B. Shackman & Company   227
85 Fifth Avenue at 16th Street
New York, NY 10003
Tel. 212/989-5162

Jim Baker   29
P.O. Box 149
Worthington, OH 43085
Tel. 614/885-7040

John Morgan Baker   73
P.O. Box 149
Worthington, OH 43085
Tel. 614/885-7040

Lindsay Frost Bandboxes   32
Box A
Avella, PA 15312
Tel. 412/587-3990

The Battered Brush   69
228 Dogwood Avenue
Quitman, MS 39355
Tel. 601/776-3180

The Bedpost   20
R.D. 1, Box 155
Pen Argyl, PA 18072
Tel. 215/588-3824

Beecham Products (Ace Combs)   205
P.O. Box 1467
Pittsburgh, PA 15230

Big Sky Leatherworks   111
Route 3
Billings, MT 59101
Tel. 406/373-5937

Black Creek Pioneer Village   218
c/o The Metropolitan Toronto
   Conservation Authority
Five Shoreham Drive
Downsview, ON
Canada M3N 1S4
Tel. 416/661-6610

The Blitz-Weinhard Brewery   117
1133 West Burnside
Portland, OR 79209
Tel. 503/222-4351

Blue Star Tipis   154
P.O. Box 2562
Missoula, MT 59806
Tel. 406/728-1738

Ed Boggis   210
Old Church Road
Claremont, NH 03743

Nancy Borden   65
P.O. Box 4381
Portsmouth, NH 03801
Tel. 603/436-4284

Bradford Consultants   61
16 East Homestead Avenue
Collingswood, NJ 08108
Tel. 609/854-1404

Briar Rose Farm   103
RR 1, Box 174
Layton Road
Woodstown, NH 08098
Tel. 609/769-1452

Broad-Axe Beam Company   8
R.D. 2, Box 181-E
Brattleboro, VT 05301
Tel. 802/257-0064

**C & D Jarnagin Company
   161-163, 165-166, 167**
Route 3, Box 217
Corinth, MS 38834
Tel. 601/287-4977 (information) or
   1-800/647-7084 (new orders only)

**Caswell-Massey Co., Ltd.   202, 204,
   205**
Mail Order Division
111 Eighth Avenue
New York, NY 10011

Charles P. Rogers Brass Beds   20-21
149 West 24th Street
New York, NY 10011
Tel. 212/807-1989

Charles Scribner's Sons   185
597 Fifth Avenue
New York, NY 10017
Tel. 212/486-2888

Chicago Albumen Works   188
P.O. Box 379
Front Street
Housatonic, MA 01236
Tel. 413/274-6901

Chop-Rite Manufacturing Company   43
P.O. Box 294
Pottstown, PA 19464
Tel. 215/326-5970

**The Coalbrookdale Company   18,
   37, 71, 87**
American Sales Office
RFD 1, Box 477
Stowe, VT 05672
Tel. 802/253-9727

Cohasset Colonials   77
834 X Ship Street
Cohasset, MA 02025

Conner Prairie Pioneer Settlement   219
13400 Allisonville Road
Nobelsville, IN 46060
Tel. 317/773-3633

The Country Iron Foundry   28
P.O. Box 600
Paoli, PA 19301
Tel. 215/296-7122

Crawford's Old House Store   27
301 McCall
Waukesha, WI 53186
Tel. 414/542-0685

**Crazy Crow Trading Post   30, 112,
   129, 131, 134, 153, 207, 209**
P.O. Box 314
Denison, TX 75020
Tel. 214/463-1366

**Cumberland General Store   40, 53,
   79, 95-96, 105-109, 116, 203, 205**
Route 3
Crossville, TN 38555
Tel. 615/484-8481

Cumberland Woodcraft Company   7
2500 Walnut Bottom Road
Carlisle, PA 17013
Tel. 717/243-0063

**Custom Blacksmithing &
   Manufacturing   173**
827 Commercial
Waterloo, IA 50702
Tel. 319/291-2095

Dairy Association Company, Inc.   100
Lyndonville, VT 05851

The Dearborn Inn   217
20301 Oakwood Boulevard
Dearborn, MI 48124
Tel. 313/271-2700

The Decoy Works   74
2601 S.W. 122nd Avenue
Davie, FL 33330
Tel. 305/472-7910

DeWeese Woodworking Company 11
P.O. Box 576
Philadelphia, PA 39350
Tel. 601/656-4951

Dixie Gun Works 166, 168, 173, 174, 192
Gunpowder Lane
Union City, TN 38261

Doll House Factory Outlet 196
325 Division Street
Boonton, NJ 07005
Tel. 201/335-5501

Dudley Kebow, Inc. 35
2603 Industry Street
Oceanside, CA 92054
Tel. 619/439-3000

Durango & Silverton Narrow Gauge Railroad 223
479 Main Avenue
Durango, CO 81301
Tel. 303/247-2733

Elizabeth Edge Studios 198
Department AH
5060 West Lake Road
Canandaigua, NY 14424
Tel. 716/394-0656

Elmira Stove Works 88
22 Church Street West
Elmira, ON
Canada N3B 1M3
Tel. 519/669-5103

Enchanted Doll House 194-195
Manchester Center, VT 05255

The Evergreen Press, Inc. 229
P.O. Box 4971
Walnut Creek, CA 94596
Tel. 415/825-7850

The Examplarery 70
P.O. Box 2554
Dearborn, MI 48123
Tel. 313/278-3282

Fancibrass 29, 71
522 Parkway View Drive
Pittsburgh, PA 15205
Tel. 412/787-2499; Telex: 812381

Folk Art Studios 198
611 West 12th Street
Bloomington, IN 47401
Tel. 812/336-5575

Folkwear Patterns 129
Box 3798
San Rafael, CA 94912
Tel. 415/457-0252

Ford's Theater National Historic Site 225
10th Street NW
Washington, DC 20001

Four Winds 33
Straight Wharf
Nantucket, MA 02554
Tel. 617/228-1597

Freedom Boat Works 215
Route 1, Box 12
North Freedom, WI 53951
Tel. 608/356-5861

Frizzel Coach & Wheel Works 104
P.O. Box 82001
Oklahoma City, OK 73148
Tel. 405/943-8038

G. H. Bent Company 115
7 Pleasant Street
Milton, MA 02186
Tel. 617/698-5945

General Housewares Corporation 37
P.O. Box 4066
Terre Haute, IN 47804
Tel. 812/232-1000

George E. Daniels Wagon Factory 110
Daniels Road
Rowley, MA 01969
Tel. 617/948-3815

Gohn Brothers 112
Box 111
Middlebury, IN 46540
Tel. 219/825-2400

Gold Bond Sterilizing Powder Company 205
745 Washington Street
Fairhaven, MA 02719

Hubbel Trading Post 223
Box 150
Ganado, AZ 86505
Tel. 602/755-3475

Jenifer House 12, 19, 38
New Marlboro Stage
Great Barrington, MA 01230
Tel. 413/528-1500

John Wright, Inc. 38
North Front Street
Wrightsville, PA 17368
Tel. 717/252-3661

Kenneth Lynch & Sons 78
P.O. Box 488
Wilton, CT 06897
Tel. 203/762-8363

L. F. Deardorff & Sons 187
315 South Peoria Street
Chicago, IL 60607
Tel. 312/829-5655

L. L. Bean, Inc. 63
Freeport, ME 04033

Levi Strauss & Company 144-145
Levi's Plaza
1155 Battery Street
San Francisco, CA 94106

Living History Farms 220
2600 N.W. 111th Street
Des Moines, IA 50322

Lodge Manufacturing Company 36
P.O. Box 380
South Pittsburgh, TN 37380
Tel. 615/837-7181

The Log Cabin Shop 35, 135-136, 139, 141, 142, 172, 207, 209
P.O. Box 275
Lodi, OH 44254
Tel. 216/948-1082

Louisville Tin & Stove Company 99
P.O. Box 1019
Louisville, KY 40201

MJA Porcelain Dolls 196
Sunset Drive
Hope Valley, RI 02832
Tel. 401/539-2209

H. McCue, Wheelwright 104
Skinner Road
Lodi, NY 14860

McIllenny Tabasco Company 118-119
Avery Island, LA 70513
Tel. 318/365-8173

McLeach 227
Box 575
Fitchburg, MA 01420
Tel. 617/836-5323

Marle Company 53
170 Summer Street
Stamford, CT 06901
Tel. 203/348-2645

Mason & Sullivan Company 79
586 Higgins Crowell Road
West Yarmouth, MA 02673
Tel. 617/778-1056

Merrimack Publishing Company 184
85 Fifth Avenue at 16th Street
New York, NY 10003
Tel. 212/989-5162

Militaria, Inc. 163
138 Kearny Avenue
Kearny, NJ 07032
Tel. 201/998-7471

Mohonk Mountain House 221
Lake Mohonk
New Paltz, NY 12561
Tel. 914/255-1000

Mountain Dulcimers 191
P.O. Box 117, Fassett Hill
Hancock, VT 05748

Mountain Lumber Company 2, 6
Route 2
P.O. Box 43-1
Ruckersville, VA 22968
Tel. 804/295-1922

Golden North Hotel 224
P.O. Box 343
Skagway, AK 99840
Tel. 907/983-2451

Good Time Stove Company 82
Route 112
Goshen, MA 01032
Tel. 413/268-3677

The Great Out O'Mystic Schooner Fleet 218
7 Holmes Street
Mystic, CT 06355
Tel. 203/536-4218

Greyfriar's Imports, Ltd. 82
65 Broadway
Greenlawn, NY 11740
Tel. 516/754-1831

The Ground Floor 73
95½ Broad Street
Charleston, SC 29401
Tel. 803/722-3576

The Hamilton Watch Company   80
1817 William Penn Way
Lancaster, PA 17603
Tel. 1-800/233-0281

Hammermark Associates   38
P.O. Box 201-SC
Floral Park, NY 11002

Hancock Shaker Village   126, 218
U.S. Route 20
Hancock, MA 01237
Tel. 413/443-0188

Harold's Cabin   120
445 Meeting Street
Charleston, SC 29403
Tel. 803/722-2766

Harrington's   116
618 Main Street
Richmond, VT 05477
Tel. 802/434-3411

Harrisville Designs   64
Main Street
Harrisville, NH 03450
Tel. 603/827-3333

The Heller-Aller Company, Inc. 90-91
Corner Perry & Oakwood
Napoleon, OH 43545
Tel. 419/592-1856 or 419/592-3216

Henry Thayer Company   66
One Main Street
Concord, MA 01742

Heritage Rugs   66
Kay and Ron Loch
Lahaska, PA 18931
Tel. 215/794-7229

**Historic Charleston Reproductions
    Shop   198**
105 Broad Street
Box 622
Charleston, SC 29402

Historical Replications, Inc.   4
P.O. Box 31198, Dept. AHSC
Jackson, MS 39206

The Hitchcock Chair Company   15
Riverton, CT 06065

Hohner, Incorporated   192
Lakeridge Industrial Park
Sycamore Drive, P.O. Box 15035
Richmond, VA 23227

Honey Acres   116
Ashippun, WI 53003
Tel. 414/474-4411

Hoppe's   158
c/o Penguin Industries, Inc.
Airport Industrial Mall
Coatesville, PA 19320
Tel. 215/384-6000

Hotel Del Coronado   224
1500 Orange Avenue
Coronado, CA 92118
Tel. 619/435-6611

House of Thoreau   3
P.O. Box 91
Concord, MA 01742
Tel. 617/259-8709

Laurence Mrock, Riflesmith   140
Box 207
Woodhill-Hooksett Road
Bow, NH 03301

**Mystic Seaport Museum Store   52,
214**
Mystic, CT 06355
Tel. 203/536-9957

**Navy Arms Company   141, 155, 157,
169, 171-172, 173, 214**
689 Bergen Boulevard
Ridgefield, NJ 07657
Tel. 201/945-2500

The Nestle-Lemur Company   202
902 Broadway
New York, NY 11010

New England Basket Works   33
Box 645
Higganum, CT 06441

Noble & Cooley Company   199
Water Street
Granville, MA 01034
Tel. 413/562-9694

Norlands   222
c/o Mrs. Alfred Q. Gammon
R.D. 2
Livermore Falls, ME 04254

Northwest Traders   131
4999 Packard Drive
Box 24305 H.H. Br.
Dayton, OH 45424
Tel. 513/236-3930

Northwood Stoneware Pottery   45
Route 4, Box 458
Northwood, NH 03261

Nostalgia Decorating Company 53, 73
P.O. Box 1312
Kingston, PA 18704
Tel. 717/288-1795

Nowell's, Inc.   56-59
P.O. Box 164
Sausalito, CA 94965
Tel. 415/332-4933

Old Dartmouth Historical Society 213
Whaling Museum
18 Johnny Cake Hill
New Bedford, MA 02740

**The Old-Fashioned Milk Paint
    Company   8**
P.O. Box 222
Groton, MA 01450

**Old Sturbridge Village   30, 48,
49-50**
Museum Shop
Sturbridge, MA 01566
Tel. 617/347-9843

**Old World Sewing Pattern Company
128**
Route 2, Box 103
Cold Spring, MN 56320

Open Cupboard   32
P.O. Box 70
Tenants Harbor, ME 04860
Tel. 207/372-8401

Pearce Woolen Mills   63
Woolrich, PA 17779

**La Pelleterie de Fort de Chartres
    35, 36, 124-125, 132-133, 142, 154,
    192, 199, 209**
P.O. Box 627
Chester, IL 62233
Tel. 618/826-4334

Peterson of Dublin   208
P.O. Box 608
Southport, CT 06490

Philomel Books   184-185
The Putnam Publishing Group
200 Madison Avenue
New York, NY 10016

The Phoenix Foundry   97-98
P.O. Box 68
Marcus, WA 99151
Tel. 509/684-5434

Piel Craftsmen   212
307 High Street
Newburyport, MA 01950
Tel. 617/462-7012

**The Pioneer Place   16, 36, 41, 95,
110**
Route 2, 9938 County Road 39
Belle Center, OH 43310

Plymouth Cheese Company   114
P.O. Box 1
Plymouth, VT 05056

Poland Spring   115
777 West Putnam Avenue
Greenwich, CT 06836

Pool Tables by Adler   199
820 S. Hoover Street
Los Angeles, CA 90005
Tel. 213/382-6334

Portland Stove Company   85
P.O. Box 377
Fickett Road
North Pownall, ME 04069
Tel. 207/688-2254

The Potting Shed   45
P.O. Box 1287
Concord, MA 01742
Tel. 617/369-2981

Prairie Edge   149-153
P.O. Box 8303
Rapid City, SD 57709
Tel. 605/341-4525

**Preservation Shops, Dept. AH   25,
    52, 64, 75, 101**
National Trust for Historic
    Preservation
1600 H Street NW
Washington, D.C. 20006
Tel. 202/673-4200

Primitive Arms   156
Route 1
Box 42-A
Ashdown, AR 71822
Tel. 501/898-2345

Products of the Past   100, 139, 172
P.O. Box 12
West Main Street
Wilmington, VT 05363
Tel. 802/464-5569

Progress Lighting   55
Erie Avenue & G Street
Philadelphia, PA 19134

Putnam Antiques   129
3 Pond Road
Middlefield, MA 01243

The Quilt Room   65
Old Country Store
Intercourse, PA 17534

R. E. Dietz Company   54
225 Wilkinson Street
Syracuse, NY 13204
Tel. 315/424-7400

R. J. Fish Publishing Company   229
P.O. Box 1771
Reseda, CA 91335

Red River Frontier Outfitters   124,
146-147, 158, 164, 172
P.O. Box 241
Tujunga, CA 91042
Tel. 213/352-0177

The Reggio Register Company   11
P.O. Box 511
Ayer, MA 01432
Tel. 617/772-3493

The Renovator's Supply   27, 28, 60
182 Northfield Road
Millers Falls, MA 01349
Tel. 413/659-2211

Rideable Antique Bicycle Replicas,
Inc.   112
2447 Telegraph Avenue
Oakland, CA 94612
Tel. 415/444-1666 or 415/541-2838

The Rocker Shop   17
1421 White Circle NW
P.O. Box 12
Marietta, GA 30061
Tel. 404/427-2618

Rowantree's Pottery   46
Blue Hill, ME 04614
Tel. 207/374-5535

Royal Windyne Limited   8
1022 West Franklin Street
Richmond, VA 23220
Tel. 804/353-1812

S. Chris Rheinschild   11
2220 Carlton Way
Santa Barbara, CA 93109
Tel. 805/962-8598

The Shaker Seed Box Company   101
6656 Chestnut Street
Mariemont, OH 45227
Tel. 513/271-7100

Shaker Workshops   22-24, 34, 66,
72
P.O. Box 1028
Concord, MA 01742
Tel. 617/646-8985

Simms & Thayer, Cabinetmakers   14
P.O. Box 35-AC
No. Marshfield, MA 02059
Tel. 617/585-8606 or 617/837-0271

Sleepy Hollow Press   176-178, 228
c/o Sleepy Hollow Restorations
150 White Plains Road
Tarrytown, NY 10591
Tel. 914/631-8200

Smith & Hawken Tool Company
92, 101
25 Corte Madera
Mill Valley, CA 94941
Tel. 415/383-4415

The Smithsonian Institution   67
P.O. Box 2456
Washington, D.C. 20013
Tel. 202/357-1826

Spruce Head Wood Products
Company   92
P.O. Box 14
Spruce Head, ME 04859
Tel. 207/594-2401

Steptoe & Wife   9
36261 Victoria Park Avenue
Willowdale, ON
Canada M2H 3B2
Tel. 416/497-2989

Stone Ledge Company   19, 86
170 Washington Street
Marblehead, MA 01945
Tel. 617/631-8417

Sunrise Specialty   10
2210 San Pablo Avenue
Berkeley, CA 94702
Tel. 415/845-4751

Time-Life Books   182, 183
Time-Life Building
Chicago, IL 60611

Transocean Limited   84
2290 Panorama Drive
Holliday, UT 84117
Tel. 801/278-3635

Tremont Nail Company   94
21 Elm Street
P.O. Box 111
Wareham, MA 02571
Tel. 617/295-0038

Henri Vaillancourt   137
P.O. Box 142
Greenville, NH 03048

Van Nostrand Reinhold Co., Inc.
180-181
135 West 50th Street
New York, NY 10020
Tel. 212/265-8700

Vermont Frames   6
P.O. Box 100
Hinesburg, VT 05461
Tel. 802/482-2722

Vintage Wood Works   3, 7
P.O. Box 1157
Fredericksburg, TX 78624
Tel. 512/997-9513

Wakefield-Scearce Galleries   48
Historic Science Hill
Shelbyville, KY 40065
Tel. 502/633-4382

Warner-Lambert Company (Sloan's
Liniment)   203
201 Tabor Road
Morris Plains, NJ 07950

Wattle & Daub's Victorian Accents
25, 29, 31, 48, 77, 184-185, 188, 189,
197
661 West 7th Street
Plainfield, NJ 07060
Tel. 201/757-8507

White House Ranch   220
Living History Program
3202 Chambers Way
Colorado Springs, CO 80904
Tel. 303/578-6777

White Mountain Freezer Company
41-42
Winchendon, MA 01475
Tel. 617/297-0015

Wilbur Chocolate Company, Inc.   122
48 North Broad Street
Lititz, PA 17543
Tel. 717/626-1131

The William G. Bell Company   120
P.O. Box 99
East Weymouth, MA 02189
Tel. 617/337-5000

Wisconsin Wagon Company   200
10 South Locust Street
Janesville, WI 53545
Tel. 608/754-0026

Woodcraft Supply Corporation   93,
138
41 Atlantic Avenue
P.O. Box 4000
Woburn, MA 01888
Tel. 1-800/225-1153 toll free
(orders only)

Woodstock Pottery   45
Woodstock Valley, CT 06282
Tel. 203/974-1673

Woodstock Soapstone Stove
Company   83
Route 4, Box 223
Woodstock, VT 05091
Tel. 802/672-5133